Sachar Paulus
Norbert Pohlmann
Helmut Reimer

ISSE 2004 –
Securing Electronic Business Processes

vieweg-it

www.vieweg-it.de

Sachar Paulus
Norbert Pohlmann
Helmut Reimer

ISSE 2004 – Securing Electronic Business Processes

Highlights of the Information Security Solutions Europe 2004 Conference

vieweg

Bibliographic information published by Die Deutsche Bibliothek
Die Deutsche Bibliothek lists this publication in the Deutsche Nationalbibliographie;
detailed bibliographic data is available in the Internet at <http://dnb.ddb.de>.

1st edition September 2004

Vieweg is a company of Springer Science+Business Media.
www.vieweg.de

Cover design: Ulrike Weigel, www.CorporateDesignGroup.de
Typesetting: Oliver Reimer, Ilmenau
Printing and binding: Lengericher Handelsdruckerei, Lengerich
Printed on acid-free paper

ISBN-13: 978-3-528-05910-1   e-ISBN-13: 978-3-322-84984-7
DOI: 10.1007/978-3-322-84984-7

Application_____ 177

Spam is Here to Stay
Andreas Mitrakas _____ 179

The Key to My On-Line Security
Paul Meadowcroft _____ 186

Dealing with Privacy Obligations in Enterprises
Marco Casassa Mont _____ 198

Trusted Computing: From Theory to Practice in the Real World
Alexander W. Koehler _____ 209

Electronic Signatures – Key for Effective e-Invoicing Processes
Stefan Hebler _____ 219

Legally Binding Cross Boarder Electronic Invoicing
Georg Lindsberger, Gerold Pinter, Alexander Egger _____ 228

SecMGW – An Open-Source Enterprise Gateway for Secure E-Mail
Tobias Straub, Matthias Fleck, Ralf Grewe, Oliver Lenze _____ 237

Web Service Security – XKMS (TrustPoint)
Daniel Baer, Andreas Philipp, Norbert Pohlmann _____ 250

EPM: Tech, Biz and Postal Services Meeting Point
José Pina Miranda, João Melo _____ 259

Preface

The Information Security Solutions Europe Conference (ISSE) was started in 1999 by EEMA and TeleTrusT with the support of the European Commission and the German Federal Ministry of Technology and Economics. Today the annual conference is a fixed event in every IT security professional's calendar. The aim of ISSE is to support the development of a European information security culture and especially a cross-border framework for trustworthy IT applications for citizens, industry and administration. Therefore, it is important to take into consideration both international developments and European regulations and to allow for the interdisciplinary character of the information security field. In the five years of its existence ISSE has thus helped shape the profile of this specialist area.

The integration of security in IT applications was initially driven only by the actual security issues considered important by experts in the field; currently, however, the economic aspects of the corresponding solutions are the most important factor in deciding their success. ISSE offers a suitable podium for the discussion of the relationship between these considerations and for the presentation of the practical implementation of concepts with their technical, organisational and economic parameters.

An international programme committee is responsible for the selection of the conference contributions and the composition of the programme:

- Jan Bartelen, ABN AMRO (The Netherlands)
- Ronny Bjones, Microsoft (Belgium)
- Alfred Buellesbach, DaimlerChrysler (Germany)
- Lucas Cardholm, Ernst&Young (Sweden)
- Roger Dean, EEMA (UK)
- Marijke De Soete (Belgium)
- Jos Dumortier, KU Leuven (Belgium)
- Loup Gronier, XP conseil (France)
- John Hermans, KPMG (The Netherlands)
- Frank Jorissen, Silicomp Belgium (United Kingdom)
- Jeremy Hilton, EEMA (United Kingdom)
- Matt Landrock, Cryptomathic (Denmark)
- Karel Neuwirt, The Office for Personal Data Protection (Czech Republic)
- Sachar Paulus, SAP (Germany)
- Norbert Pohlmann, TeleTrusT (Germany)
- Reinhard Posch, TU Graz, (Austria)
- Bart Preneel, KU Leuven (Belgium)
- Helmut Reimer, TeleTrusT (Germany)
- Paolo Rossini, TELSY, Telecom Italia Group (Italy)
- Ulrich Sandl, BMWA (Germany)
- Wolfgang Schneider, GMD (Germany)
- Robert Temple, BT (United Kingdom)

Many of the presentations at the conference are of use as reference material for the future, hence this publication. The contributions are based on the presentations of the authors and thus not only document the key issues of the conference but make this information accessible for further interested parties.

The editors have endeavoured to allocate the contributions in these proceedings – which differ from the structure of the conference programme – to topic areas which cover the interests of the readers.

Sachar Paulus   *Norbert Pohlmann*   *Helmut Reimer*

EEMA (www.eema.org):

For 16 years, EEMA has been Europe's leading independent, non-profit e-Business association, working with its European members, governmental bodies, standards organisations and e-Business initiatives throughout Europe to further e-Business technology and legislation.

EEMA's remit is to educate and inform around 200 Member organisations on the latest developments and technologies, at the same time enabling Members of the association to compare views and ideas. The work produced by the association with its Members (projects, papers, seminars, tutorials and re-ports etc) is funded by both membership subscriptions and revenue generated through fee-paying events. All of the information generated by EEMA and its Members is available to other members free of charge.

Examples of papers produced in recent months are:- Role Based Access Control – a User's Guide, Wireless Deployment Guidelines, Secure e-Mail within the Organisation, The impact of XML on existing Business Processes, PKI Usage within User Organisations. EEMA Members, based on a requirement from the rest of the Membership, contributed all of these papers. Some are the result of many months' work, and form part of a larger project on the subject.

TeleTrusT (www.teletrust.de):

TeleTrusT was founded in 1989 to promote the security of information and communication technology in an open systems environment.

The non-profit organization was constituted with the aim of:

- achieving acceptance of the digital signature as an instrument conferring legal validity on electronic transactions;

- supporting research into methods of safeguarding electronic data interchange (EDI), application of its results, and development of standards in this field;

- collaborating with institutes and organizations in other countries with the aim of harmonizing objectives and standards within the European Union.

TeleTrusT supports the incorporation of trusted services in planned or existing IT applications of public administration, organisations and industry. Special attention is being paid to secure services and their management for trustworthy electronic communication.

Table of Contents

Strategy _____ **1**

True Economics of a Security Infrastructure
Andrew Oldham _____ 3

ROI+ Methodology to Justify Security Investment
Philippe Lemaire, Jean-Luc Delvaux _____ 12

Basel II and Beyond: Implications for e-Security
Thomas Kohler _____ 23

The Role of Attack Simulation in Risk Management Automation
Avi Corfas _____ 30

Secure ICT Architectures for Efficient Detection and Response
György Endersz _____ 38

Biometric Identity Cards: Technical, Legal, and Policy Issues
Gerrit Hornung _____ 47

New Initiatives and New Needs for Privacy Enhancing Technologies
Alexander Dix _____ 58

Data Protection Aspects of the Digital Rights Management
Alfred Büllesbach _____ 66

Big Brother does not Keep your Assets Safe
Johannes Wiele _____ 75

Technology _____ 87

Identity Federation: Business Drivers, Use Cases, and Key Business Considerations
J. Matthew Gardiner _____ 89

Trusted Computing and its Applications: An Overview
Klaus Kursawe _____ 99

RFID Privacy: Challenges and Progress
Burt Kaliski _____ 108

Light-weight PKI-Enabling through the Service of a Central Signature Server
Malek Bechlaghem _____ 117

Massmailers: New Threats Need Novel Anti-Virus Measures
David Harley _____ 127

OpenPMF: A Model-Driven Security Framework for Distributed Systems
Ulrich Lang, Rudolf Schreiner _____ 138

Is Grid Computing more Secure?
Thomas Obert _____ 148

Tamper-Resistant Biometric IDs
Darko Kirovski, Nebojša Jojić, Gavin Jancke _____ 160

Practice _____ 269

Managing Trust in Critical Infrastructure Protection Information Sharing Systems
John T. Sabo _____ 271

Legal Status of Qualified Electronic Signatures in Europe
Jos Dumortier _____ 281

The Finnish Ecosystem for Mobile Signatures
Werner Freystätter, Samu Konttinen _____ 290

e-Transformation Turkey Project
Aysegul Ibrisim, Rasim Yilmaz _____ 299

Asia PKI Interoperability Guideline
InKyung Jeun, Jaeil Lee, SangHwan Park _____ 309

Recent PKI Experiences in Serbia
Milan Marković _____ 321

CCTV and Workplace Privacy – Italy
Paolo Balboni _____ 333

Enhancing Security of Computing Platforms with TC-Technology
Oliver Altmeyer, Ahmad-Reza Sadeghi, Marcel Selhorst, Christian Stüble _____ 346

Index _____ 363

Strategy

True Economics of a
Security Infrastructure

Andrew Oldham

ASPACE Solutions, Three Tuns House,
109 Borough High Street, London, SE1 1NL, UK
aoldham@aspacesolutions.com

Abstract

Fundamental to a discussion on the financial implications of implementing and running a security infrastructure is that an Identification & Verification (ID&V) solution will not make you money directly. Rather, ID&V is considered to be an enabling technology helping organisations improve operational processes and customer experiences as well as reducing exposure to risk and fraud.

When talking about Return on Investment (ROI) in the context of security, it is important to look to the tangible benefits derived from implementing a security infrastructure – the application of the solution, not the solution itself, can reduce costs and lead to increased revenue.

Due to the multi-channel nature of the financial services sector and the importance of identification and verification in undertaking financial transactions, examples included in this paper are primarily drawn from this market.

1 The cost elements

Organisations seeking to secure their customer communities are only too aware of the need to keep pace with customer demands, industry trends and technological advances.

Implementing, maintaining and using a strong security infrastructure is a costly exercise. Generally speaking, the more complex the solution, the more difficult it is to use and the greater the operating costs.

Quantifying costs versus benefits associated with introduction of security services is an abstract process, predominantly because of the intangible nature of these services.

Deciding upon the measurement criteria to build a business case for a security solution is a difficult process, often based on opinion and speculation. This approach is not dissimilar to the calculations required for BASEL-II; quantification of risk for example, is a notoriously subjective area.

Security solutions are normally implemented for a specific reason; namely to protect a valuable resource. The nature of the resource drives the scale, scope and complexity of the underlying security solution such as the manner in which it is accessed and which user communities are permitted access to it. If solution requires many different types of resources to be secured then the underlying security model becomes even more complex.

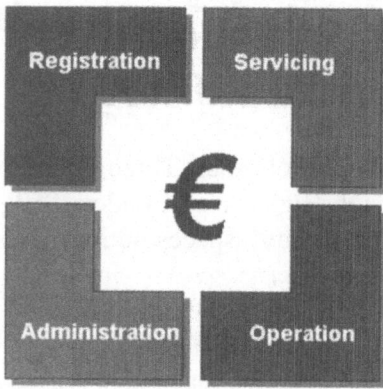

Figure 1: Cost elements of a security service.

This paper considers the tangible costs associated with the implementation and operation of ID&V services in their support of business processes. It also investigates approaches to cost reduction and identifies the intangible benefits of deploying an enterprise-wide security solution.

The cost elements of a security solution can be considered as the:

- Registration Costs – Registration of users for the security service;
- Servicing Costs – Application of security controls (identification, verification, authorisation);
- Administration Costs – Administration of registered users;
- Operational Costs – Installation and maintenance of the solution.

1.1 Registration costs

A registration process can be described as the sequence of steps required in order to provision a new user. Registration processes are typically supported by a workflow or CRM application, which serves to sequence the steps and invoke appropriate activities. In the retail financial services world, the registration process is analogous to the account opening process. For example, a new-to-brand customer will be led through a series of steps before completing a product application. Certain steps invoke a series of identification processes, such as proof of address or verification of credit worthiness – in the UK financial services sector these are termed Know Your Customer (KYC) checks. Successful completion of these checks results in the provision of a valid user identity and the establishment of trust between the customer and the organisation.

Typically, these security components will include:

- Provision of a unique identifier;
- Provision of one or more verifiers (such as passwords, PIN's or memorable facts);
- Fulfilment of a physical token (if a strong authentication mechanism is required);
- Provision of a security profile (defining privileges, roles, entitlements and restrictions);
- Enablement of one or more access channels (such as web, branch, interactive voice response (IVR) and phone)

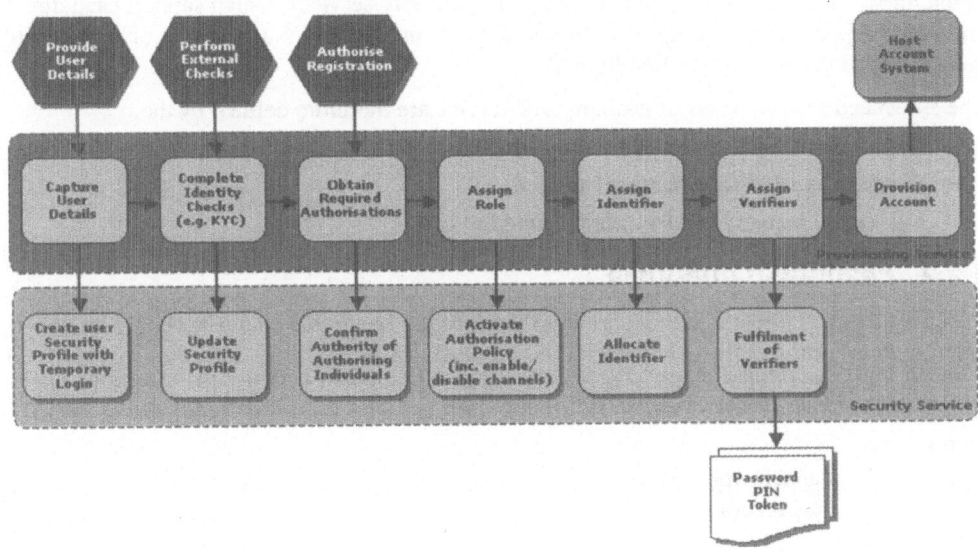

Figure 2: Generic user registration process.

Typically, organisations employ different registration processes and systems for each channel and product, thus duplicating customer interactions, systems and resources.

1.2 Servicing costs

The security components associated with the servicing of a resource relate to the way in which the acts of identification, authentication and authorisation are applied including auditing all activities.

Users access resources either directly through self-service channels (such as the web or IVR) or indirectly through facilitated channels (such as over the phone to contact centres or through branches).

1.2.1 User self-service

In order to reduce operating costs, organisations provide their customers with tools that allow them to service their own resources directly, reducing the number of service agents required.

As the transaction value becomes higher, so the financial risk increases and thus the security controls applied become stronger. Channel access must also be considered, with direct channels, such as web, perceived to be of higher risk than facilitated channels. Therefore, an organisation permitting higher risk transactions, such as a bank transfer, may require the deployment of strong verification mechanisms, for example two-factor authentication or one-time passwords.

Types of security controls applied to user self-service are typically:

- Username and password for authentication;
- Memorable facts as a back-up process for resetting verifiers;
- A second token, such as a smartcard or one time password token for secondary authentication.

Often, there are a number of different underlying security services, which support each direct channel independently, leading to a duplication of functionality (such as use of memorable data, the application of transaction limits).

The associated security costs of enabling self-service are therefore defined by the:

- Types of authentication mechanisms adopted;
- Complexity of security features applied;
- Number of security services implemented.

1.2.2 Facilitated channels

Allowing users to interact with an organisation through facilitated channels should be undertaken with the same security considerations as those for self-service. The security processes adopted must be strong enough to reduce the risk of fraudulent activity, but should be applicable to the situation. For example, it doesn't make sense to use a £10 smartcard to secure a £5 resource.

In facilitated channels, the fact that staff transact upon a resource on behalf of a user means that the audit must record not only what activity was performed, but also which staff member carried out the transaction on behalf of the user. Typically, security solutions supporting facilitated channels are geared up to record activities performed by *either* staff *or* end-users but not both.

When users call a contact centre in order access resources, they are initially identified and authenticated by the service agent. If the service query requires a hand-off to another agent, often it is not possible to transfer the authenticated user session thus requiring the user to re-authenticate. Ideally, an organisation would maintain a consistent audit record of all interactions with the user, such that it is possible to trace the initial authentication by the first agent and then subsequently transfer an authenticated user to a second agent.

The ability to perform an authenticated session transfer reduces the average call time, since a second agent does not need to re-verify the user. This is an important feature in reducing the cost of sale and improving customer satisfaction.

Supporting facilitated channels introduces the additional risk of internal fraud. To combat this threat, the security infrastructure must be capable of applying suitable controls on internal staff to restrict access and to monitor and report agent collusion.

The security costs associated with supporting a facilitated channel are therefore directly related to the complexity of services offered through each channel, coupled with the degree to which these security services are integrated with contact management applications and supporting infrastructures, such as Computer Telephony Integration (CTI).

1.3 Administration costs

In many organisations, users and customers must remember almost as many passwords as they have products; maybe more if they use multiple channels to contact the organisation. Where customers have more than one role, for example a retail account holder and business account holder, organisations tend to treat them as separate individuals. This means that the business often has to maintain multiple different identities and verifiers on different systems for the same user.

When customers forget a password, they are often forced use the telephone channel to perform a password reset, since facilities are not provided to reset their own passwords.

Due to the fragmentary nature of audit logs in a multi-channel, multi-role system, should there be a customer issue that requires an audit query, significant effort must be invested to piece together information from multiple records and systems.

The following are just some of the causes of costs that arise from having to maintain a user community served by the organisation:

- Resetting passwords;
- Re-issuing tokens or PINs;
- Enabling channels;
- Updating thresholds and access limits;
- Registering to access new services.

One way of arriving at a total cost of administration is to consider it in terms of the numbers of staff required.

For example: the cost of resetting passwords, which can account for up to 25% [Alle02] of all helpdesk calls, is significant. With speculative costs of £13 per call, a large financial services organisation serving 15 million customers has an average monthly call volume of around 4 million calls. This equates to a monthly bill in the region of £13million, just to reset users' passwords. Even considering the ambiguity of these estimates, the underlying message is that just servicing password resets is exceedingly costly and any actions that can be taken to reduce these figures will directly impact the organisation's bottom line. Statistics suggest that if a user has one password rather than five then the number of password reset calls is likely to fall by 80-85%

1.4 Operational costs

System costs associated with the deployment and maintenance of a single security solution can consider two main categories:

- Cost of implementation – these are the costs of delivering a security solution and include:
  - Physical hardware costs;
  - The cost of integrating with existing components;
  - The cost of changing internal processes and procedures often known as Business Process Re-engineering (BPR).
- Ongoing cost of system support – these are the costs of running and extending the solution once it has been delivered:
  - The cost of extending the solution – extending security services to support a new marketing initiative, an advancement in technology or a consolidation of services, sometimes means the costs of extending individual, point solutions becomes inhibitive;
  - Support and maintenance contracts – with multiple security services supporting the plethora of channels, products and services, the total ongoing support and maintenance costs are significant;

- Operational support – the staff costs associated with the daily maintenance of the system (the monitoring of logs, the maintenance of keys and daily housekeeping activities).

2 What is the ideal solution?

A Greenfield-site implementation has the benefit of no legacy system integration and the opportunity to deploy a security infrastructure capable of meeting the desired requirements. However, most real-world implementations are faced with a myriad of channels, services and, more pertinently, existing ID&V systems each supporting different parts of the business.

For example, a typical tier one retail financial services organisation is likely to be operating over 20 separate ID&V systems underpinning multiple products and services, which are used by in excess of 15 different, distinct customer communities. The underlying security infrastructure will comprise a complex mix of integrated, semi integrated and stand-alone systems, all playing their individual role in supporting discrete processes, service channels or user groups.

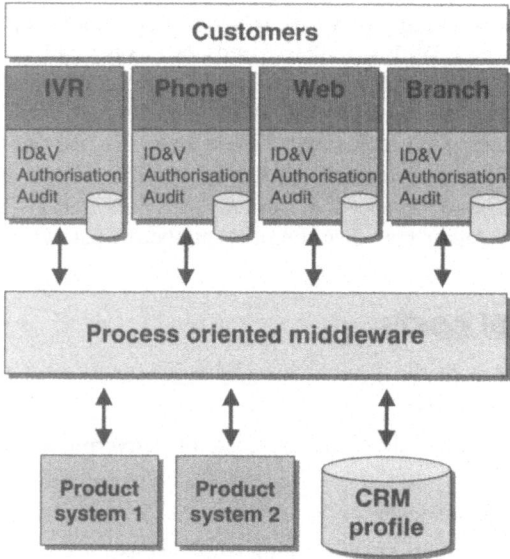

Figure 2: Silo approach to security services.

A much simpler and cost efficient solution is to implement a service orientated architecture (SOA) that adopts a single point of policy administration. This allows an enterprise-wide security policy to be deployed across an organisation administered from a single source.

Existing ID&V systems and services do not need to be replaced. The definition of user security profiles is consolidated into a central source, but the application of controls can continue to be enforced by existing services. A centralised security server provides the ability to deploy multiple security policies, concurrently from a single source. The solution provides extensible services to integrate to existing security solutions and data repositories.

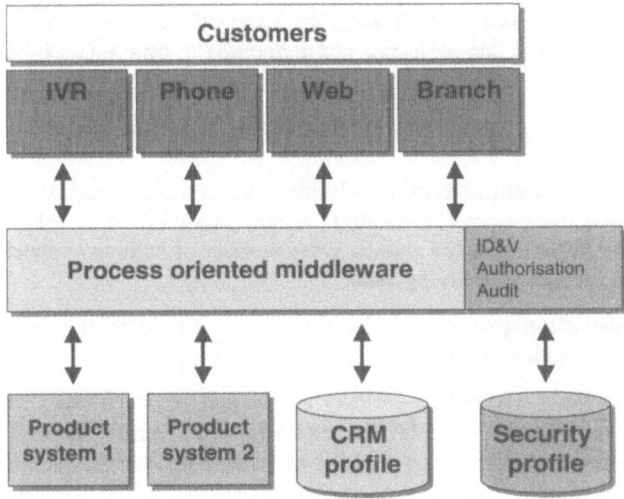

Figure 3: Multi-channel approach to security services.

This architecture has the following advantages:

- Maintainance of a single security service;
- A consistent application of security policies across all channels;
- Provision of a single source of audit data;
- Provides a framework for future expansion of security services;.
- Publishes a single set of security services that can be used by all registration systems, simplifying the provisioning process;
- Provides a a single security profile, with identifiers and verifiers that can be used across multiple channels improving customer experience.

3 How can cost savings be made?

The implementation of a solution that has a single point from which the enterprise security policy is defined produces significant cost reductions.

3.1 Registration

Reduction in the cost of registration – provisioning customers onto a security service using a single registration process and pre-registration for new-to-brand customers saves time and effort in channel-by-channel or service-by-service provision.

3.2 Servicing

Reduction in the cost of account servicing – facilitating the take up of lower cost channels and increasing call maturity – i.e. authenticating customers to a suitable level to enable agents to complete a customer request over the phone. With no process in place to allow customers to verify themselves to a level sufficient to perform an activity over low cost channels, customers are forced to complete the transaction either by post or face-to-face.

Reduction in the cost of sale – facilitating the hand-off between service agents and sales agents by pre-authenticating the customer and reducing the time taken by the agent in processing the sale.

3.3 Administration

Reduction in the cost of administration – Implementing a common ID&V solution across a large organisation, customers are less likely to forget passwords, lose tokens or mislay usernames. This has the direct impact of reducing the number of calls to support desks to reset or re-issue passwords immediately saving costs.

Simplified administration processes – by virtue of a single reset process administration processes are simpler and lower cost.

User self-maintenance – Adopting a security policy that provides users with back-up security mechanisms (such as memorable facts), empowers users to reset their own primary verifiers, reducing the number of administration calls and therefore operational costs.

Distributed administration – Having a security solution that can implement controls based upon user communities allows adminsitration of the user base to be delegated or outsourced.

3.4 Operation

Reduction in IT implementation and management costs – the costs associated with implementing and operating one, rather than many security systems (including annual maintenance, upgrade costs, systems operation, backup and recovery) is significantly lower.

4 Can security services increase revenue?

Although a security solution will not generate more income directly, enabling new processes and improving existing ones can have a significant impact on the bottom line.

Improved cross-selling – facilitating the hand-off of an authenticated customer between agents allows organisations to cross-sell through contact centres more efficiently.

Improves time to market – the ability to deliver new products and services to market, over multiple channels, quicker because of the underlying security framework.

Increased Customer retention – a single security process delivers improved customer experience and increased customer loyalty.

5 Intangible benefits?

The implementation of a centralised, common ID&V service that delivers an extendable framework for future verification mechanisms provides a number of intangible benefits such as:

Avoidance of further costs – Avoids the cost of implementing future verification mechanisms in multiple systems (e.g. two factor authentication using EMV smartcards). Avoid the cost of upgrades to existing security systems. Avoids the cost of implementing additional ID&V solutions for new products or services.

Reduction in risk – a customer with a single password is less likely to forget it than one with multiple passwords.

Risk management – manage the risk of fraud (both internal & external) against the customer, rather than within a single channel.

Reduced fraud – minimises the risk of fraud (both internal & external) through the use of ID&V mechanisms that are appropriate to specific user activities (such as facilitating KYC & supporting BASEL II requirements).

Consistent ID&V solution – used across all channels, products and services removes duplication of ID&V information for the user and the organisation.

Improved speed-to-market – facilitating the deployment of new products.

Successful implementation of security policies – enabling implementation of a complex security policy across all channels, rather than being channel aligned (such as a customer based daily transaction limit as opposed to a product or channel based limit).

References

[Alle02]   Allen, Ant: Password Management, Single Sign-On, and Authentication Management Infrastructure Products: Perspective, Gartner, 2002, p. 2, 10.

ROI+ Methodology to Justify Security Investment

Philippe Lemaire · Jean-Luc Delvaux

Telindus Corporate
Geldenaaksebaan 335
Heverlee B-3001, Belgium
{jeanluc.delvaux I philippe.lemaire}@telindus.com

Abstract

This paper covers the controversy around ROI when planning security investments. It starts with the definitions of the necessary financial terms and an outline of a CFO and CISO expectations.

It is followed by a study of the various existing approaches in security ROI and TCO, looking at: ROSI (Return on Security Investments), Value measurement, Business impacts ... An alternative method to this standard ROI calculation is to compute a differential ROI between an „As is" situation and a „Proposed" one, which adds the tangible and intangible benefits of security on a given period of time (3-5 years). This is what is called the ROI+ methodology.

To illustrate the methodology and tools, we will then apply them to concrete examples around specific security domains such as: Anti-Spam and Anti-Virus technologies, Penetration Testing, Web Security, VPNs...

1 Introduction

1.1 Market context

Following the IT investment slowdown after 9/11, there has been a growing demand for **financial analysis** using **Return On Investment** (ROI) or similar techniques, to allow organisations to take better investment decisions. With tighter IT budgets, there are simply less approved IT projects. In this context one of the most effective ways to select the 'best' projects is to look at the return they will generate for the company.

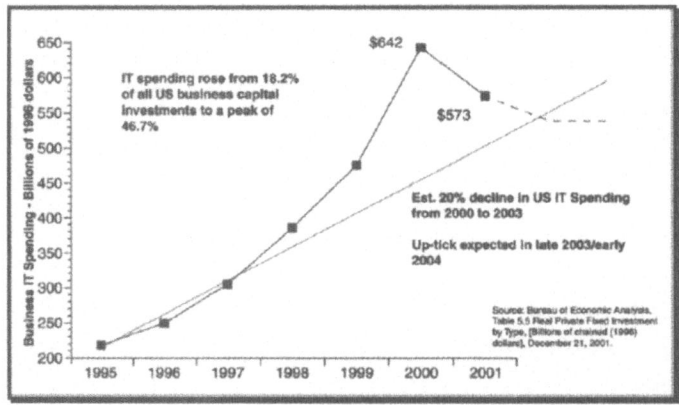

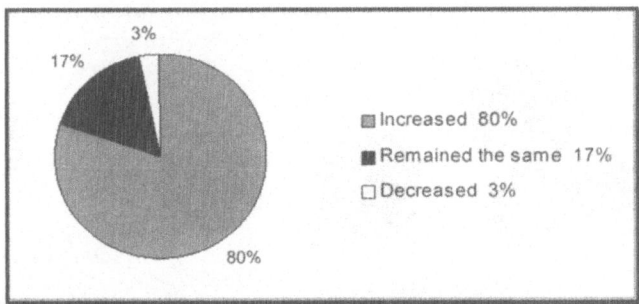

Comparing 2003 to 2002, an increase demand on ROI justification was around 80%. In 2004 analysts consider that close to 100% of IT investment will require an ROI like financial justification.

According to Gartner, C level executives are more involved than ever in the decision process:

- 60% of IT investments are controlled by business or functional managers
- And 40% by IT organizations –source Gartner 2002

1.2   R³ Magic Quadrant

When it comes to justifying and prioritising security projects, ROI is not the unique driver. However it is part of the three most significant driving factors in the purchase of Security technologies and services. These are:

- **R**eturn on Investment (ROI) associated to the project
- **R**isk Management and Mitigation
- **R**egulatory Compliance such as Sarbanes-Oxley, Basel II for banks, Data Privacy laws, etc.

To help companies prioritise their security projects, Telindus helps them to identify the relative importance of these parameters and maps the result in the form of an „R³ Magic Quadrant" . In this case R³ stands for: **R**OI, **R**isk and **R**egulatory Compliance.

This visualisation tool will obviously give very different results from organisation to organisation and will also need to be adapted over time within a same company.

In the example below we show a case where:

- Major Risk exposures are associated with Viruses, lack of Identity Management, and implementation of Wireless LANs… (The bigger the bubble, the bigger the risk)
- Regulatory Compliance is very important for Identity Management and general Security Management…
- And best ROI are achieved through Anti-Virus, Anti-Spam, Identity Management, VPNs…

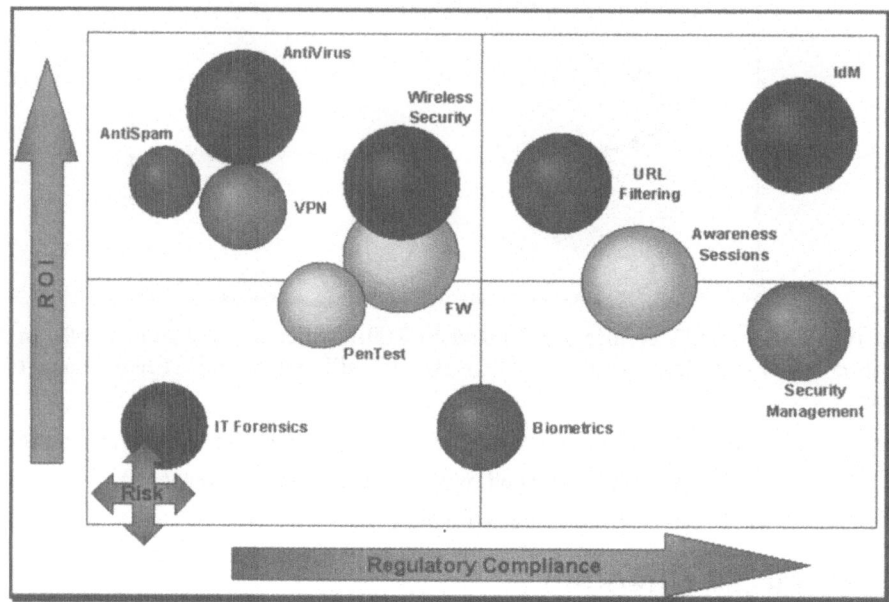

The rest of this paper will exclusively focus on the financial justification of security projects.

1.3 Controversies around Security ROI

As for any other IT project, the Security managers are under pressure to demonstrate the ROI of their projects. However, the very nature of IT security makes financial projections difficult. Indeed, the benefit of Security is difficult to quantify because the measure of its success is the absence of failure. In many cases security is seen as a basic necessity, like electricity or climate control. How can you calculate a return on investment for electrical cable or air conditioning?

At best, technology vendors and service providers will try to give an answer with immature data or un-quantifiable benefits. For this reason, many people are trying to avoid the challenge by claiming that it is impossible to quantitatively predict ROI, leading to a general scepticism on ROI in the security domain.

Last but not least, it is equally difficult to evaluate the damage of a security breach if you had not done the investment. This is sometimes quoted as 'Loss on Non-Investment' The damage can usually be related to assets but also to intangibles such as company image.

With IT security being today an essential business issue on most CEOs agenda, the ROI+[tm] approach seems more and more to be the adequate one to justify the investment in business terms.

2   ROI, TCO or an Alternative Set of Parameters...

2.1 Financial Definitions

The **ROI** is defined as being the ratio of the net gain from a proposed project, divided by its total costs. It is expressed as a percentage (also called ROI%). A good ROI analysis must take into account all the costs of a new project as well as all the benefits an organization can expect from it.

ROI% is lacking of absolute value. For example a 500% ROI project could not be considered for a 2k€ investment (too small return), or a 1000% ROI project on a 10M€ investment could also be rejected (too big investment).

The **Total Cost of Ownership** (TCO) is a concept introduced in the late 80s by Bill Kirvin from Gartner group. It was aimed at that time to justify the replacement of high cost centralized systems by decentralized ones and to show that hardware and software are just a part (<15%) of the total costs of owning computers. It is now mainly used to uncover costs issues not to evaluate a new project as it looks at only one side of the equation: the costs. TCO must be carefully used as it has serious drawbacks. For example, to obtain the lowest TCO you better throw away computers (7k€/PC/year) and replace them with pen and paper (1.5k€/year)!

The right financial parameters to be used to convince Finance Managers are the **Net Present Value (NPV)** for a given period of time, the **Internal Rate of Return (IRR)** and the **Payback period**.

The **NPV** is the net Cash Flow discounted in today's value, i.e. the sum of each year Cash Flow discounted by a given interest rate (bank interest incremented by a risk factor), meaning that time value of money is considered (e.g. 100€ in hand today is worth more than 100€ in 10 years from now).

The **IRR** is the interest rate that nulls the NPV, meaning an interest rate that will be high enough to lower future savings down to the initial spending.

The **Payback period** is defined as the time for the project to provide a positive cumulative cash flow.

The following picture explains those „magic" formulas:

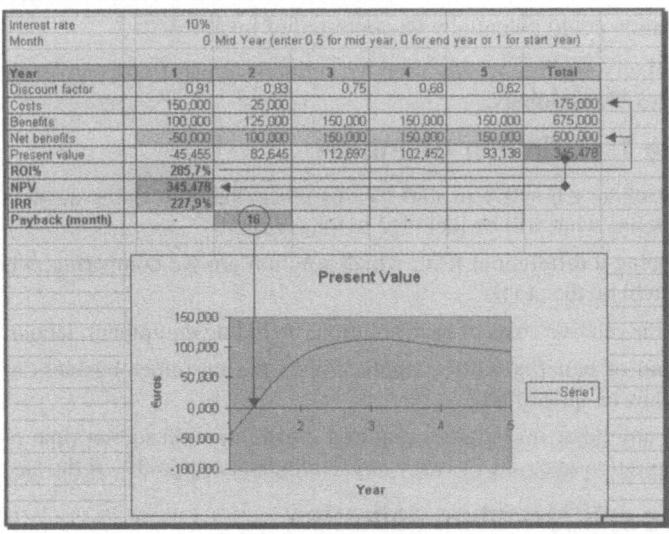

It is a good practice to provide those three parameters for a given period of 3 to 5 **years**, depending on the technology.

3 Telindus ROI+ Methodology

3.1 ROI Generic Misunderstanding

ROI is widely used by **IT managers** and most of their suppliers to justify, at the very last minute, the **costs of a technological choice**. This is mainly done in terms of costs and without either the benefits of the technology or the time value of money. In general ICT people are lacking of time, skilled resources or tools to do an extensive and complete calculation.

Financial managers are more concerned by the **Return On Invested Capital (ROIC)** meaning they want to see the business benefits of the investment as well as the value over time of it, expressed in financial terms (NPV, IRR and Payback).

3.2 What is ROI+^{tm}

To conciliate both of these demands of, Telindus proposes to its customers an **ROI+ ^{tm} approach**.

ROI+^{tm} provides a differential ROI analysis between the „as is" situation and the recommended „to be" situation. Adding the quantified tangible benefits of the project as well as intangible ones when they can be carefully quantified, complements the approach.

The **ROI+^{tm}** computation is done on a given period of time (3 to 5 years) and the results are expressed by the NPV, IRR and Payback parameters.

3.3 ROI+^{tm} Methodology: Building the Business Case

Statistics are not valid for convincing Finance Managers; they are just good enough to indicate that a project must be considered but no more. To be **compelling, an actual business case** must be developed using the **own figures specific to the customer case.** Otherwise any piece of information could potentially be contested or invalidated.

ROI+^{tm} is based on a method widely used by Telindus at pan-European level. **ROI+^{tm}** is a 4-phase consultancy methodology.

3.3.1 Phase 1: Perimeter definition

It is a good consultancy practice to start by this phase that allows the customer and Telindus consultant to finalise what will be included in the study:

- **ROI+^{tm}** being a differential ROI, which solution are we comparing, what is the „as is" and what will be the „to be".
- What are the relative costs of each solution, including equipment, labour, and training…
- Which kind of benefits will be applicable in the customer business environment and how can they be quantified,
- Are there any other investments required during the considered time period, such as a phased migration over one or two years, compulsory upgrades of the „as is" solution…

3.3.2 Phase 2: Information gathering

When the perimeter is defined it is the right time to retrieve all the information that will be necessary to quantify costs and business benefits.

This is done through specific questionnaires developed by Telindus for each considered technology solution in the new project.

This phase must not be under-estimated as it is quite often the opportunity to some internal or external people reluctant to the new project or new technology to conceal their own information in order to keep their power in the organization.

3.3.3 Phase 3: Computation

Following the numerous business cases that Telindus studied for its European customers an ROI+ spreadsheet tool was developed in order to be able to input data on:

- Generic information:
  - Financial parameters: discount rate, time period for the study (3 to 5 years)
  - Customer specific data: number of employee and burdened salaries for up to 5 personnel profiles, number of sites, square meters...
- Costs relative to the actual situation and to the proposed one:
  - Hardware and software costs
  - Installation and other services
  - Ongoing costs such as maintenance and other services
- Benefits associated to the specific proposed project including:
  - Employee productivity enhancements
  - Network costs reduction (converged network, simplified cabling, etc)
  - Communication call costs reduction (IP Telephony)
  - Asset loss reduction (Security).

3.3.4 Phase 4: Result reporting and presentation

All the detailed computations are done on a monthly basis that allows:

- To more accurately express the different figures
- And to delay some investment costs or benefits by a given number of months.

For easier understanding all the results are yearly summarized in a summary table and associated graphs giving results on a monthly basis:

- The cumulative cash flow of the project, showing the payback period after x months
- The amount of each benefit over time (employee productivity, communication cost reduction, network benefits and asset loss reduction,

And the present value over time

See in next chapter for applicable results to security.

4 ROI+^{tm} for Security

4.1 Introduction

4.1.1 Risk Management vs. ROSI (Return on Security Investments)

Risk Management is a technique that is based on loss prevention. The first step is a Risk Analysis and the second one is to implement, review and maintain safeguards.

ROSI (Return on Security Investments) mainly consider the cost of Security Investments, which is still in the IT cost centre mindset. The goal here is to minimize risks not considering either revenue generation, cost reductions or productivity increases.

4.1.3 A better approach in ROI+^{tm}

Considering the fact that business value must be considered, security can be defined as:

- Being the best protection for systems, storage, processing and transmission of information assets
- At the lowest possible cost, consistent with the value of the asset.

This approach of ROI is directly derived from risk management techniques:

> *The highest the information asset value, the highest the potential losses,*
>
> *The highest the Risk Management / Security needs will be.*

This means that security products/services must be correlated to the business value of the asset to demonstrate an ROI.

It is interesting to note that ROI only works when business makes a voluntary choice on a particular initiative, not when it hopes to reduce risks against a potential loss following industry best practices.

Prior to initiate a ROI analysis asset value must be understood. The basic components include:

- Initial and Ongoing Costs: Purchasing, licensing, developing and supporting it
- Value to production, R&D and business model viability
- Value in the external market: Intellectual property, patents, copyrights…

Once this value established, the necessary safeguards must be identified. Then we need to calculate their costs (purchase, installation, maintenance, additional investment over the considered period of time…).

Estimate the Exposure Factor (EF), i.e. the percentage of the asset value that will be lost in case of a security problem. Then the Single Loss Expectancy (SLE) is computed by:

$$\text{SLE} = \text{Asset Value x EF}$$

Refer now to industry available data concerning the Annual Rate of Occurrence (ARO), which is the probability that this event occur on a yearly basis.

This results in Annualised Loss Expectancy (ALE) given by:

$$\text{ALE} = \text{SLE x ARO}$$

In fact as the ROI+^{tm} is a differential ROI then we will consider two Exposure Factors: one without and one with the proposed security solutions, leading to a decrease in Annualised Loss Expectancy.

The following table can be used to enter data before making the computation:

Asset Valuation								
					Exposure Factor			
Asset name	Purchase value	Ongoing Costs	Internal Value	External Value	w/o security	w/ security	Annual Rate of Occurrence	Delay (mth)
Asset #1	100 000,00 €	15 000,00 €	200 000,00 €		20%	5%	2	1
Asset #2	50 000,00 €	1 000,00 €		150 000,00 €	30%	20%	1	2
Asset #3								
Asset #4								
Asset #5								
Asset #6								
Asset #7								
Asset #8								
Asset #9								
Asset #10								

One can argue that ARO is not easy to find but regulations as well as insurances being more and more pushing the industry, data will be easier to find in a near future.

Asset value is not the only way to demonstrate ROI. Additional tangible benefits must be included too, such as employee productivity per employee category (hiring is sometime difficult so re-deploying employees in other tasks can be useful), network optimisation (bandwidth, storage...).

4.2 ROI+^{tm} for Anti-Spam tools

All companies are using e-mail to communicate either internally or with customers and partners. This is a real communication channel and any dysfunction of it could lead to concrete business losses.

A large majority of companies noticed that a growing proportion of e-mails were not business related. For some of them, the volume of unsolicited e-mails has reached unacceptable levels. Spam is defined as 'any e-mail that was not requested by its recipient and has been sent out en masse'. Spam is clearly a cheap marketing tool, but it can be used for illegal e-business, political or racial propaganda, pornography, etc...

In the recent years, tools have been developed to filter Spam before it reaches its recipients. Filtering is normally based on content, source or a combination of the two.

More than two thirds (67.6 per cent) of the 840m emails scanned by filtering firm Message-Labs in April 2004 was identified as spam.

Impact of an anti-Spam tool can be quantified in terms of:

- End-user productivity enhancement, gaining time by either not retrieving and reading unexpected mails, nor calling helpdesk,
- Network bandwidth reduction due to traffic of those unexpected mails,
- Storage limitation due to useless messages storage,
- Helpdesk calls reduction.

Referring to employee productivity and considering the following population:

| Employee charges | | |
Loaded salaries	# people	Av. salary /year
Group #1	10	150 000,00 €
Group #2	50	70 000,00 €
Group #3	100	30 000,00 €
Group #4	500	15 000,00 €
Group #5	1000	10 000,00 €

The employee productivity can be the following:

Spam:reading unexpected mails		minutes /day	gain %	1	costs reduction per month
	Group #1	0	0%		- €
	Group #2	2	50%		397,73 €
	Group #3	2	50%		340,91 €
	Group #4	2	50%		852,27 €
	Group #5	1	50%		568,18 €
					2 159,09 €

With average monthly benefits on network usage of:

Cost of bandwidth used by Spam	750,00 €
Bandwidth used by e-mail	50%
Total cost of Internet connectivity per month	5 000,00 €
Percentage of spam e-mail	30%
Cost of storage used by Spam	1 141,25 €
Average message size (Kb)	50
Storage cost per GB inc. management	0,50 €
Average email number per day per employee	5

With an anti-Spam tool costing around 25K€ per year for this population, and productivity benefits of 4000€ per month the payback will be after 6,25 months.

4.3   ROI+^{tm} for Anti-Virus software

The proportion of companies that suffer virus infection is still rising. The 2004 CERT and CSO Magazine eCrime Watch Survey published recently shows that 77.2% of surveyed organisations had suffered of viruses and malicious attacks in 2003. These had various impacts:

- From a single day disruption of service and less than a man-day's investigation and remediation
- Up to several weeks of disruption of service and man-month to fix the problem.

The impacts of an Anti-Virus tool can be quantified in terms of:

- IT personal productivity avoiding to diagnose the problem, fix it and even re-install several machines, less the time spent in managing the Anti-Virus tool,
- End user productivity, time not lost in diagnosing the problem, and wait for a fix before re-starting the normal work,

- • Reduction of losses of IT assets during the incident (individual workstation, web server, database server, content of the data base…) that will be measured by the differential ALE as defined before

An example of productivity improvement is given hereafter:

Anti-Virus : IT employee productivity			gain %	cost reduction per month
Number of virus attacks per year		10	80%	250,00 €
Average time spent in fixing viruses / attack		3		
Time spent in administrating anti-virus / year		2		
Salary group		Group #3		
Anti-Virus : End User productivity		lost hours /attack		cost reduction per month
	Group #1	0,25		35,51 €
	Group #2	1		331,44 €
	Group #3	2		568,18 €
	Group #4	1		710,23 €
	Group #5	0,5		473,48 €
				2 118,84 €

4.4   ROI+[tm] for VPN

A simple example is given here where we can consider the Communication costs reduction due to the use of Internet communication through a Virtual Private Network (VPN) instead of accessing to the company network by means of a Remote Access Server (RAS).

			per month	delay (mth)			
Security	VPN instead of RAS		2 388,33 €	0			
	Usage of Remote Access Server		3 138,33 €				
	Home communication cost per mn						
			% users		mn / day		
		Group #1	10%	1	5		9,17 €
		Group #2	30%	15	15		412,50 €
		Group #3	20%	20	15		550,00 €
		Group #4	10%	50	10		916,67 €
		Group #5	0%	-	0		- €
				86			1 888,33 €
	Fixed centralised costs						
	Number of telephone lines for RAS		5	4,30			1 250,00 €
	VPN Costs						
	% of Internet access use		15%	750,00 €			

Considering the usage of remote access per user group (average number of minutes per day) and both costs of calls from employees' home and cost of line rental, this lead to average monthly cost of 1.888,33€ (same population as in others examples). Centralised costs of the RAS must be added, in that case 5 lines with a monthly cost of 1250€.

The ongoing costs of the VPN are just a percentage of the costs of the Internet access shared with other access types (mail, Internet surfing, Extranet and Institutional Web server…). It is considered in that particular customer situation as being 15% of the total use, e.g. a monthly cost of 750€.

Using the VPN induces a benefit of 2.388,33€ per month, with an initial investment of 20.000€ that leads to a payback period of 8 months.

5 Conclusion

We have seen that ROI is nowadays a „Must" to justify investment for any ICT project. Even if they are some different interpretations of the concepts between ICT staff and C-level management, ROI calculation is being used daily for IT and for Security projects.

Even if justifying the Return on Security Investments is more complex than for other domains that are more directly linked to the business, it is still possible to elaborate the right figures for very specific areas of security..

Telindus' ROI+ approach provides decision makers with some methodology:

- To properly identify the different benefits induced by the various security technologies and/or services,
- To include the risk management components in the ROI study.

Last but not least, ROI or ROI+ will not be enough to take the right decision in the security space. The use of a magic quadrant mapping the ROI impact with the risk level and with the regulatory compliance will help organisation in taking the correct decisions for their business.

Telindus is ideally positioned and has extensive experience to help organisations in their process to justify and implement security solutions.

Basel II and Beyond: Implications for e-Security

Thomas Kohler

IT & Information Risk Control
UBS AG
thomas.kohler@ubs.com

Abstract

IT and Information Security is more and more influenced by the regulatory framework of the jurisdiction(s), a company is active in. For Financial Institutions, the most common regulation is Basel II, for all companies listed at an American stock exchange, the regulation to seek compliance with, is SOX (Sarbanes Oxley). Furthermore, financial institutions serving clients in the US, have to be compliant with the Gramm Leach Bliley Act (GLBA) which is a further cornerstone in the regulatory framework of globally acting financial institutions.

My presentation will layout the most common and basic aspects of the new regulations in order to set a common ground. The main focus however, is put on the implementation aspects of the Basel II, SOX and GLBA and its' impact on the architecture and design of global applications within an internationally and globally acting Financial institution.

1 Basic Requirements of Basel II, SOX and GLBA

1.1 About Basel II

With the new framework of Basel II, the operational risks are measured and supported by financial provisions. These provisions can be calculated in three different ways (basic indicator approach, standard approach, advanced measurement approach), depending on the maturity of the risk management and risk control processes and the quality of the documentation of the losses, suffered in the past. Operational risks is understood as the risk of loss resulting from inadequate or failed internal processes, people and systems or from external events. The definition of operational risks includes legal risks but excludes strategic, reputational and systemic risks. Therefore operational risk event types that the Basel committee has identified as having the potential to result in substantial losses include:

- Fraud
  - Internal
  - External
- Employment practices and workplace safety
- Clients, products and business practices
- Damage to physical assets
- Business disruption and system failures
- Execution, delivery and process management.

S. Paulus, N. Pohlmann, H. Reimer (Editors): Securing Electronic Business Processes, Vieweg (2004), 23-29

Clearly, Basel II does also not cover the primary risks of a financial institution such as credit, market and liquidity risks. However, the financial provisioning has a direct impact onto the product prices, a financial institution is offering in the market.

Basel II sets a couple of requirements to be compliant with, such as:

- Operational risk framework

    - To be based on an appropriate definition of operational risks (what constitutes operational risks in the firm)

    - Covers the company's tolerance for operational risks

    - includes the policies outlining the firm's approach to identify, document, assess, monitor and control/mitigate the operational risks

    - defines the key processes to manage the operational risks

- Board of Directors

    - Awareness of the major aspects of the operational risks

    - Approval and review of the operational risk framework

    - Fostering a management structure capable of implementing the framework

    - Setting up clear lines of management responsibility, accountability and reporting

    - Separate the responsibilities and reporting lines between operational risk control functions, business lines and support functions

    - Ensuring that the operational risks are managed arising from external market changes or other environmental factors

    - Ensuring that the operational risk management is subject to effective and comprehensive internal audits

- Senior Management

    - Responsibility for a consistent implementation of the operational risk framework throughout the whole organisation

    - Development of procedures to effectively manage operational risks in all material products, processes and systems

    - Assignment of authority, responsibility and reporting relationships

    - Assurance of a proper communication within the organisation

    - Assurance of holistic view on operational risks

    - Giving attention to the quality of documentation control and to transaction-handling practices

1.2 About SOX

This act requires all CEOs and CFOs of companies listed at any US stock exchange to certify their financial results. Now the industry is grappling with SOX 404, but there are a number of additional requirements to be compliant with. SOX is therefore all about the integrity of the financial statement. For SOX, the following aspects become relevant and famous as the 11 Acts of SOX:

- Public Company Accounting / Oversight Board
- Auditor Independence
- Corporate Responsibility
- Enhanced Financial Disclosure
- Analyst Conflict of Interests
- Commission Resources and Authority
- Studies and Reports
- Corporate and Criminal Fraud Accountability
- White Collar Crime Penalty Enhancements
- Corporate Tax Return
- Corporate Fraud and Accountability

Not all of the 11 Acts are relevant for the IT arena, in my presentation I will focus on the impacts of SOX 404 and 80x.

- SOX 404: Companies must include in their annual reports a report of management on the company's internal controls over financial reporting
  - Statement of management's responsibility for establishing and maintaining adequate internal controls
  - Statement identifying the framework used to conduct the required evaluation of the effectiveness of the internal controls
  - Management's assessment of the effectiveness of the company's internal controls, including the disclosure of any material weaknesses
  - Attestation report on management's assessment by the independent auditors

- SOX 80x: This Act mandates a company to have the processes, tools and people in place to forensically investigate internal and external criminal fraud
  - SOX 801: Corporate and criminal fraud accountability
  - SOX 802: Retention of records relevant to audits and reviews
  - SOX 803:   Debts non-dischargeable if incurred in violation of securities fraud laws
  - SOX 804: Statute of limitations for securities fraud
  - SOX 805: Obstruction of justice and extensive criminal fraud
  - SOX 806:   Protection for employees of publicly traded companies who provide evidence of fraud (whistle blowing)
  - SOX 807:   Criminal penalties for defrauding shareholders of publicly traded companies

Having concentrated on Act 4 and 8, I have to admit that other Acts play a role for IT as well, such as e.g. „Analyst Conflict of Interests" where a so called Chinese Wall has to be built and maintained between various system within an enterprise.

1.3   About the GLB Act

The Gramm-Leach-Bliley Act was enacted on November 12, 1999. In addition to reforming the financial services industry, the Act addressed concerns relating to consumer financial privacy. The Gramm-Leach-Bliley Act required the Federal Trade Commission (FTC) and other government agencies that regulate financial institutions to implement regulations to carry out the Act's financial privacy provisions (GLB Act). The regulations required all covered businesses to be in full compliance by July 1, 2001. The main concern of GLBA is privacy and integriy of client data. The GLB Act sets therefore a hand-full of basic requirements to be observed:

- **Protect the privacy of consumer information held:**
  - Give consumers privacy notices that explain the institutions' information-sharing practices;
  - In turn, consumers have the right to limit some – but not all – sharing of their information;
  - Protect information collected about individuals (does not apply to information collected in business or commercial activities)

- **Safeguards Rule:**
  - Have a security plan to protect the confidentiality and integrity of personal consumer information;
  - Written Security Plan;
  - Employee and Management training

- Pretexting Provisions
  - The GLB Act prohibits „pretexting", the use of false pretenses, including fraudulent statements and impersonation, to obtain consumers' personal financial information, such as bank balances.

Given the amount of overlapping requirements of these regulations, Financial Instituions tend to develop a global compliance architecture rather than developing or purchasing piecemeal technology solutions to address each regulation, separately.

This is exactly what UBS has done, as well. At UBS, the formerly distinct projects to address Basel II, SOX, GLBA and further regulations (SAS, Patriot Act, ...) were tight together and amalgamated to a single project.

1.4   Impact of the Regulations

This chapter highlights the areas of concern which are specifically addressed in UBS:

- Legal and regulatory framework impacting IT architecture
- Operational Risk Framework as a process

- Self-assessment
- Review methodology

1.4.1 Legal and Regulatory Framework

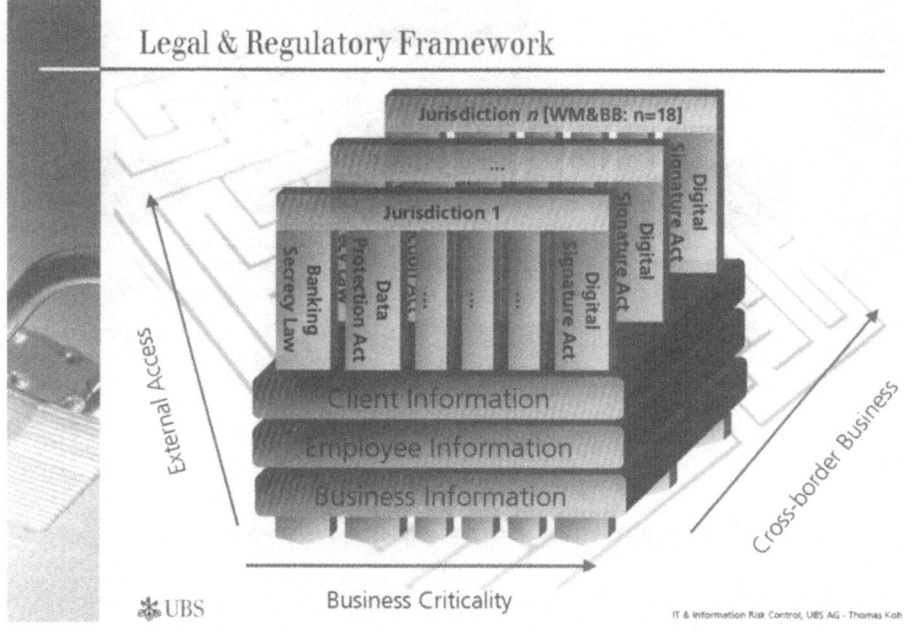

Figure 1: Legal and Regulatory Framework

A number of specific laws and regulations fundamentally influence the way on how IT architecture and the IT department's operational processes with cross-border projects are concerned with. In my presentation, I will focus on our way to deal with the amount of projects in a efficient way and I will further address this issues based on three concrete examples (global Active Directory Design, global support model, global processing platform). All three projects have different scopes however, a common criteria is certainly the sensitivity of these projects with regards to local laws and regulations.

1.4.2 Operational Risk Framework as a process

The cornerstone of our processes to comply with the various challenges from Basel II or SOX or GLBA is a stringent process which sets and enforces

- cross functional governance
- clear standards
- risk identification (self assessment)
- measurement of quality
- risk monitoring
- loss database

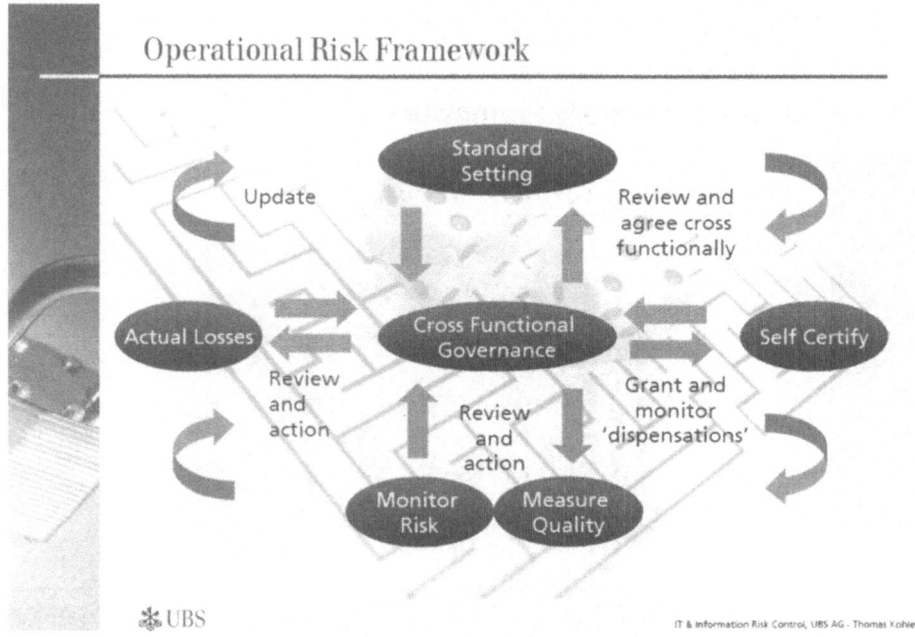

Figure 2: Process of Operational Risk Framework

1.4.3 Standards

Standards should be documented and implemented. They are the benchmark to be met and represent the path to follow. Based on incident or technology changes, standards may need revisions.

1.4.4 Cross Functional Governance

The governance in all relevant disciplines is a key element of the operational framework. It is of utmost importance that the governance model includes all risk disciplines, be it primary or consequential risks, as well as all business functions.

1.4.5 Self Certification

This is the step where users as the beginning of a cascade of certifiers will testify whether or not a specific control is performed. The questions to be answered are such that a YES or NO answer can be given. This self certification is subsequently testified, confirmed or turned-down by the users superiors. Once the self certification process is closed, the cross functional governance board will take the lead and will allow or deny exceptions from the rule. Again, the process of the decision as well as the result are documented and transparent. An exception from the rule can only be given on a temporary basis.

1.4.6 Review methodology

Self certification is the job of the risk management or the business function. Risk Control however has a different view and does not only rely on self certification, but also on their reviews. These reviews are supported by an internationally accepted methodology – in our case, ISF (Information Security Forum) which is nowadays used world-wide within approximately

280 companies. The ISF based review has to be understood as an add-on to the self certification and clearly goes beyond the latter. Strength of mechanisms, robustness of processes are evaluated and recommendations are triggered-off, where required.

Any finding be it from the self certification or the reviews or from any other source are documented in a risk tracking database the workflow engine of which ensures that no threat stored in the database is lost, but dealt with in due time.

2 Lessons to be Learnt

I'm more than convinced that many global Financial Institution has lost significant money because laws and regulations were not adhered to. Reverting from a given route in a project is very costly, cumbersome and risky. It pays off, if the conditions are identified, anticipated and implemented as part of the IT architecture and process models, and subsequently reflected in Business and technology projects.

Recent surveys (e.g. Banking Technology, issue March 2004) suggest that only a minority of the CIOs are yet actively involved in Basel II or SOX projects. Rather, the majority found that this is a sole Compliance issue. This attitude is dangerous and inappropriate and may lead many projects following the wrong path.

The Role of Attack Simulation in Risk Management Automation

Avi Corfas

Aurora House 5-6 Carlos Place
London W1K 3AP
Skybox Security, Inc.
avi@skyboxsecurity.com

Abstract

Organizations are under tremendous pressure to protect digital assets in compliance with new regulations. With ten of thousands of vulnerabilities, 10 new vulnerability types published daily and constant network changes, it takes months for enterprises to prioritize the top 1-3% of critical vulnerabilities that are accessible, exploitable and that matter – an unmanageable window of exposure. Products that help identify and mitigate vulnerabilities through automation have fallen short of delivering on their promises because they ignore the IT environment and business context. Through customer case studies, this session will introduce the role of attack simulation in the four steps to automation.

1 Overview

Operational best practices along with new government regulations requiring financial reporting accuracy and information asset privacy are making risk management a strategic imperative for enterprises. The resulting new business environment has significant implications for business, technology and security professionals in every corporation. Executives in particular need to take a strategic view of risk management, aligning the business and compliance needs of the enterprise with the technologies that support them.

The implications for security professionals are even more far-reaching: these individuals are tasked with ensuring that people, processes and technologies are implemented enterprise-wide to support all aspects of risk management in a cost-effective, proactive, non-invasive, continuous manner.

As conventional vulnerability assessment tools are operating on a component-base and ignore the business and network contexts including all the control mechanisms, new technologies, such as attack simulation, which enable the proactive security risk management process, are growing in acceptance and can be used to implement a comprehensive, automated solution. Although these technologies alone cannot replace the skills and or insight of the security professional, they can dramatically increase the accuracy and efficiency of the assessment process, reducing both the cost of and time expended in audits by as much as 90%.

2 Risk Management Defined

Security risk management is the process of identifying exposure risks, defining controls and requirements to manage those risks, and implementing controls in a cost-effective manner.

S. Paulus, N. Pohlmann, H. Reimer (Editors): Securing Electronic Business Processes, Vieweg (2004), 30-37

Risk management typically consists of three phases: Risk Assessment, Mitigation Planning, and Evaluation and Assessment[1].

Ideally, a sound risk management program answers questions such as:

- What is the risk level of each business application?
- How can critical vulnerabilities be found and mitigated in the least amount of time?
- How do infrastructure changes impact security levels?
- What is the right priority of remediation actions?
- How is regulatory compliance demonstrated?

3 Challenges in Risk Management

3.1 Assessment cycle is extremely long – typically a few months.

The security professional has many tools at his disposal: vulnerability scanners, network auditing tools, log analyzers and testing tools. While using these technologies, security teams are faced with an incomprehensible volume of information to analyze. With tens of thousands of vulnerabilities[2], ten or more new vulnerability types published daily, and constant network changes; it can take months to manually find the critical vulnerabilities that are truly accessible and potentially exploitable—an unacceptable window of exposure.

Figure 1 shows that there is a direct correlation between the assessment cycle time and risk level. The longer the assessment cycle time, the more exposed the organization is to attacks on critical information assets. Therefore, the most straightforward way to reduce risk is by completing the assessment cycle much faster – that is, shrinking the window of exposure.

Is it possible to shrink the window of exposure to a single day perhaps, while keeping required resources low?

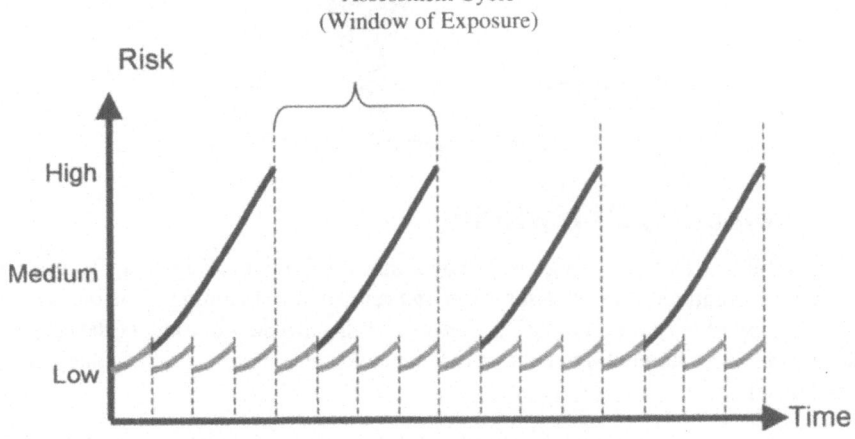

Figure 1: Risk Level and Window of Exposure

---

[1] ISSA Journal, October, 2003 "The Risk Management Process" by Michel Landry

[2] Typically, every node has 10-30 vulnerabilities

3.2 Typical Vulnerabilities Funnel

Most security professionals know from painstaking experience that only one to two percent of all vulnerabilities are truly critical from a potential business impact perspective: the ones that lie along a potential attack path to an important information asset, create a real exposure, and must be treated as a top remediation priority. In fact, most vulnerabilities are mitigated by some specific control mechanism such as a firewall, or by the network architecture itself. For example, some vulnerabilities ranked as 'severe' by a vulnerability scanner are actually already mitigated, simply because the assets in question sit behind a firewall that denies access to those assets.

The security professionals' challenge is to identify and mitigate the 1-2% of critical vulnerabilities quickly enough in order to prevent potential exploitation by attackers in a cost effective way. This is becoming increasingly crucial as the average number of days between a vulnerability being published and exploited continues to shrink and zero-day attacks become a real threat.

„IT security professionals need a way to prioritize the mitigation of vulnerabilities. With an accurate and timely way to reduce the volumes of vulnerabilities produced by scanners down to the one or two percent of risks that really matter, enterprises can protect assets and eliminate threats to business-critical applications." Mark Nicolett, Gartner Group, 2004

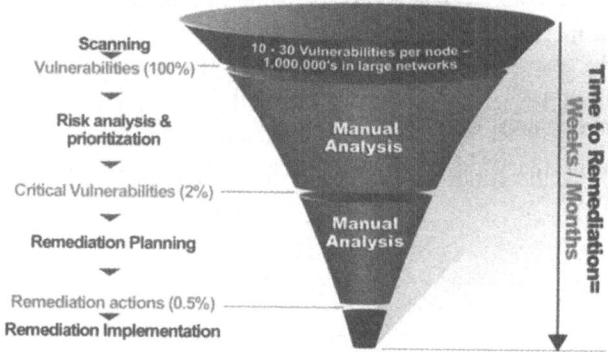

Figure 2: Vulnerabilities Funnel

3.3 Automation Opportunity

The Vulnerabilities Funnel in Figure 2 shows that the bottleneck in today's process is the manual analysis required for risk assessment and remediation planning. This bottleneck opens a significant opportunity for automation. The rest of this article will explain the crucial role of attack simulation in automating security risk management processes to 'flatten' the Vulnerabilities Funnel.

4 Attack Simulation

4.1 Attack Simulation Defined

In order to proactively identify business risks, the assessment process has to show a concrete way – an attack scenario – that the business can be impacted by a security threat – internally or externally.

The goal of an attack simulation is to find all the possible attack scenarios, by all possible threats that can impact the business.

An attack scenario, depicted in Figure 3, is a step by step recipe of the sequence of actions that an attacker could take in exploiting vulnerabilities and infrastructure weaknesses to breach the Confidentiality, Integrity, or Availability (CIA) of critical information assets. In a large complex network of thousands of infrastructure nodes, the number of potential attack scenarios can be very large[3], and cannot practically be created by hand.

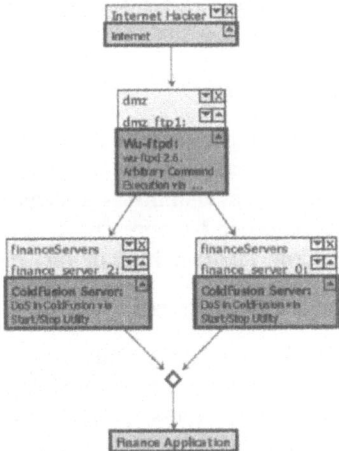

Figure 3: An Attack Scenario

Occasionally a subset of attack scenarios is worked out manually by Red teams, often as part of a penetration test or risk assessment. With the advent of new scaleable attack simulation algorithms for very large complex networks, commercialization of such a technology is now possible. This opens new options for the security professional in automating much more of the risk management cycle.

4.2 Risk Assessment and Prioritization

4.2.1 Classifying Vulnerabilities

One of the most immediate uses of attack simulation is the classification of vulnerabilities. Vulnerabilities can be classified into exposure categories, such as those that are *directly exposed* – i.e. vulnerabilities that can be directly exploited by an attacker located in one of the threat origins (i.e., no firewall blocks the access to the vulnerable services); those that are *in-*

---

[3]A large network may have of dozens of threats and thousands attack targets

directly exposed – i.e. vulnerabilities that cannot be exploited directly from the threat origins, but can be exploited using multi-step attacks that begin at one of the threat origins; and finally, those that are *inaccessible* – i.e. vulnerabilities that cannot be exploited by applying a single-step or multi-step attack from any threat origin.

Classification greatly impacts the security professional's ability to prioritize vulnerabilities and remediate only the most critical vulnerabilities. For example, vulnerabilities classified as 'directly exposed' can be addressed immediately, while those classified as 'inaccessible' can be postponed.

4.2.2 Calculating business risk

Risk to a information assets depends on two factors: 1) The likelihood of a successful attack on an information asset and 2) The potential damage that could be caused by the security loss. In a mathematical format, this risk would be represented by the equation:

$$Risk = Likelihood * Impact$$

The following section describes how to determine the impact and likelihood values, which are the key variables in calculating business risk.

4.2.3 Determining Impact Value

For each information asset, the security professional should define the impact of a successful attack using a set of impact rules. Typically, an impact rule is defined for each type of security loss – confidentiality, integrity and availability – associating an estimate of the potential damage to each loss type. The damage can be represented by an explicit monetary value or as a qualitative level, e.g., very low, low, medium, high or very high.

4.2.4 Determining Attack Likelihood

The attack simulation finds all the possible attack paths from the threat origins to the information assets, taking in account the vulnerabilities associated with network nodes and the access control. The likelihood of an attack on a business application is expressed in terms of the likelihood that attackers will successfully perform one or more of these attack paths. Each of these attack paths begins at one of the threat origins and includes a sequence of one or more attack steps that can be performed by an attacker in order to cause the security loss. An attack step can be either an exploitation of a vulnerability or a 'legitimate' usage of a service (e.g., telnet, ftp). The computation of the attack path likelihood should take into account the likelihood that an attack will be initiated from the threat origin (as estimated by the user who defined the threat origin), the number of attack steps in the attack path and finally, the success likelihood of each of the attack steps.

The success likelihood of exploiting a vulnerability is determined by the degree of difficulty in exploiting the vulnerability, the skill of the attacker, as well as the popularity or availability of the vulnerability. A vulnerability which is known to be popular among hackers carries a higher probability of success.

4.2.5 Traditional vulnerabilities ranking is misleading

Severity, ranked by current vulnerability scanners, is very different from criticality. Using just a severity ranking can be very misleading. To be accurate, a risk assessment process must consider both the technical and business contexts. From a technical perspective, this means understanding the network topology and the access control. From a business perspective, potential threats—both internal and external—the criticality of business applications and other information assets, and regulatory compliance requirements must all be modeled.

For example, the same vulnerability may reside on three separate servers – the first is mitigated by a firewall rule and thus not critical, the second may permit access to a development server, and the third may permit access to a critical finance application. Clearly, all three vulnerabilities have a different criticality, but are typically ranked by vulnerability scanners with the same severity level. Criticality can only be deduced through attack simulations and risk analysis, which is conducted in the context of the value of business assets, defined threats and the network topology itself.

4.3 Remediation Planning

The final important component in an effective, automated risk management solution is the generation and presentation of an actionable set of recommendations—based on the determination of actual risks and exposures—to aid users in decision-making and remediation efforts. These remediation plans must take into account both the nature of each identified vulnerability as well as the network context. Therefore, potential remediation suggestions should not only include patching and upgrading, but also blocking access in firewalls or changing network topology to prevent unnecessary access. The suggested remedies should be tied to the identified vulnerabilities, so that new vulnerabilities are shown with the latest information on patching and potential fixes.

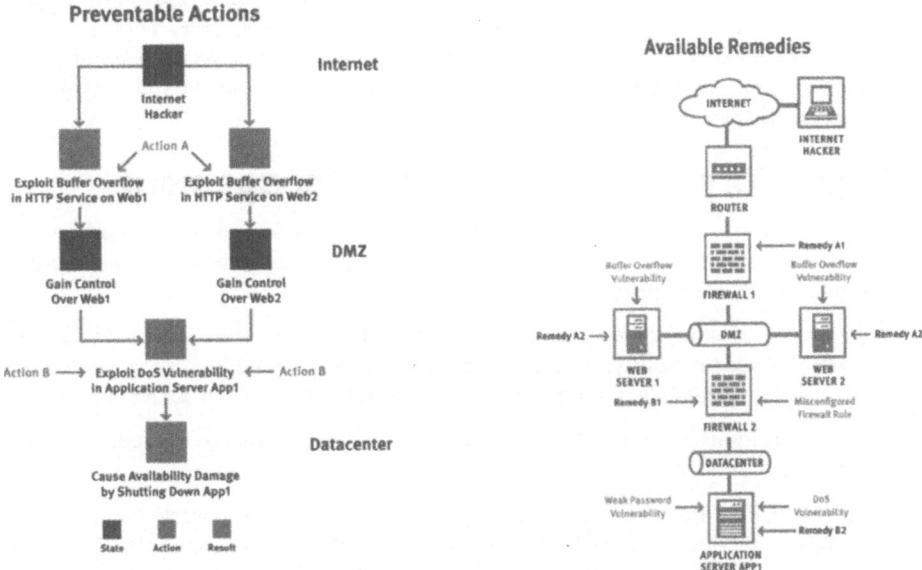

Figure 4: Preventable Actions   **Figure 5:** Available Remedies

In order to optimally mitigate an attack scenario the key is to find the minimum set of attacker's actions which, if prevented, would mitigate the entire attack. Figure 4 illustrates two sets of actions that can be prevented. The first action is exploitation of the buffer overflow vulnerability in the HTTP service (Action A). The second is the exploitation of the DoS vulnerability in the application server (Action B). Preventing any one of these actions is enough to prevent the entire attack.

Of course, not all actions are created equal. Each action might have different prevention alternatives. Figure 5 illustrates that Action A can be prevented by blocking access from the Internet to the HTTP service (Remedy A1), or alternatively by patching the HTTP services in order to remove the buffer overflow vulnerability (Remedy A2). Action B can be eliminated by adding a firewall rule that prevents access from the DMZ to the management interface of the application server (Remedy B1). As an alternative, the application server could be patched in order to eliminate the DoS vulnerability (Remedy B2).

Deciding on the *right remedy* requires the consideration of many factors. For example, if the organizational policy requires access from the Internet to the HTTP services in the DMZ, the option to block such access doesn't make sense – i.e. Remedy A1 is irrelevant.

Another example is the prevention of action B. Upgrading the application service (Remedy B2) may require shutting down the e-banking application for 8 hours, preventing customers from accessing their bank accounts. The organization may prefer to add a firewall rule (Remedy B1) instead.

Other considerations in selecting the right remedy are the cost of change, the control of the change process, and the time to remediation.

Attack simulation and modeling can be very effectively used in this phase of risk management as well. The security professional needs to be able to conduct 'what-if' modeling to optimize his choice of remediation for each critical vulnerability. This capability allows the user to choose various remediation options, apply them to a model of the environment, and then re-run attack simulation in order to visualize the impact of various remediation suggestions before actually applying any changes to the production network.

5 Regulatory Compliance Risk Management

Sarbanes Oxley Act, GLBA, HIPAA and Basel II are only a few of the regulations that require organizations and their executives to ensure that risk management programs, processes and internal controls are in place.

The implications of non-compliance are quite real and range from risk of incarceration through personal accountability, to heavy legal costs and financial losses, loss of reputation and finally, to low shareholder confidence, and thus stock value, and customer satisfaction.

How can organizations leverage attack simulation in order to proactively reduce regulatory compliance risks?

Typically, regulations are aimed at protecting organizations from a concrete security breach – confidentiality, integrity, or availability – of a certain information asset type. For example, Sarbanes Oxley Act requires the prevention of integrity breaches to financial data.

Table 1 below shows a partial list of regulations and the associated breaches they require to protection from. If attack simulation is run against information assets that are tied to legislation based on CIA, then the results of the simulation can be readily used to measure the risk that an organization may be out of compliance with a particular section of legislation, since that information asset is at risk. Simply put, the internal control has lapsed due to the presence of vulnerability, and by fixing the right vulnerabilities, in the right sequence, as revealed by the attack simulation, the organization can minimize the time it takes to return to a state of compliance.

Table 1: Regulations by CIA Breach

Regulation	Affected Segment	Details
Sarbanes Oxley	Public companies (US)	Financial data *Integrity*
BASEL II	Banks	Operational Risk – *CIA*
GLBA	Banks (US)	Customer records *Confidentiality*
FDA 21 CFR Part 11	Pharma (US)	Design & process *Integrity*
HIPAA	Healthcare (US)	Patient records *Confidentiality*
CA SB 1386	Enterprises that operate in California	Customer records *Confidentiality*
Data Privacy Act	Any company (UK)	Customer records *Confidentiality*

6 Summary

In summary, attack simulation can help the security professional enormously in the risk management process. The need for a drastically shortened assessment cycle is well understood by security professionals, yet tools that automate today's manual methods have been sorely lacking until the advent of attack simulation technologies. The benefits of automating the process using context sensitive methods are extremely compelling. Organizations can realize a dramatic reduction in risk, as well as dramatic reduction in both the time and effort taken to conduct an audit. In addition, security teams and auditors can quickly and explicitly see and correct lapses in internal controls due to vulnerabilities that may place and organization out of compliance with regulations. By proactively showing attack scenarios and shutting down critical vulnerabilities in a sequence that clearly makes sense, the IT department, security teams, business teams and executive can talk about security in the same terms and work collaboratively to continuously improve security processes, technologies and infrastructure. Finally, the true state of security can become highly visible to all stakeholders and concrete, cost-effective steps can be taken to continuously lower risk.

Avi Corfas is Vice President and Managing Director, Europe, Middle East and Africa for Skybox Security, Inc. He was previously Executive Vice President (Europe, Middle East & Africa) at @stake, Inc., a leading information security consulting company. Prior to @stake, he was Vice President, Worldwide Sales and Operations for CommerceQuest, Inc. Before that, he was Worldwide Director for Electronic Commerce at Digital Equipment, and co-founder of FutureTense, Inc. For the last 26 years, Avi has worked in four continents and held multiple technical, consulting and executive management positions. He is a former chairman (1994-6) of EEMA, the European Forum for Electronic Business, and holds an EMBA degree from France's Haute École de Commerce.

References

ISSA Journal, October, 2003 „The Risk Management Process" by Michel Landry

A typical network node has between 10-30 vulnerabilities – empirical statistics from Skybox Security, Inc.

A large network may have of dozens of threats and thousands attack targets – empirical statistics form Skybox Security, Inc.

Secure ICT Architectures for Efficient Detection and Response

Dr. György Endersz

TeliaSonera AB, Stockholm, Sweden
gyorgy.endersz@teliasonera.com

Abstract

The starting point of the present paper is the ongoing transformation of the Information and Communication Technology (ICT) environment and the consequences of this transformation for the choice and realisation of optimal strategies to protect ICT assets against malicious use. Current defence strategies emphasise preventive countermeasures and recovery, devoting less effort to detection and immediate response. This strategy may provide adequate protection for static environments, with fairly well defined actors, borders and trust domains. However, the above assumptions prove invalid in the evolving dynamic environment, exhibiting complex and rapidly changing configurations and trust relationships.

An architectural framework is needed, which can provide stronger support for detection of and efficient response to attacks and is less dependent on preventive, perimeter protection. The core of the concept is tight integration and interaction between applications, protection mechanisms and system management. This change of defence strategy is needed in order to meet security requirements posed by actors in the emerging dynamic ICT environment. The subsequent analysis and discussion will identify the main characteristics of the proposed architecture.

The second part of the paper is devoted to some key issues of trust establishment in open environments, necessary for trust in seamless, pervasive services. An attempt is made to identify experiences from the field of electronic signature infrastructures, which may be applicable to validate trustworthiness of service providers in the wider ICT context. The last section provides suggestions for future work.

1 Introduction

1.1 The evolving ICT environment

Society is becoming increasingly dependent on information and communication technology systems to provide distributed, networked and instantly available services, regardless of location. They are ubiquitous and pervasive and provide flexible and tailored services of all kinds. This dependence is accompanied by an increased vulnerability to threats.

An increasing share of electronic transactions occurs outside the home domain of trust and between actors who have no relationship prior to the transaction, i.e. between „strangers". Working in an open environment also means bridging across different authority domains. Organizational flexibility, coping with complex and changing business models are further challenges.

A specific issue underlying future requirements for e-business and e-society is the coordination of resource sharing and problem solving within and between multi-site organizations, interacting in dynamically changing patterns of programs, files, computers, networks and indi-

S. Paulus, N. Pohlmann, H. Reimer (Editors): Securing Electronic Business Processes, Vieweg (2004), 38-46

viduals. The resource sharing that we are concerned with is not primarily file exchange, but rather direct access to computers, networks, software, data, and other resources, as is required by a range of collaborative problem-solving and resource brokering technologies.

1.2 The growing vulnerability gap

Costs of protecting assets in the evolving open, dynamic ICT environment are escalating. Still, deployment of new services is slowed down or limited in scope or scale because of threats of fraud and misuse [Kvar02]. In the following are listed some of the major impediments to timely and cost-efficient adaptation to the new conditions:

- Current defence strategies emphasise preventive countermeasures and recovery, devoting less effort to detection and immediate response. This strategy may provide adequate protection for static environments, with fairly well defined actors, borders and trust domains. However, the above assumptions prove invalid in the evolving dynamic environment, exhibiting complex and rapidly changing configurations and trust relationships.

- Use of intrusion and fraud detection is increasing but their level of integration and direct interaction with other security functions and system management is still low. The same applies to most of currently available security facilities.

- Policy updates in response to changing conditions and trust establishment between different domains are commonly off-line procedures

- Response to attacks and recovery operations require in most cases human intervention.

Although considerable research and development efforts are being devoted to improved and even new security mechanisms, the overall defence strategy did not undergo any significant change.

2 Shift of paradigm

2.1 Cornerstones of the proposed strategy

The main objectives are to close the vulnerability gap, to support flexibility and mobility in a changing environment and to achieve intrusion tolerance, i.e. dependability in the presence of malicious attack. As mentioned above, research has addressed selected areas, which are important for our objectives. E.g. the MAFTIA project published contributions on intrusion-tolerant Intrusion Detection Systems (IDS) [Daci02].

In order to achieve major improvements, an architectural framework is needed. In the following a few concepts are identified and proposed as the bases of the secure ICT architecture.

- A shift of emphasis to detection and response, as compared with the current reliance predominantly on prevention and recovery. This is illustrated in Figure 1. In-depth security mechanisms, such as intrusion and fraud detection (IDS and FDS) systems are fundamental for the strategy [Kvar04].

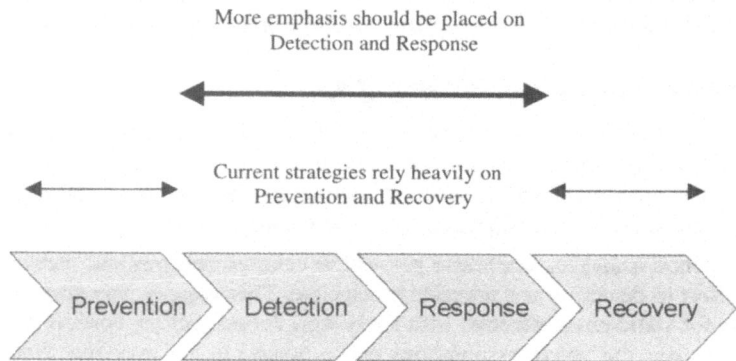

Figure 1: Security couintermeasures

- Integration of security mechanisms with key components of the ICT system in a scheme, which will improve synergy between security mechanisms and management and allow swift, automated assessment and response. The realisation of this objective means to specify a „secure ICT architecture", unlike the common notion of „security architecture".

The next section is a more detailed analysis and discussion of the necessary characteristics of the architecture.

2.2 Required properties of the architecture

The aim of this section is to bring forward some of the characteristics and features, which seems fundamental for the realisation of „secure ICT architecture".

- Security awareness and in-depth protection mechanisms

Current IDS and FDS solutions utilize reported log data. Security aware applications and communication facilities should be able to detect irregular events and generate immediate response, moving out part of the first-line defence to the distributed, low-end part of the system. Digital Right Management is one example, where the potential of close interaction between protection at the application level and the overall protection capabilities of the system has been identified and to some degree specified.

- In-depth protection and its integration

Conventional information security, when applied to networks and distributed systems, involves protecting individual data flows between system elements. Typically, encryption will be applied to protect data confidentiality, and Message Authentication Codes (MACs) or digital signatures will be used to guarantee data origin and integrity. Signatures may also be used to protect against repudiation of messages. These methods are complemented by well-understood computer security techniques, which involve building access control mechanisms into information processing platforms to prevent unauthorized access to data. These techniques are all characterized by the fact that they do not take any account of the semantics of the data that they are protecting. They are, in essence, the electronic counterparts of the physical safe, providing exterior protection to valuable resources; for example, the goal for communications security is typically to provide a 'secure pipe' for data flows, i.e. providing exterior protection.

In-depth protection aims to go beyond this limited view of information security, by including techniques aimed at interpreting the data flows and the behaviour of systems, to understand when security attacks might be taking place. In response, the existing security infrastructure can be actively managed to respond to detected threats. Thus, in-depth security includes not only all the conventional preventative (exterior protection) mechanisms, but also more active data- and system-aware techniques providing multi-layered defence against security threats. In-depth security also include the concept of situation awareness which could be guided by techniques such as intrusion and fraud detection systems giving indications of environmental threats imposed on the target system and its protection. The synthesis of these different approaches to security and privacy, and the integration of these techniques into a single management framework are the cornerstones of the proposed architecture.

Current security enhancing techniques and concepts are adapted to existing network and application environments, which are not designed for maximum efficiency and flexibility of in-depth security solutions. A majority of currently available security features are add-ons to already existing network protocols and applications, including management facilities. E.g. most of the interactions between the management of the ICT-system and security policy management of the same system occur by manual operations.

- Context (situation) awareness

User platforms (e.g. mobile terminals) and applications should be provided with capability to assess their security conditions in the actual IT environment. Based on the assessment it will be possible to adopt the user's security policy to the actual situation and activate adequate protection measures. Such capability assumes uniform technical support along networks and applications.

- Integration and interaction

As we see, interactions among the key components are essential to efficient monitoring, adaptation to changing conditions, detection of events/attacks and the subsequent response. The entities to be interconnected are distributed applications and security mechanisms, security and system management, policies – rules and decision support mechanisms.

- Adaptive security policies

Security policies at different levels control protection and response to events. While the governing high-level (e.g. corporate policy) remains stable, policies for user platforms or individual applications have to adapt to short-term or local changes.

Policy-mapping aspects between co-operating security domains have to be taken into account, which may also be reflected in the overall trust model. Trust establishment in open ICT environments is particularly important and the same time complex issue. Trust models need to be developed, able to support on-line decisions, even under complex trust relationships. Extensive work has been accomplished with regard to mutual validation of actors and trust establishment in the area of certificate based services and PKI. An overview of the problems, recent results and their possible applicability in the wider ICT context will be given in Section 3.

- Automated response and recovery

Advanced decision support and whenever possible automated response are key components of the proposed architecture. Minimizing manual intervention will enhance both the timeliness and accuracy of response.

- User experience

The major issue here is the conflict between increasing demand on the user to maintain control of the complex client environment on one side, and the user's requirement for simplicity on the other. A limiting factor to automation is the requirement by the public and by the legislator that privacy and integrity of individuals must be maintained.

It is also important to keep in mind that all context information cannot be encoded and automated. What is left to the user must be easy to understand and operate. The option to review the actual security state shall be offered to the user, in a uniform and transparent manner.

The owner of system resources wants to know the identity of the user, a requirement, which in many cases is in conflict with the user's intent to remain anonymous.

2.3 Key components and processes

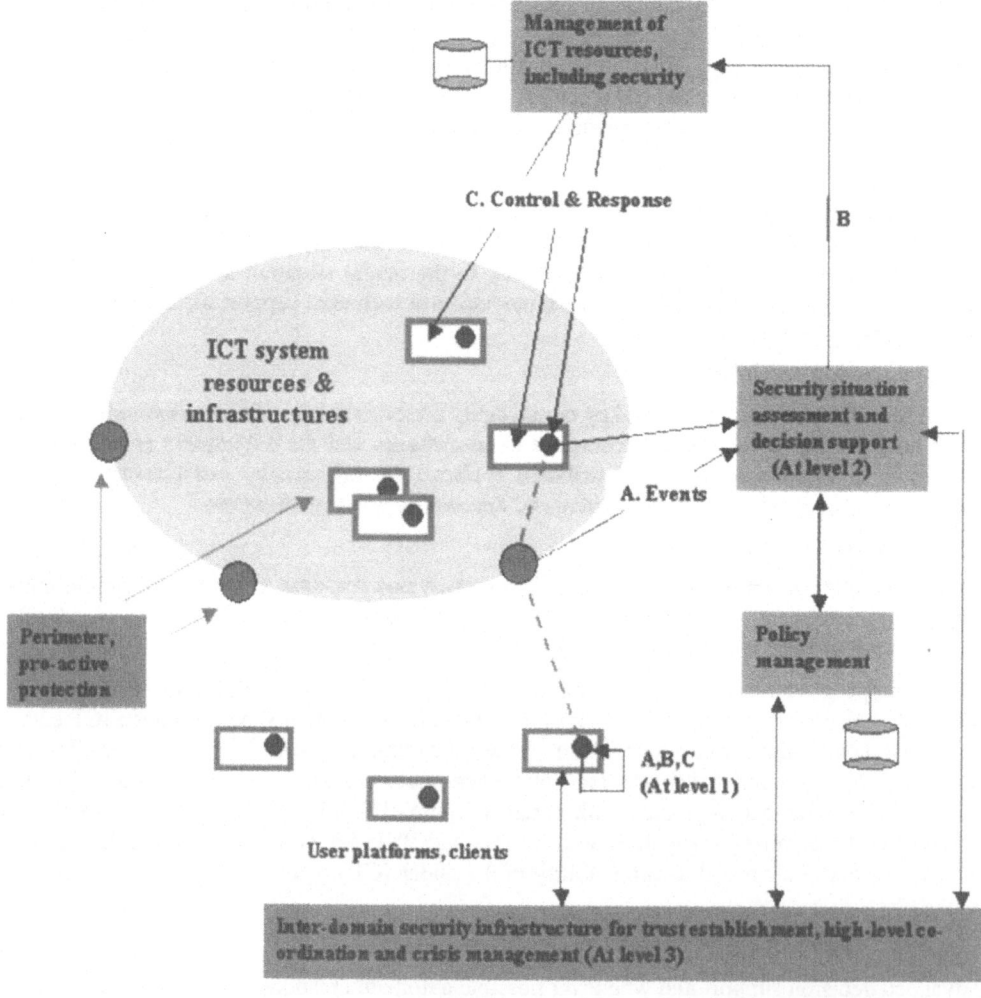

Figure 2: Overview of components and interactions of a secure architecture

Figure 2 is an overview of the major entities involved, together with their interactions and interdependencies. Security awareness is maintained at three levels. The lowest level is represented by functional units, such as application or client platforms, equipped with pro-active and reactive security facilities and with the necessary functionality for self-assessment and adaptation under varying conditions and environments. This will include the ability to communicate with supporting instances at levels 2 and 3, both for trust establishment and for incident handling.

The rectangle with orange border in the Figure represents the smallest autonomous unit, which may be a communicating user platform or a system resource, e.g. an application platform, database, etc. The orange border represents pro-active security, such as access control or secure association, protecting the unit. Similarly, the orange dots on the perimeter of the ICT system stand for firewall protection.

The circles inside the units symbolise the reactive mechanisms, which monitor and assess the security situation of the unit and generate both the local reaction and the report to the next level for tactical evaluation and response. At the highest, strategic level, co-ordinated assessment and response and support for crisis management are generated. The three phases of monitoring/reporting, assessment/decision and execution/response are denoted A, B and C, respectively. The level 1 process, including all three phases at the unit level, is illustrated with the arrow starting from and looping back to the unit.

3 Critical issues of trust establishment

A larger part of the ideas and conclusions of this chapter originates in studies and normative work, carried out under the European Electronic Signature Initiative (EESSI), between 1999-2004. Although the program addressed more specifically the requirements of the European Directive on Electronic Signatures (Directive 93/99), many of its results are applicable in a wider context.

3.1 Requirements in the open environment

An open ICT environment shall support transactions between strangers. Transactions include pervasive, ubiquitous computing, cross-domain eBusiness, etc. In our time ICT system is the major technical component and platform, a necessary but not sufficient condition. Doing eBusiness far from home we are always looking for a trust anchor. So does our counterpart in order to verify our trustworthiness. The essential requirements are:

- Instant, on-line access to relevant trust status information for assessment. This requirement implies technical interoperability.

- Trusted site to provide the information. Machine-readable information has to be concise and standardised.

- In order to interpret trust status information, the underlying evaluation criteria must be known to the evaluator. Evaluation criteria in the open environment have to be well defined, published and machine processable.

3.2 Technical and non-technical context

All transactions are associated with context information, both technical and non-technical. Not all the relevant context information can be encoded and processed by computers for the purpose of automatic decision support. A software validating an electronically signed transaction will need a whole set of information. In a closed environment many of the parameters are set as part of the rules of the business, most of them off-line, and the procedure may be simple. The more open the environment is, the more parameters need to be made available to the validating entity. There have been attempts to specify syntax and semantics and codify the context information.

One example is the work carried out on signature policies [ETSI03a] for the support of automatic validation of electronic signatures. The client who does the validation needs, among others, to know about the intentions, business and security conditions, etc. related to the signing act. There are more than one layers above the technical security and interoperability conditions and the complexity increases when trust domain borders are crossed and strangers meet in the ICT environment. The work provided valuable knowledge but no practically useful technical standard, which could encode the complex world of business context. This is what some of the participating legal experts told us at an early stage of the program.

This should serve as a warning but also as an incentive, so as to devote more effort to the study of societal, cultural and legal aspects of electronic business.

3.3   Trust without bilateral agreements

Different trust models have been developed and tested in the world of PKI, notably the hierarchical model based on a „top" CA and the cross-certification model, based on bilateral trust. A detailed analysis of alternative solutions and their pros and cons is outside the scope of this paper. For the present discussion it is sufficient to agree that the hierarchy leaves the trust in the top CA open, while cross-certification needs a bilateral case-to-case scrutiny and mapping of the respective CA policies, leading to a scalability problem. The Bridge-CA is a pragmatic combination of the two, involving a multi-part agreement to create a common reference and to cover business context, one step towards a more generic scheme, which may prove useful for large, open environments.

The European Telecommunication Standards Institute (ETSI) has studied the issue and proposed the publication of a standardised Trust Service Provider Status List (TSL) [ETSI03b]. The list is available for public access and provides actual information about numerous aspects of the service in question, including those relevant for the establishment of trust. Contents and formats of the list are standardised in [Ref].

The following are some of the main features of a trust infrastructure, based on the TSL:

- The party providing the status information is independent of the service provider („third party"). In the business sector well-known auditors may provide this service, while in the public sector, e.g. in healthcare, the task is more likely to be allocated to public authorities.

- Confidence in the TSL-based scheme is further improved if the TSL is available from a multiple of sites.

- Status information may cover a wide range of aspects and properties of the service and its history, as opposed to a revocation list for CA certificates.

- In order to be machine readable and processable, syntax, semantics of the TSL and relevant interfaces have to be interoperable. In the open environment this means open standards.

- Interpretation and decision based on the TSL is only possible if the underlying evaluation criteria are well understood by all involved parties. Again, in the open environment this means well defined, widely adopted and recognised classes of trust, which allow consistent evaluation results by independent auditors. In the PKI area this can be achieved by reference to standardised CA policy requirements, but the agreement to do so is in the policy domain, not technical.

- The use of TSLs can be extended to any service requiring confirmation/validation of status, regarding trust and operation in general, that is, to cover both trust services and other kinds of services, based on ICT.

However, it may take considerable time before the more precise minimum requirements for trust establishment in the ICT world have been identified and agreed by the general public, the business community and public authorities. Different application and service areas require different levels and will emphasise different aspects of security. For trust service provider infrastructures, e.g. for PKI, such needs are addressed by CA policies, each addressing a different trust level and application area.

In a more general sense, for transactions, resource sharing, etc in the evolving ICT environment, security requirements need to be defined and measured with finer granularity and differentiation. The security metrics for this end is still to be developed. Nevertheless, the model based on third-party audit and pre-defined sets of standardised security requirements will likely to become a way to support real-time situation assessment and trust establishment.

4 Conclusions and future work

Analysis of the evolving new ICT environment and its security problems demonstrates that there is a growing vulnerability gap. A successful strategy, able to counter the negative trend and create „secure ICT architectures", requires qualitative improvements at the architecture level as well as in the field of security mechanisms and trust models. Some key areas suggested for increased R&D efforts are:

- Secure architectures, providing a framework for integration and automation
- Security aware applications and generalised in-depth protection mechanisms
- Trust models for the dynamic ICT environment
- Non-technical aspects of security context (societal, cultural, legal)
- User aspects
- Security metrics

Acknowledgements

The author likes to thank Dr. Chris Mitchell, Dr. Håkan Kvarnström, Dr. Lars-Erik Eriksson and Dr. Riccardo Genghini for stimulating discussions and comments about subjects related to this paper.

References

[Daci02]   Dacier, M. (editor). Design of an Intrusion-Tolerant Intrusion Detection System, Deliverable D10. *Maftia European Project IST-1999-11583*, IBM Zurich Research Laboratory, 2002

[Kvar04]   Håkan Kvarnström. On the Implementation and Protection of Fraud Detection Systems. Thesis for the degree of doctor of philosophy (ISBN 91-7291-461-0), June 2004, Department of Computer Engineering, Chalmers University of Technology, SE-412 96 Göteborg.

[Kvar02]   Håkan Kvarnström, Ulf Larsson, Erland Jonsson. New security issues in emerging computing environments – A reflection. *Technical Report 04-02*. Department of Computer Engineering, Chalmers University of Technology, SE-412 96 Göteborg, Sweden.

[ETSI03a]   ETSI Technical Report, Signature policy for extended business model, TR 102 045 v1.1.1, 2003-03.

[ETSI03b]   ETSI Technical Specification, Provision of harmonised Trust Service Provider status information, TS 102 231v1.1.1, 2003-10.

Biometric Identity Cards: Technical, Legal, and Policy Issues

Gerrit Hornung, LL.M.

Projektgruppe verfassungsverträgliche Technikgestaltung (provet),
University of Kassel
Mönchebergstr. 21a, 34109 Kassel, Germany
gerrit.hornung@uni-kassel.de

Abstract

It is very likely that in a few years time, most persons travelling around the world will possess a travel document that includes a biometric identifier. This development could have a major impact on research in the field of biometrics, as well as on the market of ID solutions. However, the use of biometrics poses highly controversial technical and legal problems. The technical issues are addressed by standardisation activities, which are conducted by the ISO/IEC JTC 1 SC 37 and 17, as well as the International Civil Aviation Association (ICAO). From the legal perspective, states have to comply with privacy requirements enshrined in constitutions and international treaties when implementing biometric data in ID cards. The most important questions concern the choice of the biometric, the storage in central databases, the use in private applications, and the installation of back-up procedures to avoid discrimination. In the end, the question of whether a project as identity cards with biometric data will be accepted in the population should not be underestimated.

1 Introduction

In the aftermath of the terrorist attacks of September 11, 2001, states around the world have started *programmes for the implementation of biometrics* in passports. In the US, visa applicants already have to present their fingers and faces at ports of entry. Furthermore, US laws were introduced which required passports from countries participating in the visa waiver programme to include biometrics if they are issued after October 26, 2004 (sec. 303 (c) (1) and (2) Enhanced Border Security and Visa Entry Reform Act [US02]). This deadline has now been extended in the meantime. However, the visa procedure will nevertheless apply to people from visa waiver countries until those countries have started to issue passports with biometric data.

Biometrics are a means to ensure a secure connection between a person and a travel document. By including such data in passports, states try to enhance their border security. By the same token, some of them consider a new generation of compulsory identity cards. While there is a debate in some states (*e.g.* the United Kingdom, the US, and Canada) whether there should be ID cards at all, others have *already implemented some form of electronic identity card*, although the meaning of the term differs widely. In Europe, most projects so far only include the possibility of electronic signatures, while no biometric data is stored on the chip. On the contrary, some Arabian and Asian countries collect fingerprint data for their ID cards.

In Germany, a first legislative step was taken in 2001. Yet there is still *no comprehensive legal basis* for a new identity card, the so-called „Digitaler Personalausweis". To foster the plans, the Government launched a feasibility study which was completed in January 2004 [RRM04].[1] A second report [TAB03] was carried out for the German Parliament by the Büro für Technikfolgenabschätzung (office of technology assessment), which had already submitted a first general report on biometric systems [TAB02].

The study for the government focuses on the feasibility of a new ID card, which would include biometric data, as well as the possibility to use the card as „secure-signature-creation device" in the meaning of Art. 2 (6) of the European Union Directive on Electronic Signatures [EU99]. This card would, primarily, be a national identification document. In most countries around the world however, this type of identity document is – at least for some other countries – a valid travel document as well. In the European Union in particular, citizens are allowed to use national ID cards instead of passports when travelling abroad. Therefore, it must be possible for other countries to read biometric data from the card. To this end, national identity cards must *comply with international technical standards*.

2 Technical Issues

Biometrics are the automated means of recognising a living person through the measurement of distinguishing physiological or behavioural traits. [WOH03, 7].

Standardisation activities are conducted by the ISO/IEC JTC 1 SC 37 and 17, as well as the International Civil Aviation Association (ICAO). In the field of machine readable travel documents (MRTDs), both are working closely together. There are ISO standards for smartcards (ISO/IEC 7816) and contactless interfaces (ISO/IEC 10536, ISO/IEC 14443, and ISO/IEC 15693, depending on the distance between the chip and the card reader). ISO/IEC 19785 (Common Biometric Exchange Formats Framework, CBEFF) and ISO/IEC 19784 (BioAPI) apply to biometric data. Further documents (ISO/IEC 19794-1 to 7 concerning a general framework, finger minutiae, finger pattern, finger image, face image, iris image, and signature image) are in different stages of the standardisation process, which should be completed by October 2004.

While the standards and recommendations of the ICAO are not legally binding, almost all states have committed themselves to comply with them. *Several documents apply to biometric ID cards*:

* The basic document is the three-part ICAO DOC 9303 [ICAO03a] on Machine Readable Travel Documents which was first published in 1980 and has been updated since.

* As for the choice of the biometric, the ICAO Technical Report on Biometric Deployment of Machine Readable Travel Documents endorses the use of face recognition as the globally interoperable biometric for machine assisted identity confirmation with machine readable documents, while the states may elect to use fingerprint and/or iris recognition as additional biometric technology [ICAO03b, 15]. The decision was mainly based on several advantages of face recognition: it can be used by virtually every person, it is non-intrusive (in the sense that the user does not have to touch or interact with a physical device), it is already collected and verified as part of MRTD applications, and it does not require new and costly enrolment procedures. The ICAO also claims that face recognition does not disclose information that the person does not routinely disclose to the general public. The organisation suggests using image data instead of templates to ensure global interoperability.

---

[1] The author is one of the contributing authors of this study.

- Another ICAO Technical Report is concerned with the Development of a Logical Data Structure for optional Capacity Expansion Technologies which will be used to store biometric data on travel documents [ICAO03c].

- With reference to the interface of the chip, the ICAO Technical Report on the Use of Contactless Integrated Circuits in Machine Readable Travel Documents recommends this contactless type because of durability advantages [ICAO03d, 7].

- To ensure the integrity and authenticity of the biometric data, the ICAO Technical Report on PKI Digital Signatures for Machine Readable Travel Documents proposes a „simplified PKI infrastructure for ICAO MRTDs" [ICAO03e]. Every participating state will generate private and public keys for each issuing location. The public keys will be collected by the ICAO, signed with its own private key, and made available to all other countries. Thereby, the organisation acts as de-facto certification authority. The private keys of the issuing locations will not be released from a central location in each state, to which the biometric data will be send by the issuing locations for the signing process.

3 Legal issues

3.1 Applicability of data protection laws

National and international data protection laws only apply to „personal data". By way of example, this term is defined by Art. 2 a) of the EU Data Protection Directive [EU95] as „any information relating to an identified or identifiable natural person ('data subject')", while an identifiable person is one „who can be identified, directly or indirectly, in particular by reference to an identification number or to one or more factors specific to his physical, physiological, mental, economic, cultural or social identity". There is some dispute about the question in which circumstances biometric data falls in the ambit of this definition (for the German discussion, see [Horn04a]). However, the biometric data in an identity document is, in any case, personal data, because it is inseparably linked to the name which is printed on the surface of the document.

3.2 Legal basis for the implementation of biometrics

According to Art. 3 (2) and recital 13, the EU Data Protection Directive does not apply to the processing of personal data in the course of an activity which falls outside the scope of European Community law, such as those provided for by Titles V (provisions on a common foreign and security policy) and VI (provisions on police and judicial cooperation in criminal matters) of the Treaty on European Union and in any case to processing operations concerning public security, defence, state security and the activities of the state in areas of criminal law. Therefore, all matters related to national ID cards are not regulated by the Directive and left to the national laws of the member states.

Nonetheless, there is a *considerable amount of concurrence among those laws* due to the harmonisation process induced by the Directive. Furthermore, there are other international treaties which contain data protection safeguards. The European Court of Human Rights has held since *Leander ./. Sweden* [ECHR87], that the right to respect for private life in Art. 8 of the European Convention for the protection of human rights and fundamental freedoms [ECHR] includes, *inter alia*, the processing of data against the will of the person. According to the United Nation's Human Rights Committee [HRC94, 21], the same holds true for Art. 17 of the International Covenant on Civil and Political Rights [ICCPR]. The Charter of Fundamental Rights of the European Union [EU00] even encloses an explicit provision on data protection in Art. 8, although the Charter is not yet legally binding.

General principles of data protection law include:

- Interferences authorised by the state can only take place on the basis of law, which itself must comply with the provisions of constitutions and international treaties. The relevant legislation must specify in detail the circumstances of the lawful interference.

- As in all state action, the processing of the data must be proportional in relation to the interference.

- The purpose of the data has to be specified before it is collected, and the subsequent use is restricted to those purposes; unless the consent of the data subject or the law provide for this use.

- Unless there are express legal provisions, data has to be collected with the knowledge or consent of the data subject (principle of transparency).

- The data subject enjoys certain rights against the data controller, namely the right to obtain information of whether or not the data controller has data relating to him, the right to have such data communicated to him in a reasonable time and manner (or to be able to challenge a decision which denies the communication), the right to challenge data relating to him, and, if the challenge is successful, to have the data erased, rectified, completed or amended.

- Appropriate security measures have to be taken for the protection of personal data against inadvertent or unauthorised destruction or accidental loss, as well as against unauthorised access, alteration or dissemination.

3.3 Data protection issues

3.3.1 Choice of the biometric identifier

The biometric identifier has to be suitable for the purpose of a general identity card, *i.e.*, the secure verification of a large group of cardholders. Thus, the biometric has to be universal, while the system must operate with low failure rates: false acceptance rate (FAR) and false recognition rate (FRR) should be less than 1 %.

While this is the point of view of the state, data protection law requires the biometric to meet the proportionality test. According to the *principle of proportionality*, preferred biometrics do not include additional information, are not permanently left in one's environment, and require the cooperation of the card holder. However, these criteria do not conclusively lead to one biometric feature.

The main problem of *face recognition* is that it is non-cooperative. The picture can be captured, stored and processed without the knowledge of the data subject. As long as face recognition is not suitable for 1:n matches with large databases, this is not too critical. However, this restriction is likely to change in the future. The German Bundesverfassungsgericht has decided in its famous Volkszählungsurteil [BVER83, 43] that a situation in which citizens do not know if the state secretly collects information about critical behaviour would be incompatible with a democratic society because this could deter from making use of political rights (*e.g.* the rights to freedom of expression, assembly and demonstration). Some authors [RAEF02, 511; WOOD01, 6], as well as the ICAO [ICAO03b, 15], claim that the use of face recognition is preferable because the face is an „open" biometric which is routinely disclosed to the public. However, this argument is flawed. While it is true that it will always be possible for a motivated attacker to capture a high-quality picture of a person and use it for fake attacks on biometric systems, this scenario is unrealistic for a large group of persons or even the whole population of a country. In contrast, the use of facial data for identity documents would give the state authorities access to high-quality images of every citizen, thereby enabling them – on condition that there will be technical process in the future – to track public behaviour (see also [AGRE03; MCCO03, 135ff.; NGUY02, 2ff.]).

The use of *fingerprint recognition* reduces this risk, because it is not possible to collect the data at control station without the knowledge of the card holder. However, fingerprints are involuntarily left on everyday objects, which makes it feasible to trace individual moves and actions for a long time. Furthermore, there are indications that it is possible to infer certain diseases (*e.g.* breast cancer, Rubella syndrome, and certain chromosomal disorders such as Down syndrome, Turner syndrome, and Klinefelter syndrome) from fingerprint data [WOH03, 202f.].

Iris recognition avoids the main disadvantages of face and fingerprint data: iris data cannot be collected without the knowledge of the data subject, and is not left involuntarily in the environment. However, the iris is the biometric which – at least potentially – discloses the most additional information about the holder of the identity card. Medical scientific research suggests that iris data could be connected to diabetes, arteriosclerosis und hypertension [WOH03, 203], HIV and misuse of alcohol and drugs [ALBR03, 173], or even homosexuality [HAKI94, 1203ff.; LEVA96, 157f.]. While the latter might be speculative, any sole suspicion could lead to disadvantages for the person affected.

On the whole, each type of biometric data has its own special risk. From the standpoint of data protection, the iris seems to have certain advantages. Furthermore, this biometric is, generally, the one with the lowest failure rates. However, data protection issues are only one of many considerations when it comes to the decision which type of data should be preferred.

3.3.2 Central databases

Concerning the *storage of the data*, most countries use central, nationwide biometric databases or plan to do so in the future. The aim is to prevent citizens from establishing more than one identity by obtaining several identity cards with different names, particularly in those states which do not possess a general register of residents or are introducing it at the same time as the new identity card.

On the contrary, the German legislative has already *ruled out the possibility of a nationwide database* (see § 1 (5) Pesonalausweisgesetz [PAG]). Furthermore, the constitutional requirements in Germany are tighter than in most other countries. That is to say, a central database (and de-central equivalents) would be incompatible with the „Recht auf informationelle Selbstbestimmung" (right to informational self-determination) which forms part of the fundamental rights of the German Grundgesetz (see also [ULD03, 66ff.] Furthermore, there seems to be less necessity for a database, given the highly developed system of residents registers.

3.3.3 The use in private applications

In Germany it is currently *not legally possible* to use prospective biometric data on the national ID card in private applications. If the government deems this desirable, it needs to establish legal requirements.

Generally, it is debatable *if and to which extent* private actors should be given access to the biometric data on the ID card. On the one hand, this could pose additional problems, especially if the data contains medical information. Moreover, the biometric could be used as a general identifier to collect and accumulate other personal information of the data subject, thereby building up detailed profiles of each person. On the other hand, it is in the interest of the holder of the ID card to securely establish his/her identity in private applications as well. Therefore, he/she should be given this opportunity, if there are safety measures in place. Privates must not have access to the data without the consent of the holder, and there should be a mutual authentication procedure to record authorised and prevent unauthorised access.

3.3.4 Back-up procedures

Every biometric system has to face the problem that, for various reasons, a certain percentage of the population will permanently or temporarily be *unable to present the biometric feature*. While almost everybody is able to use facial recognition, this failure to enrol rate (FER) is estimated to be 1 to 4 per cent (finger) and 1 per cent (Iris), respectively [WOH03, 22, 99; FENN03]. Face, fingerprint, and iris recognition can also be momentarily hampered by body injuries.

It is currently unclear how many people will be confronted with these problems. Yet it is apparent that states will have to *install back-up procedures* to both ensure the secure identification of all persons, and avoid discrimination of those unable to enrol in the system. Therefore, it will not be possible to only rely on biometric identification at checkpoints. Additionally, back-up procedures must be effective to prevent delays. In any case, the body of the ID card needs to be forgery-safe and usable without a chip, because its content could be destroyed without the owner's knowledge.

3.3.5 Matching on Card?

If the ID card operates with matching on card, there are *two possibilities*. Either the card itself is equipped with a biometric sensor, or the data is captured by an external sensor and transmitted to the card for the matching. The first case has the advantage that the card holder is in total control of the biometric data. However, sensors on cards are only feasible for fingerprint recognition. If the data is captured by an external sensor, then the matching on card has no additional safeguard in normal control situations, because the controller will in any case be able to store the newly collected raw data. Thus, there is no need to read the data from the chip. There remains the advantage that this scenario cannot arise, *i.e.* unauthorised access to the data is prevented.

Critically, with both types of matching on card, the controller at the checkpoint *has to trust the chip*, which could be forged to always produce positive matching results. Therefore, states are unlikely to choose matching on card for authentication purposes. On the contrary, additional applications may even require this type of matching to securely identify the holder when providing access to his/her data.

3.3.6 Contactless Interfaces

As stated by the ICAO, contactless interfaces (which operate at radio frequency) should be preferred if the ID card is valid for a longer period, because contact smartcards suffer from failure due to dirt or moisture. Conversely, contact or dual interface chips are essential, if high-security applications (such as advanced electronic signatures in accordance with Art. 2 (2) of the European Union Directive on Electronic Signatures) are added on the card.

While the use of contactless chips has durability advantages, data stored on those chips *poses transparency problems* for the card holder, who is hardly able to notice whether data is read from the card [RPG01, 185]. In this situation, it is preferable to use chips which operate at a close range to the card reader ("close-coupled" and "proximity" cards in accordance with ISO/IEC 10536 and 14443, respectively). Besides, the access to the data could be restricted by the use of mutual authentication between the chip and the card reader, although this would require the distribution of certificates between the participating states. As a last resort, the card holder could keep the ID card in a metal jacket (such as aluminium foil) which will prevent the radio frequency reader from reading the data.

3.3.7 Templates

The use of templates in biometric systems is usually due to storage space restrictions. However, this use also has *data protection advantages*, on the conditions that

- Firstly, the meaning of "template" is restricted to data which encompasses only certain extracted features from the raw data (sometimes biometric image data is called "template" as well)

- Secondly, the template is constructed in a way that either excludes some sort of additional (and sensitive) raw data information or that makes it impossible to deduce the identity of the person from the template itself

- Thirdly, it is impossible to reconstruct the original raw data from the template (on the possibilities and restrictions of this reconstruction, see [BROM03]).

Generally speaking, the use of templates is preferable from the viewpoint of data protection law. However, it should be stressed that this way of storing biometric data *still requires the use of raw data* for each matching, which significantly reduces the advantages for the data subject.

In the specific case of international travel documents, the use of templates is, in part, held back by the *lack of template standardisation*. Card readers around the world must be able to read and match data from passports, whereas European national ID cards have to be compatible with readers at least in the European Union. In the short term, template standards are likely to be achievable for fingerprint data (ISO/IEC 19794-2 and 3), while there is a de-facto standard for iris templates, due to the limitation to only one patentee for these systems. In contrast, there are only proprietary template solutions for facial data.

In this situation, states have no choice but to use image data, if they deem facial data the most suitable biometric identifier. At the same time, however, they should endeavour to push ahead with standardisation activities. In any case, fingerprint and iris templates have to be employed if this kind of data is stored on the ID card.

3.3.8 The use of encryption

One possibility to protect the personal data of the card holder could be the use of encryption. However, the *use of symmetric encryption* is hampered by the fact that it appears to be impossible to ensure the nondisclosure of the keys if there are numerous checkpoints on the international plane.

Therefore, encryption cannot protect the data from highly motivated attackers. Nonetheless, it would at least prevent a situation in which every person equipped with a card reader could read the biometric data from the ID card. Furthermore, the cracking and distributing of the key is likely to be a criminal offence in most countries, which constitutes a significant deterrence. Besides, it should be possible to keep the encryption keys secret from unauthorised persons if they are only used at a limited number of control stations. Thus, national identity cards in Europe might be suitable for encryption because of the limited number of states and the abolishment of border controls in the Schengen Acquis.

4 Policy Issues

Data protection issues are only one, albeit important, aspect for the implementation of biometrics on ID cards. *Organisational and financial aspects* are equally important.

Every control station must be provided with the necessary biometric equipment, and employees need to be trained for the matching procedures. Similarly, every issuing location (6.500 in Germany) must have the equipment, because even if the enrolment takes place at a central location, the card needs to be tested before it is handed out to the holder.

It is currently difficult to estimate the total cost for a national system of biometric ID cards. The German Büro für Technikfolgenabschätzung suggests that the initial expenditure could be up to 600 Million €, with annual costs up to 610 Million €, depending on the technology of the card and the distribution process [TAB03, 81ff.]. In states where, as in Germany, the validity period of the existing ID card is ten years, the implementation of biometrics itself (*i.e.* regardless of the actual technology) could double the expenses: The ICAO recommends that the states consider moving to five year validity periods for reasons such as technical flexibility and technology and security feature turnover [ICAO03b, 36].

In the end, the question of whether a project such as identity cards with biometric data will be accepted by citizens should not be underestimated. Given the potential to overcome legal and technical problems, this factor could be decisive for the realisation of such projects.

5 Outlook

The implementation of biometrics in passports and national ID cards seems to be inevitable. However, major technical, legal, and policy problems are yet unsolved. Those concerned with the execution of the projects should seize the one year extension by the US to develop and test interoperable technical solutions which both ensure the secure identification by the state and create maximum protection for the sensitive biometric data of the card holders.

In the end, depending on each state, the projects *have to be connected to other technological developments*. In Germany, the new identity card is related to the issuing of a new, highly sophisticated patient data card, envisaged for January 2006 [Horn04b], and the so-called „Job-Card" programme, which will require every applicant within the social security system to posses a secure signature-creation device when making a claim for social benefit [HoRo04].

References

[AGRE03] Agre, Philip E.: Your Face Is Not a Bar Code. Arguments against Automatic Face Recognition in Public Places, available at http://polaris.gseis.ucla.edu/pagre/bar-code.html, 2003.

[ALBR03] Albrecht, Astrid: Biometrische Verfahren im Spannungsfeld von Authentizität im elektronischen Rechtsverkehr und Persönlichkeitsschutz, Nomos, Baden-Baden, 2003.

[BROM03] Bromba, Manfred: On the reconstruction of biometric raw data from template data, available at http://www.bromba.com/knowhow/temppriv.htm, 2003.

[BVER83]   Bundesverfassungsgericht: Decision of 15 December 1983 („*Volkszählung*"), Amtliche Sammlung, Vol. 65, pp. 1-71.

[ECHR]   European Convention for the protection of human rights and fundamental freedoms, available at http://conventions.coe.int/treaty/en/Treaties/Html/005.htm.

[ECHR87]   European Court of Human Rights: *Leander ./. Sweden*, Decision of 26 March 1987, Series A no. 116.

[EU95]   Directive 95/46/EC of the European Parliament and of the Council of 24 October 1995 on the protection of individuals with regard to the processing of personal data and on the free movement of such data, Official Journal L 281, p. 31, available at http://europa.eu.int/comm/internal_market/privacy/law_en.htm.

[EU99]   Directive 1999/93/EC of the European Parliament and of the Council of 13 December 1999 on a Community framework for electronic signatures, Official Journal L 13, 19. 1. 2000, p. 12, available at http://europa.eu.int/eur-lex/pri/en/oj/dat/2000/l_013/l_01320000119en00120020.pdf.

[EU00]   Charter of Fundamental Rights of the European Union. Official Journal 2000 L 364, p. 1, available at http://europa.eu.int/eur-lex/pri/en/oj/dat/2000/c_364/c_36420001218en00010022.pdf.

[FENN03]   Fenner, Michael: Ready for the big Leagues?, Card Technology 9/2003, available at http://www.cardtechnology.com/cgi-bin/readstory.pl?story=20030902CTMC484.xml, 2003 .

[HAKI94]   Hall, J. A. Y. / Kimura, D.: Dermatoglyphic Asymmetric and Sexual Orientation in Men. In: Behavioral Neuroscience 108 (1994), pp. 1203-1206.

[Horn04a]   Hornung, Gerrit: Der Personenbezug biometrischer Daten. Zugleich eine Erwiderung auf Saeltzer, DuD 2004, 218ff. In: Datenschutz und Datensicherheit (DuD), to be published in 2004.

[Horn04b]   Hornung, Gerrit: Der zukünftige Einsatz von Chipkarten im deutschen Gesundheitswesen. In: Horster, Patrick (Ed.), D-A-CH Security 2004, Syssec 2004, pp. 226-237.

[HoRo04]   Hornung, Gerrit / Roßnagel, Alexander: Die JobCard – „Killer-Applikation" für die elektronische Signatur? In: Kommunikation & Recht (K&R) 2004, pp. 263-269.

[HRC94]   United Nations Human Rights Committee: General Comment 16/32 on Art. 17 ICCPR, UN-Doc. HRI/GEN/1/Rev. 1, available at http://heiwww.unige.ch/humanrts/gencomm/hrcom16.htm.

[ICAO03a]   International Civil Aviation Association (ICAO): Doc 9303. Machine Readable Travel Documents. Part 1: Machine Readable Passports. 5fth Edition, 2003; Part 2: Visa, 1994; Part 3: Size 1 and Size 2 Machine Readable Official Travel Documents. 2nd Edition, 2002.

[ICAO03b]   International Civil Aviation Association (ICAO): Biometrics Deployment of Machine Readable Travel Documents. Technical Report, Version 1.9, 2003, available at http://www.icao.int/mrtd/Home/Index.cfm.

[ICAO03c]   International Civil Aviation Association (ICAO): Development of a Logical Data Structure – LDS for optional Capacity Expansion Technologies. Technical

Report, 1st Edition, 2003, available at
http://www.icao.int/mrtd/Home/Index.cfm.

[ICAO03d] International Civil Aviation Association (ICAO): Use of Contactless Integrated
Circuits in Machine Readable Travel Documents. Technical Report, Version 3.1,
2003, available at http://www.icao.int/mrtd/Home/Index.cfm.

[ICAO03e] International Civil Aviation Association (ICAO): PKI Digital Signatures for
Machine Readable Travel Documents. Technical Report, Version 4.0, 2003,
available at http://www.icao.int/mrtd/Home/Index.cfm.

[ICCPR]   International Covenant on Civil and Political Rights, available at
http://www.unhchr.ch/html/menu3/b/a_ccpr.htm.

[LEVA96]   LeVay, Simon: Queer Science: the Use and Abuse of Research into Homosexuality, MIT Press, Cambridge, 1996.

[MCCO03]   McCormack, David: Can corporate America secure our nation? An analysis of
the identix framework for the regulation and use of facial recognition technology. In: 9 Boston University Journal of Science and Technology Law (2003),
pp. 128-155.

[NGUY02]   Nguyen, Alexander T.: Here's Looking at you, Kid: Has Face-Recognition
Technology Completely Outflanked the Fourth Amendment? In: 7 Virginia
Journal of Law and Technology (2002), p. 2.

[PAG]   German Gesetz über Personalausweise of 21. April 1986 (Bundesgesetzblatt I,
548), last amended on 25. March 2002 (Bundesgesetzblatt I, 1186).

[RAEF02]   Rankl, Wolfgang / Effing, Wolfgang: Handbuch der Chipkarten. Aufbau – Funk-
tionsweise – Einsatz von Smart Cards, 4. Edition, Hanser, München, 2002.

[RPG01]   Roßnagel, Alexander / Pfitzmann, Andreas / Garstka, Hansjürgen: Modernis-
ierung des Datenschutzrechts. Gutachten im Auftrag des Bundesministeriums
des Innern, Berlin 2001.

[RRM04]   Reichl, Herbert / Roßnagel, Alexander / Müller, Günter: Machbarkeitsstudie
„Digitaler Personalausweis", to be published in 2004.

[TAB02]   Büro für Technikfolgenabschätzung beim Deutschen Bundestag (TAB): Biometrische Identifikationssysteme – Sachstandsbericht. Bundestags-Drucksache
14/10005 (available at http://dip.bundestag.de/btd/14/100/1410005.pdf), 2002.

[TAB03]   Büro für Technikfolgenabschätzung beim Deutschen Bundestag (TAB): Ar-
beitsbericht Nr. 93: Biometrie und Ausweisdokumente. Leistungsfähigkeit, poli-
tische Rahmenbedingungen, rechtliche Ausgestaltung. Zweiter Sachstandsbericht, available at
http://www.tab.fzk.de/de/projekt/zusammenfassung/ab93.pdf, December 2003.

[ULD03]   Unabhängiges Landeszentrum für Datenschutz Schleswig-Holstein: Datenschutzrechtliche Anforderungen an den Einsatz biometrischer Verfahren in
Ausweispapieren und bei ausländerrechtlichen Identitätsfeststellungen. Stand
Juli 2003, available at
http://www.datenschutzzentrum.de/download/Biometrie_Gutachten_Print.pdf.

[US02]   United States Enhanced Border Security and Visa Entry Reform Act of 2002. Available at http://frwebgate.access.gpo.gov/cgi-bin/getdoc.cgi?dbname=107_cong_public_laws&docid=f:publ173.107.pdf.

[WOH03]   Woodward, John D., Jr. / Orlans, Nicholas M. / Higgins, Peter T.: Biometrics. Identity Assurance in the Information Age, McGraw-Hill/Osborne, New York, 2003.

[WOOD01]   Woodward, John D., Jr.: Super Bowl Surveillance. Facing Up to Biometrics, available at http://www.rand.org/publications/IP/IP209/IP209.pdf, 2001.

New Initiatives and New Needs
for Privacy Enhancing Technologies

Dr. Alexander Dix, LL.M.

Commissioner for Data Protection and Access to Information
Landesbeauftragter für den Datenschutz und
für das Recht auf AkteneinsichtBrandenburg
dix@lda.brandenburg.de

Abstract

The concept of privacy enhancing technologies is central to modern data protection regulation. Systematic protection of privacy has to be built into the design of technology from the outset. The fast development of new technologies and the modification of existing technical solutions makes a continuous privacy impact assessment indispensable. Legal regulation should encourage the development of privacy friendly technical solutions (and standards) and international standardisation should in turn take into account the necessary legal framework rather than trying to replace it. Legal and technical regulation (standardisation) need to be harmonised in order to reinforce each other. Technology must not be allowed to outstrip legal protection. The paper exemplifies this with reference to camera phones, RFID tags and Voice over IP.

Technology is playing an increasingly important role in ensuring the protection of privacy. Traditionally society and data protection regulators have tended to perceive technological developments as a potential threat to privacy which needed to be contained. More recently the technological potential for safeguarding and indeed improving privacy protection has been recognized/realized (RoGB95). The impacts of technology on privacy may vary depending on the circumstances of deployment. Technology – if not designed properly – can be extremely privacy invasive but it can also – with privacy enhancing features – support the protection of personal privacy. It is all the more important that a certain default level of privacy and additional options for enhanced privacy are built into the technology design from the very start.

To what extent privacy is or is not sufficiently taken into account when designing new technology may be studied in three examples:

- Camera phones
- RFID
- Voice over IP.

1 Camera phones

Most mobile phones nowadays are sold with camera functions. Sales of these small-size devices have skyrocketed to such an extent that some analysts believe that camera phones will soon replace digital cameras altogether. Camera phones are the basis for multimedia messaging services which allow for the taking and instant sending of pictures and sounds to an unlimited number of recipients (ultimately by publishing them on the Internet). This technology has already led to a vast amount of pictures being made available online in „moblogs" (mobile blogs, i.e. websites where anyone can post pictures with or without comments).

The privacy implications of this technology arise from the fact that pictures may be taken without the person depicted noticing it. The available hardware features lenses which are so small that individuals in the vicinity of the person holding the camera phone will not even notice whether the mobile phone has a camera function and whether the camera function is in operation. Although many camera phone owners take a specific posture when using their phones as cameras it is possible to make a phone call or to pretend to do so and take a picture at the same time.

For reasons of commercial secrecy a growing number of companies such as BMW, Rolls Royce, Volvo and British Aerospace have banned the use of camera phones inside their factories. In Saudi-Arabia the use of these devices is illegal in the entire country. In Australia and Japan they are banned from changing rooms (ITUB04). The Italian Garante per la protezione dei dati personali (Data Protection Authority) has issued guidelines in which it stresses that taking pictures of a person without his or her consent is illegal. The state of the law in Germany is basically the same.

However, legal regulation in a global economy does not – at least not on its own – solve the underlying problem of privacy enhancing or privacy invasive technology design. It is therefore necessary to think about a whole set of measures to tackle this problem.

The International Working Group on Data Protection in Telecommunications in recent Working Paper has recommended the following options:

- Improvement of education of the users, particularly taking into account their youth and inexperience;
- Improvement of the information given by manufacturers about the appropriate use of camera phones;
- Implementation of technological supports to facilitate application of the relevant principles of data protection an enhance awareness. Possible means to achieve this target might include the issue of a sound signal whenever the camera function is operated and developing technologies allowing the camera function to be disabled in certain marked areas („safe havens", e.g. health club) (IWGD04a).

The latter options are relevant in the context of privacy enhancing technologies discussed here. They have already been implemented in South Korea where the government has ordered manufacturers to ensure that all camera phones send a beeping signal of at least 65 decibels when a picture is being taken. A similar technological design is followed by Japanese manufacturing industry on the basis of voluntary self-regulation.

The „safe haven"-technology is not supported by the current generation of mobile phones. Safe havens send a signal to mobile phones telling them that they are in a privacy zone. The imaging system of the phone then switches itself off. The phone can still be used for voice communication. This nascent technology could equally be used to deactivate digital cameras or the camera function in PDAs and notebooks. But it would require the corresponding hardware which is not available yet. There may be a certain incentive for manufacturers to produce it once the demand for safe havens on production premises is rising. It is probably more acceptable to ban phones which cannot respond to safe havens than to ban mobile phones altogether. The need for protection of production secrets could have privacy enhancing technology as a by-product. Gyms and health clubs will then have to install safe haven-technology and ban camera phones and mobile computers with camera function which do not comply with this technology. The incentive for doing so could be the rising demand by customers for an environment in which they can relax without being subject to „digital stalking". Privacy enhancing technology could bring a competitive advantage to those using and advertising it.

2 RFID technology

Radio frequency identification (RFID) technology was originally developed for military applications during the Second World War (CAVO04). Allied aircraft were the first to be equipped with RFID sensors which were then named Identify Friend or Foe (IFF). Today this is an essential feature on every civilian and military airplane in the world. The technology is at present rapidly gaining ground in a different area due to miniaturisation and the falling costs of tags (transponders, transducers) and readers. Tags now cost between 50 cents and 1 Euro and readers cost around 1000 Euro. Although the prices are still quite high and a number of standardisation issues still have to be solved on an international level large retail companies (Wal-Mart) are introducing this technology on the case and pallet level first to reduce costs of logistics and controlling the supply chain. The economic pressure to introduce this technology may be illustrated by the fact that savings for retail industry are estimated at 20% of the present costs of logistics, i.e. several billions of US-Dollars.

The Auto-ID Center at MIT (sponsored by Procter & Gamble and other companies) has developed the Electronic Product Code Standard (EPC) in September 2003 which is designed to lead to an „Internet of things" by assigning Internet addresses to individual (unique) objects and link them to individual persons. This is probably the most important step towards ubiquitous computing, a scenario which has also been called „ambient intelligence". RFID tags will in the foreseeable future replace the barcode but it would be a mistake to simply equate it with barcodes. There are several crucial differences which make RFID tags much more powerful than conventional barcodes:

- RFID tags can be assigned to and identify individual objects (a certain vehicle, a razor blade) whereas barcodes are the same for a specific type of product (a type of vehicle, Gillette razor blades); this would e.g. allow a car manufacturer or dealer to quickly locate cars on their premises which are due for delivery. The RFID of a specific item may be linked to an individual who buys this item by using his or her credit card;

- RFID tags may be read contactless (and therefore unnoticed and unnoticeable) from a distance whereas line-of-sight is required for barcodes; miniaturisation will lead to „smart dust" which can be embedded in any material („wearable, invisible computing")

- RFID tags may be read outdoors even in harsh weather conditions (snow, fog, ice) or though paint (unlike barcodes); but even RFID tags cannot be read if shielded by metal substances (therefore it is still impossible to have an automatic check-out in a supermarket where items are buried in a shopping basket under tins etc.);

- Objects with RFID tags can communicate with readers („speak to them") during their entire lifecycle thus allowing the manufacturers (or indeed anyone controlling an infrastructure of readers) to register and monitor consumer behaviour and even their location as long as they are carrying the tagged object. A tag can transmit inter alia information about the date and place of purchase, the price, a possible link to the buyer and the present location of the tagged object.

There are numerous other fields of possible application of RFID technology, especially the integration in:

- passports and identity cards
- Euro-banknotes

- tickets (e.g. für the Soccer World Championship 2006)
- credit or loyalty cards.

The Veripay project in the US even provides for the voluntary implantation of subdermal chips for payment purposes. Considerable publicity has also concentrated on the Florida family who agreed to have VeriChips implanted in their bodies to ensure proper and quick medical treatment in case of severe diseases or unconsciousness.

Other applications of RFID tags include:

- tracking of hospital staff when fighting infectious human diseases (SARS)
- tracking cattle (mad cow disease) or pets
- tracking luggage and containers
- road pricing
- tagging of poisonous substances e.g. in PC to facilitate recycling.

The privacy implications of implanted chips are obvious. They will not be dealt with in this paper since the issue is more related to informed consent freely given rather than to privacy enhancing technology (although after valid consent has been given there may still be issues of privacy-friendly or privacy- invasive technological alternatives).

Since RFID technology will probably first hit the market in the retail and logistics scenario mentioned above privacy considerations should be taken account of at the earliest possible stage here. There has been an instance of a retail store using this technology (e.g. Metro in Germany) where the company misled the public about the fact that personal data were in fact processed by RFID tags in conjunction with a personal loyalty card. This led to public protests in Germany so that the company had to stop the trials (at least as far as the loyalty card is concerned). Transparency and sincerity are therefore essential when deploying this technology. Hidden devices for data collection will always (once detected) cause mistrust. Two recent Bills in Utah and Missouri emphasise transparency by requiring information to be given to the data subjects whenever RFID tags are used.

But transparency is only a necessary but not sufficient step to protect privacy. If the person concerned is informed that his or her data are being collected but nothing can be done about it (except perhaps leaving the shop and not buying tagged items as long as there are alternatives) this will not be enough to comply with data protection principles. The RFID Bill currently before the California legislature (sponsored by Sen. Bowen) therefore goes further by setting out conditions under which RFID tags may be used legally (only in shops or libraries for specific purposes). A number of problems still arise as to how define the admissible timespan in which personal data may legally be collected (Bowen's Bill would forbid the use of tags „before a customer *actually* initiates a transaction or a borrower *actually attempts* to borrow an item…and after the transaction is completed."). These regulatory difficulties can perhaps be solved but legal safeguards need to be accompanied by privacy enhancing technical solutions.

The Data Protection and Privacy Commissioners at their International Conference in 2003 adopted a resolution which called for the implementation of these recommendations:

a) any controller – before introducing RFID tags linked to personal information or leading to customer profiles – should first consider alternatives which achieve the same goal without collecting personal information or profiling customers;

b)   if the controller can show that personal data are indispensable, they must be collected in an open and transparent way ;

c)   personal data may only be used for the specific purpose for which they were first collected and only retained for as long as is necessary to achieve (or carry out) this purpose, and

d)   whenever RFID tags are in the possession of individuals, they should have the possibility to delete data and to disable or destroy the tags (25IC03).

The manufacturers of RFID tags have suggested the use of „blocker tags" which enable the consumer to disrupt the communication between tag and reader or at least the transmission of specific information. Such devices – which are not yet available – however have a number of severe disadvantages. They would only disable tags within their reach so if a tagged item is separated from the blocking device the tag could be read by any reader in the vicinity. The most important argument against blocking devices is a principal one: the burden to protect one's privacy is shifted to the data subject (CONS03). He would have to get acquainted with the technology and once he did not use the blocker for whatever reason the collection of data and tracking of objects and persons possessing them would go ahead unhindered.

Privacy enhancing technology should be designed in such a way that the data subjects can decide autonomously whether their data should be collected or transmitted. Any such collection or transmission should depend on their consent and should be initiated by them. What is known in terms of legal regulation as the „opt-in" with regard to the processing of personal data has to be supported by a „technical opt-in" rather than a mere „technical opt-out". Whereas the blocker tag would be a technical opt-out of limited value the technical opt-in can be provided for if as a default no personal data are collected at all.

This has been the case with the „R-click"-service at a trial in a new Tokyo shopping district between November 2003 and February 2004. NTT DoCoMo, the Japanese carrier, issued about 4.500 RFID tags embedded in small handheld terminals which can be attached to user's mobile phones. 200 stores participated in the trial. Subscribers could inform the network that they wish to be located by pushing a button, but the default setting was off. In case they pushed the button the R-click service delivered area specific information to a user's location transmitted by the RFID tag (ITUB04).

Privacy enhancing RFID technology would therefore require that any communication (i.e. any disclosure of personal information) between the tag and the reader be initiated and controlled by the data subject carrying the tagged item. Japanese researchers have described an interesting system how this user control of RFIDs could be achieved (InYa03). In a simplified manner the system can be described as using personal keys (user-defined IDs) for RFID tags thereby preventing the reading or use without the cooperation of the owner of the tagged item. This idea is primarily addressing the problem of RFID tags on items on display in shops (what happens at the point of sale). But it could equally be applied to RFID tags in passports and identity cards since there is no need to read or check these documents without the cooperation or even the knowledge of the passport- or ID-Card-holder.

3 Voice over IP

The third example shows the urgent need for privacy enhancing technologies before a new and far reaching technical development may outstrip legal protections. According to the Wall Street Journal by the end of 2004 20% of all new phones being delivered to U.S. businesses will use Voice over IP technology. By 2007 that figure will rise above 50% and eventually almost all new phones will use Voice over IP. Which consequences does this have on existing legal protection, especially secrecy of telecommunications ?

Whereas conventional voice telephony does not normally lead to the storage of content data on the part of the called person (except in special circumstances where the conversation is being taped) with Voice over IP a technological change takes place: IP-based telephony leads to the same ease of storage on both the sender's and the recipient's end as with e-mail (SWIR04). Contents of the conversation are stored routinely on the computers used for this communication (unless the content data are deleted). The relation between unrecorded conversations as a rule and recorded conversations as exception is reversed: storage of content data becomes the rule and their deletion requires specific action. The ephemeral telephone conversation would resemble more an e-mail-communication with systematic storage at both ends.

In most jurisdictions the lawful access to content data of telecommunications requires a judicial warrant which will only be granted under specific circumstances. The reason for this is the protection of telecommunications secrecy. But this protection does not extend to content data which have been stored after the end of the communication. The interception of letters on their way to the recipient comes under the secrecy of mail communications; once the letter has reached its destination it may be seized under less strict conditions. The same applies to taped telephone conversations (which are not made systematically). Although there may be an issue if the telephone conversation could have been taped legally in the first place once that has happened the tape may be seized even if the telephone conversation itself may not have been overheard legally.

With Voice over IP not only the contents of telephone conversations will be stored routinely on individual users' computers but also on the network level for groups of users such as company employees or university staff. At least one such product is already on sale ("CacheEnforcer").

Whereas with conventional telephony there has always been what the U.S. Courts used to call „a reasonable expectation of privacy" this expectation will no longer be „reasonable" with Voice over IP in view of the systematic and easy storage of content data. In the discussion on routine retention of traffic data on the national and European level it has always been stressed by the proponents of such retention duties that no retention of content data is envisaged. What the regulators may not dare to provide for expressly may very soon be the factual side-effect of a new technology.

The obvious privacy enhancing technical answer to this development would seem to be *usable* end-to-end-encryption. This has been called for by data protection experts long before anyone could think of Voice over IP. But now there is an urgent need and at the same time perhaps a chance for user-friendly encryption to be available on a global level because this would protect stored content data even after the communication has ended.

A further step for privacy enhancing technology could be to let the caller determine whether his message may be stored by the recipient at all (encrypted or unencrypted). But this would probably have to be applied to e-mail-communication as well (which would mean in increased autonomy of the sender of a message and a decreased autonomy of the recipient).

4 Conclusion

The three examples of camera phones, RFID tags and Voice over IP are rather different. But they illustrate the importance of privacy enhancing technology design from the start. What the U.S. Congress has mandated for e-government projects, i.e. an explicit privacy impact assessment (USEG02, sec.208), is equally necessary for technological innovations. The International Organisation for Standardisation (ISO) is at present discussing a Draft Privacy Framework Standard and has formed a Privacy Study Group. Whereas ISO had envisaged to adopt this Draft following a fast track procedure the International Working Group on Data Protection in Telecommunications has called for a more thorough discussion (IWGD04b). It is to be hoped that this discussion will lead to an international standard on privacy which includes more than references to the OECD Guidelines of 1980. Since the adoption of these Guidelines the principles of scarcity and minimisation of personal data have become central to a modern systematic concept of privacy protection. As a default rule they should be integrated in any modern privacy standard.

Ambient intelligence; camera phones; content data; barcode; data minimisation; data retention; data scarcity; encryption; International Standardisation Organisation; privacy standard; RFID tags; secrecy of telecommunications; traffic data; ubiquitous computing; Voice over IP; wearable computing

References

Cavoukian, A., Tag, You're It: Privacy Implications of Radio Frequency Identification (RFID) Technology, Information and Privacy Commissioner, Ontario, Toronto, February 2004 (CAVO04)
http://www.ipc.on.ca/scripts/index_.asp?action=31&P_ID=15007&N_ID=1&PT_ID=113 51&U_ID=0

Consumers Against Supermarket Privacy Invasion and Numbering (CASPIAN) et al., Position Statement on the Use of RFID on Consumer Products, November 2003 (CONS03)
http://www.privacyrights.org/ar/RFIDposition.htm

Inoue, S./Yasuura, H., RFID Privacy Using User-controllable Uniqueness, Paper presented at the RFID Privacy Workshop @ MIT: November 15, 2003 (InYa03)
http://www.rfidprivacy.org/agenda.php

International Telecommunications Union, Social and Human Considerations for a More Mobile World, Background Paper, ITU/MIC Workshop on Shaping the Future Mobile Information Society, Seoul, March 2004 (ITUB04)
http://www.itu.int/osg/spu/ni/futuremobile/SocialconsiderationsBP.pdf

International Working Group on Data Protection in Telecommunications, Working Paper on ptivacy and processing of images and sounds by multimedia messaging services, Buenos Aires 2004 (IWGD04a)
http://www.datenschutz-berlin.de/doc/int/iwgdpt/index.htm

International Working Group on Data Protection in Telecommunications, Working Paper on a future ISO privacy standard, Buenos Aires 2004 (IWGD04b)
http://www.datenschutz-berlin.de/doc/int/iwgdpt/index.htm

25th International Conference of Data Protection and Privacy Commissioners, Sydney 2003, Resolution on Radio Frequency Identification (25IC03)
http://www.privacyconference2003.org/resolutions/res5.DOC

van Rossum, H./Gardeniers, H./Borking, J.J., Privacy-Enhancing Technologies: The Path to Anonymity, Vols. I-II, ed. by Registratiekamer, The Netherlands & Information and Privacy Commissioner Ontario, Canada, 1995 (RoGB95)
http://www.ipc.on.ca/scripts/index_.asp?action=31&N_ID=1&P_ID=11361&U_ID=0
http://www.ipc.on.ca/scripts/index_.asp?action=31&N_ID=1&P_ID=15313&U_ID=0

Swire, P., Has Technology Outstripped Telephone Legal Protections ? Privacy Journal, Providence, June 2004 (SWIR04)

U.S. E-Government Act of 2002, H.R.2458 (USEG02)

Data Protection Aspects of the Digital Rights Management

Professor Dr. Alfred Büllesbach

Chief Officer Corporate Data Protection
DaimlerChrysler AG
70546 Stuttgart
alfred.buellesbach@daimlerchrysler.com

Abstract

The application of DRM-methods frequently has a potential to conflict with issues of data protection, because a substantial amount of personal data is usually processed. The constitutionally protected position of the copyright holder, who wants appropriate protection against any circumvention of copyright protection and the modification and erasure of his works, collides with the basic right of informational self-determination of the user. The article will examine the possibility to develop DRM-systems which conform to the demands of data protection and will present the conditions, which have to be met.

1 The conflict between copyright protection and data protection

The widespread distribution of powerful hardware and world-wide networking facilitates a simple digital copying technique which preserves the quality of copyright protected works. This has led to significant losses in revenue in particular for the music industry. But the film industry and the publishing sector, to a minor extent, have also felt the consequences of this development.

For this reason the industry is keen to restrict, apart from legal limitations for the use of protected works, the use of copyright protected works through technical procedures so as to bring tighter control and more efficiency in terms of use and distribution. The technical procedures used therefore are summarised under the term Digital Rights Management (DRM).

But the currently established IT-infrastructure has to be regarded all in all as insecure. Especially the systems used by the users could easily be attacked and corrupted. This complicates the allocation of interactions and therefore the certain possibility of allocation in e-commerce and DRM. Therefore, on the part of the software and hardware industry techniques under the keyword „Trusted computing" are developed to ensure a secure infrastructure.

The progress in the Trusted Computing sector opens up questions regarding data protection. In this respect, especially the issue of data security has to be mentioned.

The application of DRM procedures conflicts with data protection since normally a substantial amount of personal data is processed. The constitutionally protected position of the author, who wants an appropriate protection against the circumvention of the copyright protection and against the alteration or erasure of his works, collides thereby with the basic right to informational self-determination of the user. In particular the transparency of data processing

S. Paulus, N. Pohlmann, H. Reimer (Editors): Securing Electronic Business Processes, Vieweg (2004), 66-74

often does not seem to be given. It is however an important prerequisite to be able to decide by oneself about the processing of the own data. Furthermore, the basic principle of data reduction and data economy implemented for instance through an anonymous or pseudonymous possibility to use DRM-protected works, only finds inadequate consideration.

2 Trusted Computing

There are different efforts to make the employed platforms – in particular those of the users – more secure, so that, on the one hand, programs causing damages cannot access the systems or cannot being implemented into the systems and on the other hand, an authentication of the system is made possible both locally and externally (e.g. via internet).

On the hardware side, there is a pooling of manufacturers in the Trusted Computing Group[1], who aims on the basis of a so called Trusted Platform Module (TPM), to bring evidence to the integrity of the used platform.

TPM is a hardware security module, which is bound to the computer platform. It supervises the state of the system by controlling the integrity of the starting process and based on that producing a pre control of the integrity for each starting program.

TPM contains a unique key pair (Endorsement keys) and could therefore be used for authentication. The Endorsement keys can be used for the generation of further keys, the so called Attestation Identity Keys (AIK). However, an conclusion from the AIK to the Endorsement keys is not possible. A possible application of the AIK is in electronic trade as a pseudonymous identity.[2] Another functionality is the cryptographic function for other system components. On the basis of a key which is equally protected through the TPM, a key hierarchy is established. The keys can be linked to certain states of the system so as, for example, the encrypted data can only be decrypted again on the condition of a state of the system similar to that during the encryption.

For the functions to be fulfilled certification authorities are additionally necessary which certify that an Endorsement key belongs to a TPM (presumably the producer), that an AIK belongs to a person and that integrity features of the programs are correct. Trustworthy certification authorities are decisively important for the over-all concept.

There is currently a development by Microsoft under the name „Next Generation Secure Computing Base" (NGSCB) for operating systems. The core was originally supposed to be a protected sector within the operating system and memory in which applications or services run completely separated from other sectors. However this variant would probably have led to a significant slowdown of the system. Therefore, small protected sectors per application or per service respectively are to be set up instead. Simultaneously, an integer system environment from the input to the output was devised. The realisation of this plan nevertheless is questionable as it is difficult to implement it in reality. Namely, it would require a complete conversion of the entire IT-terminal equipment-infrastructure of the users. That requires apart from the secure operating system core additional secure hardware that could be based upon a TPM.

---

[1] www.trustedcomputinggroup.org

[2] [KöNe03], p. 696

2.1   Trusted computing as a basis for identity management?

A conceivable application of Trusted Computing would be its employment as a basis for identity management. Identity management plays an important role in businesses and could also be used in DRM systems as well as in e-business.

Identity management can also be used to administer several identities of one and the same person. Thus a person can act under his/her name or under a pseudonym.

The precondition of the application for identity management is a sufficient security of all components used for Trusted Computing. A security vulnerability could lead to an identity theft or it could cancel the functionality of the administration of identities at least.

Trusted Computing contains by itself no reference to a person. Therefore there is a need for further components, like for example a Trust Centre, which undertakes an allocation to the person.

2.2   Dangers for data protection

The creation of an integer system environment, which prevents the intrusion and the running of programs causing damages, is also from the point of view of data protection favourable. Data protection can only be implemented effectively by using accompanying measures. Trusted Computing can contribute to that.

Admittedly there are also negative aspects to data protection. The user loses the sole control over the infrastructure implemented by him/her, as he/she does not have any influence on the Endorsement key. It therefore has to be claimed that the user keeps full control over the functionality of his/her computer.[3]

Another problem is the fact that the Endorsement key can be created outside of the TPM. Producers state for that cost reasons. Therefore, the user has to rely on the uniqueness of his/her Endorsement key.[4]

A further weakness is the certification infrastructure. The user has to trust in this infrastructure. The user has neither an alternative nor a competence to check or control. A compromising which could occur because of failures in the implementation could endanger the data processing of all the computers taking part in Trusted Computing Systems and therewith in particular the data. On top of that, in a case of a compromising the actions of an attacker could possibly be assigned to the attacked user. This can then lead to virtual „identity theft".

Furthermore, the Trusted Computing procedures must not be used to enforce the disclosure of the identity of the user.[5] Whether the user only wants to authenticate himself/herself or whether he/she does indeed wish to identify himself/herself must be subject to his/her own decision.

---

[3] see: Entschließung der 65. Konferenz der Datenschutzbeauftragten des Bundes und der Länder, 27./28th March 2003

[4] generally concerning that: Pfitzner, R., TCPA, Palladium und DRM-Technische Analyse und Aspekte des Datenschutzes (state: Juni 2003),
http://www.lda.brandenburg.de/sixcms/detail.php?id=88160&template=allgemein_lda

[5] see [DiPf03] p. 562

Additionally, it is prohibited to compile a use-profile of identified users without the consent of the user which was provided in advance.

If the user wishes to be completely protected against the possible risks, then he/she has to switch off the TPM. Consequently, the user will not, at the same time, be able to make use of the benefits of Trusted Computing.

3 Digital Rights Management

With the implementation of Digital Rights Management (DRM) systems in particular the Music and Film industry anticipates the prevention of the production of (illegal) copies of copyright protected works. With the help of DRM it should be ensured that unauthorised contents cannot be consumed. Moreover, works protected by DRM should not be unauthorised altered. The precondition is the identifiability of both the copyright protected works and the scope of the legitimation of the respective user to use the works.

The spreading of DRM is only at an early stage although different systems already exist. The mode of function can basically be explained as follows:

First of all, regularly a registration is necessary to access the service. Then, data can be loaded or the program can be installed. A digital identity will be created, which will be registered with a licence server. If a payment is required the necessary transaction will be done. The user will thereafter receive the licence and he/she can use the contents or the applications within the scope of the licence.

In particular, the binding of the utilization to a certain computer plays an important role. For this purpose procedures of the Trusted Computing can be used which ensure the binding either through the operating system or through the hardware.

3.1 Data protection in case of the employment of Digital Rights Management

Most of the DRM applications will require that the user logs in with his/her personal data before he/she is authorised to use protected works. In comparison to the purchase in a shop this presents a procedure which is not conducive to privacy since an anonymous or pseudonymous use of works is no longer possible. Also considering the aspect of freedom of opinion, the loss of anonymity during the use of works is regrettable as this could lead to a diminished use in particular of works critical of society as users could fear to be observed by security agencies.

Apart from the collection of personal data when logging into a DRM system (basic or contractual data), utilization data can be collected as well. Conceivable is the collection of utilization data whilst downloading of protected works for example from the Internet and in the course of every use of protected works. In this way personal use and interest profiles can be compiled even without the attention of the user.

The main application case for the employment of DRM systems is presumably the downloading of copyright protected works via the Internet. While doing this, potentially personal data is sent via unprotected channels. Therefore, from the viewpoint of data protection, a SSL-encryption has to be used for these connections.

If the use of DRM protected works takes place through demand e.g. from the Internet then the offer has to be classified as a teleservice. To assess the compliance with data protection regulations, the Act on the Protection of Personal Data Used in Teleservices (TeleServices Data Protection Act – hereinafter TDDSG) is applicable.

3.1.1 The processing of contractual data

The processing of contractual data, meaning the basic data of the user is governed by Sec. 5 TDDSG. Accordingly the contractual data can only be used for the conclusion, the determination of the terms and the modification of the contractual relationship.

A processing of contractual data for other purposes than those mentioned is only possible on the basis of consent.

For Content-providers who offer DRM protected contents, this means that the basic data (user IDs, name, email address, if so postal address, information about mode of payment) can, at first, only be processed for the provision of the service and only this data necessary for the provision of the service can be collected. Further processing requires the consent of the data subject.

3.1.2 Processing of utilization data

3.1.2.1 Principles

The processing of utilization data is regulated by Sec. 6 TDDSG. According to this provision processing of utilization data is principally permitted for the provision of the service, to charge the user, and to the fight against misuse. There is an obligation to delete or anonymize utilization data insofar as it is no longer needed for accounting purposes or for the investigation of misuse. Anonymized utilization data may be disclosed to third parties for the purposes of market research.

3.1.2.2 Use-profiles

Sec. 6 para. 3 TDDSG allows a service provider to compile use-profiles under the use of pseudonyms. The provider may only compile pseudonym-based use-profiles for purposes of advertising, market research, or structuring the services to comply with the demand. However the provider must grant the user the possibility to object to the compiling of use- profiles and he has also to inform the user about her/his right of objection. Moreover the service provider may not combine use- profiles with data on the bearer of the profile. Aim of this regulation is to avoid that interest profiles are compiled about specific users. This is of particular importance in the field of DRM since utilization data is generated while downloading as well as during the actual use of one of the works protected through DRM systems. Through this way an extensive interest profile about the user could be compiled.

If the provider wishes to compile use-profiles beyond the scope of Sec. 6 para. 3 TDDSG, he needs the consent of the user.

3.1.3 Data processing based on the consent

Apart from the legitimation of a data processing by a legal provision the data subject can allow a data processing by providing his/her consent.

Sec. 4a Federal Data Protection Act provides for the requirements of a consent and Sec. 4 para. 2 TDDSG for the electronic declaration of consent. The data subject has to understand the content of his/her declaration. For this reason he/she needs to be informed about the purpose as well as the type and scope of the data processing. He/she also has to be informed if his/her data is processed outside the EU. Under certain circumstances the level of data protection in states outside the EU is not comparable to the level of data protection in place in Germany and if so the data subject must be informed about this situation before he/she gives his/her consent. Moreover he/she has to be notified that he/she has the right to withdraw the consent at any time in the future according to Sec. 4 para 3. TDDSG.

An electronic declaration of consent requires an unambiguous and deliberate act by the user. It has to be particularly taken into account that the user himself/herself has to become active. A tick box in front of a declaration of consent must initially be un-ticked. Rather the user must tick it himself/herself.

The so called coupling ban according to Sec. 3 para. 4 TDDSG prohibits coupling the service provision with the consent to the data processing for other purposes if the user does not have any other reasonable possibility to use the service. An example in this respect is to make the use of a DRM protected work contingent upon the consent to data processing for advertising purposes, which in each specific case requires a detailed consideration from a privacy prospective.

3.1.4 Data reduction and data economy

The basic principle of data reduction and economy aims at processing as little data as possible. This is regulated by Sec. 3a Federal Data Protection Act. More concrete is the postulation provided by Sec. 4 para. 6 TDDSG in so far as the user needs to be granted the utilization of teleservices and their payment anonymously or under a pseudonym, provided that this is technically possibly and reasonable for the provider.

Data reduction can be achieved in two different ways. The provider can design the system in such a way that as little data as possible is processed (systemic data protection) or the user can be given tools so that he/she himself/herself can serve for protection of his/her own data in the wanted scope (self data protection).

The providers can support the systemic data protection approach by allowing an anonymous or pseudonymous use. With respect to DRM systems this would mean that a personal related log in to the (technical) producer of the DRM-system, at the Content provider, or at the legal owner is not required.

Another approach for the systemic data protection is the separation of the accounting from the use of the DRM protected content. Hereby the user can use the offer of the content provider under a pseudonym and the payment takes place at another provider who then again does not know which content has been used.

An important aspect of systemic data protection is especially data security. If it is absolutely necessary to collect personal data then they need to be protected on transport through insecure networks like the Internet and also at the provider himself they have to be protected against misuse.

The possibilities of the offer of self data protection tools should not be underestimated. The utilization of such tools can be performed by the user whereas the measures of the systemic data protection are normally outside of the perception of the user. The transparent presentation of data processing, the possibility for an easy execution of the rights of data subjects like for example the right to information, the right to object and to withdraw as well as the opening of other possibilities to choose from for the user, lead to a positive feeling on the side of the user regarding the compliance with data protection regulations by the service provider. Nevertheless it shall not be pleaded for an ostensible „data protection to feel good" which has no substance in the backend. Rather it has been thought of an extra offer for the user under utilization of the existing technical tools which apart from a duly data processing while observing the aspects of systemic data protection, leads to acceptance from the user. This will then spill over to sectors in which data processing of personal data is necessary for the provision or desirable for the provider.

3.1.5 Impact of the Directive on privacy and electronic communications

Contractual data may be processed according to the regulations of the Directive on privacy and electronic communications[6], for advertising and market research purposes. However the data subject has the possibility to opt out of the data processing for such purposes. The TDDSG requires consent for the processing of contractual data for advertising purposes.

The requirements of the German law go beyond the requisitions of the directive. In this context it therefore has to be questioned if the legislator has leeway which allows him to decide on stronger regulations in spite of the differently provided guidelines. Moreover the question needs to be asked why the legislator keeps the stronger regulation for teleservices while in other sectors along with Sec. 28 para. 4 Federal Data Protection Act also only a right to object exists. As regards contractual data no higher threat is discernible compared to other sectors of the economy with respect to the utilization of contractual data for advertising purposes. Insofar the possibility to opt out seems an appropriate solution considering the balance of interests of the economy on the one side and the data subject on the other side.

Regarding the sending of electronic mails for purposes of direct marketing, the directive prescribes that a sending is only allowed if there is an existing business contact. Also then the data subject has the possibility to opt out. A sending without an existing business contact is only permitted with the consent of the data subject. The German legislator has incorporated corresponding regulations into the Law on Unfair Competition (Sec. 7 of the Law on Unfair Competition).

At this point it shall be mentioned that the American Digital Millennium Copyright Act (DMCA) also provides for an opt out against the use of basic data for advertising purposes in relation with DRM systems.

---

[6] Directive 2002/58/EC of the European Parliament and the Council of 12 July 2002 concerning the processing of personal data and the protection privacy in the electronic communications sector (Directive on privacy and electronic communications), Official Journal p.201/37.

3.2 Designs of DRM systems which are supportive of data protection

Due to networking the offer of copyright protected works is no longer a local but a world-wide offer. World-wide the data protection law is extremely heterogeneous. Companies, associations, and other organisations try to cope with this diversity through measurements of self-regulation.[7] For world-wide offers of copyright protected works under the use of a DRM system an own Privacy Policy is a possibility to react to this heterogeneity.

The use of DRM systems for the protection of the owner of copyrights does not necessarily result in compiling profiles about the user and therefore violating his/her right to informational self determination. In fact such systems can be designed supportive of data protection.

The preferred solution in terms of data protection would be that no personalised log in is necessary. However problems would then possibly evolve at the enforcement of copyrights.

If a personalised log in is necessary then data may first only be processed according to Sec. 5 TDDSG for executing a contract. In such a case it has to be however checked if processing of personal data is really necessary for the utilization and accounting or if such a service can also be performed through pseudonymous procedures.

For instance a service provider could be employed for the payment who does not get to know the utilized content. In spite of the provider knowing which work is used he does not find out about the user standing behind a pseudonym.

The provider has to get the consent of the user if he wants to process data beyond the scope necessary for the provision of the service. Hereby the presentation and therefore the creation of transparency of data processing is a crucial aspect. When the user feels honestly informed about the data processing then this leads to acceptance and to preparedness to consent to data processing. Thereby the user's rights to withdraw and to object as well as the right to get informed about the data concerning the own person have to be observed. Also the offer of graduated identities linked with an identity management system can lead to a better acceptance by the user.

4 Conclusion and outlook

Trusted Computing procedures as well as the use of DRM systems technically provide the possibility to compile profiles about the interests of the user.

Systems and applications which are supportive in terms of data protection therefore stand out in particular through transparency vis-à-vis the user regarding the data processing. Measures of the systemic data protection, like a graduated identity management or pseudonymous payment procedures and offers for self data protection, boost the acceptance of the user. As it has been shown numerously[8] data protection can develop to a competitive component or even a competitive advantage.

---

[7] More detailed: [Büll03] p. 390 ff.

[8] e.g. [Büll97], p. 239; [Büll99] p. 162; More detailed [Büll03] p. 394; [Büll04], p. 175 ff.

References

[Büll97]   Büllesbach, Alfred: Datenschutz und Datensicherheit als Qualitäts- und Wett-
             bewerbsfaktor, RDV 1997, p. 239 ff.

[Büll99]   Büllesbach, Alfred: Datenschutz als prozessorientierter Wettbewerbsbestandteil,
             PIK 1999, p. 162 ff.

[Büll03]   Büllesbach, Alfred: Datenschutz in der Informationsgesellschaft, in
             Klumpp/Kubicek/Roßnagel (ed.) next generation information society?, Mössin-
             gen –Talheim 2003, p. 386-397.

[Büll04]   Büllesbach, Alfred: Datenschutzrechtliche Bewertung der Verarbeitung und
             Nutzung von Kundendaten, in: Taeger/Wiebe (ed.) Informatik – Wirtschaft –
             Recht; Regulierung in der Wissensgesellschaft, Baden-Baden 2004, p. 175 –
             187.

[DiPf03]   Dix, Alexander/Pfitzner, Roy: Trusted Computing und Datenschutz in Deutsch-
             land, in: DuD 2003, p. 561 – 562.

[KöNe03]   König, Christian/Neumann, Andreas: Anforderungen des EG-Wettbewerbsrechts
             und vertrauenswürdige Systemumgebungen, in: MMR 2003, p. 695 – 700.

Big Brother does not
Keep your Assets Safe

Johannes Wiele

AWi Verlag
Redaktion LANline
johannes_wiele@csi.com

Abstract

There seem to be many reasons today to increase employee and user monitoring as a measure of security. The well-known insider threat is the first one: Statistics tell that security breaches caused by employees or internal users of information systems outrun the attacks of external hackers in number and severity. In connection to this aspect another motivation to implement workplace surveillance is the fact that in many countries a CEO or a board member of a company can be held responsible for the use employees make of the communication systems provided by their employers.

Nowadays a third reason has become even more important than the two already mentioned. Organisations struggling with the increasing pressure by law and by financial regulations to implement risk management realise that the behaviour of employees is a source of „uncertainty and unpredictability in any organisation's environment" [StSt03, p. 153]. The best measure to minimise this risk seems to watch every person working in an organisation as closely as possible to predict what he or she is up to. Companies try to make starting lawsuits against insiders as easy as possible. As a result of these considerations preventative security measures like access control are often devaluated. Employee monitoring is presented as the key to secure IT environments and communication systems.

Unfortunately, technicians and managers tend to overlook the drawbacks and unwanted side effects of surveillance. This article will focus on these aspects. It aims to show that monitoring can undermine the power of an organisation and its chance to be a learning organisation, because the unpredictable elements of the employees' behaviour are not only a source of uncertainty, but also a source of creativity desperately searched for in a period of weak economy. Furthermore, surveillance itself poses new security threats to those who use it thoughtlessly.

1 Dealing with The Insider Threat

It cannot be denied that the insider threat is real. Sometimes disgruntled employees or internal users of IT infrastructure, networks and information systems attack these systems themselves. For insiders it is comparatively easy to do harm to an organisation, as they do not have to get over the perimeter security walls before starting their attacks.

But it is also true that the statistics providing information on the insider threat are often misinterpreted. Many stories based on these statistics only reveal part of the information which can be found in the figures and details, especially when these stories are told by the vendors of surveillance systems and their lobbyists. Therefore, before taking current statements on the insider threat as granted, it seems to be a good idea to ask a simple question from the toolbox of a journalist: „Who says what to whom under what circumstances to achieve what?" The answers are intriguing.

S. Paulus, N. Pohlmann, H. Reimer (Editors): Securing Electronic Business Processes, Vieweg (2004), 75-85

1.1 Statistics Fuel Fears

No company likes to talk about information security breaches which really took place. There are several well-known reasons to be discreet: Companies fear a loss of trust by their customers, they do not want to be involved in investigations and lawsuits and they do not want to reveal information on their IT infrastructure that might help attackers to find vulnerabilities.

Analysts know that. That is the reason why they often try to avoid direct questions in their questionnaires on IT security incidents. Instead of asking: „What has happened?", they help the addressees by giving them a chance to wrap their experiences in an envelope of personal opinion. Most questions are worded as variations of: „What kind of incidents do you fear most?" The analysts hope that the fears of their interview partners reflect reality good enough to build a picture of what really happened.

If a survey is done honestly, the questions are revealed when it is published. But in most cases the executive summaries do not mention these details. Because of that, many readers who are interested in the results never learn that some security surveys have weak links to reality. If the results find their way into the press releases of vendors selling monitoring tools, it is even more likely that the weaknesses of the questioning tactics will not be mentioned.

It is also questionable whether the fears themselves are a good starting point for decisions, because IT security risks are often misjudged. To mention a well-known example, security specialists often complain that CEOs of small and medium enterprises still do not believe that their company may be subject to industrial espionage, even if they wonder why a certain competitor around the corner or from another continent always presents similar products a little bit earlier and a little bit less expensive. Many decision makers cannot imagine that information stored in their networks could be of interest for anyone. The threat from the outside seems to be extremely mysterious for many managers, because they cannot rely on experience when trying to understand it.

On the other hand, most managers can too easily imagine the existence of disgruntled employees in their organisation. It is not easy to manage an organisation without annoying someone from time to time, and in most cases there are no procedures implemented to help disappointed employees with some kind of compensation. A lot of CEOs and board members therefore will easily find members of their staff who are unhappy with their working conditions and who at the same time are capable of launching an attack. If this is the case, they tend to forget that in most cases even the disappointed employees are loyal. Asked for their opinion, anxious managers will then check the box in the questionnaire which says: „Internal attacks are likely to happen".

And there we have the endless chain of fear. The same CEOs and board members who give their fearful input on the insider threat to the surveys find themselves confirmed when reading the results. Asked to answer the next questionnaire, they will be happy to rely on approved knowledge on the threat. They do not realise that they are already running with a crowd of lemmings. Even those who never experienced any incident caused by a dishonest employee and those who would never fail to be loyal to their employer themselves will nod without thinking twice each time someone points out that employees have to be monitored closely. In this atmosphere of fear it is easy to sell employee monitoring solutions, and it is even easier to sell certain types of surveys to the vendors of monitoring solutions.

Finally, it has to be mentioned that many surveys show that information security breaches caused by employees in most cases are based on mistakes, not on criminal energy. Given that this result is correct, it is strange that initiatives to improve the usability of software in order to reduce risks so far have failed to reach as much popularity as efforts to increase user surveillance. It is also strange that the role of mistakes and the reasons for making mistakes are often mentioned, but seldom discussed at security events. The reason for that is simple: Improving existing software does not open new markets and does not help to make a vendor's business grow. Selling monitoring is more profitable.

1.2 Access Control vs. Monitoring

In his article „Security Monitoring – Why and How?" [Arno04], published in issue 3, Volume 9 of the Information Security Bulletin 2004, John Arnold takes up the cudgels for what he calls „reactive security". He devaluates preventative security mechanisms like access controls and firewalls, because they do not prevent legitimate users of IT systems from misusing them. As a second reason not to rely on high-standard access control Arnold points out that identity management systems are too complex and too expensive to be implemented by an average company. It is worth discussing some of his arguments in detail, as they represent the opinion of a constantly growing number of IT security specialists in the world.

Arnold pleads for security monitoring which he describes as a bunch of measures that include employee monitoring as a key element, whereas other security specialists like Bruce Schneier insist on drawing a line between security monitoring as an administrative practise of monitoring technical systems and employee monitoring as the permanent surveillance of human beings. Asked for a statement on this topic, Schneier wrote: „I think employee monitoring is invasive. I think security monitoring is essential. It's the difference between a security camera in the deserted hallway and a camera trained on the employee while he is working." The third sentence quoted introduces the topic of personal mistrust which has to be discussed later.

The reason why Arnold describes access control systems as too expensive and too complicated is that they are difficult to manage when access to several resources in an heterogeneous environment has to be provided. He even points out that for companies in general it may be too difficult to determine which services every single employee needs to have access to [Arno04. p. 86]. This argument is a frightening one. If Arnold is right, then most companies in the world are not able to use their IT resources professionally at all. Finally, Arnold lists difficulties resulting from having to deal with more than one person carrying the same name, and he does not fail to mention all the well-known basic problems of binding a digital identity to a real person.

It is worth a comment that Arnold misses to mention some arguments which do not support his preference for monitoring systems. At first, the vendors of authentication and authorisation solutions have already started to improve their products significantly. Standardisation processes like the one driven by the Liberty Alliance open the door to identity management systems which are manageable and suitable for businesses of any size. These initiatives are even benevolently discussed by privacy groups [ICSN03], because user-controlled identity management systems are capable of providing consumers and employees with the means to actively control the usage of their personal data. The systems empower the users to enforce their right to communicational self-determination [ICSN03, p. ii].

It is also strange that Arnold implicitly demands that every access control solution should be able to identify every single person in this world. When he talks about technical limitations of identity management, he quotes Dan Geer who once spoke on those limitations in general [Arno04, p. 85]. But it is questionable whether virtual identities used within a company will have to be used anywhere else. Additionally it has to be emphasized that according to identity management specialists the personal use of different roles and different virtual identities seems to be one of the key enabling factors of future online services. Scientists and privacy specialists point out that „the amount of digital identities per person will even increase in the next years" [ICSN03, p. i]. The concept of one single digital identity to be used everywhere seems to be outdated.

Arnold actually does not present a solution to information security breaches at all. Monitoring makes it easier to prosecute suspects, and it helps to hold criminals accountable for what they did. But it does not prevent incidents. Amazingly, Arnold recommends that companies should implement reactive security systems in order to be compliant with privacy regulations which hold businesses responsible for storing customer data securely. But if, for example, an employee makes sensible customer data accessible to the public, the victim still suffers from the fraud even if the lawsuit against the employee can be won. From the customers' point of view, any company which stores personal data should at least invest as much money in preventative security as in reactive systems.

Finally there is one strong argument left. Arnold is right to say that access control systems cannot prevent a legitimate user from misusing rights. But in contrast to Arnold I believe that the remaining risks are worth to be taken, not only from a business point of view, but also from a security point of view. In the next chapters, I will explain why.

2 The Drawbacks of Monitoring

The legal and technical advantages of employee monitoring are often discussed. In Europe and especially in Germany the use of employee surveillance systems is limited by law, but lobbyists are already working hard to weaken the chains. It is helpful for them that the business world still tries to solve most security problems by technical solutions.

Today most German companies try to comply with employee privacy regulations. Vendors of content security solutions report that nearly every customer asks them if the log files written by their products can be encrypted and if flexible access control can be applied to them.

This situation may change. Law and financial regulations require enforced risk management, so that companies desire to minimise the uncertainty and unpredictability introduced by the employees. There is a growing interest in proactive forensic tools, and more and more companies ask their employees to allow monitoring of email, telephone calls and web access. Lawyers tend to recommend that the consent to being monitored should be made a part of every contract of employment. In Germany, a reason to do so is that monitoring of the employees' email and internet communication is forbidden unless the employer himself has interdicted personal use and the employees have signed an agreement on being monitored. Otherwise, surveillance under certain circumstances could be handled similarly to a breach of the secrecy of letters [Bitk04, p. 20].

Generally speaking, today companies tend to trade communicational self-determination at the workplace for security more easily than before. This seems to be reasonable, but it has unwanted side effects.

2.1 Why the Hell Do They Resist?

Security specialists sometimes are brilliant technicians, but poor psychologists. „Why the hell do those employees accept video surveillance at the train station, but resist monitoring tools at the workplace?" is a common but stupid question. Being monitored while walking through the city may be annoying and worth fighting against, but the victims do not suffer so much from this type of surveillance because they have voluntarily entered the public. The cameras introduce a disturbing new capability of profiling someone's moves in the public, but they operate in areas where nobody expects to be left alone completely.

In the office, at least most Europeans still expect a certain amount of privacy to feel well. This fact was first observed when in the sixties the open-plan offices came up. Soon after having built the first of this kind of offices and having forced the employees to work in them, the number of notifications of illness to the employers began to grow, and health problems probably caused by psychological reasons began to show up [Ropo96, p. 47]. For a certain time the companies tried to ignore this, but then architects began to modify the offices and they found solutions to provide more privacy again. Today, these lessons seem to be forgotten, as some companies follow a new trend to provide employees with movable working desks. Sources tell that many employees have already started to undermine this concept by working out strategies to conquer the same desk at the same place every day.

Monitoring employees by logging their PC-related activities, their email and their network communication is even more invasive because in this case, employers spy on work in progress.

2.1.1 Monitoring Work in Progress

PCs and network terminals today provide an employee with tools which make creative work much easier than in the past. If a specialist of any kind starts working on a project, the computer will be used to store the first notes and thoughts. First contacts will be made by email and first information sources will be searched for in the internet.

Especially if a project requires new strategies or if an employee works on a project for the first time, at the beginning not every step he or she takes will lead to the right direction. Some actions perhaps will look stupid, some efforts to seek for help may look naïve or unprofessional.

Monitoring his kind of work in progress is simply unfair. The feeling of being spied on when struggling to find a path across unexplored terrain is annoying, even if the employees have given their consent to surveillance. If an employee knows that he or she is being monitored when doing work which is not pure routine, he or she will either suffer, try to get away from this situation or limit all efforts to steps which seem to be approved. Creativity and entrepreneurial spirit soon are chained up.

Using only well-known methods or the favourite methods of their superiors, employees will not be able to find new ways to do business. The learning organisation will learn nothing new. Employees should have the right to choose if their work is ready to be presented to others or not, at least to a certain extend.

2.1.2 Deviation as a Chance

The risk of losing creativity is increased by the fact that more and more monitoring systems are based on anomaly detection [Noga01, p. 161]. It is striking that this technical development appears at a time when psychologists already register in society a growing mistrust of deviation of any kind. Children are treated with medicine if they appear to be more vivacious than the average or when they are shy, people call the police or the landlord if neighbours behave oddly and foreigners are more often watched with suspicion again. Couples try to design their children before they are born, and from the United States first efforts are reported to clone the favourite pet of a family to avoid the effort of having to get used to another one after the old one has died. The general change of the western world to societies of fear seems to be mirrored by the business world and has already found its way into methods to handle security threats technically.

From the employees' point of view, the best way to avoid drawing the attention of an anomaly detector simply is always to choose the average way to do their job. It is a common misjudgement that this could only influence the work of high-level managers who decide on business strategies. On the contrary, it also affects for example sales persons or support engineers.

Under constant surveillance, a sales person who knows a way to get in touch with a new customer by chatting with him about golf, tennis or football will perhaps avoid this because this kind of communication could alarm a content scanner which is trained to detect forbidden personal use of email. A support engineer who knows an unbureaucratic shortcut to help a customer at once may avoid taking the necessary steps if he or she fears to be questioned on that approach.

A general mistrust of deviation and anomaly will sooner or later lead to bureaucratic businesses anxiously keeping away from any risks and any chances. The value of conformity differs in different environments. In a nuclear power plant, a creative way of using the dashboard might be extremely dangerous. In an average company, the same experimental spirit may be crucial to keep the business alive. Biologists know that plantations, on which only one type of plant is grown, are more likely to be wiped away by a single pest than those on which different fruits are cultivated.

2.1.3 If they don't trust me, I won't help

Constant surveillance may pose a new security risk to companies which so far has been seldom discussed. It is well known that security mechanisms sold and implemented today still have poor abilities to react properly to new threats. Anomaly detection produces lots of false positives and automatic countermeasures too often miss the targets they should hit. For the same reason why NASA still sends astronauts into space, companies should try to involve all their employees in the struggle to control security risks. Computers are simply too stupid.

But if these employees feel that the security systems of a company spy on themselves, they will be reluctant to support the security measures of their employers. „If they do not trust me, why should I help? Let them do that stuff alone!" The philosopher Moses Mendelssohn once stated that every kind of despotism provokes opposition or resistance [Bats89, p. 9]. Surveillance can easily be understood as a kind of despotism. But if employees understand security measures as signs of mistrust, they will probably do not care about security. This is risky, because if this is the case, a company is left alone by its strongest allies.

2.1.4 Employees under Pressure

The new trend to increase workplace surveillance happens to meet a weak economy which puts more pressure onto most employees. The growing risk of dismissal meets decreasing social security and increasing costs of insurance and health. The number of employees in Germany who suffer from depression increases significantly [Reic04]. Workforces have been hearing quite a lot about being too expensive and not flexible enough. This demoralising situation fortifies the paralysing side effects of employee monitoring even more, and it produces exactly the kind of disgruntled employees the businesses are afraid of.

Providing a good working atmosphere is one of the strongest preventative IT security measures that can be taken, but the art of providing it is unfortunately not taught to managers and technicians at universities. American CSOs, who are required to be skilled technicians and psychologists at the same time, for example know that constantly confirming employees in good behaviour is more effective than punishing misbehaviour. But this knowledge seldom finds its way into security concepts because making use of it requires a real preventative approach and engaging someone to work on it. Buying another appliance seems to be easier.

2.2 Philosophical Background

Philosophy is seldom used to work on IT security problems, but it is worth a try. Some ideas of great philosophers are amazingly practical.

2.2.1 Lessons from Dialogic Philosophy

Many scientists who try to apply ethics to technical environments first have a look at the works of Immanuel Kant. The thoughts of a philosopher of the enlightenment period with an appreciated knowledge of law seem to be easily applicable to technical or economic problems. Unfortunately, Kant's key statement from the „Fundamental Principles of the Metaphysic of Morals" („I am never to act otherwise than so that I could also will that my maxim should become a universal law", translated into English by Thomas Kingsmill Abbott) only provides a general guideline. Employers and employees are communicating actors in a certain hierarchy, and therefore additional thoughts from other philosophical disciplines must be taken into consideration.

Dialogic philosophy is one of the disciplines often quoted. An opinion peace written by Luca D. Introna, published in „Surveillance & Society", for example uses the work of Emmanuel Levinas to argue that workplace surveillance is unethical and unfair [Intr03, p. 210]. The article starts with the statement that from Levinas' point of view „the force of ethics lies in the irreducibility of the Other facing me" [Intr03, p. 210]. This means: I can only act ethically, if I do not reduce a person I communicate with to fit into a category. To act ethically, I must understand that my behaviour has an influence on others and vice versa. No system of common rules or justifications ever reduces the responsibility for what we do to others. Implicit in these thoughts is that all individuals share the same human dignity which is especially violated by not giving them the possibility to speak face-to-face to any kind of persecutor in any kind of conflict.

Workplace surveillance presses individuals into categories. First someone decides who is subject to monitoring and who is not. Secondly, for each category and its members appropriate behaviour has to be defined.

Furthermore, systems like key loggers, content scanners and surveillance cameras are one-way mechanisms which do not allow the subjects monitored to explain why they are doing this or that. „Surveillance in its operation renders the Other faceless and speechless" [Int03, p. 212]. The individual is devaluated to an object which must be cared for because it is not capable of deciding what is good or bad in certain circumstances. From these aspects Introna concludes that using surveillance mechanisms is unfair. It seems as if they cannot be used ethically.

The meaning of this is easier to understand when comparing network-based workplace surveillance to a variety of surveillance which is widely accepted. The two pilots of a passenger flight are constantly monitoring each other. The superiority of the captain is relative. Both pilots face each other and they always can explain to each other every step they take and the condition they are in.

The topic of devaluation caused by categorisation is often discussed controversially. It seems to be so common to look which categories someone fits in that the effects resulting from this practice seem to be negligible. But most individuals spend most of their lives in their jobs and use all their creativity and knowledge to make the best of it. What happens to them at the workplace is crucial to their self-confidence and has a strong influence on their lives. Furthermore, no one likes to be categorised only by what he or she is able to show in the office or cubicle when working at a certain project which has been laid upon him or her by someone else. Everyone wishes that others could see his or her potentials, even the hidden ones. Referring to the judgements we make of each others' characters, Simone Weil once found the words „Every being cries out to be read differently" to describe this situation [Weil65, p. 10]. Workplace surveillance strongly hits the hearts and the self-confidence of every person who is monitored.

In his book „Ethik und Technikbewertung" (Ethics and Technology Assessment) Günter Ropohl, a specialist in technology assessment, lists six rules based on human rights which in his opinion may be helpful to ensure the ethical use of technology in society. The fourth of these rules states that no person should be inhibited in his self-determination of his personal lifestyle and that no person should be limited in his well understood choices of personal development. The fifth rule says that no one's trust in other people should be shaken [Ropo96, p. 321]. Interestingly, both rules would be broken by modern employee surveillance systems which did not exist when Ropohl wrote down his ideas. Frederick S. Lane shows that today especially the right of employees to separate their private lives from their business lives is in danger: „We are steadily approaching the time when nothing is irrelevant to an employer's protection of its business interests" [Lane03, p. 232].

Note: It would be an interesting exercise to discuss how Martin Buber's concept of the „I" and the „Thou" and his works on human interrelation and dialogue [Bube84] can be used to understand modern ideas of the „I", „Me", „Implicit Me" and „Explicit Me" that are presented in surveys on modern identity management [ICSN03, p. 6]. A first look reveals that user-controlled identity management at least hands over control of their virtual identity to the individuals taking part in net-based communications. The interesting fact is that in e-business staying faceless by relying on anonymous communication sometimes is the only way to secure communicational self-determination, because the „You" someone is connected to from time to time turns out to be a faceless profiling mechanism.

2.2.2 Philosophy of Trust

For many managers, trust is no more than a nice idea from the times of romanticism. Interestingly enough, one of the best known in-depth analysis of the trust phenomenon describes it as some kind of economic idea. For Niklas Luhmann, trust reduces the need for doing things alone. It also reduces costs by making it unnecessary to constantly monitor those who take over a part of some work. On the whole, trust is a mechanism which reduces the complexity of social systems [Luhm89]. By scientists, trust today is discussed as an economic principle of organisation [Ripp98], and popular management guidebooks present it as the most effective principle to manage the workforce of an organisation [Spre02].

At first glance, technical workplace surveillance seems to be inexpensive. But as soon as the unwanted side effects are taken into consideration, surveillance may cause real losses. The employees' resistance to monitoring not only affects security, it also decreases the work-intensifying potential of surveillance. The absence of empirical studies on this issue makes it difficult to calculate the effects in detail, but in many cases the investment in monitoring tools perhaps turns out to be less remunerative than estimated. Relying on trust may be less expensive.

It is interesting that John Arnold, who strongly recommends surveillance-based security, tries to save the advantages of trust when explaining his concepts. From his point of view, only a person under surveillance can easily be trusted because he or she cannot do the wrong things. He argues that every employee under surveillance feels „more trusted/empowered" and therefore will „likely behave better" [Arno04, p. 88]. Too bad, trust does not work that way. Trust implies accepting the risk that it might be misused. Whenever a company implements monitoring systems and does not take some precautions which will be discussed in the last section of this article, it will lose the benefits of acting as a trust-based community.

One of these advantages was discovered when research on the „learning organisation" stepped forward. Individuals who trust each other are more likely to share information and knowledge than those who think that they must always safeguard their own assets. Because of that, monitoring as an evident sign of mistrust can easily undermine information sharing. Another aspect to think about is what happens if the public learns about a case of an employee punished without reason caused by a false positive alarm of a monitoring system. Trust in the communication systems of this company would come to an end. Customers would perhaps try to avoid stepping into the same trap and therefore stop using the web services of the company.

3 Conclusions

Under the growing pressure to implement risk management procedures, it is difficult for companies to decide which of the risks they are facing are worth to be taken. There is a strong enticement to reduce the uncertainty employees introduce to a company, and the promise of the vendors of employee monitoring solutions to solve the problem technically using digitised patterns of approved behaviour sounds intriguing. It seems to be a good idea to implement employee monitoring as a part of security systems and to pull down the walls which separate it from security monitoring.

Nevertheless, the side effects of monitoring have to be calculated when a company steps into risk assessment. Surveillance without doubt limits creativity and trustful communication to an extend that may have a measurable bad influence on a business. It is a risk.

This is the reason why Big Brother does not keep your assets safe. He paralyses the potential of a company by turning the business into a prison and employees into inmates.

The first strategy to avoid this risk is to give preventative security measures priority. It is not true anymore that they are always too expensive and too hard to manage. Implementing strong authentication and authorisation also will be honoured by customers, insurers and investors. Furthermore, in contrast to employee surveillance, talking about preventative measures can be part of a public relation strategy.

Where monitoring has to be implemented because of no alternative, it can be modified to comply with human rights. Encrypting log files and allowing to access them only when there is reason for suspicion is the most important measure. Bruce Schneier therefore suggests introducing warrants into IT security techniques [Schn04]. Access to sensible log files should only be granted if a trusted intermediary elected by the workforce is present. This kind of solution is often implemented into content scanning products.

The most effective way of reducing unwanted side effects of employee monitoring is to hand over controls to the users themselves and to change the monitoring tools into personal policy compliance tools used by the employees [Wiel01]. If this technique is combined with methods to prevent actions which appear to be really risky, security can be effective and humane at the same time. To be able to use these methods, it is necessary that companies accomplish an in-depth risk assessment which helps them to distinguish low-risk action from high-risk action. It is also important that the security systems are able to reflect individual ranking orders of risks.

If, for example, an employee tries to access a web side which seems not appropriate or if some content he or she tries to send by email looks like confidential information, the actor should be warned first without logging the incident. In most cases, it will turn out that the incident was caused by mistake. In this case, the warning itself is a sufficient measure to stop the risky action.

If the security system detects an action which is labelled as a high-risk one, it should be able to hold it up. Again it should inform the user why he or she was prevented from doing what he or she started to do. In addition to that, all information on how to go on should be provided. If the user thinks that what he or she wants to do is legitimate, the person who is entitled to decide about it and to possibly enable it should be mentioned.

If the monitoring system is implemented this way, surveillance avoids rendering employees faceless and speechless. False positives are less damaging, and the reactive system turns into a preventative one which rises awareness. To achieve this, not only companies who use IT security are required to hold human dignity dear. It is also necessary to ban a certain type of marketing by fear which misrepresents employees as the main culprits of the IT world.

References

[Arno04]   Arnold, John: Security Monitoring – Why and How? Implementing a Real-World Monitoring System. In: Information Security Bulletin, Volume 9, Issue 3, April 2004, p. 85-94.

[Bats89]   Batscha, Zwi: »Despotismus jeder Art reizt zur Widersetzlichkeit«. Die französische Revolution in der deutschen Popularphilosophie. Suhrkamp, 1989.

[Bitk04]   Bitkom: Die Nutzung von Email und Internet im Unternehmen. Rechtliche Grundlagen und Handlungsoptionen. Bitkom 2004 (http://www.bitkom.org/de/publikationen/1357_7594.aspx)

[Bube84]   Buber, Martin: Das dialogische Prinzip. Wissenschaftliche Buchgesellschaft Darmstadt, 51984.

[ICSN03]   Independent Centre for Privacy Protection (ICPP) / Unabhängiges Landeszentrum für Datenschutz (ULD) Schleswig-Holstein and Studio Notarile Genghini (SNG): Identity Management Systems (IMS): Identification and Comparison Study 2003 (http://www.datenschutzzentrum.de/projekte/idmanage/index.htm).

[Intr03]   Introna, Lucas D: Opinion. Workplace Surveillance 'is' Unethical and Unfair. In: Surveillance & Society 1 (2) 2003, p. 210-216 (http://www.surveillance-and-society.org/).

[Lane03]   Lane, Frederick S. III: The Naked Employee: How Technology is Compromising Workplace Privacy. AMACOM American Management Association, 2003.

[Luhm89]   Luhmann, Niklas: Vertrauen. Ein Mechanismus der Reduktion sozialer Komplexität. Enke, 31989.

[Noga01]   Nogala, Detlef: Der Frosch im heißen Wasser. Wie in der informatisierten Gesellschaft des 21. Jahrhunderts Überwachung trivialisiert wird. In: Schulzki-Haddouti, Christiane: Vom Ende der Anonymität. Die Globalisierung der Überwachung, Heise, ²2001, p. 149-165.

[Reic04]   Reicherzer, Judith: Ausgebrannt und angefeindet. In: Süddeutsche Zeitung Nr. 133, June 12th/13th 2004, p. 28.

[Ripp98]   Ripperger, Tanja: Ökonomik des Vertrauens – Analyse eines Organisationsprinzips. Mohr Siebeck, 1998.

[Ropo96]   Ropohl, Günter: Ethik und Technikbewertung. Suhrkamp, 1996.

[Schn04]   Schneier, Bruce: Warrants as a Security Countermeasure. In: Cryptogram, May 15, 2004 (http://www.schneier.com/crypto-gram.html).

[Spre02]   Sprenger, Reinhard K.: Vertrauen führt. Worauf es im Unternehmen wirklich ankommt. Campus, 2002.

[StSt03]   Stanton, Jeffrey M. and Stam, Kathryn R.: Information Technology, Privacy, and Power within Organizations: a view from Boundary Theory and Social Exchange perspectives. In: Surveillance & Society 1 (2) 2003, p. 152-190 (http://www.surveillance-and-society.org/).

[Weil65]   Weil, Simone: Gravity and Grace. Routledge and Kegan Paul, 1965.

[Wiel01]   Wiele, Johannes: Content-Filter als persönliche Assistenten. In: Nadin, Mihai: trust://das.prinzip.vertrauen. Beiträge zum internationalen Kolloquium »Vertrauen. Das 21. Jahrhundert und darüber hinaus«. Synchron Publishers, 2001, p. 207-226.

I'd like to thank Betty, who made the confusing bunch of notes I wrote down understandable to others.

Technology

Identity Federation: Business Drivers, Use Cases, and Key Business Considerations

J. Matthew Gardiner

Netegrity, Inc.
201 Jones Road Waltham, MA 02451
Product Marketing Division
mgardiner@netegrity.com

Abstract

Finding ways to more efficiently and intelligently coordinate business and integrate business processes with trading partners to keep up with the ever-accelerating pace of business has long been a dilemma faced by many companies. Identity federation and the industry standards that comprise it were invented to address this cross domain, application interoperation challenge. This paper introduces and defines identity federation, the benefits that companies can reap by leveraging it, the typical use cases that can be enabled by it, the sometimes competing industry standards and specifications that underlie it, and finally the business issues that must be addressed for federated applications to be successfully delivered at scale.

1 Federation – Introduction & Business Value

Basic access to applications and data over the Internet has existed for years; however the ability for a user to easily and securely access services from multiple security domains within an enterprise or from multiple companies has remained a challenge. Finding ways to efficiently and more intelligently coordinate business with trading partners to keep up with the ever-accelerating pace of business has long been a dilemma faced by many companies. Twenty years ago many pinned their hopes on electronic data interchange (EDI), which has been used successfully in the automotive, retail, and manufacturing industries, but has generally failed to reach a broader corporate audience primarily because of its cost, inflexibility, and proprietary nature.

Today, the Internet, Internet-compliant technology, and standards have matured to the point that effective coordination and mass integration between trading partners is now achievable and affordable. Moreover, the advent of general purpose and industry specific standards are easing the extension of today's enterprises by lowering the barriers to connecting disparate business applications both within and across corporate boundaries. This enables businesses to substantially reduce costs, create new revenue opportunities, and provide greater convenience, choice, and control for its users.

By integrating applications and business processes across corporate boundaries, trading-partners, business customers, and outsourcers can automatically link processes and take part in transactions across multiple companies – eliminating the business interruption associated with traditional means of information exchange, such as phone, fax, and email. The ubiqui-

S. Paulus, N. Pohlmann, H. Reimer (Editors): Securing Electronic Business Processes, Vieweg (2004), 89-98

tous network (the Internet) and high-scale transactional applications already exist at most organizations. They can and should be further leveraged to drive cost and time out of doing business. Federation standards and the security systems that implement them were invented explicitly for this purpose.

2 Securing Federation

However, the aforementioned gains can fail to materialize if the information exchange is not conducted securely. For example, a government agency could risk damage through a leak of a citizen's private information. A financial institution might incur financial penalties and brand degradation due to an unauthorized trade or withdrawal. A health care firm might suffer damaging lawsuits with the release of personal health information to the wrong parties. With federation, as really with most IT efforts, organizations need to have security as a front-of-mind item. In the end though, a balance must be found between letting business in and keeping risk out.

In a federation scenario a key way to address these security challenges is to integrate partnering companies' security systems so that user, security, and entitlement information can be shared in a defined and controlled way between partners in a trusted business relationship. Integrating applications across independent security domains is defined broadly here as „federation". Furthermore, the sharing of digital identities to enable federation is defined as „identity federation". Federation enables users to work with autonomous internal business units, external business partners, and other third-parties seamlessly as if they were part of the same security domain, while in fact the domains remain largely independent.

Cleary, since cross-company federation is the ultimate goal, the only way to effectively accomplish this is through the development and use of open standards, since by definition multiple products will need to interoperate to deliver cross-company federations between given companies. Fortunately, many standards have and are being developed to address various aspects of identity federation (single sign-on (SSO), trust, attribute sharing, Web services security, privacy etc.). Some of these standards, when combined, provide the basis for an identity federation framework, but there are still overlaps and competition between emerging standards, making selection decisions challenging.

3 Federation Requirements

Given the intense focus on personal privacy and control of digital identities, the existing identity infrastructures that can be found in today's organizations, and the high-value of customer information that is often housed within them, it is virtually impossible to expect organizations to collaborate on creating and maintaining a universal, shared point of identity information. Requiring organizations to first merge their user's digital identities as a prerequisite to federating their applications for use by those users, is a non-starter. This is one of the basic requirements driving federation standards and why the space is termed „federation" (as in a „federal" government of individually sovereign states – as is the case in the USA) in the first place.

Companies involved in identity federations establish trusted relationships allowing their respective users to access resources operated by their business partners. To do this companies issue „security tickets" for their users that can be processed by relying business partners. Essentially, to over simplify, federation standards boil down to defining these security tickets;

what their structure is, what is in them, how they are passed, how they are administered, how they are validated, and what services they can and should enable.

4 Federation Use Cases

There are many potential federation use cases. The use cases presented in this paper are not intended to cover all the potential scenarios, but are intended to be generically illustrative of typical federation use cases to get the reader thinking about federation and how it may be leveraged by their organizations.

More specifically, identity federations can be conducted in two basic forms, browser-based or document-based. The browser-based mode of federation is focused on supporting live users that are using Web applications presented to them via standard Internet browsers. Federation in this case enables an authenticated user to move from one Web security domain to another without needing to provide credentials again. Browser-based federations essentially provide the user with SSO between two sets of applications or portals that live in two separate security domains, without requiring the synchronization of the user's digital identities in the two domains.

By contrast, document-based federations use XML documents transported between two security domains leveraging Web services. With document-based federations the activity is driven either by a live user sitting on some „client" application or by some client application in the absence of direct human involvement. Federations in document-based scenarios involve defining XML document structures, locations and definitions of credential information, and other factors.

Both modes of federation, browser-based or document-based, nonetheless hinge on the development and use of standards to simplify how two independent security domains can easily work together for the benefit of their common user.

4.1 Browser-Based Scenarios

The following use cases demonstrate different ways of using user identities to provide browser-based, end-users with SSO across multiple companies involved in a partnership.

4.1.1 Federation Based On Account Linking

In this use case, Workplace.com contracts the management of its employees' health benefits to a partner company called Health.com. To access her account, an employee of Workplace.com authenticates at the employee portal (www.workplace.com) and clicks on a link to view her health benefits at www.health.com. The employee is taken to Health.com's Web site and presented with all of her personal health benefit information without having to sign-on to Health.com's Web site.

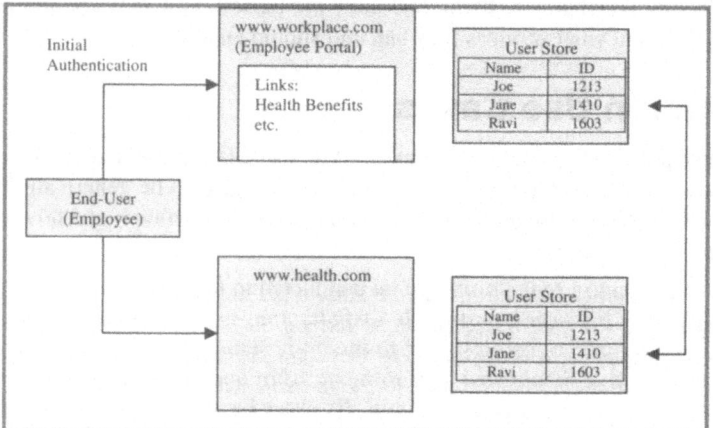

Figure 1: Federation Based On Account Linking

Health.com maintains all health-related information for the employees at Workplace.com. Health.com thus maintains user identities for every employee of Workplace.com a priori. When an employee of Workplace.com accesses Health.com as part of the federation an identifier for the employee is passed from Workplace.com to Health.com in a secure manner. This identifier allows Health.com to determine who the user is and thus what access to provide them. The security systems at Workplace.com and Health.com are linked (federated) to provide a SSO experience to their shared users.

Account-linking is the most typical browser-based use case being currently pursued by customers and prospects of Netegrity. However, the following additional use case is illustrative of another important browser-based federation scenario that is useful in some business situations.

4.1.2 Federation Based On Roles

In this use case Workplace.com buys parts from a partner company PartsSupplier.com. An engineer of Workplace.com authenticates at the employee portal (www.workplace.com) and clicks on a link to access information at PartsSupplier.com.

Because the user is an engineer (has the role of engineer) at Workplace.com, he's taken directly to the technical documentation and troubleshooting portion of PartsSupplier.com's Web site without having to sign-on.

In contrast when a purchaser for Workplace.com authenticates at Workplace.com and clicks on a link to access information at PartsSupplier.com they are taken directly to the order portion of PartsSupplier.com's Web site without having to sign-on.

In either case, PartSupplier.com's Web site can be personalized with information such as the user's name, leveraging whatever information is sent over from Workplace.com in the security token.

In this roles-based scenario PartsSupplier.com does not want to maintain user identities for all of Workplace.com's employees. However, PartsSupplier.com must control access to sensitive portions of their Web site. To do this, PartsSupplier.com maintains a limited number of profile identities (mapping to roles) for Workplace.com's users.

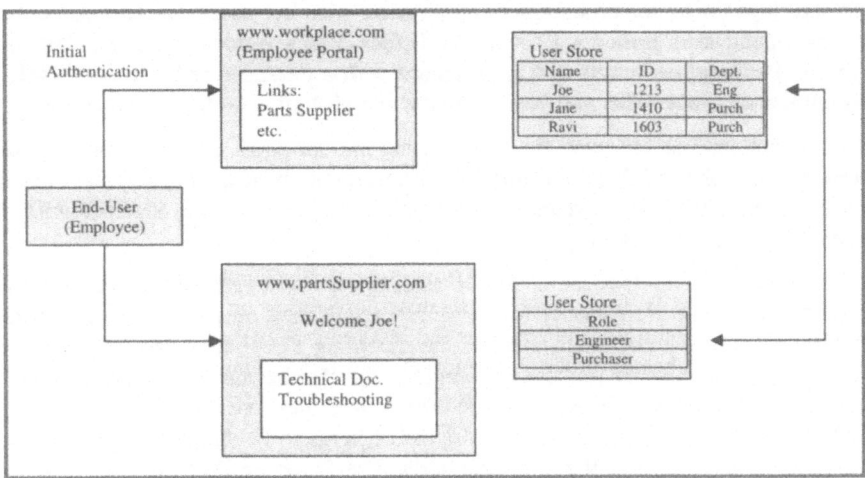

Figure 2: Federation Based On Roles

In this case, one profile identity is maintained for engineers and one profile identity is maintained for purchasers. When an employee of Workplace.com accesses PartsSupplier.com, user attributes are sent from Workplace.com to PartsSupplier.com in a secure manner, leveraging federation standards. These attributes define the role of the user and determine what profile identity is used to control access at PartsSupplier.com.

4.2   Document-Based Scenarios

Document-based federations are realized using Web services flows. As with browser-based federations there are many possible usage scenarios, I highlight one to convey the basic concepts that are involved.

4.2.1   Chained Web Services

In this use case, Workplace.com has a purchasing agreement with PinSupplies.com, and Pin-Supplies.com has a business relationship with E-Ship.com.

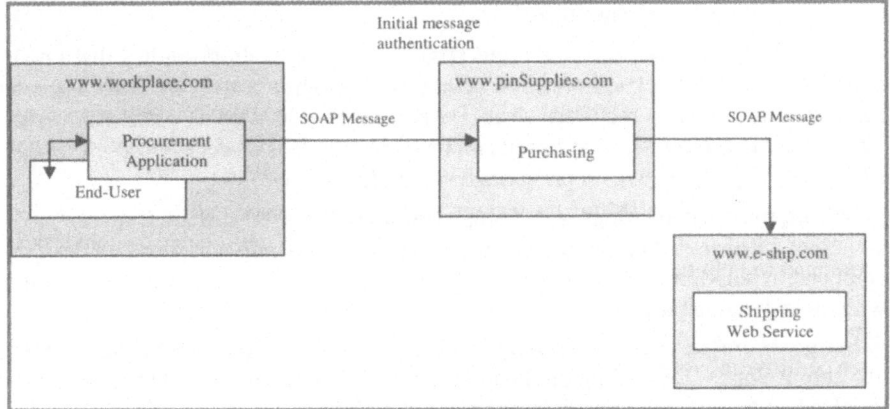

Figure 3: Chained Web Services

The end-user logs-on to her procurement application with her username and password. The procurement application provides a list of Workplace.com's various suppliers. The end-user clicks on the PinSupplies button and is presented with a purchase order in an HTML page. She fills out the purchase order and then clicks the submit button on the HTML form.

The procurement application turns the HTML form into an XML document that it inserts in the envelope body of a XML/SOAP message. The procurement application then inserts the end-user's credentials in the envelope header of the SOAP message, together with Workplace.com's organizational identity.

The procurement application posts the SOAP message to PinSupplies.com's purchasing Web service. The Purchasing Web service (or a security application on its behalf – the more scalable and manageable solution) authenticates the incoming SOAP message and processes the request. When the purchasing process is complete, the Purchasing Web service makes a request to E-Ship.com using a SOAP message. The SOAP message includes a PinSupply.com security token in the envelope header and the list of items to be shipped as well as the end-user's shipping information in the envelope body. The Shipping Web service (or a security application on its behalf) authenticates the request and processes the shipment order.

One of the keys to creating federated applications, as with any application really, is to think in terms of the users, what experience you are trying to provide them and how best to accomplish it, given your current infrastructure. When thinking about potential federated applications thinking in terms of browser-based versus document-based federations should help focus your thinking.

5 Key Federation Business Issues to Consider

While identity federation holds the promise of delivering significant benefits to users and organizations alike, the reality is that industry standards and specifications, such as SAML, Liberty Alliance, and others (discussed briefly below) can only go so far in resolving issues that are inherent when two or more organizations attempt to integrate their systems and business processes. The standards introduced below go a long way to make organizations' security infrastructures work together, but do not by themselves resolve the business issues inherent in federation. Early federation adopters will need to resolve the following issues, and probably others, in a form satisfactory to the federating partners, before they can launch their federation projects and scale them in any significant way.

- **Legal and contractual issues around trust** – Since federation implies that one-party depends on the security systems and practices of another party, any enabling contract needs to define what is required, what is expected, how liability is dealt with, what service levels are promised, what happens if and when there is a security breach, what controls does the partner have on providing user credentials, etc.

- **What happens when things go wrong, who does the user call?** – If a user can't get what they need for whatever reason, there needs to be a call-center or helpdesk that is equipped to help them and a process for managing customer issues that might originate with the federation partner.

- **What government regulations may apply? How can the partners ensure that they are complying?** – Depending on the industry, region of the world, and the personal data involved, different government regulations may apply. Which regulations apply and how to meet their requirements needs to be addressed as part of any identity federation.

- **Who pays for the federation?** – Given that by definition federated applications are shared and both sides often gain some benefit, it is not unreasonable to expect that both sides might need to pay for the federation to occur. How this gets sorted out depends highly on the existing economic relationship between the parties. It is certainly possible that one side or the other might handle all the federation costs, but this is clearly a non-technical issue that must be resolved before the specific federation can occur.

- **Privacy policy compliance.** – In most scenarios for federation to occur some amount of personal data about the user will need to be „shared" with the federation partner. Not only does this sharing need to be legal, but it also needs to comply with the privacy policies of both federating organizations.

- **Technical infrastructure/savvy of the federating parties.** – For two organizations to federate they need to integrate their security infrastructures using a standard of their mutual choosing. This assumes that both sides understand what that means and have the ability to acquire or build the required systems. Like any new technology, it is certainly recommended to start with the highest priority business partners that also have the highest level of IT and security expertise.

- **Scaling of the federation deployment** – While system scaling is certainly a technical issue, the engineers who are tasked with designing and deploying the federation infrastructure, on both sides, will need to be provided the business requirements regarding how many counter-parties will need to be supported, what the estimated transaction rate will be, and a number of other factors. The bottom line is this; the federation system that is built to support 1 federation counter-party might be dramatically different from that which would be required to simultaneously support 100 federation partners. The planned growth of the federated services will thus need to be addressed as part of the initial federation system design so that this system can scale to meet the organization's business needs.

- **Administration of the federated users** – Federation generally does not eliminate the need to administer the digital identities of the federated users on both sides of the federation. This administration requires more than a technical solution; it requires that organizations somehow create a cross-company process, perhaps enabled by identity management tools, that supports the digital identity data management. Said another way, organizations need to supply some process that supports the lifecycle of the user identity, from creation, modification, to ultimate deletion, for the federated applications of one or both parties.

- **Rights to audit federation partner** – Auditing and security systems naturally go hand-in-hand. Shouldn't one assume that this applies to federated security systems as well? However, given that one-half of the security system of the solution is housed at a business partner, getting access to their audit data (assuming they have it) is something that would have to be negotiated up-front.

The listing of the above business issues was not intended to scare the reader off from considering identity federation projects. It was provided to help set the right expectations for all participants. It is important to understand what business issues will have to be faced with identity federation in addition to the technical issues. Going into a federation project without addressing the business issues is a recipe for a disaster.

Like any new IT initiative in most organizations, effective execution of the first project is critical to making usage grow over time. Success breeds more demand, more funding, more attention, and hopefully growth of the initiative over time. The best advice I can give is to pick your best, most motivated partner first. Get all aspects of your federation, both business and technical issues, right with them and then expand to more partners as time, demand, and resources allow.

6 Federation Standards

There is no single industry standard that meets all federation requirements, whether browser-based or document-based. As mentioned in this paper, federation involves description of identities (i.e., security tokens), protocols to exchange security tokens, preservation of privacy, and methods for the establishment of trust.

This section briefly describes four standards and industry initiatives that in the opinion of the author are most immediately important to identity federation and trust initiatives:

- SAML
- Liberty Alliance
- WS-Federation
- WS-Security

6.1 Security Assertion Markup Language (SAML)

SAML is an open, application-level, framework for sharing security information on the Internet through XML documents. In January 2001, Netegrity along with other companies, created the OASIS Security Services Technical Committee (SSTC) which culminated in the adoption of SAML as an industry standard in November 2002. SAML 1.1, the current version of SAML, was approved by the OASIS Board in September 2003. SAML is probably the single most important, supported, and implemented federation standard currently in existence.

6.2 Liberty Alliance

The Liberty Alliance Project (loosely referred to as Liberty Alliance or Liberty) is an industry organization started in September 2001 that currently includes over 150 member companies worldwide, including Netegrity. The purpose of the Liberty Alliance is to create a set of specifications for identity federation.

The ID-FF module is the foundation of the Liberty architecture and is the portion of Liberty most commonly in current use. I thus focus on it further.

6.2.1 ID-FF

A basic ID-FF environment minimally includes three parts: an identity provider (e.g., a telecommunication company), a service provider (e.g., an online retailer, a financial institution, a government agency), and a user agent. The user agent is a thin client (e.g., a standard browser) or a Liberty-enabled client or proxy (LECP), e.g., a wireless (cellular) telephone handset. Use cases under ID-FF fall into the Federation Based on Account Linking use case described in the Browser-Based Scenarios section above.

With ID-FF, upon successful authentication of the principal, the identity provider produces a SAML Assertion including an authentication statement describing the principal's security context, together with a name identifier (or „handle").

6.3 WS-Federation

Web Services Federation Language (WS-Federation) is a specification jointly developed by IBM, Microsoft, BEA, Verisign, and RSA. WS-Federation will no doubt be of interest to most readers since Microsoft has announced that a WS-Federation supporting product, formerly codenamed TrustBridge, will come to market sometime in 2005 and be called Active Directory Federation Service (ADFS). The plan as of this writing is for Microsoft to include ADFS as part of the Windows Server 2003 Update, codenamed R2.

WS-Federation provides support for secure propagation of identity, attribute, authentication, and authorization information. In many ways WS-Federation is quite similar to the SAML standard. WS-Federation enables brokering of trust and security token exchange, support for privacy by hiding identity and attribute information, and federated sign-out. The practical advantage of WS-Federation is with its future release in Windows, and the massive world-wide distribution that inevitably will follow, the ability to find technically enabled federation counter-parties will be dramatically improved.

6.4 WS-Security

The Web Services Security specification (WS-Security) was originally developed by IBM, Microsoft, and Verisign. It is now hosted by the OASIS Web Services Security Technical Committee (WSS TC). WS-Security specifies SOAP security extensions providing data integrity and confidentiality and is thus useful in the context of document-based federation scenarios. WS-Security defines how to attach signature and encryption headers to SOAP messages. It also provides profiles that specify how to insert different types of binary and XML security tokens in WS-Security headers.

7 Conclusion

Enterprises are faced with an increasingly complex set of challenges as they balance the need for security and the growing requirement for seamless access to information from a large and diverse set of users. Integrating partners and their heterogeneous security systems and infrastructures to securely share and administer user information, profiles, and entitlements requires a solution that supports scalable, inter-enterprise security that stretches across many partnerships. Federation standards and the security products that implement them are focused on providing exactly these services.

Today, the Internet, Internet compliant technology, and federation standards have matured to the point that effective coordination and mass integration between trading partners is now achievable and affordable. The immediate benefits of this are available to those organizations with the vision and the focus to take advantage of the building blocks and make it happen for their organizations. The question to the reader is how are you going to let business in while keeping risk out?

Technical References

A roadmap for message delivery in Web services:
http://www-106.ibm.com/developerworks/webservices/library/ws-rmdev/

Security Assertion Markup Language (SAML):
http://www.oasis-open.org/committees/tc_home.php?wg_abbrev=security

The Liberty Alliance Project:
http://www.projectliberty.org/

Web Services Federation Language (WS-Federation):
http://www-106.ibm.com/developerworks/library/ws-fed/

Web Services Policy Assertions Language (WS-PolicyAssertions):
http://www-106.ibm.com/developerworks/library/ws-polas/

Web Services Policy Attachment (WS-PolicyAttachment):
http://www-106.ibm.com/developerworks/library/ws-polatt/

Web Services Policy Framework (WS-Policy):
http://www-106.ibm.com/developerworks/library/ws-polfram/

Web Services Secure Conversation (WS-SecureConversation):
http://www-106.ibm.com/developerworks/library/ws-secon/

Web Services Security (WS-Security):
http://www.oasis-open.org/committees/tc_home.php?wg_abbrev=wss

Web Services Security Policy (WS-SecurityPolicy):
http://www-106.ibm.com/developerworks/library/ws-secpol/

Web Services Security Trust (WS-Trust):
http://www-106.ibm.com/developerworks/library/ws-trust/

XML Encryption:
http://www.w3.org/TR/xmlenc-core/

XML Signature:
http://www.w3.org/TR/xmldsig-core/

Trusted Computing and its Applications: An Overview

Klaus Kursawe

Katholieke Universiteit Leuven,
ESAT/COSIC
Kasteelpark Arenberg 10, 3001 Leuven-Heverlee
klaus.kursawe@esat.kuleuven.ac.be

Abstract

Since two years, the term „Trusted Computing" has caused quite some controversy in the media, on the Internet, and even in the German Parliament. In spite of all that attention, surprisingly few people actually know what Trusted Computing does, what the benefits are and where the problematic issues lie.

This paper provides a high level survey explaining the concepts behind trusted computing, highlighting some of the use-cases and finally addressing some of the problematic issues.

1 Introduction

Over the last two years, several industry leaders in information technology started developing and deploying the „Trusted Computing" concept, which is supposed to provide a cheap basis for security applications and to enable a trust relationship between different computing device which is independent of the entity controlling the device.

This property has the potential for a rather large impact on the way electronic transactions may be done in the future, and so far it is not fully understood which impact this may have on the IT-Infrastructure, market behaviour and the legal framework. Unfortunately, the public and academic debate is largely distracted by early misconceptions, which inhibit a constructive approach to Trusted Computing and to understand its benefits and problems.

This paper provides a short overview on the background of Trusted Computing as well as some applications, and summarises the status of the current attempts to understand and direct the future of Trusted Computing.

2 Trusted Computing Overview

2.1 Essentials of Trusted Computing

The basic idea behind the trusted computing technology specified by the TCG is twofold. One aspect is that software means are insufficient to protect a platform from malicious software. TCG offers a last line of defence if everything else failed, i.e., it allows to protect important keys and to detect alterations of the system.

S. Paulus, N. Pohlmann, H. Reimer (Editors): Securing Electronic Business Processes, Vieweg (2004), 99-107

In this, complements other recent hardware approaches to common security problems, such as the non-execution mode in new AMD processors that allows preventing buffer overflow attacks, which are by far the most common source of security holes.

More importantly, however, is that Trusted Computing allows building a trust relationship between the different parties using one platform and between networked platforms. On a traditional system, the administrator of a system has a godlike status; in principal, there are no limits on what the administrator can do (there where some early approaches to build an administrator-less system, as well as some new additions to Linux to restrict the rights of the super-user; however, a software solution can only go so far).

With trusted computing, the administrator (the „owner") of the machine can give up some power completely. For example, cryptographic keys managed by the TCG hardware can have individual owners, and thus can be protected from anyone else, and they can be bound to the machine in a way that they can never be exported.

Beyond that, trusted computing allows the user to make provable statements about the properties of keys and the configuration of the machine. Thus, with the corresponding software support it is now possible to build a trust relationship between networked computers that may be under the control of different entities, and thus to bind transactions -- such as access to private or otherwise sensitive data -- to certain properties.

This is also the property that has lead to the greatest controversy, as it may be misused to „lock-in" a user – a user that cannot lie about his software configuration can easier be bullied into using a specific configuration.

2.2   The Trusted Computing Group (TCG)

The Trusted Computing Group (TCG) is a consortium of about 70 IT companies, including IBM, Sun, Sony, HP, AMD, Intel and Microsoft. The official mission is to

> „develop and promote open, vendor-neutral, industry standard specifications for trusted computing building blocks and software interfaces across multiple platforms,"

i.e., to specify the necessary hard-and software to implement trusted computing on various devices ranging from cellular phones up to large servers; for the time being, only specifications for PC Platforms have been finalised, but adoptions to further platforms are currently developed, and first prototypes – such as the IBM Arctic 2 PDA – are available.

The Trusted Computing Group emerged out of the Trusted Computing Platform Alliance (TCPA) in May 2003. As opposed to its predecessor, TCG membership implies duties as well as rights; for example, a significant membership fee is to be paid, and all patents on the technology (though not its applications) has to be licensed to other members at fair and non-discriminatory terms.

The TCG sees itself as a standard body only. Neither does it provide any infrastructure needed to fully utilize the technology, nor does it perform certifications of any kind.

On the one hand, this disarms critics who feared that the TCG would have to much influence on the way we will do computing in the future. On the other hand, this way the TCG has little means to influence the use of their technologies for good, which again has caused criticism.

2.2.1 Some Technical Details

The TCG specifications [TCG03] define three components that form a „Trusted Platform". The core is usually implemented as a smartcard-like chip, the „Trusted Platform Module" (TPM). Like most smartcards, this chip can perform some cryptographic operations – such as RSA signatures and encryption – and has a limited amount of non-volatile memory for internal use.

Unlike a smartcard, however, the TPM is required to be bound to the platform – it may not be possible to remove the chip from one platform and use it in another one – the focus of this technology is authentication and security of the platform rather than of the individual user.

The TPM is designed for simplicity and only provides a minimal functionality. This is on one side to reduce the cost – the goal is about one dollar per TPM – and also decreases the risk of a dangerous security monoculture and of the possibility of bugs in the chip.

To compensate for the lack of functionality of the TPM, the TCG specifies a *TCG software stack* (TSS), which fills in some of the non-critical functionality and provides standard interfaces for high level applications, such as PKCS#11 and Microsoft's Crypto API.

The final component is called *Core Root of Trust for Measurement* (CRTM), and is the first code the TCG compliant platform executes when it is booted. This component is needed as the TPM is completely passive, but needs to collect information about the boot sequence to detect modifications of the platform. In a PC, the CRTM is the first part of the BIOS, which can not be flashed or otherwise be modified. In a nutshell, the system provides five basic functions:

User management

The TCG Specification differs between an Administrator („Owner") and normal users of the TPM. The specification goes a long way to balance the rights between owner and user; for example, it is always possible for any user to deactivate the TPM, after which it cannot be remotely activated even by the owner. Also, the owner can surrender rights to the user, such as the control over a key, such that he can not take it back anymore.

Generic Security Mechanisms

As most cryptographic tokens, the TPM supports a number of generic functions that are needed internally or that provide a useful service to security aware applications. Examples provided by the TPM are a monotonous counter, a random number generator, RSA key generation, signatures and encryption, a clock, and some non volatile memory that can be associated with various access policies.

Key Management

To reduce the amount of non-volatile memory needed inside the TPM, only one key – the *Storage Root Key* (SRK) needs to be permanently stored inside the TPM. Other keys maintained by the TPM can then be encrypted under the SRK (or by any other key that is already maintained by the TPM, thus creating a hierarchical key-tree) and stored outside of the TPM, for example on a hard disk.

This allows the TPM to maintain a virtually unlimited number of keys, at the price that it gives up the control over the lifetime of keys – neither can the TPM revoke individual keys itself (outside the SRK, deleting which destroys all keys maintained by the TPM), nor can it prevent the operating system (or other software) from destroying keys maintained by the TPM.

Keys can have various properties, such as an individual owner (i.e., even the owner of the platform has no access to that key), binding to a particular platform configuration (see below) or migratable / non-migratable. A non-migratable key may not leave the TPM at all; the specification does suggest an optional mechanism to move the entire content of one TPM to another, but this mechanism is rather complex and so far not supported by any producer.

Due to cost limitations and potential export problems, the TPM is specifically not designed to support bulk encryption; encryption of large amounts of data should be made outside of the TPM by the operating system or the TSS.

Reliable Boot

One of the main properties of a TCG-Compliant platform is that the hardware monitors the Boot process and can thus be used to reliably detect what was booted, i.e., what operating system is running and whether there were any low-level modifications. Being a passive system, the TPM does not react on changes or have a notion of the „right" operating system; it can just report what it has seen, and it can lock keys to a specific boot sequence which are not available if the boot process changed.

Attestation

Attestation allows a TPM make provable statements about the results of the reliable boot or properties of the TPM-maintained Keys. To this end, it has to be able to prove that it is a genuine TPM – otherwise, its statements have no significance at all.

For this reason, the TPM contains a second RSA key, the „Endorsement key" (EK). The Endorsement key is generated when the TPM is produced and comes with a number of certificates issued by the chip manufacturer, the platform manufacturer, and potentially a third party that verified the production process.

As a lesson from the bad public reaction to the processor serial numbers introduced by Intel in 1999, the Endorsement key – which is unique to each TPM – is not used directly for transactions involving the TPM. Rather, it is used to demonstrate the genuine of the TPM to a trusted third party, which then certifies one or more pseudonyms the TPM may use in the future. However, the dependency on a third party was also seen as rather problematic [BuRe04,EuCo04]. Thus, the latest version of the specification includes a rather complex zero-knowledge proof, the „Direct Anonymous Attestation", that allows a TPM to demonstrate that it is genuine directly without revealing its identity. It is possible for the manufacturer to allow the Endorsement key to be deleted. As all certificates are bound to this key, this option disables the TPMs ability to prove it is genuine. Mostly to satisfy the security requirements for cryptographic modules as defined by the National Institute of Standards and Technology [NIST94], which require every key to be erasable.

To make attestation fully work, some PKI -like infrastructure will be required. It is not clear yet who will provide this outside of a corporate network, which implies that the utilization of this feature in generic Internet applications may need a rather long time.

2.3 Next Generation Secure Computing Base (NGSCB)

Another approach towards trusted computing that is often wrongfully mixed with the TCG specification is Microsoft's Next Generation Secure Computing Base (NGSCB).

The basic idea here is that many security problems are deeply embedded into the design of the common operating systems -- such as the lack of strong process isolation and a huge, monolithic kernel containing third party components. Those problems cannot easily be solved without rendering most of the existing software useless, either because it won't run or because of a more than significant performance loss. The idea behind NGSCB is to virtually split the computer into two parts. In one part (called „the left-hand side" by Microsoft, the insecure operating system operates as before. In the „right-hand-side", a new micro-operating system with limited capacities is build which applies all modern security techniques. The two sides are separated by extra hardware and can only communicate via dedicated channels, completely protecting the secured applications from any malicious code on the platform. Unfortunately, it is very difficult to give a precise description, as the NGSCB technology is both a fuzzy and a fast moving target. Most of the detailed information is not available to the public, and after negative reactions of application designers a major redesign of the technology has recently occurred which may implement a significantly different architecture. Although the approach is fundamentally different, NGSCB shares some property and even some hardware with the TCG technology.

The relationship between TCG and NGSCB is a bizarre hybrid between competition, dependency and orthogonal goals. The TCG hardware – or part of it – is an integral part of NGSCB, and some improvements proposed by the TCG as a result of the public debate have thus found their way into NGSCB too. In some parts, the technologies are orthogonal; TCG allows to harden the existing Operating system, while NGSCB allows to run secure applications in spite of it. Finally, there is some competition; especially for the attestation part, many problems can be solved by one technology or the other, and – at least in principle – an NGSCB like system can be implemented in software using only the TCG hardware [SaSt03].

3 Applications

The Trusted Computing technology as defined by the TCG is a rather simple and generic building block that does not do much on its own. Therefore, it is rather difficult to define „the use-case"; different participants have different applications in mind, and it cannot be assumed that a cell phone producer such as Nokia shares the same vision as a server and services company like Sun. Also, as all use-cases are also business-cases in a highly competitive market, the participants do not tend to be too eager to communicate their detailed. The TCG has published a document containing available solutions provided by its members [TCG03b]. Most of those early solutions use the TPM to secure various keys and thus do not utilize the full potential of the concept. On the academic side, the first prototypes of secure operating systems already utilize the reliable boot function [MSNW03,SaSt03]

3.1 Securing and Managing Intranet Resources

The application that is most obvious and likely to happen in the near future is the administration and protection of corporate intranets. Currently, the administrator of such a network has little reason to trust his own machines. Users may have willingly or unwillingly tampered with the system, and machines of home-workers may be accessed by third parties and used heavily for non-business purposes. As a result of this, system administrators spent a lot of their time practically fighting their own users to keep the security guidelines in place. Failure to do so may have significant consequences. In September 2001, the Swiss Post had to shut down its Internet service portal due to the Nimda Virus. While the administrators had applied up-to-date virus scanners and firewalls on all machines, one single user had installed his own operating system, thus creating a gateway through which the Virus could attack the intranet and force the system to be shut down.

The TCG-technology – if applied correctly – would allow the administrator to have much more control on who accesses the critical resources with significantly less work. A machine that cannot prove that it is still in the configuration it initially had will simply be denied access, and the administrator may be alerted and check up on the corresponding machine.

3.2 Key Management

The traditional way of maintaining keys is to either have a (password protected) key somewhere on a disk, or to issue smart tokens to each user that store the key and perform the necessary operations. The former solution is clearly to avoid, as it is relatively easy to steal the key. The latter solution is clearly superior, but due to the overhead in management of the tokens it is rarely deployed.

The key-management mechanism specified by the TCG allow it to handle the keys of all users that want to use a machine, and thus offer a solution comparable to the smart tokens, but with less management overhead. Furthermore, it is possible to restrict the transferability of the keys; an employee may use the signature key of his company in his office, but not take it home. The disadvantage of the TPM approach is that the key is bound to a machine rather than to a user. Thus, if a user is likely to work on several machines, a copy of the key has to be put into each machine.

3.3 Digital Rights Management (DRM) and Privacy

In the public debate, no discussion of Trusted Computing use-cases can afford to not mention Digital Rights Management (DRM), i.e., attaching policies to data and enforcing it even if the data is given to external, untrusted parties. While this is not a bad thing in itself – it could be used to, for example, enforce privacy guidelines and protect confidential documents – many critics fear that this feature will be used to enforce „unfair" policies on digital data, e.g., restrict the user from producing a private copy or lend a piece of music to a friend (there also seems to be a major disagreement on what a fair policy is in the first place, which does not help the debate). Many critics (mistakenly) go so far to claim that DRM was the main intention behind TCG altogether. So far, some concepts exist, such as Microsoft's document management system (which would attach policies on written documents) and Nokias Superdistribution (which would allow file-sharing on mobile devices, but ensure that the producer of the content receives some payment), but both appear to be in rather early stages.

On the other side, there is currently active research on using TCG for data protection purposes, i.e., to guarantee that private data given to a company or a government agency is treated according to some privacy policies. This too, however, currently is in an early research phase and it is not clear yet how a final solution would look like.

3.4 What's to come?

The use-cases above are the more obvious use-cases, but once the technology is sufficiently wide spread and further developed, new applications will appear. Some examples on technologies that may profit from Trusted Computing on the long run are:

The Grid

Grid Computing allows sharing resources (such as CPU cycles) with other computers, which may greatly enhance utilization. However, this implies running a program with potentially critical data on somebody else's machine. This requires some high levels of trust; an assurance is required that the other machine actually does the computation, rather than just claiming it did and sending a bill, and in many cases the data or even the program should not be revealed to the party that does the actual computation.

Mobile Devices and Ad-Hock Networks

Mobile devices are currently rapidly evolving, and location based services may create whole new market. This raises many security and privacy concerns. While the importance of mobile devices as well as the value of the data stored on them is increasing, so is the number of vulnerabilities. It already is possible to hack a number of cellular phones via the Bluetooth connection, and the first experimental cell-phone viruses have just been discovered. With the increasing openness and complexity of their operating systems as well as use of cellular phones as PDAs and gaming devices is likely to make attacks both easier and more critical in the near future.

Opening Proprietary Platforms

Many computing systems that used to be closed and proprietary – such as car-internal systems and systems for military use – are now becoming increasingly connected and base on open platforms. There are good reasons to go down that road. However, as some of those systems are literally vital, it is important to deal with the security problems implied by the openness in an early stage – a situation which is currently experienced in the area of personal computing would be absolutely unacceptable in the area of, for example, car electronics.

4 Criticism and Risks

Even though much of the initial critic on Trusted Computing was based on misunderstandings and can safely be ignored, some points remain and which deserve some further elaboration. Resolving those issues may not necessarily be the responsibility of the TCG itself; both politics (most notably the German Ministry for Economics and the Department of the Interior as well as the European Union data protection agencies) and academia (both Law and Computer Science) have now started to work with the TCG, and the first results already entered the latest version of the TCG Specification.

Privacy

The TCG has learned a lesson from the problems with Intel's processor serial numbers in 1999 and thus introduced pseudonyms to hide the TPMs identity. This turned out to be still insufficient, as the pseudonym system requires a trusted third party that still learns the TPMs identity. The TCG responded to the criticism by implementing the Direct Anonymous Attestation protocol, which allows proving the necessary properties without revealing any identity information. Discussions currently go even further to ensure even more user privacy. In the current concept, a user would prove to a service provider what operating system he booted, allowing the service provider to determine the properties of the platform. However, this gives the service provider more information than needed; by seeing the entire boot-sequence, the service provider learns details about the users platform that may contain information such as the price range of the platform. This operation could be offloaded to a trusted third party or even into the TPM itself, which also has the advantage that service providers have to be explicit about the properties they want from a platform, rather than accepting or rejecting the platform on the base of a hidden policy.

Attestation

The concept of remote attestation lies in the core of trusted computing and is one of the main factors that distinguish a TPM from today's smartcards. Being able to make provable state-

ments without the ability to lie, however, may have its drawbacks. If the user has a weak position with respect to a service provider and cannot simply choose an alternative – e.g., because
she wants to buy a particular song that is only offered by one provider – this allows the service providers to enforce arbitrary policies. Also, attestation makes it easier to discriminate
against specific operating systems or applications, thus fostering monopolistic structures
[KoNK03]. First technical proposals to allow the owner of the TPM to „lie" under controlled
circumstances exist [Scho03, KuSt03], but are unlikely to find a majority within the TCG, as
this ability may also destroy valid and intended use-cases. Basing the attestation on properties
of the system rather than on the system itself as described above may ease the problem and
make it easier for the lawmaker to enforce fairness, but a technical solution does not seem to
exist for the moment.

Infrastructure

The TCG and its members understandably do not want to create unnecessary obligations. This
implies that it is undefined by whom and how large parts of the necessary infrastructure will
be provided that is needed to use some of the functionality – such as attestation – in a large
scale. In order to take positive influence the implementation of the infrastructure, the TCG
has set up a working group to define „best practices", i.e., guidelines for providers that build
on these systems. Unfortunately, however, these best practices have no binding character, and
the TCG itself has little means to enforce them.

Manageability

As with the global infrastructure, the TCG specification leaves open a number of problems in
terms of manageability of the platform. As keys may be bound to both a physical machine and
an operating system, it may become a rather complex procedure to change one or the other.
So far, no satisfying solution exists, especially for the issue of moving all keys to a new TPM
– the (optional) mechanism requires active participation of the manufacturer – as a result of
which no manufacturer has implemented that mechanism for the time being. Most issues
could be resolved by the higher level applications, but a more complete solution on the level
of the TPM that does not require application programmers to get everything right would be a
more satisfying solution.

5 Summary

With the increasing reliance on networked computers, as well as an even more increasing risk
of attacks by various means, new security mechanisms such as TCG are clearly welcome.
With the concept of remote attestation of platform properties, it delivers a powerful tool
which can significantly reduce the effort of managing a large network, but whose impact on
electronic transactions is not fully understood yet.

Unfortunately, while the basic concepts of trusted computing date back about 10 years
[Gros90], the public discussion about its potential uses, abuses and impact did not happen until the first devices where actually sold two years ago. Furthermore, the initial debate suffered
from major misconceptions which blocked a lot of capacity on both the side of the TCG and
of the corresponding stakeholders. Only recently some constructive discussions as well as
first research projects on the topic have started, which may help utilizing the new concept
without negative side effects on privacy and free choice.

References

[BuRe04]   *Stellungnahme der Bundesregierung zu den Sicherheitsinitiativen TCG und NGSCB im Bereich Trusted Computing.* Available at http://www.bsi.de/trustcomp/stellung/StellungnahmeTCG1_2a.pdf

[EuCo04]   *Working Document on Trusted Computing Platforms and in particular on the work done by the Trusted Computing Group,* 11816/03/EN WP86, European Commission, January 2004. Available at http://europa.eu.int/comm/internal_market/ privacy/docs/wpdocs/2004/wp86_en.pdf

[Gros90]   Michael Groß. *Vertrauenswürdiges Booten als Grundlage authentischer Basissysteme.* Internes Arbeitspapier, GMD, June 1990.

[KoNK03]   König, Neumann and Katzschmann. *Trusted Computing.* Verlag Recht und Wirtschaft, Heidelberg, Dezember 2003.

[KuSt03]   Kursawe and Stüble: *Improving End-User security and Trustworthiness of TCG-Platforms.* GI Jahrestagung 2003, Frankfurt, Oktober 2003.

[MSNW03]   MacDonald, Smith, Marchesini and Wild. *Bear: An Open-Source Virtual Secure Coprocessor based on TCPA.* Technical Report TR2003-471, Department of Computer Science, Dartmouth College, August 2003.

[NIST94]   Security Requirements for Cryptographic Modules, Federal Information Processing Standards Publication (FIPS) 140-2, January 1994. Available at http://csrc.nist.gov/cryptval/140-2.htm

[Scho03]   Schoen. *Trusted Computing: Promise and Risk.* Oktober 2003. Available at http://www.eff.org/Infra/trusted_computing/20031001_tc.php

[SaSt03]   Sadeghi and Stüble: Taming „Trusted Computing" by Operating System Design; Proceedings of the 4th International Workshop on Information Security Applications (WISA'03), LNCS 2908, Springer Verlag, Berlin, pp. 286-302, August 2003.

[TCG 03]   Trusted Computing Group. *TCG Main Specification.* May 2003. Available at http://www.trustedcomputinggroup.org

[TCG03b]   Trusted Computing Group. *Trusted Computing: A Solutions Guide for Personal Computers.* 2003. Available at http://www.trustedcomputinggroup.org

RFID Privacy: Challenges and Progress

Burt Kaliski

RSA Security
bkaliski@rsasecurity.com

Abstract

Recent proposals for widespread deployment of Radio Frequency Identification (RFID) systems have raised significant concerns about consumer privacy. With current low-cost tag technology, these concerns are somewhat unavoidable, as the tags aren't designed to differentiate between authorized readers and unauthorized ones, and likewise the readers can't directly distinguish between tags they're allowed to identify and those they aren't. Moreover, the privacy risks for consumers translate directly into the potential for industrial espionage in supply-chain implementations, undermining the competitive advantages that businesses aim to realize by deploying RFID systems in the first place. This article outlines some of the recent research results in RFID privacy that attempt to address these concerns without significantly impacting the cost of the tags.

1 Introduction

Radio-Frequency Identification (RFID) technology, already more than 30 years old, has received considerable attention in the last few years because of the convergence of two effects: the ability to manufacture ever cheaper tags, and the ability to manage ever expanding information about them. As these trends continue, RFID systems will likely be widely deployed in a variety of applications, just as Internet and wireless technology are at present.

As a basic model, an RFID system consists of the following components:

- *Tags*: individual devices containing an antenna and a chip that embeds a unique *tag identifier*
- *Readers:* appliances also containing an antenna and a more powerful chip, which interact with nearby tags over a defined radio protocol, and report *tag events*, i.e., data about which tags have been seen
- *Applications:* Software that controls readers and processes tag events and other information about tags
- *Tag databases:* Information stores that manage the volumes of information about tags

Generally, a tag only stores an identifier; other information about the tag (where it was manufactured, where it was last read, etc.) is kept in the databases. However, some tags may also provide information about their environment, for instance their temperature; these are more like sensors.

In the low-cost versions, the tag has no battery, and instead relies on the reader for power. This significantly limits the capabilities of the tag. Since these are the type of tags that will be most widely deployed initially, they are the focus of this article. The general principles will apply to some extent to more powerful versions as well.

S. Paulus, N. Pohlmann, H. Reimer (Editors): Securing Electronic Business Processes, Vieweg (2004), 108-116

The ability to read a tag easily at it moves or is at rest (modulo various practical limitations about radio transmission — such as metal and water), has tremendous implications for industry. A warehouse or a store can now maintain an accurate real-time inventory; an operator can learn the contents of a container without opening it; a pharmacy can verify that received medication is authentic; a store can quickly process returned goods. However, the very same convenience of tracking individual items, in the wrong hands, translates into less desirable consequences. For instance, a thief can find out who is carrying a valuable product, or a corporate spy can track a competitor's shipments.

With initial RFID systems involving RFID tags, the threats are a somewhat unavoidable side-effect of enabling the desired applications. But RFID technology in general is still maturing, and research on privacy-enhancing technologies has yielded some preliminary results that help to mitigate the risks. The privacy challenges as well as the some of the recent research progress are outlined further in this article.

2 Tag privacy

As an ideal, one may define tag privacy as follows:

> **Tag Privacy:** Only authorized applications should be able to identify tags.

Identify means „associate with other information": for instance, determine the actual identity of the object (or user) with which the tag is associated, and/or link to previous events involving the tag. A reader may be able to scan a tag, but the result should not be meaningful to the application employing the reader unless the application is authorized.

(Without sophisticated spread-spectrum communications, it seems difficult to prevent a reader from detecting the presence of an RFID tag and obtaining some response from the tag, hence the focus on whether the reader can understand what it has seen.)

Authorized means „having permission according to some security policy." That policy will depend on the application and on local regulations. One example of a policy relates to consumer privacy: A store can identify the tags on its unpurchased items, but not on purchased ones, except with user consent. Another example relates to industrial espionage: A company can identify the tags on its own items, but not on those belonging to another company.

The tag privacy goal is an ideal; it is not necessarily a requirement of every application, and there are sure to be cost/benefit tradeoffs in achieving it. As an example of the tradeoff, it is relatively easy to prevent an application from determining the actual identity of the object with which the tag is associated, simply by employing a random (but static) tag identifier. However, this will not protect against linkage to previous events, since the identifier is the same each time it is read.

Tag privacy occurs at one level as a consumer concern, in anticipation of future uses of RFID technology on retail products worn or otherwise borne by consumers. (In fact, there are already substantial uses of RFID technology in consumers' hands — proximity cards for building access, payment cards, and electronic toll-payment devices being three current examples.) At another level, however, tag privacy is also a business concern. Unauthorized scanning on tags in a supply chain is a kind of industrial espionage. Unscrupulous organizations may well be tempted to spy on one another's RFID-tagged shipments in the future, just as unscrupulous retailers may be tempted to spy on their customers. The broad definition of tag privacy given above encompasses both concerns.

3 Privacy challenges

RFID privacy is a challenge today primarily because low-cost RFID tags have very little security. A typical low-cost RFID tag will respond to any reader that requests its identity, and the identity will be the same every time the tag is scanned. Moreover, the tag identity may include information about the object with which the tag is associated for the convenience of the application. Even if the tag identifier is a random value, however, tag privacy is only partially achieved if the identifier is static.

The privacy challenge is fundamentally a result of two complementary limitations of current technology.

First, tags aren't designed to differentiate between authorized readers and unauthorized ones. A given tag responds the same way to every reader (assuming the reader runs the appropriate frequency and communications protocol, of course). This is very useful for the widespread deployment of RFID technology, but challenging for privacy. But unless a tag can decide whether to respond to a reader based on some property of the reader, privacy protection will have to rest elsewhere in the system.

Second, readers can't directly distinguish between tags they're allowed to identify and those they aren't. Every tag responds the same way to a given reader (again assuming compatible frequency and protocol). This makes it difficult for a reader itself to follow a privacy policy such as in the example above, where it can identify tags on unpurchased items, but not on purchased ones; the tag doesn't say which kind it is. Unless a reader can decide whether to identify a tag based on some property, privacy protection again will have to rest elsewhere.

4 Conventional solutions

Many protocols have been developed to address security concerns in more conventional systems, e.g., Web-based applications. They have some applicability in RFID privacy, but also limitations.

4.1 Public-key protocols

One way to address the privacy problem is with a public-key protocol, like TLS [DiAl99]. The tag establishes a secure session with the reader using the reader's public key, where the reader is authenticated to the tag (but not necessarily vice versa). The tag maintains a list of trusted readers; as long as the reader is on that list, the tag can safely reveal its identity to the reader.

Just as in Web-based applications, it may not be so easy to manage the trust list. Preferably, each reader should have a different public key / private key pair, to reduce the impact should one reader's security be compromised. This means that the tag would need to store a large list of trusted readers, or else follow a certificate hierarchy. This is known to be one of the more complex parts of today's conventional public-key infrastructure.

Furthermore, the trust list may change over time as the tag moves through the supply chain. For instance, initially, the tag manufacturer should be able to identity the tag, but perhaps later only the consumer packaged goods manufacturer that employs the tag should be able to do so, and then later only a distributor or a retailer.

On a low-cost tag, the storage, management, and cryptography in a public-key protocol is likely to be too expensive in any case. For higher-cost tags such as proximity and payment cards, the cost may be more acceptable, and in these cases the trust list is likely to be less variable as well.

4.2 Symmetric-key protocols

Another way one might try to address the problem is with a symmetric-key protocol, where the tag establishes a secure session with the reader using a shared symmetric key. This shared key itself effectively expresses the trust relationship — as long as the reader demonstrates its knowledge of the key, the tag can safely reveal its identity to the reader.

But there is somewhat of a „chicken-and-egg" („Huhn oder Ei") problem: If the reader interacts with many tags, how does the reader know which shared key to employ when communicating with a particular tag? The reader cannot ask the tag for its identifier until the reader has demonstrated knowledge of the shared key; but the tag can't reveal its identity until the reader has authenticated itself to the tag.

This problem is related to the following *reactivation dilemma*. A common solution to consumer privacy concerns is to deactivate or „kill" a tag at the point of sale. But if the product with which the tag is associated is something that will later be returned — for instance, a library book, or a video rental — then the tag will need to be „reactivated" at a later time.

The deactivation operation is protected by a „kill code" shared between the tag and the reader to prevent unauthorized deactivation of tags (see [WeSE02] below). The reactivation operation should likewise be protected by some „resurrect code". But how does the reader know which code to provide? When deactivating the tag, the reader can first identify the tag and then lookup the corresponding kill code. But when reactivating, the tag identity is by definition unavailable.

5 Research progress

Research in security and privacy for low-cost RFID tags has been of growing interest over the past two years as the widespread tag deployment has begun, and as the cryptographic community has begun to focus on the security concerns as well as the tag limitations. The article by Weis, Sarma and Engels at CHES 2002 [WeSE02] outlines many of these issues; see also [WeSE03][WSRE03]. Here, some of the recent research results are summarized.

5.1 Privacy bit

As noted above, one of the two fundamental limitations of low-cost RFID tags with respect to privacy is that a tag does not indicate to a reader whether it is allowed to be identified by the reader; all tags appear the same in this regard. One simple way to improve on the situation is for tags to have a *privacy bit*. The bit would indicate whether the tag is „private" or „public" — for instance, whether it is on a purchased item or an unpurchased item, and therefore whether it can be identified or not, assuming a particular privacy policy.

When the tag is first manufactured or programmed, the privacy bit would be cleared, indicating that the tag is public. The tag would be marked as private at the point of sale, where the command to set the privacy bit is protected by a „privacy code". This is analogous to the „kill code" for deactivating a tag at the point of sale. Thus, the privacy bit relies on the same infrastructure for access code management as is already required for deactivation; no significant new management functionality is needed.

In order for the privacy bit to have its full effect, the reader's interactions should be verifiably different depending on whether it is interacting with a private tag or a public one. One approach to varying the interactions is described in [JuRS03], where the privacy bit is the first bit of the tag identifier, and where tags are individually addressed through a tree-walking protocol that partitions the search space for tags according to successive bits of the tag identifier. Since the privacy bit is the first bit searched, a reader's preference for private or public tags is expressed in terms of the half of the tree it searches. A reader can explicitly avoid private tags by not searching the private half of the tree.

Another approach is to have different commands for interacting with private and public tags. This has the advantage that it does not assume a tree-walking protocol, though it could be used with one.

The privacy bit alone does not prevent an unauthorized reader from identifying a tag, of course. Any reader can read private tags. But the privacy bit does make such identification detectable: an auditor can determine whether the readers in a store, for instance, are straying into tag regions they shouldn't be. By extension, the privacy bit makes the store's honesty verifiable: Because a store can be audited, it can be certified as respecting privacy policy, thereby increasing consumer confidence. Dishonest stores still might find a way to pass inspection, but surprise audits will make this more difficult.

Without the privacy bit, a dishonest store would look the same as an honest one in terms of reader interactions: both would read all tags they encounter. The honest store just wouldn't use the ones it's not allowed to see, but this is harder to audit and therefore harder to convey to consumers.

The privacy bit is just a binary starting point to tag privacy. More sophisticated policies can be supported with more specific privacy fields in tags, and additional protection is also available through the methods described next.

5.2 Blocker tag

The fact that a reader's attempts to interact with private tags can be detected and distinguished from attempts to address public tags has an important side-effect: It becomes possible for interactions with the private tags to be *blocked*, without interfering with the reader's public operations. Reader/tag interactions can be blocked universally, of course, by jamming the reader with sufficient noise at the reader's transmission frequency. But such universal jamming is akin to mounting a denial-of-service attack on a Web site that is suspected to be compromising privacy; it eliminates the bad as well as the good.

Selective blocking is much more desirable. If one is concerned that a reader may stray into private tag territory, such blocking can be a useful countermeasure. This is particularly so when one is concerned about suspected readers outside a store environment, which unlike the store readers may not be subject to auditing. While the near-term threat of illicit tracking by such readers is uncertain, it is important to have tools available in the long term in case this kind of tracking becomes common.

Briefly, the *blocker tag*, described in [JuRS03], interferes with a reader's attempt to identify private tags by simulating the presence of *every* possible private tag. The blocker tag, which would involve only slightly more circuitry than an ordinary RFID tag, does this by a special non-compliant response to the standard tree-walking protocol. The reader will perceive that every private tag is present, which effectively prevents the reader from operating and hides the actual private tags. If the reader only searches for public tags, however, the blocker tag remains silent — so ordinary operations are unaffected.

The blocker tag's peculiar behavior — namely the simulation of so many tag identifiers, all at the same physical location — makes the blocker tag itself easy to detect. It may also make it possible for a sufficiently careful reader to overcome the blocker tag. This remains an interesting area for research, as well as a potential motivation for further improvements in the blocker-tag concept.

5.3 Pseudonym tag

The privacy bit and the blocker tag are primarily oriented toward consumer privacy since they assume there is a point of sale at which the tag can be marked „private" and also that some user intervention is involved, e.g., to activate the blocker tag, or to consent to the reader identifying the tag. Industrial espionage calls for somewhat different countermeasures that are more suitable to supply-chain operations.

A first step to defend against industrial espionage is to employ random identifiers while products are in the supply chain; this will prevent an attacker with an illicit reader from directly determining information about the tag from the tag identifier itself. However, linkage of tag events remains a concern. For instance, an attacker who plants readers at several companies' warehouses may be able to discern shipping-flow patterns by correlating the tag identifiers observed in the different locations. (This could be of special concern in defense applications.)

A second step is to vary the identifier. If done effectively, this will address the concern about tag event linkage. Clearly, the legitimate participants in the supply chain for a particular tag need to be able to link the different identifiers provided by a given tag. This is relatively straightforward, given that the participants would typically be sharing data with each other about the items they are shipping and receiving. The multiple identifiers for a given tag could be part of that data. The key to effective implementation is to ensure that the identifier changes regularly and that successive identifiers for a given tag are not obviously related to one another.

One method for achieving these goals is an approach developed by Juels called *minimalist cryptography* [Juel03]. „Minimalist" refers to the fact that the tags involve no cryptographic operations — only memory reads and writes, counter updates, and comparisons. This is important to maintain the desired low tag cost, at least with tag technology over the next few years. (It is not clear, however, that reliably writeable memory is altogether less expensive than implementing a cryptographic algorithm.)

A tag following the minimalist approach may be called a *pseudonym tag* due to the varying identifier. A pseudonym tag has a small set of identifiers. In one version of the tag, each reader requests a different one of these identifiers. This protects against passive eavesdropping, since an attacker who listens to the legitimate readers in the supply chain (if that were possible) will observe different identifiers in different places. However, this version does not protect against an active, illicit reader, which could itself always request the same identifier.

In another version, the tag rotates through a set of identifiers, so that a different one is returned each time. Identifier rotation can be combined with simple reader authentication and a „throttling" mechanism to prevent an illicit reader from obtaining more than one tag identifier at a time. For instance, the tag could require that the reader present a „confirmation code" after the tag provides an identifier to the reader, where the confirmation code is preprogrammed and specific to that identifier. If the confirmation code is not received, the tag would shut down for some period of time. The identifier provided by the tag at the next point in the supply chain would therefore be less likely to have been seen beforehand by an illicit reader.

Several other versions are also available including one where the pseudonyms on the tag are updated periodically by the reader to provide proactive security against any potential previous compromises.

Interestingly, pseudonyms seem to be a reasonably effective way to address the reactivation dilemma mentioned above. Deactivation could conceivably be replaced by the step of changing the tag's identifier to a pseudonym, and reactivation achieved by the reverse step of changing back to the original one. While this would not prevent all event linkages, it would break the association between the tag's identifier before and after the point of sale. This would at least partially mitigate concerns such as illicit tracking of library books and video rentals outside a store environment, since an attacker would not be able to correlate tags previously read in the store with those found in a consumer's possession.

5.4 Policy (soft blocker) tag

The blocker tag addresses privacy concerns by interfering with the tag-to-reader protocol, while the pseudonym tag changes the protocol. A *policy tag*, referred to as *soft blocking* in [JuBr03], achieves some improvement without altering the protocol interactions by giving information to the reader about the user's preferences. Like user preferences in the Platform for Privacy Preferences specification [W3C02], a policy tag is a convenient way for a user to express preferences to an honest reader — for instance, to indicate that the user consents to having the reader identify a private tag. While not preventing illicit tracking by dishonest readers, the policy tag can still improve the consumer's experience in a store, much as P3P does (in principle) for user interactions on the Web.

5.5 Physical countermeasures

Privacy concerns can be reduced considerably if the read-range of a tag is sufficiently small, such that a consumer would easily notice when a reader is within range. Fishkin and Roy [FiRo03] propose an interesting and more flexible variant on this concept whereby the tag (or perhaps a set of tags working together), by analyzing the radio signal from the reader, estimates the distance of the reader and thereby its trustworthiness. A tag could identify itself automatically to nearby readers (assuming that the consumer would not have approached so close to a reader without intending to have the tag identified). In contrast, a tag might only identify itself to a distant reader with the user's consent.

6 Other security issues

Privacy has been the most widely discussed of the security issues surrounding RFID systems, likely because it is personally perceived as an issue by many users. RFID privacy as defined in this article also encompasses industrial espionage, so it is a fairly comprehensive topic. A number of other security issues also need to be addressed in RFID systems. Although outside the principle focus of this article, they are summarized here for completeness. These issues follow the outline in [Kali04].

6.1 Tag access management

Tag access management is the assurance that only authorized applications can read or modify information stored on a tag, or instruct the tag to perform some operation. An example is the kill function on a tag. Only authorized applications should be able to perform this operation, and the access is typically governed by a „kill code" stored in the tag that is distributed only to authorized applications.

6.2 Tag authenticity

Tag authenticity is the assurance that only authorized applications can produce valid tags, where a valid tag is one that has an identity recognizable by an authorized application. As an example, only a particular manufacturer should be able to produce tags recognizable as being from that manufacturer.

Tag authenticity addresses the threats of cloning, where an adversary copies an existing tag, and forgery, where an adversary makes new a tags with a valid identity without necessarily seeing an existing one.

6.3 Reader security

Reader security consists of two kinds of assurance. First, only authorized applications should be able to interact with readers, for instance to obtain information about tag events. As an example, a company should be able to obtain information from its own readers, but not from a competitor's readers. Second, only authorized readers should be able to provide information about tag events to an application. As a converse of the example just given, only a company's readers should be able to provide information to the company's applications; a competitor's readers should not be able to do so.

These assurances address further (and more conventional) threats to RFID security, including eavesdropping on reader-to-application communications, and insertion, deletion and modification of tag events, for instance by bogus readers.

6.4 Tag database security

Finally, *tag database security* is an assurance related to the stored tag information itself. The goal here is that only authorized applications and users should be able to access (read, modify and use) the information about tags. This is perhaps the most complex part of RFID security, due to the variety of parties who may need access to information about a tag, the diversity of potential attackers interested in that same information, and the dynamic nature of that information as tags move through the supply chain. Accordingly, these issues are a quite appropriate topic for a more detailed article.

7 Conclusion

RFID systems present significant challenges to consumer privacy because of the anticipated widespread deployment of tags and readers, and the very limited capabilities of low-cost tags, at least for the foreseeable future. Simple measures are available that can offer some improvements in consumer privacy without significantly impacting the cost of the tags.

It is likely that some basic concerns about consumer privacy as well as the companion concerns about industrial espionage can be addressed by improved RFID technology itself — but only if privacy-enhancing technologies are appropriately and early integrated into the system design.

RFID privacy is clearly still a young and rich area of research, with perhaps even more interesting results ahead. Continual assessment of privacy concerns is well advised as new threats may emerge as new applications are introduced. At the same time, tag capabilities may well increase to accommodate at least some portions of more conventional cryptographic solutions.

References

[DiAl99]   Dierks, T. and Allen, C.: The TLS Protocol Version 1.0. IETF RFC 2246, January 1999. Available via http://www.rfc-editor.org/.

[FiRo03]   Fishkin, K.P. and Roy, S.: Enhancing RFID Privacy via Antenna Energy Analysis. Presented at MIT RFID Privacy Workshop, November 2003. Also Intel Research Seattle Technical Memo IRS-TR-03-012, November 2003. Available via http://seattleweb.intel-research.net/people/fishkin/.

[Juel03]   Juels, A.: Minimalist Cryptography for RFID Tags. In submission, 2003. Available via http://www.ari-juels.com/.

[JuBr03]   Juels, A. and Brainard, J.: Soft Blocking: Flexible Blocker Tags on the Cheap. Manuscript, 2003. Available via http://www.ari-juels.com/.

[JuRS03]   Juels, A., Rivest, R.L., and Syzdlo, M.: The Blocker Tag: Selective Blocking of RFID Tags for Consumer Privacy. In Atluri, V.: 8th ACM Conference on Computer and Communications Security, ACM Press, 2003, p. 103-111. Available via http://www.ari-juels.com/.

[Kali04]   Kaliski, B.: Security and Privacy in RFID Systems. Presented at RSA Conference Japan 2004. Available via http://www.rsasecurity.com/rsalabs/.

[WeSE02]   Weis, S., Sarma, S.E., and Engels, D.W.: RFID Systems and Security and Privacy Implications. In Kaliski, B.: Cryptographic Hardware and Embedded Systems, Lecture Notes in Computer Science Volume 2523, Springer, 2002, p. 454-470. Available via http://theory.lcs.mit.edu/~sweis/.

[WeSE03]   Weis, S., Sarma, S.E., and Engels, D.W: Radio-Frequency Identification: Risks and Challenges. In: CryptoBytes, Volume 6, No. 1, Winter/Spring, 2003. Available via http://www.rsasecurity.com/rsalabs/cryptobytes/.

[WSRE03] Weis, S., Sarma, S.E., Rivest, R.L., and Engels, D.W: Security and Privacy Aspects of Low-Cost Radio Frequency Identification Systems. In: Security in Pervasive Computing, Lecture Notes in Computer Science Volume 2802, Springer, 2003, p. 201-212. Available via http://theory.lcs.mit.edu/~sweis/.

[W3C02]   World Wide Web Consortium: The Platform for Privacy Preferences 1.0 (P3P1.0) Specification. W3C Recommendation, 16 April 2002. Available via http://www.w3.org/TR/P3P/.

Light-weight PKI-Enabling through the Service of a Central Signature Server[1]

Malek Bechlaghem

CRYPTOMAThIC N.V., Interleuvenlaan 62/19 B-3001
Leuven/Belgium
mbe@cryptomathic.com

Abstract

The main complexities, for an organization considering PKI-enabling, are related to the constraints inherent to performing the validation of digital signatures and certificates. So PKI-aware applications must support the complex logic to perform certificate path construction and validation, and retrieval of certificates. Such operations require lots of communications with directories and databases, each of them using different protocols that the PKI-aware application should implement to access them.
In this paper, we consider an organization willing to PKI-enable its applications. We study the issues related to PKI-enabling in the point of view of the organization presenting the reasons why we think that PKI adoption and rollout has not become a reality yet. Then we propose a model where we are able to resolve most of the issues related to PKI-enabling. Our model relies on server-generated signatures that relieve the application from most of the tasks related to signature validation.

1 Introduction

PKI-Enabling provides applications with the capability to rely on digital certificates, replacing existing technologies such as usernames and providing additional services such as digital signatures support.

The primary mean for PKI-Enabling applications is to authenticate users and transactions based on digital certificates and associated private keys. Certificate-based authentication consists of two steps as described in figure 1 below: (1) performing a challenge-response protocol between the business application and the client[2], and (2) validating the end-user's signature and certificate.

1. **Performing a challenge-response between the server and the client**. The business application generates a challenge and sends it to the client. The client digitally signs this challenge using the private key of the user and returns it to the server. The server can use the user's certificate to verify the signature on the challenge.

2. **Validating the user's certificate**. In summary, the server validates that the certificate was issued by a CA that the server trusts, that the certificate has not expired and that the certificate has not been revoked. For checking the revocation status of the user's certifi-

---

[1] This work was supported by the funding of IWT Flanders project: "ITEA 02011 SATURN : Security applications and technologies for universal information networks"

[2] The client is software acting on behalf of the end-user.

S. Paulus, N. Pohlmann, H. Reimer (Editors): Securing Electronic Business Processes, Vieweg (2004), 117-126

cate, the relying party[3] relies on CRL[4] downloaded from the CA directory or on online servers implementing OCSP[5] protocol.

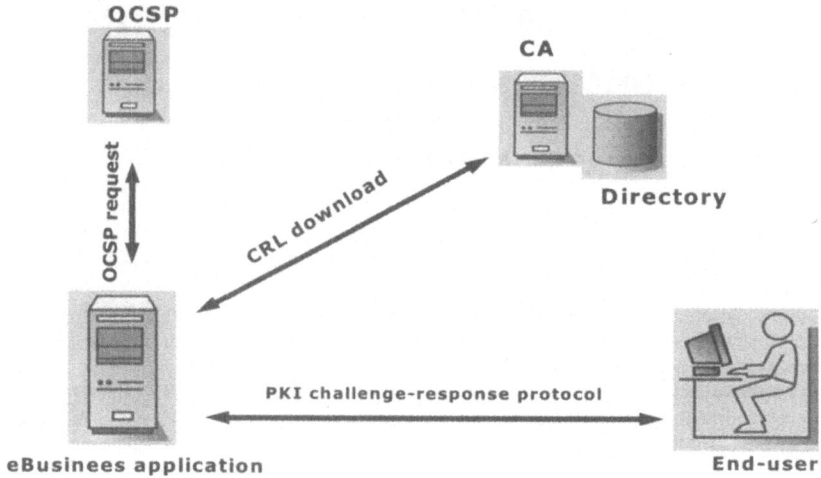

Figure 1: Certificate-based authentication process

In this paper, we address the general question of PKI-Enabling business applications. In section 2, we discuss the pitfalls and issues of PKI-Enabling from the point of view of the organization willing to PKI-Enable it's applications. In section 3, we describe the goals and motivation of the organization explaining that we need a PKI-Enabling process that resolves the issues addressed in section 2. Sections 4 and 5 are dedicated to the description of a centralized signature server and to its benefits that allow light-weight PKI-Enabling process for organizations.

2 PKI-Enabling issues

We sumsmarize hehreunder the issues that are faced by an organization willing to PKI-Enable its applications:

2.1 Issues inherent to certificate and signature validation

The main complexities, for an organization considering PKI-enabling, are related to the constraints inherent to performing the validation of digital signatures and certificates. So PKI-aware applications must support the complex logic to perform certificate path construction and validation, and retrieval of certificates. Such operations require lots of communications with directories and databases, each of them using different protocols (such as OCSP, HTTP, LDAP) that the PKI-aware applications should implement to access them.

The complexity of dealing with certificate validation is further increased in the case of a network of PKI's , instead of a single hierarchically structured PKI [EAH+01]. In such a case,

---

[3] The relying party relies on the validity of a certificate to take critical decisions. In this document, the relying party corresponds to the business application accessed by the user.

[4] CRL format is standardized in RFC 3280.

[5] OCSP protocol is defined in RFC 2560.

the problem is to find a trusted certification and validation path between two or more persons who belong to different PKI's. All the above issues lead to longer application development times, increased costs, the need for powerful client platforms and client configuration.

2.2 Application-interoperability issues

For an organization willing to PKI-Enable all its applications, application-interoperability issues might occur. So in general an application is developed to work with the certificates issued by a particular CA (or a limited set of CA's). This is related to the fact that even with the use of standard tools and certificate format, it is difficult for application developers to anticipate the potential constraints that certificate issuers (CA's) will impose on its certificate profile. Therefore, the application will only have the logic to interpret the certificates issued only by the list of supported (and hence trusted) CA's and when a PKI-Enabled application decides to trust certificates issued by other CA's, the application's interface to the PKI components has to be flexible enough to interpret the certificates from the new CA's. And assuming that a newly supported CA has a slightly different certificate profile, and uses one of the fields differently, changes will become necessary for the application. One application change may be acceptable. And in case multiple CA's are involved, the technical impacts will get higher and higher.

In addition to the integration efforts related to supporting several CA's, application developers need to understand the various PKI standards and primitives in order to program effectively with the PKI toolkit. This causes further strains to the development resources, which should be focusing their efforts in delivering the application functionality to meet the business requirements.

2.3 Non-repudiation issues

When a user signs a digital document, he is using his private key that is linked to his public key certificate. The validity of the signature on documents relies on a validation chain consisting at minimum of two certificates. The first one is the end user entity public key certificate. The second one the Certification Authority (CA) root certificate which is bound to the CA master signing key (used to sign the user's public key certificate). Unfortunately, a signing private key can become compromised or may simply reach its expiry date (in which case it should be considered as a compromisable or compromised key). The compromise of the private key is even simpler if the user is using soft keys stored on his machine. Moreover, if the end user is willing to repudiate some signature he has generated, he can simply compromise his private key in which case, it won't be clear anymore for the business application verifying the signature whether a signature generated using a „compromised" (e.g. revoked) key has been generated before or after the key compromise occurred.

The issue we have just raised has impacts on organizations that will be reluctant to PKI-Enable their applications.

2.4 Issues related to maintaining long-term signature validity

Another issue that has to be faced by an organization willing to PKI-Enable its applications is related to keeping valuable signed transactions for years and years such that they can be used each time needed (i.e. typically for dispute resolution). The trivial solution would be to record the data and archive it on whatever available storage medias. Unfortunately, electronic documents, can be easily edited, modified without having a way to trace the original document and being able to say who created it, modified it, at what time. It becomes more problematic if there is a signature that is attached to a data that changes causing the signature to be no longer valid.

To solve the above issue, organizations rely on Time-stamping to enhance the signature validation procedure by allowing signatures to be verified long after the expiry of the signing certificate. For obtaining a time stamp the business application should send a request to a third party – the Time-Stamping Authority (TSA). The TSA is an on-line party who issues time stamps for any kind of documents and implements the standard PKIX timestamping protocol [ACPZ01]. However, for the business application, relying on a TSA authority induces several problems. Apart from being obliged to understand and support the timestamping protocol, several liability and legal issues need to be resolved by the organization running the business application before beginning to rely on the services of the TSA.

2.5 PKI-Enabling does not provide Single sign-on (SSO) services

Organizations often wrongly believe that PKI-Enabling provides single sign-on (SSO) where a user authenticates once towards an application that can vouch for the identity of the user towards other applications provided by the organization. The fact is that SSO is not a mechanism-specific paradigm where PKI might be the preferred authentication mechanism towards business application.

3 The challenges of PKI-Enabling for the organization

3.1 Bypassing certificate revocation checking

We explained in the previous section that the most important issues raised by PKI-Enabling are related to digital certificate validation covering the revocation status checking.

On the business application side, the best way to handle certificate revocation checking is to be able to avoid it as much as possible. So the organization running the business application will be interested in a PKI-Enabling model where certificate revocation checking is no longer mandatory for the business application authenticating a user via a challenge/response PKI protocol.

3.2 Bypassing certification path building and validation

The logic required to find certificates and build certification paths able to validate digital signatures is often costly and complex especially when considering implementing the path building and validation algorithm described in PKIX standard RFC 3280 [HPFS02].

So the organization will be interested in PKI-Enabling where path building and validation are no longer required.

3.3 Bypassing Timestamping services

In section two, we explained why timestamping can be employed to prove the existence of and to guarantee the legal validity of digital documents. We also explained that relying on the services of a TSA induces some constraints on the organization willing to PKI-Enable its business applications.

So for this organization, it would be very convenient to rely on a PKI-Enabling model allowing the application bypassing requesting timestamping services from the TSA. Of course the PKI-Enabling model should allow maintaining the long-term validity of signed documents (or transactions).

3.4 Limiting non-repudiation issues

An organization would like to be immune from end-users repudiating transactions that took place. So the organization will be interested in a PKI-Enabling model where it will be difficult for a user to claim that his private key has become compromised. Such scenario typically happens if users are using soft keys stored on their machines.

The PKI-enabling model should enforce the protection of users' private keys so that the probability that a transaction is repudiated, due to key compromise, is reduced.

3.5 Single sign-on (SSO) services

Another added-value service that can be provided by PKI-Enabling would be to guarantee that within a same security domain, a user will authenticate once and then obtains access to all the applications available inside that security domain. So an organization willing to PKI-Enable its business application will certainly be interested in a PKI-Enabling model providing SSO services.

4 Central signature server

4.1 Traditional methods for PKI based authentication and signature

Traditionally private keys used for digital signatures are stored on the owner's PC protected by a password or in a smart card. A software only solution is not always sufficiently secure for high-value transactions, as it will normally be easy to recover the private key using exhaustive search on the password. Moreover, PC-protected keys do not offer mobility since once installed, key cannot be exported to other machines.

For security and applicability reasons the physical protection offered by a hardware token (such as smart card) is attractive. The downfall of this solution is that it requires smart card readers, which are still not widely available. The issue with mobility is not resolved entirely since the user needs always to use the token on a machine equipped with the corresponding drivers. Finally, hardware tokens-generated signatures do not relieve the PKI-Enabled application from all the tasks related to performing signature and certificate validation.

4.2 An innovative approach: Central signature server

As an alternative to the above traditional methods, we are considering a novel approach which consists in performing digital signatures via a Centralized signature server.

A signature server is a network application that generates the user keys in tamper resistant hardware and generates digital signatures. Both processes are initiated and fully controlled by the owner. The signature server maintains a database over individual signature keys. Given proper identification, the signature server can be requested to sign a document or a transaction on behalf of the user whose signature key it stores.

Authentication and security are major issues for the signature server but we believe that the security level of a signature server can be at least as high as that of alternative solutions such as using smart cards, and much higher than storing the signature key on a PC. This is achieved by using two independent channels. A request for a signature, typically submitted from a browser, is authenticated by traditional means, e.g. based on passwords and using SSL protection, but in addition an independent channel, e.g. based on mobile communication, is applied to confirm the request.

4.3   Workflow of authentication using the signature server

The figure below describes the workflow of signing a transaction via the signature server.

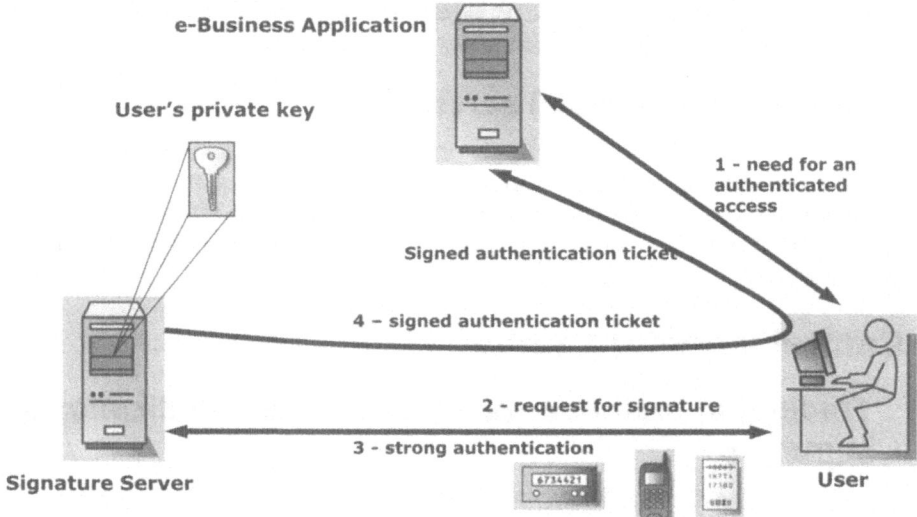

Figure 2: Workflow of authentication via the signature server

The business application needs to authenticate the user before giving him access to the requested service. The business application generates a transaction id (for the sake of simplicity, this transaction id is called "authentication ticket" in this paper) and requests a signature on this transaction id[6].

The user's application[7] (typically the browser) receives the authentication ticket from the business application and relies on the signature server in order to have the ticket signed. After a strong two-factor authentication, the user's private key is unlocked by the signature server and the ticket is signed and returned back to business application. The user's authentication towards the signature server can be summarized as follows:

1. **Identity claim:** The user's application will get the user's username and static password from the user. This is sent to the signature server together with a request to use some au-

---

[6] The authentication ticket might also include the user id and possibly other parameters.

[7] The user's application might be an applet.

thentication method (e.g. OTP[8] via SMS). If the user has been successfully identified by the server, the server randomly generates an OTP and sends it to the user via an independant channel (via SMS for instance).

2. **Authentication:** The user's application will request the user to type in the OTP (e.g. in our example, the OTP is received via SMS). The user is successfully authenticated towards the signature server if he is able to provide the correct OTP.

The user's application will then request a signature on the an authentication ticket. The signed authentication ticket is sent from the signature server to the business application via the user's application. Finally the business application verifies the signature on the authentication ticket.

4.4 Workflow of transaction signature via the signature server

Figure three below describes the workflow of signature transaction via the signature server:

The overall workflow for generating a digital signature is as follows:

1. The user authenticates himself to signature server

2. A secure connection is set up between the signature server and the user

3. Over the secure connection, the user sends the data necessary for generating the signature – a hash value of the data to be signed

4. Signature server generates the signature and returns it to the user

5. The user sends the signed data to the business application.

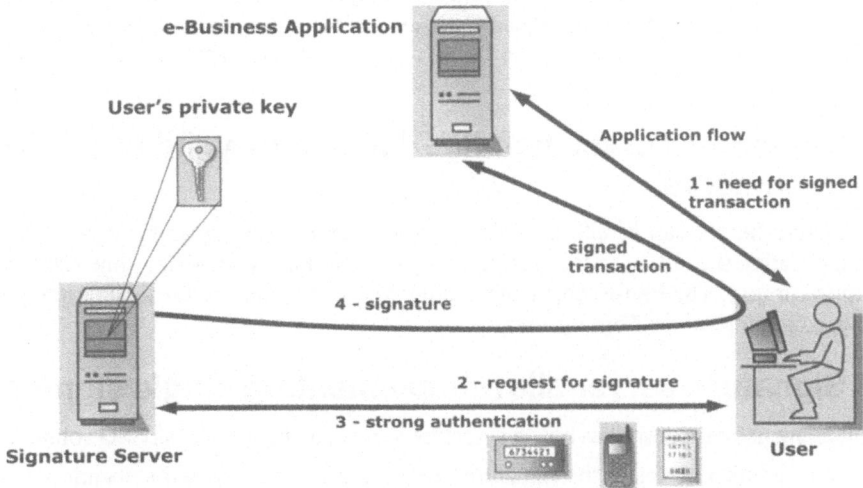

Figure 3: Workflow of transaction signature via the signature server

---

[8] One Time Password

5 The benefits of the signature server

We recall that this paper addresses the issues encountered by an organization willing to PKI-Enable its applications. In the previous section, we have described a central signature server and shown how it can be used to perform signature operations during authentication and transaction signatures operations. We describe hereunder how the signature server can offer the services that we described in section 3 allowing to cope with most the PKI-Enabling issues we discussed in section 2:

5.1 Signature server allows bypassing certificate validation

The signature server handles all critical key management operations such as key generation and certification key revocation. Key pair creation and certificate creation is done when a user is registered to the signature server. At that stage, the signature server verifies that the CA certificate is valid. The key pair is revoked when the user account is definitely blocked or when the CA certificate is no longer valid. In both cases, the signature server will no longer allow signing with the user's private key. In such a configuration, it is fair to consider that if a signature exists, this means that it is valid. The business application receiving a signed transaction is neither required to perform a certificate revocation status check on the end-user certificate nor to build and validate any certification path.

5.2 Signature server enforces non-repudiation

We recall that the signature server generates the user keys in tamper resistant hardware meaning that the physical security of the private key is no longer the user's responsibility, as it is not stored on the user's PC or hardware token. Taking into consideration this fact, the probability that a user repudiates some signed transactions due to key compromise is very low especially if we consider that the signature server can log all the operations performed by the user.

5.3 Signature server handles long-term validity of signed documents

The Signature Server can handle timestamp requests as part of signature requests from the user's application (i.e. a flag in the signature request determines whether a time stamp should be supplied or not). The PKI-Enabled application will then be relieved from timestamping the signed message it receives from the user.

5.4 Signature server allow implementing single sign-on

The following use case describes how a signature server can be used as an SSO solution:

- A client authenticates to the signature server in order get a signed authentication ticket requested by application 1. We assume that the user application is able to specify to the signature server that the user needs an authentication ticket for accessing multiple applications.

- Under a successful authentication towards the signature server, the user's private signature key is unlocked and used to sign the authentication ticket. The signature server adds to the ticket a validity period and the time of the signature. The signed authentication ticket. The signed ticket is sent to application 1 via the user's application.

- Application 1 performs these steps in order to validate the authentication ticket and provide access to the client:
  - Verify that the signature has been applied on the ticket she generated
  - Verify the freshness of the ticket by extracting and checking the signature time and validity period.
- If he wants to access application 2, the user is only asked to show a valid authentication ticket. The application will validate the signed ticket provided by the user in same way.

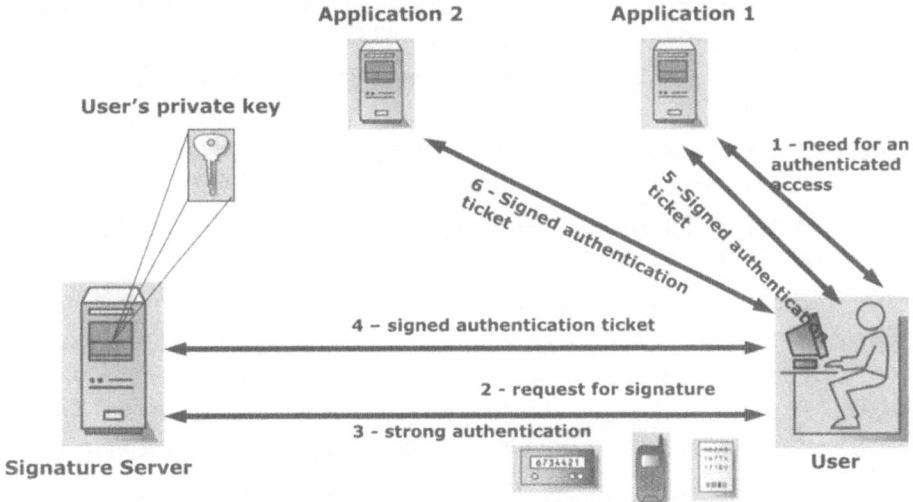

Figure 4 Workflow of transaction signature via the signature server

6 Related work

Up to our knowledge, there is no published paper addressing the general issues of PKI-Enabling and trying to describe alternatives to bypass certificate revocation and time-stamping using the services of a central signature server. We are aware of few initiatives in order to allow broader PKI adoption by organizations but none of them is similar to ours. IETF has drafted protocols allowing obtaining PKI validation services from a centralized server [PiHo02, MaHF02, Pink02, ASZZ01]. These protocols addresses only the issues related to certificate and signature validation and don't address the general issues related to PKI-Enabling we described in this paper. Other authors [JaEb02, BaLi02] addressed the needed PKI services for mobile devices that are scarce in computational and network resource.

7 Conclusion

We analyzed the issues related to PKI-enabling in the point of view of an organization. We presented the reasons why we think that PKI adoption and rollout has not become a reality yet. Then we introduced the concept of central signature, which is an on-line service generating signatures on behalf of users. We then explained how it allows relieving the organization application from most of the issues tasks related to PKI-Enabling. One possible limitation of an on-line service is that it has the potential of becoming a single point of failure, since its availability is essential for the correct functioning of communication between the end-users and the application they are accessing. We believe that this specific issue is inherent to modern PKI where most of the PKI-Enabled applications rely on on-line Trusted Third Parties such as OCSP responders and Timestamping authorities.

References

[ACPZ01]   C. Adams, P. Cain, D. Pinkas, R. Zuccherato. RFC 3161 – Internet X.509 Public Key Infrastructure Time-Stamp Protocol (TSP).

[HPFS02]   R. Housley, W. Polk, W. Ford, D. Solo. RFC 3280 – PKIX Certificate and CRL Profile

[PiHo02]   D. Pinkas and R. Housley. *Delegated Path Validation and Delegated Path Discovery Protocol Requirements*. IETF, RFC 3379, September 2002.

[MaHF02]   A. Malpani, R. Housley, and T. Freeman. *Simple Certificate Validation Protocol*. IETF, Internet draft, June 2002.

[Pink02]   D. Pinkas. *Certificate Validation Protocol*. IETF, Internet draft, June 2002.

[ASZZ01]   C. Adams, P. Sylvester, M. Zolotarev, and R. Zuccherato. *Data Validation and Certification Server Protocols – RFC 3029*. IETF, 2001.

[EAH+01]   Y. Elley, A. Anderson, St. Hanna, S. Mulla,, R. Perlman, S. Proctor. *Building Certification Paths: Forward vs. Reverse, Proceedings of NDSS 2001*, 2001.

[JaEb02]   M. Jalali-Sohi, P. Ebinger. *Towards Efficient PKIs for Restricted Mobile Devices, Proceedings of IASTED International Conference Communications and Computer Networks, Cambridge MA*, November 2002.

[BaLi02]   D. Barbecaru, A. Lioy. *Towards Simplifying PKI Implementation: Client-Server based Validation of Public Key Certificates, Proceedings of IEEE ISSPIT 2002*, 2002.

Massmailers: New Threats Need Novel Anti-Virus Measures

David Harley

National Health Service Information Authority
Aqueous II, Aston Cross, Rocky Lane, Birmingham B6 5RQ
United Kingdom
david.harley@nhsia.nhs.uk

Abstract

This paper considers changes in virus technologies and dissemination, and their impact upon anti-virus strategy and mail-management practice. Gateway products handle spoofing viruses inconsistently. The industry's continued emphasis on reactive detection of known viruses, supplemented by generic drivers and limited heuristics, has been used by virus writers to widen the window of opportunity between virus release and the availability of specific detection. Can the enterprise wait for the industry to adapt, or are broader-based strategies required? In this paper, we review some of the recent developments in virus technology and the responses of anti-virus vendors and service managers, and consider their current and long-term efficacy.

1 Introduction

While it is commonly assumed and agreed in general security circles that what is commonly (though not altogether accurately) referred to as signature scanning is failing to meet the needs of the consumer, it often seems that the industry is drawing a correct (or at least defensible) conclusion from inadequate or misunderstood data, and assumptions about what anti-virus software does or should do.

Virus writers have widened the window of opportunity between virus release and anti-virus detection by reducing the efficacy of generic drivers and heuristics (for example by recompiling or re-packing executables until they are no longer recognised as variants, and by reducing the efficacy of generic filtering by the use of encrypted archive files, limited polymorphism and the rediscovery of parasitism to confound detection techniques using message digests closing parenthesis. Inconsistency in mailer daemon configuration has resulted in the increased propagation of virus messages, sometimes with attachments, as non-delivery reports, resulting in confusion and even secondary infection. So what do we do next?

1.1 A Brief History of Anti-Virus

Most current anti-virus scanning is primarily based on a reactive model: we learn about the existence of a new virus or variant, and add detection to the virus definitions database used by the scanner. In the early 1990s, this worked relatively well, sometimes supplemented by change detector software, which scanned executable files for any sign of tampering, and behaviour monitoring. Older virus types spread comparatively slowly, and the use of electronic communications to increase spread was mitigated by the comparatively light take-up of Internet connection. However, this approach was dealt several blows in the latter part of the dec-

S. Paulus, N. Pohlmann, H. Reimer (Editors): Securing Electronic Business Processes, Vieweg (2004), 127-137

ade. The first macro viruses required significant re-engineering of most anti-virus products to address the new infection vector, a process which took weeks rather than hours, and by redefining „executable" reduced the efficacy of change detection. Newer file infectors made increasing use of Internet vectors, especially newsgroups. However, anti-virus vendors started to make use of other more-or-less proactive technologies such as heuristics (scanning for code suggesting the presence of a virus using a scoring mechanism to evaluate probability of infection and techniques such as emulation to monitor the effects of code in safe isolation) and the use of generic drivers, increasing the possibility of detecting new but fairly close variants. The near-universal take-up of Windows and the increasing sophistication and dynamic nature of operating environments generally, though, dealt something of a blow to the viability of integrity checking/change detection: system and application files may be opened and modified many thousands of times in a comparatively short time, and few end-users would be prepared to evaluate and confirm each such change.

The reinvention of the mass mailer towards the end of the decade introduced further complexity: they used some novel file types, and they were rarely parasitic (so technology based on change detection became even less useful). They also accelerated the pace of propagation. The quarterly/monthly definitions update became totally obsolete with the arrival of „Lovebug". Indeed, anti-virus vendors struggled for a while to keep pace with variants and copycat malware appearing at a rate of several per day.

End-sites began to filter emails with executable file types, and eventually virus-specific gateway scanners incorporated this approach, and the first signs of a more broad-based approach appeared: one particular ISP spin-off started to supplement multiple known-virus scanners with their own heuristic scanner based on a spam detection engine, considering message text analysis and traffic analysis as well as code analysis, an approach that most mainstream antivirus vendors are only now starting to take on board.

However, virus writers did not stand still. Mass mailers got more technically challenging, using spoofing (header forgery) to confound standard gateway scanner technology. Viruses could still be filtered generically, but it grew harder to notify the real sender that they were infected. Gateway scanners and managed services continue to assume that the sender and intended recipient should still always be notified, as had been good practice in the age of the macro virus, even when more than 99% of all email-borne viruses are mass mailers with no useful message content, and more than 99% of those are spoofers, and therefore result in misdirected alerts. [Burr04; Harl03a; Harl03b]

1.2 Email and Viruses

While email as a virus vector is indelibly associated with recent mass mailer epidemics, viruses and email have been associated almost since the first replicative malware [Harl04]. Indeed, the history of mass mailers did not, as it is sometimes believed, start with Melissa or LoveLetter, but with an earlier generation of malware such as the Morris Worm, which exploited multiple exploits including a buffer overflow in sendmail [Hrus92] and CHRISTMA EXE which included many of the characteristics seen in the mass mailer epidemic of the late 1990s and later [HaSG01]. It may useful to recap on where we are right now in relation to the main classifications of malware in the email context.

1.2.1 Boot Sector Infectors

Most of the effective early viruses were BSIs or MBR infectors. A few of these are still occasionally reported, but don't normally spread via email, but rather when a system is booted with an infected diskette. However, it is possible to transport such viruses in dropper form or as a disk image, normally with the knowledge and consent of the recipient. There have been instances where malware has used this technique as a means of covert propagation, however.

1.2.2 File Viruses

File viruses (parasitic viruses) infect files by attaching themselves to them in some way, so that when the file is run, the virus code is also run. The transmission of such a virus by email is uncommon, but from time to time a modern mass mailer virus/worm may be distributed infected by an older parasitic virus such as CIH.

1.2.3 File and Boot (Multipartite) Viruses

„File and Boot" viruses, since they use both methods of infection, in many cases can, in principle, be spread by email, though in real life they are rarely seen now at all. These are often referred to as multipartite viruses, though strictly speaking this term refers to a virus that uses more than one infection method, not only to viruses that infect program files and boot sectors only [HaSG01].

1.2.4 Macro Viruses

Macro viruses normally infect documents. The most common macro viruses infect Microsoft Word or Excel documents, but there are other vulnerable applications, not all of which are Microsoft Office applications (mostly, however, these are Proof of Concept viruses rather than truly „in the wild". Macro viruses can be multi-platform – most of the very few viruses to cause problems on Macintoshes in recent years have been macro viruses rather than Macintosh-specific malware [Harl97] – and some can affect more than one application. They are still commonly found transmitted by email, but are much less prevalent than they were in the mid-to-late 1990s, and generally form a tiny percentage of all infected messages.

1.2.5 Mass Mailers

Mass mailers are designed explicitly to disseminate (usually as fast and far as possible) via email. They maximize their own spread by seeking new target addresses from a victim's address book, files on an infected system, and other sources such as web pages. They generally rely on social engineering to persuade the recipient to execute the malicious program, though there have been successful mass mailers that used a vulnerability in the mail delivery mechanism to execute without the intervention of the recipient (using embedded scripts, for example).

1.2.6 Mix and Match Malware

More modern malware making use of multiple vectors (email, network shares and broadcasts over ports associated with known vulnerabilities, for example) may be referred to as multipolar rather than multipartite. Where multiple vectors and malware types are combined in the same package, these are often referred to as convergent [HaSG01] or blended threats [Harl02].

1.2.7 Semi-Malware

Increasingly, end-users are frustrated by the insistence of some anti-virus vendors on strict delineation of what they feel obliged to detect (i.e. viruses and, sometimes under protest, most worms and some Trojans) and what others feel they should detect [Skou04]. Such malware types may include the following: adware, dialers (inc. porn-dialers), hack tools, rootkits, joke programs, objects that appear to exploit known vulnerabilities (in Outlook, for example), remote access tools (RATs), and spyware (this list is not necessarily exhaustive!). In fact, some AV vendors do indeed detect this range of threats (not to mention garbage files, „intended" but non-functional viruses, code fragments, test files, and a number of other miscellaneous objects that are known to turn up from time to time in often poorly-maintained virus collections). However, detection of many of these objects is usually not enabled by default, and not available across all products and platforms in a vendor's product range. (Symantec refers to this functionality as „expanded threats", while McAfee refer to „potentially unwanted programs".) A similar consideration may apply to the detection of viruses not native to the platform on which the product is being run: for instance, Macintosh or Linux malware on a Windows PC.

2 The .ZIP Problem

Conventional anti-virus technology is based on the model of finding a new virus or variant, analysing it, and adding detection to the scanner's capabilities. So in principle, however good an anti-virus scanner is, every virus to make it into the wild has a window of opportunity between the time it's launched and the time detection becomes available. Recently, virus writers have, fairly successfully, used a number of techniques to widen that window of opportunity. Such techniques include, for instance, the simultaneous release of single variants recompiled, or compressed with different runtime packers, with the aim of reducing the effectiveness of anti-virus heuristics and/or generic detection drivers.

Anti-virus administrators, on the other hand, use several techniques to narrow it. One of the most effective is generic blocking of attachment file types that are more likely to be used by viruses than as part of a genuine business process. This includes such file types as .EXE, .COM, .BAT, .SCR, .LNK, .PIF etc. (Categorisation of file type by risk level is considered in some detail in the next section.)

Recently, virus writers suddenly realized that compressed, archive files such as .ZIP files could be used as a means of impeding the efficacy of both generic and virus-specific countermeasures.

2.1 Evading Generic Blocking

Many generic filters use simple-minded checking of an attachment's filename to determine whether it should be stripped, or the message discarded or quarantined. This has the advantage of being cheap and simple to implement – it can often be done with simple scripting at the mail-server. However, it has disadvantages, too. One obvious problem is that a file called innocentfile.txt is not necessarily a text file at all, and could be a dangerous executable. It is, of course, often possible to check that a file is what its filename suggests, for example by checking the file header to see if it conforms to the specification for an .EXE. There are products and services that perform this sort of check, but they go far beyond simple scripting.

ZIPs are popular not only because they provide efficient compression and almost universally used, but because there is so much free, near-free or shareware software that supports the format. It is possible to get free compressing/decompressing software using formats other than .ZIP. However, virus writers have already turned their attention to other encryption and compression packages: compression formats such as RAR, *gzip* and *tar* have already been exploited, and other packages and formats such as .CAB (cabinet files), ARJ, LZH, a host of Unix and Mac archives could just as easily be exploited. Since major compression packages such as WinZip, WinRar and StuffIt address, between them, a wide range of compression formats apart from .ZIPs (many of which themselves support encryption), there is scope for a wide range of future exploits using not only compression tools, but encryption tools and coding/decoding tools such as UUE.

2.2 Virus-Specific Problems

Another problem affects all known-virus (virus-specific) scanners, to a greater or lesser degree. The encryption used routinely for .ZIP files is not particularly secure, but it's too secure for the scanner to break the encryption and scan the file on the fly: it would take too long. Recent versions of zipping software may include enhanced encryption, which only make this particular problem worse! The solutions now being used by anti-virus vendors involve a certain element of sleight-of-hand, and involve combinations of techniques including searching for the password within the message, checksumming, and textual analysis of the message. Virus writers have responded by obfuscating the password (e.g. by presenting it as a graphic rather than as text) and reintroducing a minor form of polymorphism so that simple hashes of the zipped attachment are insufficient to guarantee detection, even where the actual malicious code remains static.

In fact, even where the code itself is polymorphic, this does not, in principle, constitute a major barrier to virus-specific detection, which has not been based on simple string signature scanning for many years, despite the ongoing misuse of the term: anti-virus search strings are usually algorithmic, not static. Surely, then, such obfuscation doesn't matter as long as there's anti-virus on the desktop, so that the actual code is scanned when it's decrypted?

This is more-or-less so, as long as desktop anti-virus is installed, active in memory, and kept up-to-date (not forgetting, of course, that the fact that a scanner is up-to-date does not mean the system is safe from a *new* virus or variant). However, if we could be sure that this was the case, we wouldn't necessarily *need* to scan email at the gateway.

2.3 Workarounds

As previously indicated, much generic blocking is just simple-minded blocking by filename extension, not file type checking by scanning the file headers and comparing to the apparent file type indicated by the filename extension. This can therefore be simply evaded by renaming compressed files with a filename extension that doesn't indicate their nature. This loophole is as available to virus writers as it is to legitimate end-users, so its use is not particularly recommended.

It is possible and even simple, even with an encrypted .ZIP, to check on whether the archive contains an .executable file, without having to decrypt it, since the .ZIP format contains filenames in clear. Thus, archives could be checked by using a utility such as *strings* to extract ASCII text then using *grep* or *findstr* to check for strings such as „.EXE", „.PIF" etc. This technique is usable with some other encryption/compression formats.

Another filtering technique available to some but by no means all users of a specific gateway anti-virus or filtering product is to discriminate between encrypted .ZIPs and unencrypted .ZIPs. This allows the blocking of encrypted .ZIPs (this is also reasonably simple: it can be done checking just the first 7 bytes of a file, so might be done on a D-I-Y basis where a product or service does not itself have the capability). This reduces but does not eliminate the generic risk.

2.4 Taking the Long View

The .ZIP format has long been used for rough and ready encryption, and experience within the author's work environment suggests many users think of it as an encryption facility rather than as a compression utility. Notwithstanding the enhancement of the encryption facilities of some of the main compression packages, the current binding of viruses and .ZIP encryption suggests that where an organisation has not already moved towards PKI, it would at least be worth encouraging or mandating standardisation on another encryption package such as PGP or GPG.

However, in terms of breaking that association and evading generic blocking to transfer files where there is no particular confidentiality or sensitivity, the answer is not necessarily to use full-industrial-strength encryption. In such a case the intention is not encryption as such, but the use of a person-to-person exchange not susceptible to spoofing by a virus, however good its social engineering. However, if files are transferred in an encrypted form (however trivial, using techniques such as inverting the file, or using a simple substitution cipher, or prepending a non-standard header that can be stripped by the recipient), a form of exchange needs to be arranged out-of-band. In other words, agree a password in person or over the phone rather than by email. Furthermore, any use of encryption formats is subject to the caveat that encryption by itself is no indication of the safety of the encrypted object in terms of malware. In fact, the use of even trivial encryption should not be contemplated unless all parties in the transaction are meeting the highest standards of malware management hygiene.

In the longer term, though, it's likely that organisations will have to face the fact that email isn't primarily intended for or best suited to secure file transfer/exchange, convenient though it has been up to now. At best, it is subject to restrictions and delays from time to time, and it might be more appropriate to use a safer channel such as SCP or SFTP, or secure HTTP download/upload access, or a tightly controlled or proprietary email service. Organisations that continue to use uncontrolled, minimally authenticated email need to consider that the cost of a single infected machine could be considerable. Not just the cost of direct damage to files and data, or the presence of a compromised machine controlled via a backdoor or virus allowing remote access and exploitation by a remote vandal, but the damage to reputation of the organisation if it became known that such a machine was responsible for large scale spamming, for example (it's believed that a high percentage of current spam is broadcast by PCs controlled remotely without the knowledge of the PC owner/user) [Kota04; Hypp03], or used as an agent for a denial of service attack on another site. Most of the problematic viruses and variants around at present are not actively destructive to data or file systems, but there is no guarantee that this will remain the case, and damage to reputation and credibility may have more impact than data damage, in some cases.

The risks are likely to increase rather than diminish, now the bad guys have seen how successful this particular class of stratagem is at circumventing anti-virus measures and creating confusion. It's possible that anti-virus vendors will respond quickly to lessen the risk by (for example) paying more attention to the message content rather than concentrating on the actual attachment, or by enhancing the way they handle zips, or by paying as much attention to traffic analysis as to code analysis, but in some cases this will require significant re-engineering.

3 Anti-Malware Solutions

Generic virus management largely consists of discarding or quarantining objects that are capable of carrying or consisting entirely of a pre-determined range of malicious code. In email terms, this range usually consists of file attachments of file types often used by the writers of mass mailer viruses, including .PIF, .SCR, .VBS, .EXE, .BAT, .COM and so on, though exactly which file types are blocked will depend partly on local usage. Most sites do not block Microsoft Office documents, despite the risk of macro viruses, since (in most corporate environments) legitimate business processes would suffer seriously from the blocking of Office documents. A Technical Note published by the UK's National Infrastructure Security Coordination Centre examines the relative risks of common file types. [NISC04]. However, from a systems administration point of view, the following categorisation of attachment types by risk level may be more immediately useful.

3.1 Very High Risk

1. File types almost never exchanged legitimately by email but are executable file types used by mass mailers: e.g. .PIF, .LNK, .BAT, .COM, .CMD, .SHS. The .EXE file type is also heavily used by mass mailers, and is very frequently blocked by generic filters for this reason (and with good reason). However, it is possible and may be convenient for legitimate .EXE files to be exchanged, so whether to block remains a local decision.

2. Filenames with two or more extensions, especially where the first type is a non-executable and the last one isn't: for example, myfile.txt.scr

3. File types that don't match the filename extension, when the file type is more dangerous than the filename extension suggests. (Some products simply check for a simple match, which can lead to anomalies such as what appears to be a Word document (.DOC – medium risk) being diagnosed as high risk because it turns out to be simple text.)

4. Filenames with double or multiple extensions where an attempt has been made to mask the presence of the real file type, for example by inserting several spaces between the penultimate extension and the real, final extension .

5. Files with a deceptive icon suggesting a non-executable file type, but identified as executable.

6. Filenames that include the characters { }, suggesting an attempt to disguise an executable file type by using its CLSID (class ID extension).

7. Filenames containing a colon character, suggesting an attempt to pass through an executable as an NTFS stream.

3.2 Medium High Risk

This category includes file types heavily used by mass mailers, but which may also be exchanged legitimately and conveniently, for example, .EXE, .SCR, .VBS, and .ZIP. It may, therefore, be decided locally not to block these file-types: .EXE attachments may denote data rather than a „real" executable, but in the form of a program file: for example, self-decompressing archive files and self-decrypting files. These are often convenient because they obviate the need for the recipient to own the archiving or encryption utility that generated them. While no security-conscious organization is still likely to consider it desirable to allow end users to trade screensavers (.SCR files are structurally .EXE files) but the final decision must be local. New VBScript (.VBS) mass mailers are still seen from time to time, but such scripts may be used to install system patches, for example. If any of these file types are exchanged by email, precautions should be taken to ensure that only trusted and trustworthy code is allowed through, and possibly restricted to internal mail, where this is technically feasible.

Compressed archive files, especially the .ZIP file type associated with PKZip and WinZip, pose an increasing risk. Virus-specific software is almost always capable of scanning the contents of a .ZIP file (and a variety of other archive formats). However, virus-specific scanners are not able to scan the contents of encrypted archives in real time and have been forced to apply less satisfactory search criteria as more viruses have exploited this loophole. Some generic filters are unable to check inside a compressed file for the presence of archived executables. Also, multiply-nested archives containing unusually large compressed files may constitute an effective Denial of Service attack on anti-virus scanners and email servers.

3.3 Medium Risk

This class includes file types not frequently used by mass mailers, but capable of carrying executable/malicious code. Most file infectors, Trojans etc. would be caught by the previous categories, but documents that can contain macros (especially Office documents) fall here. Note that exchange of some documents will often be seen as impacting too heavily on normal business practices to override the moderate increase in security (.DOC, .XLS), but others may be borderline high risk, such as those file types associated with Microsoft Access. People don't exchange full databases as often as they do more concise forms of data.

3.4 Medium-Low Risk

This category includes executable files of types not currently associated with virus action, or only with extinct viruses, zoo viruses, or proof-of-concept viruses.

3.5 Low Risk

Non-executables. Technically, this should be „no risk". However, it's probably not feasible to ascertain automatically and incontrovertibly under all conceivable circumstances that a file contains no executable code.

3.6 Uncategorized

1. Files whose executability (and infectibility) status can not be determined.
2. Files of unknown file type (or no file type: for instance, Mac data files are often not given a filename extension).
3. Encrypted files
4. Archives that can't be unpacked (fully or at all) for scanning, due to encryption, unknown packing format etc.

Categories 3 and 4 can be said to include some file types in preceding categories, but no presumptions are made in this case about filename extensions.

4 Spoofing Viruses and Gateway Configuration

The following recommendations should mitigate the worst social impacts of spoofing viruses:

- Mailer daemons should not default to bouncing undeliverable mail complete with attachments.

- Filters that reject executable files should not, if they send a notification to the apparent sender, return a copy of the attachment. Some gateway anti-virus products may not recognise viruses transmitted in this form, a problem often associated with MIME boundaries, and, of course, recipients of misdirected notifications may not have any anti-virus protection at all! If such filters do send an alert, they should include a statement along the lines of the following. „Because of the number of viruses that forge headers, this alert may have been sent to you in error." It is strongly recommended that sites consider not sending an alert message at all under these circumstances, as the confusion and traffic volumes arising from such messages is likely to exceed any advantage by orders of magnitude.

- Virus-specific anti-virus software at the gateway should never be configured to send an alert to the intended recipient or apparent sender of mail infected with a virus known to forge headers:

  - If possible, it should send an alert only where the virus is known not to forge headers. This involves either blacklisting known spoofers or whitelisting known non-spoofers. Many products and services remain unable to apply this degree of granularity, or prefer not to because of the degree of additional administration required. In fact, nearly all current mass mailers forge headers (at least the From: field).

  - If the software cannot discriminate, it should be configured never to send alerts to either the apparent sender or the recipient. In fact, it might be argued that there is rarely a justification for notifying the intended recipient that an infected message was intercepted, and that services that continue to do this are doing so either because of lack of understanding of the issues or because they prioritise the advertising potential over the actual usefulness of the notification. Some services can only turn off alerts to both parties (recipient and apparent sender), that is, they can't turn off alerts to just one. Some are now starting to ship with alerts turned off by default, but system administrators often turn them back on: clearly, there is an education issue here. The only defensible argument here is that it is socially responsible to advise someone who clearly has a virus problem of the fact. In email terms, this scenario is almost entirely restricted to macro viruses. Clearly, if it is possible to discriminate non-spoofers, notification in such cases is recommended. If not, administrators should at least be made aware that the proportion of unspoofed infected mail is, generally, a tiny fraction of 1%, and most will probably concede in those circumstances that it's better to risk missing notifying occasional individuals with a macro virus than to flood the Internet with confusing, panic-inducing, misdirected notifications. Even in this scenario, the macro virus scenario is only significantly problematical if the product/service is unable to forward the cleaned document with an appropriate message. Where the cleaned document is forwarded, the recipient is in a position to advise the sender of the problem. (There may, however, be an issue with signed messages, since the attachment and the message will be modified. This issue is not explored further here.)

  - If complete shutdown of notifications isn't possible either, the software should be regarded as unfit for purpose.

- If possible, the software should be configured not to send an alert to the intended recipient for any mass mailer, spoofing or otherwise: it accomplishes no purpose since, if it is possible to discriminate, the „sender" of a non-spoofing virus can be notified without it being useful to the target recipient. Obviously, if the virus spoofs, it is worse than useless to tell the target that the apparent sender was responsible for a virus message that had nothing to do with them.

  - If it isn't possible to discriminate between mass mailers and other malware, it shouldn't notify the recipient at all.

  - If this isn't possible, it should be regarded as unfit for purpose.

- Wording of non-delivery reports where the mail is undeliverable for reasons that may be totally unrelated to possible virus content, such as addressing to non-existent accounts, exceeded quotas, server problems etc., should take into account the fact that the NDR may be misdirected due to virus action. Wording might include something along the lines of: „If you did not send this message, it may be that it originated elsewhere, such as with a spammer or a virus that forges message headers. You can get further general advice on spam and virus issues from [local contact] or check [appropriate URL]."

- All alerts should include a local contact point for resolution of queries.

5 Conclusion

This paper does not present a range of innovative, hot-off-the-press solutions. The core technologies considered here have been around in some form for a while, in some cases almost as long as viruses. The real issue here is the need to expand anti-virus technology beyond its traditional borders, to take advantage of techniques that are often considered anti-spam rather than anti-virus – for instance, filtering on message content, message content heuristics, traffic analysis – and to take a step backward towards generic alternatives to virus-specific detection: not just the basic checksumming and behaviour monitoring of the 1990s, but approaches informed by more recent security approaches: intrusion detection and prevention, firewalling, access control management and advanced filtering, and a realistic view of what is possible within the limits of a fundamentally insecure protocol.

References

[Harl04]   Harley, David: Email Threats and Vulnerabilities. In: The Handbook of Information Security. Editor: Bidoli, Wiley, 2004 (in preparation).

[Harl97]   Harley, David: Macs and Macros: the State of the Macintosh Nation. In: Proceedings of the Seventh International Virus Bulletin Conference, Virus Bulletin Ltd, p.67-98.

[HaSG01]   Harley, David; Slade, Robert; Gattiker, Urs: Viruses Revealed, Osborne, 2001.

[NISC04]   NISSC: Technical Note 03/04. Guidance on Handling Files with Possible Malicious Content. Issued 19 March 2004.

[EEMA03]   EEMA: „Spam and eMail Abuse Management".
             https://www.eema.org/SProjects/spam.asp, 2004.

[Skou04]   Skoudis, Ed: Your desktop antivirus product may be leaving you wide open to attack.

http://searchsecurity.techtarget.com/tip/0,289483,sid14_gci967559,00.html, 2004.

[Hrus92]   Hruska, Jan, 1992. Computer Viruses and Anti-Virus Warfare. Chichester: Ellis Horwood.

[Harl03a]   Harley, David: Fact, Fiction and Managed Anti-Malware Services – Vendors, Resellers, and Customers Divided by a Common Language. In: Proceedings of the 13th Virus Bulletin International Conference, Virus Bulletin Ltd, 2003, p.83-91.

[Burr04]   Burrell, Bruce: The Plague of Viruses That Send Email with Forged „From:" Fields. http://www.itd.umich.edu/virusbusters/forged_from.html, 2004.

[Kota04]   Kotadia, Munir: Zombies may sabotage spam fight. In: ZDNet Week, CNET Networks Inc., 2004, p. 3.

[Harl03b]   Harley, David: Virus Incident Management at the Gateway. http://www.aavar.org/avar2003/presentations/David_Harley.pdf, 2003.

[Hypp03]   Hypponnen, Mikko: F-Secure Corporation's Data Security Summary for 2003: The Year of the worm. http://www.f-secure.com/2003/

[Harl02]   Harley, David: The future of malicious code: predictions on blended threats, e-mail exploits, social engineering and more. In: Information Security, 5/5, 2002, p.36-38.

OpenPMF: A Model-Driven Security Framework for Distributed Systems

Dr. Ulrich Lang · Rudolf Schreiner

ObjectSecurity Ltd.
St. John's Innovation Centre
Cowley Road, Cambridge CB4 0WS
United Kingdom
{ulrich, rudolf}@objectsecurity.com

Abstract

The wide-spread use of different distributed systems platforms and security technologies today makes the integration of distributed applications and the migration of existing applications to new technologies increasingly difficult. Model driven software development approaches try to tackle this problem by first modelling the application logic independent of technologies, and then by mapping this model to the technology. Security in distributed systems faces a similar problem because there are many different platforms and security technologies that need to be integrated. This paper illustrates how the concepts of model driven software engineering can be applied to security, and we present OpenPMF, our flexible, model-driven security framework in which a technology-independent abstract representation of the security policy is stored in a technology-independent policy repository, which is integrated with the underlying platform and security technology in a well-defined and flexible manner. Our architecture takes into account the separation of functional and non-functional properties of distributed applications. We also discuss the integration of our system with CORBA and CORBA Components.

1 Induction

Interoperability and portability of distributed applications has been a concern for the IT industry for some time because new and incompatible software platforms are developed every couple of years. In the 1990's, the software industry believed that eventually one common software platform for distributed systems would emerge that enables application interoperability, portability, scalability and other useful properties. In the early 90's, the Common Object Request Broker Architecture (CORBA) was thought to become this common middleware platform. After that, component-based middleware has evolved, e.g. Enterprise Java Beans (EJB) and the CORBA Component Model (CCM), and recently XML Web services (e.g. as part of Microsoft's .NET) are advocated to connect distributed applications. With all these technologies, the idea was that if everyone agreed on the same middleware platform then all applications could be easily integrated. However, no universal, all-encompassing distributed systems platform has emerged so far, instead several technologies have been developed with different focus in mind, such as language independence or platform independence.

A couple of years ago it was finally accepted that there will probably be a „next best thing" for the foreseeable future that is incompatible to the old platforms. Consequently there is a need to integrate applications across heterogeneous platforms and to migrate existing applications to new technologies. To do this manually is expensive, labour-intensive, time-consuming, and error-prone. This problem can be solved by using a model driven software development approach in which the application logic is specified and maintained undistorted by underlying technologies and can therefore be migrated to new technologies with less effort.

The described problem also applies to security in distributed systems because in a typical organisation there are different security technologies enforce different security policies on different platforms. Moreover, new security technologies are developed regularly. All this makes it hard to enforce and administer a coherent, organisation-wide security policy. Instead it is advantageous to store a technology-independent security policy in a central location (e.g. this allows policy optimisation and correctness validation), and map this policy to the underlying technologies in a well-defined manner.

The OpenPMF security framework presented in this paper has been designed to meet the requirements of the real-world distributed systems that we have identified in various practical projects. It tries to avoid the weaknesses of security systems for existing distributed systems, such as the Common Object Request Broker Architecture (CORBA) security services, Enterprise JavaBeans (EJB) security, and the security features of the CORBA Component Model (CCM) [Lang03].

Some other work is related to our approach. In [LOBD02], Lodderstedt et al present a UML-based modelling language called SecureUML that supports role-based access control with authorization constraints (in OCL). It is restricted to role-based access control, and the security policy is tied into the application model, while our framework supports several security models and allows the specification of the policy separate from the application model. Epstein and Sandhu propose in [EPSM99] another UML notation for role-based access control with an informal notation for defining constraints, but they do not consider the actual generation of the security system from the model. Our framework can automatically generate a policy repository from the model. Jürjens proposes in [Jürj01] an alternative UML-based approach called UMLsec for specifying requirements on confidentiality and integrity in analysis models. It incorporates concepts from formal methods regarding multi-level secure systems and security protocols into UML, and allows the identification of possible vulnerabilities in diagrams.

The paper is structured as follows: Section 2 introduces model driven software development. Section 3 briefly outlines the EU part-funded research project as part of which our OpenPMF framework and the CORBA/CORBA Component Model (CCM) mappings have been implemented. In section 4, we present the OpenPMF framework and show how it is inspired by model-driven concepts. Further work is briefly described in sections 5. Finally, some conclusions are given in section 6.

2 Model Driven Software Development

The Model Driven Architecture (MDA) [Obje03a] has been advocated by the Object Management Group (OMG) consortium since the late 90's as an approach to language-, vendor- and middleware neutral model driven software development. We argue in this paper that the concepts of model driven software development can be applied to security, and that this yields a number of advantages (see section 6). The essential idea behind MDA is the separation of the technology-independent application model and the concrete application code. Analogously, a centralised, coherent, technology-independent security policy is first modelled and then mapped to different underlying distributed systems platforms and security technologies.

The MDA is based on OMG's modelling standards [Obje03b]: The Unified Modeling Language (UML) is the most widely-used modelling standard today; we use UML to model the structure of the policy repository for our security framework. The Meta-Object Facility (MOF) standardizes a facility for managing models in a repository. The Common Warehouse Meta-model (CWM) standardizes how to represent database models (schemata) etc. XML Metadata Interchange (XMI) is an interchange format for models, based on MOF and XML.

The MDA process consists of three basic steps: In the first step a Platform-Independent Model (PIM) of the application is created in UML by the application specialist.

After that, platform specialists convert the PIM into a Platform-Specific Model (PSM) for a particular distributed systems platform, such as CORBA, CCM or EJB. This process produces two results: platform-specific artefacts (e.g., IDL, deployment descriptors) and a platform-specific UML model that can express both business semantics and technical run-time semantics of the platform-specific solution better than IDL or XML (because of the nature of UML).

Finally, the application code is created. For example, for component-based environments, the MDA process will have to produce interface files, program code files, and various descriptor files.

The crucial idea behind MDA is that the application logic has been modelled in the stable PIM and can therefore be migrated from one middleware platform to another (future) middleware platform with acceptable effort. However, all supported middleware technologies have to be integrated by defining PIM-PSM-Code mappings.

3 COACH Project

The OpenPMF policy management framework has been designed and implemented as part of the COACH (Component Based Open Source Architecture for Distributed Telecom Applications) project [Coac03], a part-funded European Commission Information Society Technologies (IST). At this time of writing, OpenPMF supports CORBA, the CORBA Component Model (CCM), and the Common Secure Interoperability version 2 (CSIv2) security protocol. Support for other platforms is planned, such as XML Web services, EJB, and firewalls. Primarily, COACH produced two complete CCM implementations (Qedo [Qedo03] for C++ and OpenCCM [Open03] for Java) for mission critical application domains such as telecommunications and air traffic control. In addition, the CCM specification was improved (e.g. support for streaming and quality of service), and it was contributed towards OMG specifications for deployment, modelling, and security. OpenPMF is available in both Java and C++.

4 OpenPMF Policy Management Framework

OpenPMF borrows some concepts of model driven software engineering and applies them to security. One of its main design features is that a technology-independent, human-readable security policy is stored centrally, consistently, and flexibly. This allows easy administration, policy optimisation, and correctness verification. Also, both legacy and future distributed systems platforms and security technologies can be integrated with PMF.

4.1 OpenPMF Architecture

Figure 1 shows an architectural overview of the OpenPMF framework. It illustrates how the technology-independent security policy is specified and stored in a repository. At start-up time, this policy is transformed into an efficient internal representation optimised for the evaluation of abstract attributes obtained from the underlying security technology and platform. The policy decision is enforced on the particular underlying platform. This approach is inspired by the model-driven concept in that the abstract model is specified undistorted by underlying technologies. The current version of OpenPMF is only used to secure incoming requests on the target side. Future versions will also protect outgoing requests on the client side or outgoing replies on the target side.

OpenPMF supports different security models, such as role-based access control or discretionary access control. The policy is expressed using our Policy Definition Language (PDL) (see section 4.2). The policy is fed into the Policy Repository using a policy compiler (soon also GUI-based) and is stored in an OMG MOF based Policy Repository (see section 4.3). The technology-independent security policy compares to the PIM of the MDA.

The described technology-independent part of OpenPMF has to be integrated with the underlying distributed systems platforms (e.g., CORBA, CCM, EJB) and security technologies used (e.g., SSL, OMG CSIv2, OMG ATLAS, firewalls, intrusion detection systems). To do this, so-called Transformers (see section 4.5) need to be implemented that obtain the relevant security attributes from the particular underlying security technology and distributed systems platform. To achieve platform-independence of the evaluator, these Transformers also provide the comparison functions for attributes. In addition, an Adapter has to be implemented that is integrated in the invocation path on the target side. It intercepts each invocation and calls the Policy Evaluator. An important feature of OpenPMF is that Transformers and the Adapter have to be developed only once per platform, not for each application. After that, the mapping from the technology-independent policy to the particular underlying technologies is automatic. This integration process compares to the PSM and code generation steps of the MDA.

At this time of writing, the areas marked with solid lines in figure 1 have been implemented in Java and C++, i.e. the CCM/CORBA mappings (e.g. MICO CORBA and Qedo CCM in C++, as well as JacORB CORBA and OpenCCM in Java). The dotted boxes are planned as further work in the near future. The boxes shaded in light grey are platform specific, while the white boxes are platform independent. The dark grey boxes in the diagram represent the underlying CCM and CORBA platforms.

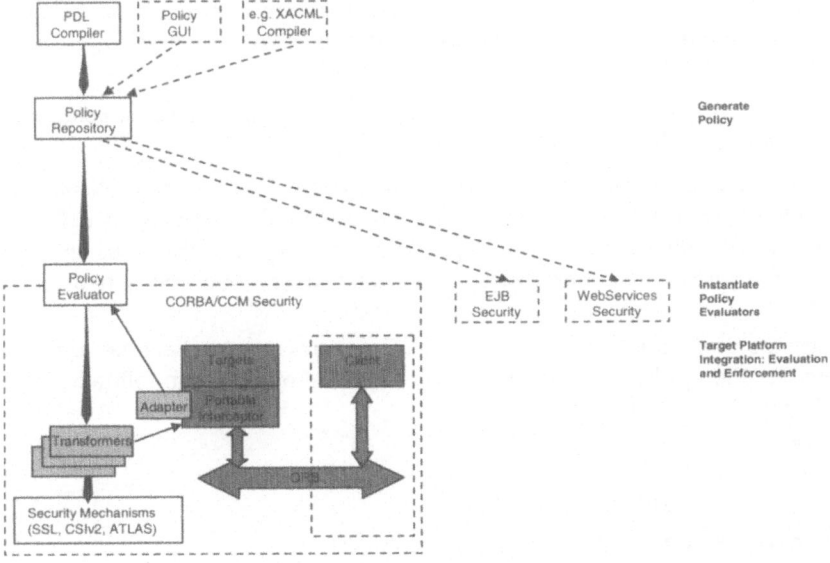

Figure 1: OpenPMF Architectural Overview

4.2 Policy Definition Language (PDL)

Policy Definition Language (PDL) is a human-readable, technology-independent language to specify security policies. It is somewhat inspired by Ponder [DDLS00] and uses concepts of the Principal Calculus [LABW92]. The Principal Calculus is based on the notions of principal and two different privilege delegation relations between principals. There are simple and compound principals. A simple principal either has a name or is a communication channel; a compound principal can express an adopted role or delegated authority. The calculus shows how to reason about a principal's authority by deducing the other principals that it can speak for.

Although PDL comprises a rich set of features, the actual policy that can be enforced on the platform is limited by the features supported by the underlying technologies.

The remainder of this section describes the main PDL features. Consider the following first bank account access control and audit logging policy example:

```
policy /OS/Bank {
   /OS/uli invokes create on /OS/Bank: allow;
   * invokes open on /OS/Bank: allow;
   /OS/uli invokes * on /OS/Account: {allow, log};
};
```

All policies start with the keyword policy and the name of the policy (e.g. /OS/Bank). After that, the actual policy follows in curly brackets. In OpenPMF, the evaluation process starts at the top of the policy file and works its way down. If a rule matches, the corresponding decision (and optional actions) is enforced and the evaluation terminates.

Next, each access rule states which actions should be carried out if the specified one or more callers invoke one or more operations on one or more targets. For example, the first rule above states that /OS/uli is allowed to invoke the operation create on the target /OS/Bank. The second and third rules illustrate how wildcards can be used to define policies that apply to any caller and operation. Furthermore it shows how several actions that are carried out if the rule matches can be specified as a comma separated list of individual actions at the end of a rule, as shown in the third rule. It is also possible to use wildcards for targets. If a match cannot be found, a default deny is applied.

In order to allow structuring the policy after the organization's management structure, it is also possible to nest policies hierarchically.

Furthermore, PDL supports the concepts of groups and roles to cluster multiple clients. This information is obtained from a directory services (LDAP) using a flexible mapping defined in a configuration file. This allows an easy reuse of already existing user databases and management tools in an organisation. For example, /OS/uli and /OS/ras both belong to the group /OS/staff.

Groups and roles are used in policy rules as follows: To express that a client has to be in a group, the client is followed by the keyword in and the name of the group followed by the operation, the keyword on, and the target:

```
* in /OS/staff * on /OS/CVS: allow;
```

Analogously, roles are used with the keyword as:

```
* as /OS/admin invokes * on /OS/testserver: allow;
```

As far as PDL is concerned, there is no difference between roles and groups. The difference is only relevant in the context of the particular mapping implemented by the so called Transformers and the underlying security mechanisms. For example the group information can be obtained directly at runtime from a directory server with different cache strategies, or, if the security mechanism supports it, from an authorisation token.

Not only clients, but also targets and operations can be clustered. While traditional domains cluster targets into domains, PDL allows more fine-grained grouping of individual operations from different targets. This concept is called „application" in PDL. An application definition starts with the keywords define application followed by the structured name of the application. The application members are then provided inside curly brackets. Each operation and target specification starts with the keyword invoke, followed by the operation, the keyword on and the structured name of the target. Again, curly brackets can be used to encapsulate both operations and targets:

```
define application /Banking {
    invoke read on /Tax;
    invoke {open, create} on /Bank;
    invoke create on {/Bank, /Account};
    };
```

One of the most advanced features of PDL is its extended support for delegation. Delegation means that some party (called the intermediate of an invocation) carries out an action on behalf of the original initiator of an invocation. In other words, there is a chain of invocations, and the initiator typically delegates (some of) its privileges to the intermediate. This privilege delegation is particularly important in complex distributed systems because typically parts of the system delegate some of their work to other parts of the system.

Inspired by the Principal Calculus [LABW92], PDL supports two delegation modes: weak and strong delegation. With weak delegation, it is the duty of the target to obtain evidence that the intermediate is really authorised to be a delegate of the initiator. Weak delegation is specified using the keyword quotes between the intermediate and the initiator:

```
/OS/ras quotes /OS/uli invokes * on /OS/Account: allow;
```

This differs from strong delegation, where the initiator of the invocation provides the proof in the form of a (digitally signed) delegation token that states that the intermediate is authorised to be a delegate. The exact functionality of strong delegation depends on the support by the underlying security technology. Strong delegation is expressed in PDL using the keyword speaksfor instead of quote:

```
/OS/ras speaksfor /OS/uli invokes * on /OS/Account: allow;
```

Weak delegation is useful if the intermediate and the target trust each other. The intermediate does all the cryptographic checking of the initiator's credentials, and then just sends these verified credentials to the target where it can be used for the access control decision without any further expensive cryptographic checks (e.g. for validity of a public key certificate).

Strong delegation is useful when there is no sufficient trust between intermediate and target, because there is a proof that the initiator's credentials are correct. It does not mean that the intermediate is really working on behalf of the initiator or that the arguments of the invocation are really correct. This is a general problem of delegation that PDL cannot solve.

The following final example shows how different elements of PDL can be combined to a complex policy rule:

```
/OS/ras as /OS/root quotes /OS/uli as /OS/admin invokes * on
    /OS/Account: {allow, log};
```

It states that if the intermediate /OS/ras (that possesses the role /OS/root) is a weak delegate of the initiator/OS/uli (that possesses the role /OS/admin), and if this intermediate
wants to invoke any operation on the target /OS/Account (on behalf of the initiator /OS/uli),
then the invocation is allowed and the invocation is logged.

4.3 Policy Repository

OpenPMF's Policy Repository is based on the MOF 1.4 standard [Obje03b] and stores the
technology-independent security policy. The policy that is stored in the Policy Repository is
derived from the textual PDL representation. Conversely, a textual PDL representation of the
policy can be generated from the policy stored in the Policy Repository.

Storing a technology-independent security policy centralized (ideally for the whole organisation) has several advantages: Primarily, the policy can be kept consistent more easily and can
be optimised because redundant policy enforcement can be detected. Moreover, having a
technology independent representation of the policy allows the easy mapping to different (and
future) technologies and technology versions.

OpenPMF uses MOF mainly because tools are available that automatically generate CORBA
IDL interfaces or XML descriptors for the policy repository from the MOF model, such as the
IKV medini Meta Model Management software [Ikvm03]. Another advantage of MOF is that
it allows to easily exchange policy models between tools via XMI.

When the application that is protected by OpenPMF is started, an efficient tree representation
of the policy is instantiated based on the information obtained from the Policy Repository.
Each branch represents one policy rule. After that, OpenPMF is ready to protect the application. Each time an invocation arrives at the target side, OpenPMF evaluates the policy by iter-
ating through the tree (see section 4.4). Storing the policy in a tree structure is more flexible
than the traditional access control lists (ACL) or access control matrices (ACM). For example, it is not possible to capture delegation with traditional ACLs or ACMs, while our policy
tree can include separate nodes for the initiator and the intermediate (because different
branches can have a different number of levels from the root to the leaf) and therefore supports the „speaksfor" and „quotes" delegation modes discussed in the Principal Calculus. Another weakness of traditional ACLs and ACMs is that all subjects and objects, respectively,
are of the same uniform type and have to be compared using the same comparison function.
Our approach allows different nodes to be of a different type, and different compare operations for each node. This increases the flexibility of the policy. In summary, while the security
model is effectively hard-coded in traditional ACLs/ACMs, our tree-based approach can represent more flexible security models.

4.4 Policy Evaluator and Adapter

The Policy Evaluator is placed into the OpenPMF architecture in such a way that it can remain independent of the underlying platform and security technologies. During the instantia-
tion of the tree, the function calls to the target security technology specific Transformers (see
section 4.5) are set up. The Policy Evaluator is called by the so-called Adapter, a platform
specific piece of code that is interposed in the invocation path and intercepts all invocations.

The Policy Evaluator is an interpreter for security rules that makes security policy decisions at
runtime based on abstract attributes. It iterates through the policy tree that has been instanti-

ated at application start-up and calls so-called Transformers (see section 4.5) at each node to obtain the relevant security attributes (each node has a type, e.g. the client transport level peer). In addition to delivering the attributes, Transformers also implement the compare relations for the particular attribute that allow the Policy Evaluator to compare the attribute from the underlying platform and security technology with the entry in the policy. OpenPMF has been designed to allow the use of arbitrary compare relations, such as equality, greater-than, smaller-than, or regular expressions.

For each node in the tree (or subtree for the particular application), the Policy Evaluator calls the Transformer, which compares the security attribute obtained from the underlying platform and security technology with the policy entry. If there is a match, then it iterates to the next tree element. If the Policy Evaluator reaches a leaf of the tree, it checks again if the security attribute matches. If there is a match, then the function(s) in the action list are executed.

4.5 Transformers

OpenPMF is also connected with the underlying technology through so-called Transformers. Transformers have several purposes: Firstly, they obtain the security attributes used during policy evaluation from the underlying platform and security technology. Secondly, they translate technology-specific security information into technology-independent security attributes. Thirdly, Transformers can apply additional mappings on a higher level of abstraction, such as identity-to-role mappings or clustering into application domains. Finally, Transformers provide the Policy Evaluator with the required comparison functionality (equality, greater-than, smaller-than etc.) used to compare the particular obtained attribute with the entry in the policy.

In each node of the policy tree, a Transformer chain is invoked to obtain and transform the relevant attributes. Each Transformer in the chain only carries out one particular attribute mapping. Consider for example that the underlying security mechanism is CORBA Security Level 1 (based on SSL), then the lowest-level Transformer would obtain the X.509 identity of the invoking client. The next Transformer up would then obtain the abstract client identity from the X.509 identity, typically using a directory service and an appropriate caching strategy. The next Transformer up would then carry out the mapping from the abstract identity to the corresponding group. This chaining together of Transformers facilitates code reuse because, e.g. in the example, if the underlying security mechanism changes, then only the bottom two transformers need to be replaced

Transformers have to be hand-coded by platform specialists (once per platform, not once per application) and need to be integrated manually with the underlying technologies. The current OpenPMF version includes Transformers for CORBA/CORBA Security 1.x, CCM, and CSIv2, which will be described in the following.

For CORBA, OpenPMF includes a Transformer for obtaining target-side security information (in particular the called target object and the invoked operation) through the Portable Interceptor interfaces. The current version integrates with our MICOSec [Mico03] CORBA Security implementation (for the MICO ORB), which can obtain type or instance information about the target (the target type is insufficient for many common security policies [Lang03] [LaGS01]). An additional CORBA Transformer extracts client and target security mechanism identifiers from the underlying SSL/TLS protocol through the MICOSec CORBA Security Level 1 interfaces.

OpenPMF also provides Transformers that integrate with the CORBA Components Model (CCM) [Obje03b], a programming language independent specification for creating server-side, scalable distributed applications. CCM is a good example of a complex component-based distributed systems platform and thus demonstrates the applicability of our framework well. The improved CCM container specified as part of the COACH EU-IST project (see section 3) includes interceptors that allow the CCM Transformers to obtain component specific information, such as per-component instance names.

In addition, OpenPMF includes Transformers for the OMG Common Secure Interoperability version 2 (CSIv2) protocol [Obje03a], which adds privilege delegation and authorization token transfer (as well as client-side authentication) on top of SSL/TLS. The protocol and upcoming API are inspired by the Principal Calculus, just like our PDL policy language. Delegation is a particularly important requirement for component-based applications because there are typically numerous and complex invocation chains between various components that comprise a distributed application than in traditional client-server systems [Lang03].

OpenPMF is also integrated (although not through Transformers) with a Public Key Infrastructure (PKI), a Privilege Management Infrastructure (PMI) based on the OMG Authorization Token Layer Acquisition Service (ATLAS) [Obje03b], directory services based on OpenLDAP for storing user data and an IIOP Domain Boundary Controller (DBC)

5 Further Work

In the near future, OpenPMF will be integrated with several other distributed systems technologies (e.g. J2EE, XML Web Services, Web servers, .NET Remoting) and security mechanisms (Kerberos, SAML). To achieve this, new Adapters and Transformers need to be developed (e.g. SAML Transformers for XML Web services). It is also planned to develop a tool that translates between XACML and PDL to allow the integration of upcoming XML Web Services security products into OpenPMF. Furthermore, future PDL versions will support constraints expressed in the Object Constraint Language (OCL), fined grained information filtering, Mandatory Access Control (MAC), more advanced role-based access control models, and a new approach to the „owner" concept.

6 Conclusion

In OpenPMF, a technology-independent security policy is stored in a centralized, standardised policy repository for a number of distributed applications, platforms, and security technologies. The policy is expressed using a technology independent policy definition language. OpenPMF, which is available in Java and C++, is then integrated with the underlying technologies through well-specified interfaces.

This approach has a several advantages: First, security policies across many different platforms and security technologies can be integrated and stored centrally in one place, which ensures the policy consistency and optimisation across multiple platforms and security technologies. Secondly, the technology-independent policy language is easier to administer than the intricate details of the underlying technologies, and also makes the validation of the semantic correctness of the technology-independent policy feasible.

From a more theoretical perspective (and related to the CSIv2 mapping) it is an advantage of OpenPMF that the same security theory based on the Principal Calculus is used from the abstract security policy language (PDL) down to the line-level protocol (CSIv2).

In summary, our OpenPMF policy management framework shows that the concepts of model driven software development (such as the OMG Model Driven Architecture) can be successfully applied to security. OpenPMF reduces the effort for the development of secure distributed applications, and helps to achieve integrated, consistent and correct security policies.

References

[Coac03]   COACH Consortium. Component Based Open Source Architecture for Distributed Telecom Applications. (http://www.ist-coach.org). May 2003

[DDLS00]   Damianou , N., Dulay, N., Lupu, E., Sloman, M. Ponder: A Language for Specifying Security and Management Policies for Distributed Systems, Imperial College (UK) Research Report DoC 2000/1, October 2000

[EpSa99]   Epstein, P, and Sandhu, R. Towards a UML-Based Approach to Role Engineering. In *Proceedings of the Fourth ACM Workshop on Role-Baased Access Control*, pages 135-143, ACM Press, 1999

[Ikvm03]   IKV. Meta Model Management – M³ (http://www.ikv.de/content/Produkte/ meta%20model%20management_e.htm), May 2003

[Jürj01]   Jürjens, J. Towards Development of Secure Systems using UMLsec. In H. Hussmann, editor. *Fundamental Approaches to Software Engineering, 4th, International Conference, Proceedings, LNCS,* pages 187-200, Springer, 2001

[LABW92]   Lampson, B., Abadi, M., Burrows, M., Wobber, E. Authentication in Distributed Systems: Theory and Practice. *ACM Transactions on Computer Systems 10,* 4, pp 265-310, November 1992

[LaGS01]   Lang, U., Gollmann, D., and Schreiner, R. Verifiable Identifiers in Middleware Security. *17th Annual Computer Security Applications Conference (ACSAC) Proceedings,* pp. 450-459, IEEE Press, December 2001

[Lang03]   Lang, U. Access Policies for Middleware, PhD Dissertation, Computer Laboratory, University of Cambridge, UK, February 2003

[LoBD02]]   Lodderstedt, T., Basin, D., and Doser, J. SecureUML: A UML-Based Modeling Language for Model-Driven Security, In: J.-M. Jézéquel, H. Hussmann, S. Cook (Eds.): UML 2002 – The Unified Modeling Language. *5th International Conference, Dresden, Germany, September 30 – October 4, 2002. Proceedings, Lecture Notes in Computer Science, LNCS 2460,* Springer, September 2002.

[Mico03]   MICOSec Team. MICOSec CORBA Security Service Web Page, http://www.micosec.org/, May 2003

[Obje03a]   Object Management Group. Model Driven Architecture Web Page. www.omg.org/mda. Needham, MA, May 2003

[Obje03b]   Object Management Group. Catalog of OMG Specifications. November 2003, (www.omg.org/ technology /documents/spec_catalog.htm)

[Open03]   OpenCCM Team. OpenCCM Project Web Page, http://www.objectweb.org /openccm/, May 2003

[Qedo03]   Qedo Team. Qedo (Quality-Enabled Distributed Objects) CCM Implementation Web Page, http://qedo.berlios.de/, May 2003

Is Grid Computing more Secure?

Thomas Obert CISM, CISSP

Deutsche Bank AG
CTO-SMT
Alfred-Herrhausen-Allee 10
65760 Eschborn
thomas.obert@db.com

Abstract

Grid computing is a relatively new discipline for IT Manager. Several research areas are already working on grid computing solutions and many of grid computing environments have already been established in research networks, where a lot of computing power is required and university budgets are low. More and more, large IT companies like IBM, HP and Sun are emerging in the grid computing technology and develop real life applications. The target is to provide solutions, which could be of high benefit for companies. A commercial use of grid computing requires many aspects like stability, scalability, reliability and of course security. The current research activities are focussing on architectural issues mainly and the interdependencies with Web Service research and development. Security is crucial especially when using shared resources of geographically far distributed grid nodes which also underly local security policies and should remain in a autonomous computing mode.

1 Introduction

1.1 Provides grid computing the next generation of Information Technology?

In days where organizations are short of money and resources and underlie high pressure in global competition, new opportunities have to be discovered, which allow the efficient and effective use of existing resources without additional costs. Again, in 2003 the bankruptcy filings in US rose to 1,654,847 which is a slight increase of 2.6 % compared to the same 12-month period in 2002 [AOUS04]. In Europe, the number of insolvencies also climbed 3.9 % compared to 2002 to a total number of 157,138, in Germany the percentage increase was even above with 5.5 % (total: 39,700) [CRED04].

Information Technology has grown to a basic requirement to succeed in global markets. Future-oriented companies can not survive in a highly diverse market without highly automated and efficient information processing technologies and strategies. Information Technology is anywhere, anytime. The Internet enables even small and medium businesses to compete in global markets, independent from the time zone of the company's head office. „Faster and cheaper" revealed the main survival strategy of the new millennium.

In the late 80's and 90's, business process re-engineering promised large companies to gain more profitability by optimizing existing weaknesses. They focussed mainly on the human factor. How do people perform within their job? What measures could reduce dependencies of human interfaces? How many people are required to perform a certain task or process within a minimum of time (and hopefully with best quality)? Many companies have learned where the limits are and that human always acted differently are.

The number of transistors per integrated circuit still doubles every couple years. This observation has been made already in 1965 by Gordon Moore as part of his research at Fairchild Semiconductor and is since then well known as „Moore's law".

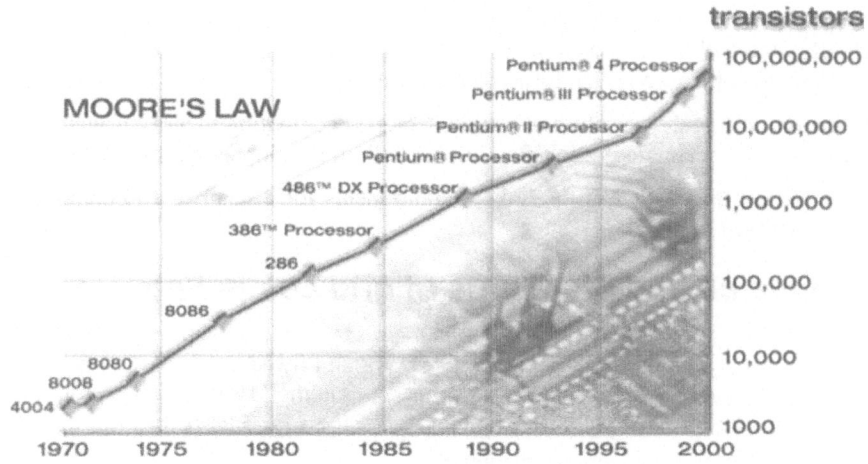

Figure 1: Moore's Law is still valid!

Derived from this law, the performance of computer processors are increasing exponential, sometimes faster than the software available. Today's Desktop PCs and Laptops have more performance than a mainframe in the 70's. But the mainframe filled large rooms and required a complex water cooling system to reduce the temperature to an acceptable level. These „number cruncher" had more communities with a radiator than with a PC equipped with an x86 processor.

A usual Desktop PC in companies is equipped with a Pentium Processor, with at least 1 Giga-Hertz, 128 MB RAM and a hard disk with several GBytes. A lot of resources, a company have invested in, but which is not used very efficiently. The most processor-consuming application running on nearly every PC is a fancy Screensaver. This is waste, isn't it? Often, at least 50% of hard disk space is generally unused. In a company with 250 PC's and 40 Giga Byte hard disks a potential disk space of 5 Tera Byte (!) are available and ready to be consumed.

This discovery is not astonishing to IT manager at all. It is a fact from the beginning of growing IT infrastructures ruled by Moore's law. But business manager realize especially in tough times seemingly opportunities as the solution for all their problems. Grid computing is the relatively new IT discipline which provides solutions to utilize the existing but unused computing resources within a certain physical or logical area, e.g. within a company's intranet.

Grid computing is highly distributed among different technologies and platforms. Increased distribution across borders leads directly to different rules and policies. Especially security is affected and must be guaranteed in a system that utilizes computing resources from several different intelligent calculators and information stores. Information security can be handled by install methods to achieve confidentiality, integrity and availability of the managed information.

1.2 Goals

After reading this article you will know, what the current status of grid computing research is, which grid computing groups are important to know and what their current working topics are.

Additionally, you will have a detailed understanding of the major challenges of grid computing, especially in coherence with information security aspects.

Finally, the recent research results and activities of grid computing security is well-known by you decide how this technology can advance your activities to increase information security.

Especially the existing risks and the linked requirements for a security grid computing base have been discussed in detail.

1.3 Research and Standards of grid computing

The Globus Alliance [GLOB04] comprises reputed research facilities from all over the world. 5 universities and research institutes from U.S., U.K., and Sweden are flanked by several institutions in the Globus Alliance Affiliates program. Another 15 universities contribute via this program to the research activities. Among these the Max-Planck Institute for Gravitational Physics represents the German chapter.

The common goal of all research institutions is to conduct research and develop fundamental technologies behind the „Grid". Grid computing let people share computing power, information stores and information itself with a highly distributed infrastructure without ruling over local autonomy. The alliance is working in four main areas:

- With fundamental *Research* the basic problems and questions of grid computing are addressed, discussed and proper solutions and standards are developed.

- To validate the concepts developed in research area, *Test beds* are required to under grid the assumptions and findings with real world experience. The alliance helps in planning and building test beds.

- *Software Tools* are outcome of excessive tests and serve as valuable programs to design and implement real world applications.

- To gain business value out of research results the alliance also develops large scale grid-enabled *Applications*.

To avoid that marketing manager will create several new product series with Trademarks and Registered properties based on the word „Grid"; the Globus Alliance gives some advice for a practical definition. Already in 1998 a still valid definition has been given by Carl Kesselmann and Ian Foster [Fost02]:

„A computational grid is a hardware and software infrastructure that provides dependable, consistent, pervasive, and inexpensive access to high-end computational capabilities."

In further research activities, the definition has been revised and enlarged to address also social and political issues, which is described in detail in [KeFo01]. The conclusion of the authors is that grid computing is concerned with „coordinated resource sharing and problem solving in dynamic, multi-institutional virtual organizations."

The birth of the World Wide Web in the early 90's, commonly called the Internet, was based on the idea of virtual information domains. With the exploded growth of the Internet founded on the commercial use of it, marketing bubbles like business 2 business (B2B) already created virtual organizations distributed through the whole world sharing not only information, but also collaborate in an automated manner in cross-company business processes.

The Global Alliance provides a three-point checklist which needs to be fulfilled to provide solutions that could be considered to be a grid:

„... a Grid is a system that:

3. *coordinates resources that are not subject to centralized control* ... (A Grid integrates and coordinates resources and users that live within different control domains—for example, the user's desktop vs. central computing; different administrative units of the same company; or different companies; and addresses the issues of security, policy, payment, membership, and so forth that arise in these settings. Otherwise, we are dealing with a local management system.)

4. *... using standard, open, general-purpose protocols and interfaces...* (A Grid is built from multi-purpose protocols and interfaces that address such fundamental issues as authentication, authorization, resource discovery, and resource access. As I discuss further below, it is important that these protocols and interfaces be standard and open. Otherwise, we are dealing with an application specific system.)

5. *... to deliver nontrivial qualities of service.* (A Grid allows its constituent resources to be used in a coordinated fashion to deliver various qualities of service, relating for example to response time, throughput, availability, and security, and/or co-allocation of multiple resource types to meet complex user demands, so that the utility of the combined system is significantly greater than that of the sum of its parts.)"

The final question still to be answered is then, what is *the Grid*? The Grid itself is a set of open and general-purpose standards that allow any interested party to establish resource sharing arrangements dynamically.

Another interest group in grid computing is the Global Grid Forum. As part of the open source software project development platform „Source Forge", the Global Grid Forum is a meeting point for open source developer with the common target to develop open source based applications and tools for grid computing. The forum is partitioned in different categories:

- Applications and Programming Models Environment (APME),
- Architecture (ARCH),
- Data (DATA),
- Grid Security (GRID SEC),
- Information Systems and Performance (ISP),
- Peer-to-Peer (P2P) and
- Scheduling and Resource Management (SRM) [GrFo04].

Working groups are focused on a special technology while *research groups* are long-term focused to address fundamental questions and provide standard proposals.

1.4   Grid computing and Web Services

One major target of the Global Grid Forum [OGSA04] is to define and standardize to *Open Grid Service Architecture (OGSA)*. Services in a Grid are generally formed as Web Services. The Open Grid Service Infrastructure (OGSI) [OGSI04] specifies which general functionality Grid Services must provide to achieve a standard compatibility among them. This includes requirements like machine-readable interface definitions, extensibility of services, lifetime of services etc [ReSc04].

1.5   Grid Applications

Research often requires number crunching calculations of complex mathematical equations, e.g. in chemistry or physics. It is no miracle that some scientist already formed a public grid community. A desktop client can be downloaded by anybody who has interest in participation in the grid and so passively supporting diverse research activities [GRID04]. The research grids comprise projects focusing on cancer, anthrax and smallpox. Additionally a Patriot Grid is available which let you participate actively in fighting bioterrorism. Currently over 2.5 million devices are connected to the global research grid.

Another very famous grid computing application is SETI@Home. A screen saver installed on a Desktop PC which is connected to the Internet starts calculation when activated. The goal is to evaluate signals received from anywhere in the universe to „Search for Extraterrestrial Intelligence". This global network of 3 million computers averages about 14 TeraFLOPS, or 14 trillion floating point operations per second, and has garnered over 500,000 years of processing time in the past year and a half. It would normally cost millions of dollars to achieve that type of power on one or even two supercomputers.

IT leader like Sun, HP and IBM already offer grid computing solutions. They differ often in the variety and complexity of their solution. In general, grid computing is still a research area which means, that the available applications are still immature.

2   Grid computing Security

Security is a major requirement to achieve reliable results from a computer program. The following chapters will focus on the threats, grid computing environments have to face. The discussion starts with a threat and risk assessment which leads directly to an overview of current standardization activities and working groups in the grid computing Security arena. The conclusion will provide an outlook and will give you an impression, what security architects have to prepare for within the next 2-5 years.

2.1   Threat and Risk Assessment

A grid computing Infrastructure is characterized by:

* High amount of various devices,
* Different computing environments and operating systems,
* Mainly autonomous local (security) policies,
* Geographically span over the whole globe,
* Grid device owners with all conceivable political and ethical attitudes.

This enumeration already gives enormous space for discussion of possible threats a grid computing environment has to face. In the following the most important (and likely) threat scenarios will be discussed:

1. Unauthorized access to local grid devices

To contribute with local resources in a global grid, a program has to be installed and run locally. The software provides the required services to be stand-by all the time the device is up and online. In today's' operating systems, most applications run in a user or administrator mode which allows the software to access local resources with required privileges. Even if the privileges have been cut to shape, software is always in risk of lacks and bugs. Thousands of times in past has shown, that software leakages enable malicious attacker to gain unauthorized access to devices located anywhere in the world.

2. Gain privileged access in an unauthorized way

With privileged access permissions, data and information theft as well as hijacking of personal transactions are feasible consequences. With adequate methods, a hacker could gain control over the device by using stealth methods. These are hard to identify, especially for a usual computer user. Controlling a device remotely leads today to a lot of misuse, e.g. in while creating and sending unsolicited mail (SPAM) to thousands of e-mail account al around the world. And this is a very friendly scenario.

3. Misuse of general available grid services

Open architectures and standards are a preferred lecture of professional hacker. Reading between the lines, hackers have a gut feel where and how possible misuse could lead to more authorization, the standard is aimed to provide to a user. Supplemental experience of typical implementation mistakes helps an attacker also to identify possible weaknesses. The fact, that normally a large amount of devices participate in a grid enables the bad guys to test different weaknesses only once on a device or in a way, that possible local log files or alerts could not easily lead to the conclusion, a hacker is testing your grid service for weaknesses.

Another feasible scenario focuses on the fact, that a grid computing environment provides methods, which are implemented in today's' generation of computer virus. An automatic distribution of the viral code makes a virus really dangerous. Especially the latest exemplars like Sasser have shown that fast distribution over a public network can create damage of millions of Euros within hours. What if a viral code would hook on standard functionality of general grid services to distribute through the whole grid?

4. Implementation weaknesses

As with all new technologies and strategies, immaturity is a well-known accompanist with the first versions. The major challenge for the developer is focussing on the establishing of the expected functionality: Make the thing happen and run! Sure, standards play here the major role. But if the grid service could execute a task as expected, security is second thing to reconsider and check in detail. Remember, the current standards are still under construction and design mode, also the ones focussing on security.

5. Falsify results of individual grid nodes

As already mentioned above, the Patriot Grid has already been established to investigate and evaluate hints and facts to fight against bioterrorism. In the world of the early 2000, terrorists are able to use computer also as a kind of weapon. An attacker could identify and assault individual grid nodes with the aim to falsify computing results in a way, that the final conclusion, drawn by the central unit creates a misleading result.

6. Misuse of anonymity requirements

A system owner should be able to grant access to his grid node based on different purposes like research areas, lawsuits, content sharing, etc. This requires a reliable authentication mechanism. A bad guy could undermine such authorizations to gain unauthorized access to computing power of nodes which do not fit the respective task to perform.

2.2 Security Architecture of Open Grid Services

The Global Grid Forum is working on Security standards for an *Open Grid Services Architecture* (OGSA) to avoid misuse of grid services which could lead to a lack of confidentiality, integrity or availability of grid nodes and authorities. Because grid services rely on web service architecture and technology, the working groups are watching the activities in the related web service security working groups and other standardization bodies. This is necessary to avoid the creation of conflicting standards and not to delay application development. Working activities are heavy in the OGSA itself, while the security working group has defined and discussed a first draft of an architecture paper in first quarter in 2003.

The primary outcome of the Open Grid Security Architecture Security Working Group (OGSA-SEC-WG) will be two documents [OGSC03]:

1. *The Security Architecture for Open Grid Services*: This document will describe a security architecture intended to be consistent with the security model that is currently being defined for the Web Services framework used to realize OGSA's service-oriented architecture.

2. *OGSA Security Roadmap*: This document is a roadmap enumerating a set of proposed specifications to be defined in the Global Grid Forum in order to ensure interoperable implementations of the OGSA Security Architecture. This group will discuss topics related primarily to the development of these two documents

Because the grid services are defined as completely relying on web services, the OGSA-SEC-WG is referencing within all their architecture topics to the respective web service standards. They assume that the respective WS-standards will provide the necessary functionality to make grid services secure.

In detail, the Security Architecture for Open Grid Services is structured by describing the security challenges in a grid environment, followed by definition of the grid requirements. After a short introduction into the grid security model principles, the model is discussed in detail. Another important reference part within the architecture draft is the reference to other related security standards.

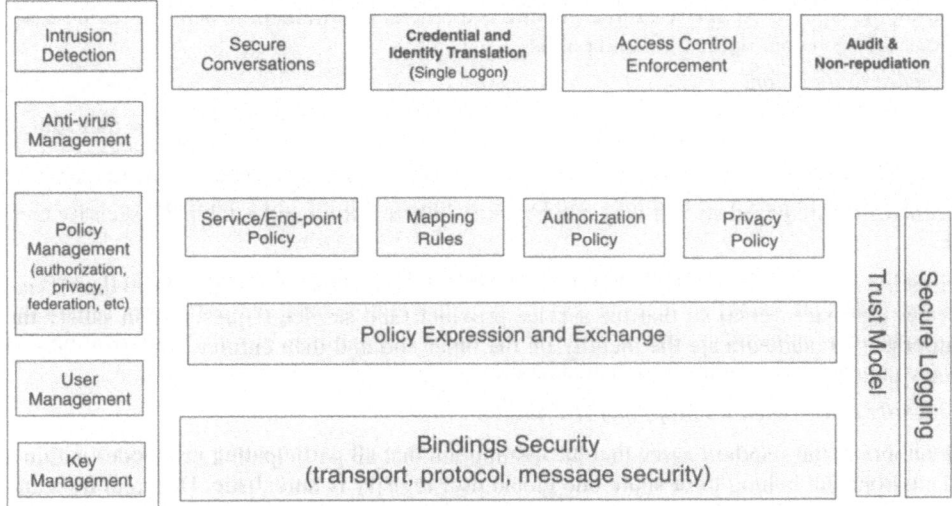

Figure 2: Components of Grid Security Model [OGSA03]

Integration, Interoperation and Trust are the main challenges, the Grid Security Model has to face and to provide fundamental answers. A grid environment is characterized by a virtual organization, independent from geographical, political, cultural and commercial boundaries. The integration of grid nodes into a virtual organization requires an extensible architecture, the use of existing services and an implementation agnostic approach with respect to local autonomy. Interoperability is described best by protocol and interface standards. In case of grid services a strong reference to existing web services standard is pretended. Federation of identities and secure inter-communication between grid service nodes completes the interoperability principle. Finally, trust elementally completes the requirement principles. A virtual organization requires an anchor to which all operation requests could be aligned to without going to risk confidentiality and integrity violations.

The Grid Security Model is described completely by 9 distinct areas:

1. Binding Security

This section considers the use of web service oriented protocols for inter-service communication like SOAP over HTTP, message queue or any other protocol. When using HTTP, which is of course the preferred method in current web service implementations and considerations, SSL is recommended as mechanism to provide secure communication between grid nodes.

Additionally IIOP bindings based on CORBA are considered to be another meaningful implementation path. Finally IPSec provides high security on packet level out of the TCP/IP stack and is another option to be supported.

2. Policy Expression and Exchange

Grid services are provided by autonomous grid nodes. The communication and security policies have to be considered from all communication partners when establishing connections. Each participating node within a grid service is asked to provide its local policies to each other. Finally, mechanisms have to be found, which enable the grid service provider and grid service requester to agree on a common policy ad hoc.

Securing the Open Grid Service Infrastructure is a crucial requirement to achieve secure associations between communication end points.

3. Secure Association.

A service requester and a service provider are likely to exchange more messages and submit requests subsequent to an initial request. In order for messages to be securely exchanged, policy may require service requester and service provider to authenticate each other. In that case, a mechanism is required so that they can perform authentication and establish a security context.

Facilitating secure association is required to establish the identity of a requestor to the service provider (and vice versa) so that the service provider (and service requestor) can satisfy the requirements to authenticate the identity on the other end and then enforce authorization and privacy policies based on the established identity

4. Identity and Credential Mapping/Translation

The authors of the standard agree that the assumption that all participating grid nodes within a grid environment belong to or share one global user registry is unrealistic. Different trust and security domains will emboss the heterogeneous grid environment. It is recommended to provide support of federation based on industry standard specifications, e.g. Liberty Alliance [LIAL04].

5. Authorization Enforcement

Each participant within a grid environment will have its own authorization enforcement to allow a service requestor proper access rights to local services and resources. Differently to identity sharing, authorization will remain a local domain.

6. Privacy Enforcement

In respective cases it must be possible for a requestor to access a grid service anonymously. Minimum authorizations shall be granted to unnamed identities required to execute the requested service order. The protection of private information is important in certain service environments, e.g. medical patient information. According to well defined privacy policies the grid services within a given grid environment must respect the restrictions given.

7. Trust

The members of the virtual organization (grid environment) have to agree to a trust model they all belong to. Trust is necessary to enable uncomplicated and secure service execution among different security policy domains. Trust models should be based on existing trust strategies as implemented in Kerberos or PKI applications.

8. Secure Logging

For high-level audit-related service secure logging is required. Especially when performing business critical process steps using grid environments, auditors will have an inherent interest to pursue all relevant activities.

9. Management of Security

Security Management embraces all functions applicable to various aspects of binding, policy, federation and trust. These include key management for cryptographic functions, user registry management, authorization, privacy and trust policy management and management of mapping rules which enables federation

2.3 Security-related WS specifications and standards

Because Grid Services rely mainly on Web Service technology, a list of most interesting and important security-related Web Service specifications and standards is given in the next paragraphs:

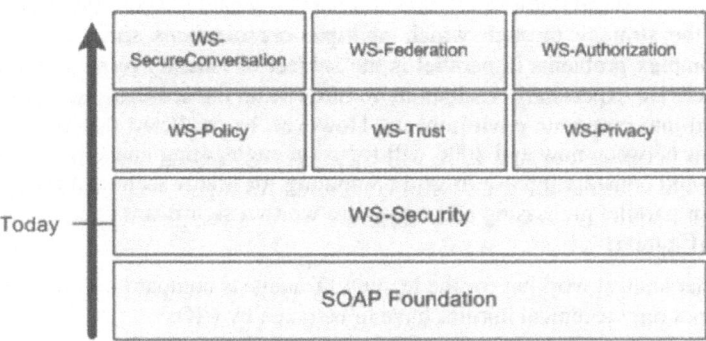

Figure 3: Overview of security-related
Web Service specifications

Initial Specifications

WS-Security: describes how to attach signature and encryption headers to SOAP messages. In addition, it describes how to attach security tokens, including binary security tokens such as X.509 certificates and Kerberos tickets, to messages.

WS-Policy: will describe the capabilities and constraints of the security (and other business) policies on intermediaries and endpoints (e.g. required security tokens, supported encryption algorithms, privacy rules).

WS-Trust: will describe a framework for trust models that enables Web services to securely interoperate.

WS-Privacy: will describe a model for how Web services and requesters state privacy preferences and organizational privacy practice statements.

Follow-On Specifications

WS-SecureConversation: will describe how to manage and authenticate message exchanges between parties including security context exchange and establishing and deriving session keys.

WS-Federation: will describe how to manage and broker the trust relationships in a heterogeneous federated environment including support for federated identities.

WS-Authorization: will describe how to manage authorization data and authorization policies.

3 Future of grid computing

Ian Foster, member of the Globus Alliance and globally one of the leading researchers in the grid computing area, was interviewed by CIO.com. The main focus was set on the future of grid computing and the benefits of commercial applications of the future. Foster advices CIOs, to start „… internally on a small level is the most promising direction." [HiFo03]. Foster said further on grid computing's impact on the enterprise applications market: „Increasingly, people will work out how to build various forms of service provider offerings. No one has been able to do that effectively to this point." It seems that there is a real market.

In 2003 grid computing was named in the TOP 10 list of strategic IT topics CIOs are going to take a deeper look in commercial use within the next 18-24 months. Gartner Inc. vice president Carl Claunch has been interviewed in 2003 and here is, what CIO.com finally published: „Grid computing, the strategy through which multiple organizations share computing resources to solve complex problems in parallel is the subject of industry hype at the moment, according to Claunch. He expects grid computing to move from the academic and government research sectors and into corporate environments. However, he predicted that most commercial implementations between now and 2006 will focus on engineering and scientific applications. Managers should consider the use of grid computing for highly technical problems that can be broken up for parallel processing and which are worth a significant amount of systems integration work." [Conn03]

Anne Powell, another analyst working for the leading IT analysts company Gartner Inc. wrote in an abstract, that not only technical hurdles have to be taken by CIOs:

„In addition to the technical issues to be resolved, there are business issues to address. If an application is run on 10 systems owned by 10 different organizations, it is important to establish who pays the costs and how those costs are charged to the organization deemed to be responsible for them. Another question to address will be whether all the systems are secure enough to allow competing companies to use the same grid." [Powe03]

As of today, grid computing is still a more scientific than commercial solution. Large companies like IBM, HP and Sun as well as some smaller ones like Platform and United Devices are working intensively on commercial solutions. IBM uses its global research capabilities to integrate customer wishes and to develop first applications. Certainly it is a good advice for CIOs to have a deep look into the grid computing activities within these companies. Nevertheless, security remains on major topic not really solved as of today for a reliable and commercial grid computing environment.

References

[AOUS04]   Administrative Office of the U.S. Courts: Bankruptcy Filings 2003,
            http://www.uscourts.gov/Press_Releases/pr02252004.pdf

[CRED04]   Creditreform, Wirtschaftsanalysen, Insolvencies Europe 2004,
            http://www.creditreform.de/angebot/Downloads_Analysen/Wirtschaftsanalysen/
            Europe.pdf

[GLOB04]   http://www.globus.org

[Fost02]   Ian Foster: What is the Grid? A three point checklist,
            http://www.globus.org/research/papers.html#Overview%20Papers

[KeFo01]   Carl Kesselmann, Ian Foster: The Anatomy of the Grid,
            http://www.globus.org/research/papers.html#anatomy

[GrFo04]   http://forge.gridforum.org/projects/sourceforge/document/All_Groups

[GRID04]   http://www.grid.org

[ReSc04]   Alexander Reinefeld, Florian Schintke: „Grid Services", Informatik Spektrum
            April 2004, Pages 129-135

[OGSA04]   https://forge.gridforum.org/projects/ogsa-wg

[OGSI04]   https://forge.gridforum.org/projects/ogsi-wg

[OGSC03]   https://forge.gridforum.org/projects/ogsa-sec-wg

[LIAL04]   http://www.projectliberty.org/

[Loft04]   Jack Loftus: „Grid computing gaining attention, but not security"
           12 Apr 2004, SearchSecurity.com
           http://searchsecurity.techtarget.com/originalContent/0,289142,sid14_gci959316,
           00.html

[HiFo03]   Matt Hines in interview with Ian Foster: „Expert charts future for grid comput-
           ing"
           22 Apr 2003, SearchCIO.com
           http://searchcio.techtarget.com/qna/0,289202,sid19_gci895039,00.html

[Conn03]   James M. Connolly, „Gartner: IM hot, grid computing getting warmer"
           27 Mar 2003, SearchCIO.com
           http://searchcio.techtarget.com/originalContent/0,289142,sid19_gci890867,00.ht
           ml

[Powe03]   Anne Powell: „A Down-to-Earth View of Grid computing „"
           31 Mar 2003
           http://www3.gartner.com/DisplayDocument?id=390263&ref=g_search

Tamper-Resistant Biometric IDs

Darko Kirovski · Nebojša Jojić · Gavin Jancke

Microsoft Research, One Microsoft Way,
Redmond, WA, 98052, USA
{darkok | jojic | gavinj}@microsoft.com

Abstract

We present FaceCerts, a simple, inexpensive, and cryptographically secure identity certification system. A FaceCert is a printout of person's portrait photo, an arbitrary textual message, and a 2-D color barcode which encodes an RSA signature of the message hash and the compressed representation of the face encompassed by the photo. The signature is created using the private key of the party issuing the ID. ID verification is performed by a simple off-line scanning device that contains the public key of the issuer. The system does not require smart cards; it can be expanded to encompass other biometric features, and more interestingly, the ID does not need to be printed by a trusted or high-end printer, it can be printed anywhere, anytime, and potentially by anyone. The ID verifier uses a single scan process which does not require the use of displays. We detail system's components and present a preliminary performance evaluation using an in-field experiment.

1 Introduction

A typical identity certification such as a driver's licence, passport, or visa, consists of a personal portrait photo, an arbitrary message, and one or more features whose purpose is to guarantee authenticity. Commonly, authenticity is assured using sophisticated printing procedures that are difficult to replicate: holograms, watermarks, micro-printing and threading, special print paper, and chemical coating [1]. However, the wide availability of such technology has rendered forging most personal ID documents a relatively simple task with results often perceptually comparable to the originals. Authentication of imprinted features via electronic devices is complex and most importantly, expensive [1].

In all-digital environments such as smart cards or lasercards [2], authenticating the source of a personal ID is an easy task using off-the-shelf public cryptography [3] and one-way authentication protocols [4]. Typically, the stored photograph as well as other biometric features are concatenated to the textual message and hashed. The resulting hash is then signed using the private key of the issuer. In-field authentication is performed using the public key of the issuer by a verification device (e.g., smart card reader), which also must display the signed data. While the security of such systems can be made to follow even the strictest security standards, the cost of supporting systems makes them undesirable for widespread identity certificate applications such as national ID cards, driver's licences, or passports. A simple smart card costs about $5-35, while a lasercard reader costs about $2400 [5].

In this paper, we combine best of both worlds into a new technology we call FaceCerts and show how sophisticated specialized compression algorithms can allow the use of paper as an inexpensive hybrid analog/digital domain on which both the human readable information, i.e., text and photo, and the secure digital information can be stored in a way that allows a single-scan verification.

S. Paulus, N. Pohlmann, H. Reimer (Editors): Securing Electronic Business Processes, Vieweg (2004), 160-175

1.1 FaceCerts

Instead of relying on the sophistication of the printing process to impose difficult forging, FaceCerts rely on public-key cryptography for provable security, while deploying a standard-quality low-cost color printing process which keeps the cost of printing a FaceCert two orders of magnitude lower than that of a smart card or a lasercard. Issuing and verification of FaceCerts is illustrated[1] in Figure 1.

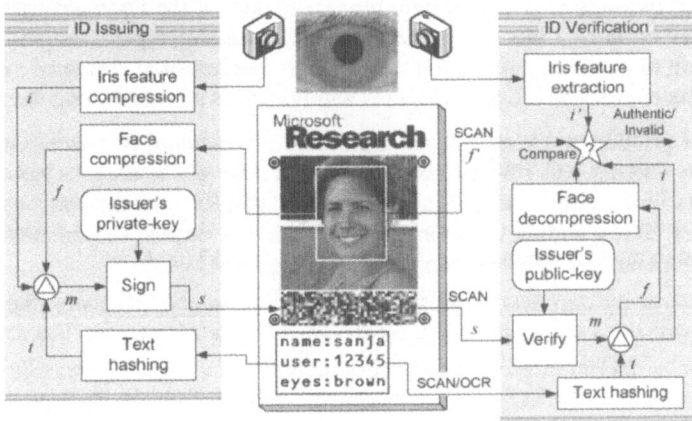

Figure 1: Functional block diagram of the actions taken at the issuer and verifier of FaceCert IDs.

The information certified on a FaceCert is both biometric and textual. The biometric data can encompass facial, iris, and/or other features. The digital photo that represents a portrait of the FaceCert holder, is the only biometric feature printed in plain-text on the ID. The textual data can be of arbitrary length and is also printed on the ID. The ID is certified in the following way. First, the textual data is hashed using a cryptographically secure hashing algorithm such as SHA1 [7]. The resulting 160-bit hash is denoted as t. Next, the facial features on the photo are identified and compressed using an algorithm partially described in this manuscript in Section 3. The best-effort output of the face compression step, denoted as f, is constrained to 1-2Kbits. The actual compression rate can be adjusted to meet the desired balance of picture quality vs. barcode size, which is mandated by the application. Picture quality affects system performance for two main reasons: first, to impose low likelihood of a false negative or positive during detection and second, to set the desired level of facial feature detail which an adversary, whose photo has not been taken for the ID, must resemble in order to use the authentic FaceCert.

Other biometric information such as iris or fingerprint patterns can be also certified and verified using a FaceCert ID as illustrated in Figure 1. For example, details of a FaceCert system that encompasses person authentication via iris patterns is described in [8]. We omit the details of the feature extraction and compression process for iris patterns in this manuscript; instead, we recognize a string of bits, i, as an output of this process. The iris digest can be typically compressed down to 700-1.5Kbits [8] depending upon the desired balance of error rates vs. barcode size.

---

[1] The iris scan in this figure has been taken from the CASIA iris database. Portions of the research in this paper use the CASIA iris image database collected by Institute of Automation, Chinese Academy of Sciences [6].

Messages $f \| i^2$ and t are merged into a message $m = (f \| i)\Delta t$ t using a reversible non-commutative operator Δ such that $(\exists\Delta^{-1}) f \| i = m\Delta^{-1} t$. Note that $f \| i$ are not hashed because their plain-text values must be retrieved during FaceCert verification. Also it is safe to assume that message t can be recovered error-free from a printed FaceCert because of deployed high-performance optical character recognition engines [9], [10]. Shortly, we review this operator in more detail.

In the next step, message m is signed with the private key of the FaceCert issuer. We use an RSA private key of $|m| + 1$ bits to sign/decrypt m. Considering typical lengths of f and i, we bound the length of m within $1300 < |m| < 3400$ bits. The resulting signature s is encoded using Reed-Solomon error correction codes [11] and printed as a barcode onto the FaceCert.

Two aspects of printing and scanning are important: *degradation of printed color* and *scanning reliability*. Independent studies have shown that state-of-the-art inks have an estimated life of 65 years on a cotton paper in average indoor display without noticeable fading and several years of corresponding outdoor lifetime [12]. The second requirement has been already addressed in modern barcode standards such as PDF417 [13].

A FaceCert verifier initially scans all three printed components: the photo, the text, and the barcode. The barcode is decoded into the originally printed signature s. The scanned textual data is also converted into a text-string using reliable optical character recognition. For successful verification of a FaceCert, the text and the barcode need to be read without errors. Next, after verifying/encrypting the signature with the corresponding public RSA key of the issuer [3], the verifier obtains the signed message m. After the verifier hashes the text to obtain t, it computes $f \| i = m\Delta^{-1} t$. Then, the verifier decompresses f into a subimage of the original photo that contains the facial features. Finally, the verifier quantifies the level of similarity between the decompressed and scanned face. If the two images are similar within the maximum tolerable compression-print-scan noise, only then the FaceCert is declared as authentic.

In case additional biometric features such as iris patterns are required for person authentication, the FaceCert verifier captures a photo of person's iris, extracts its features, and compares them to the features decompressed from i. If the feature comparison yields positive identification, the FaceCert is declared as authentic. Since the FaceCert verifier does not query a trusted database with iris digests (i.e., does not perform the traditionally error-prone iris recognition procedure), the detection threshold in the FaceCert system can be set to adjust for much lower false positive error rates than „classic" iris recognition systems [8]. In general, two verification procedures are recognized in the FaceCert system: (*a*) low-cost, where only facial features are verified, and (*b*) high-security, where both facial and iris (possibly, fingerprint and retina) patterns are verified in order to decide upon FaceCert's authenticity.

Finally, we revisit the selection of the operator Δ. Its purpose is to prevent adaptive existential forgery on the signing primitive, e.g., RSA, where the adversary creates a valid signature with no control over the message [14], [15], [16]. This problem is well known to the cryptography community and has been addressed in several protocols including the probabilistic signature scheme with message recovery (PSS-R) [17], which is based upon optimal asymmetric encryption padding (OAEP) [18]. Although several integrity check mechanisms for RSA signatures can be used with different security properties, the exemplary PSS-R achieves provable security with near-optimal redundancy used in order to achieve a desired level of security. In

---

[2] Operator $\|$ denotes concatenation.

case Δ = PSS-R, then message m is created by setting $M = f\,||\,i$ and hashing $M||t||r$ to obtain $w = h(M||t||r)$, where $h()$ is a hash function and M, w, and r refer to the corresponding variables in Figure 2 in Section 5 of [17]. PSS-R derives $m = b||w||r*||M*$ where b is a single bit set to 0 and variables $r*$ and $M*$ are created as in Figure 2 in Section 5 of [17]. Signature's integrity check in this case is performed according to the *RecP SSR* procedure presented in Section 5 of [17] with the last step altered to: if $h(f\,||i||t||r)= w$ and $b = 0$ then return $f\,||\,i$ else return REJECT. The signed message m has bit-length $|(f\,||\,i)| + 2hLen + 16$, where $hLen$ is the length of the output of the hash function $h()$ in bits (160 bits for SHA1 [7]).

Under the assumption that the cryptographic functions are signing the biometric properties and the associated text in a provably secure manner, the security of FaceCerts stems from the fact that changing a single bit of the textual message or altering the photo beyond the print-scan noise causes a global change in the barcode that appears to be random without the knowledge of the issuer's private key.

In this manuscript, we focus on the two crucial components of the system, a novel face compression algorithm and a statistical metric for computing similarity between an original and a corresponding compressed face in the presence of print-scan noise. The basic requirement for the face compression algorithm in the FaceCert system is to compress an image of a face into only several thousand bits with preserved sharpness of the main facial characteristics. We present a novel face compression technology based on eigenfaces [19] and improved variants of principal component analysis [20], [21]. We show that our technology achieves desired compression rates even when the component analysis is trained on a small database of images.

2 Related Work

The idea of using digital technology and cryptography as key to enabling low-cost photo identification is not new. For example, one centralized card authentication system which relies on displays has been developed and marketed by Kodak [22]. It stores a users photograph on a card in a highly compressed code on the magnetic stripe or smart-card memory. The authentication procedure entails reading the encoded photograph, comparing it against its database entry, and displaying it on a screen for comparison against the cardholder.

System presented by O'Gorman and Rabinovich [23] is the most related to our work as it aims at the same goal – however, it relies on signing *image digests which are tolerant to scanning errors* instead of *actual compressed images*. In this manuscript, we show a successful attack on the O'Gorman-Rabinovich system that manipulates an image using a simple procedure so that its digest equals the digest of another distinct facial photograph. By using a compressed version of the facial structure within an image instead of the image digest, in the case of FaceCerts such attacks are reduced to seeking perfect human look-a-likes. Since this is a limitation of the distinctiveness of a human face, the FaceCert system supports additional biometric information such as iris patterns.

2.1 Comparison with Existing Solutions

Biometric Recognition. Another alternative to FaceCerts is biometric recognition. Biometrics has been defined as a process of automatically recognizing a person using distinguishing traits. Several biometric solutions have been proposed via face, speech, fingerprint, handwriting, iris, and retina recognition. Solid survey of these techniques can be found at [24]. Just as Face-Certs, a person identification system that relies on biometric solutions *must* involve a human verifier who must ensure the identification system is not fooled. For instance, an adversary can show a realistic size photo of the face of an authorized person to the face detector or play a voice recording to a speaker detector.

While some types of biometric identification such as fingerprint detection are reliable, they can be used maliciously to incriminate innocent users [25]. A malicious detector can record a person's fingerprint, create its physical copy, and then, incriminate this person at will. This renders fingerprint detection systems relatively undesirable for most person authentication scenarios. Some biometrics systems are commonly subject to complaints for invasion of privacy [5]; e.g., wide-spread face detection points can disclose at any time one's location to a party who gains control over such a system. Nevertheless, the three most important disadvantages of almost all biometric recognition systems are:

- *reliability*, in particular in face and speaker recognition, does not stay constant as the system scales up, which commonly renders these systems highly prone to false alarms and false positives [26], [27], and

- *centralized decision making*– the verifier needs to be connected to a central trusted server which actually performs the identification, which in a sense implies:

- *high cost*– the equipment performing the verification is costly.

For most applications, such solutions are inconvenient, costly, and most importantly, unreliable.

Smart cards. Smart cards represent an effective solution to person identification. A big advantage of smart cards is all-digital communication with the verification device. A simple scenario is to have a smart card which contains a digital photo, personal biometric and description data, and a signed hash of this information using the private key of the issuer. Verification is performed by hashing the photo and the personal description data and then verifying this hash against the signature using the public key of the issuer. Finally, the verifier *must* display the verified digital photo, so that a human can acknowledge that the person being identified is on the photo. Note that a printed photo on the smart card is ineffective because a malicious party can trivially extract the contents of a valid card, then create another one with the same digital contents however with a different printed photo.

Smart cards just as FaceCerts, cannot be used to store private information (e.g., private keys which are revoked if smart card is lost). It has been demonstrated so far that smart cards cannot be considered a secure storage because it is relatively easy to extract the hidden information even without reverse engineering the smart card [28]. Exemplary attacks that have successfully identified encryption keys (both symmetric and private keys), have been based on analyzing smart card's I/O behavior via differential power analysis [29] or timing analysis [30].

Finally, there are several differences that strongly favor FaceCerts to smart cards.

- A smart card based system must display the photo, whereas FaceCerts only scans the ID with no requirement to display any imagery. Medium-quality displays are significantly more expensive than CCD (charge-coupled device) scanners (up to a factor of 5), which reduces significantly the cost of the verifying infrastructure.

- Personal IDs are frequently lost or damaged. Replacing a FaceCert involves only reprint, whereas replacing a smart card involves purchase of another hardware device in addition to burning this device with the appropriate identification contents – two orders of magnitude differential in replacement cost.

It is important to stress that smart cards should not be understood as competition to Face-Certs; on the contrary, the information printed on a FaceCert can be stored in its digital format on a smart card and verified in an "all-digital manner" without scanning. The main benefit of FaceCerts is that they enable the inexpensive paper ID version.

Watermarks. Another technique for authenticating content is to hide an imperceptible secret information, watermark, in the digital photo. One serious disadvantage of this type of ID authentication is the fact that in most watermarking systems, the secret hidden in the photo must be present in the verifier. Hence, a single broken verifying device renders the entire system broken. A public-key watermarking system has been developed, however, with a different target application [31]. This system requires significantly longer host signals than a single photo to reliably detect the existence of a given secret. Also, such a system would require that the secret used to mark a photo is renewed after issuing several distinct IDs. In summary, using modern watermark-based technologies results in the least robust and secure performance for secure identity certification.

3 FaceCerts -Face Compression

The computer vision community has studied various models of faces in the past. The system we are proposing in this paper does not need to encode the face image to facilitate recognition of the person when observed under various new conditions, such as angle of view and illumination changes, aging, or facial hair changes, but rather in the very same photograph from which the face code has been extracted. Thus, we do not face the difficult issue of over-training that is present in a typical face recognition application. Rather, our needs are simply for a very efficient face image compression.

As faces form a class of images with substantially smaller variability then the class of all natural images, they can be compressed better by using a class-specific compression scheme than using general-purpose compression algorithms, such as JPEG. To develop such a scheme, we need to model the variability of facial images, i.e., the probability distribution $p(\mathbf{g})$, where $\mathbf{g}$ denotes the vector of pixel intensity in a facial image. Then, according to Shannon's coding theorem, the code length for the image g is bounded bellow by $- \log_2 p(\mathbf{g})$ bits. To build this distribution, we focus on 2D subspace models.

The problem of subspace learning can be elegantly defined in terms of a generative model that describes joint generation of the subspace coordinates, or factors, $\mathbf{y}$ and the image $\mathbf{g}$ by linearly combining image components in the factor loading matrix Λ:

$$p(\mathbf{g}, \mathbf{y})= N (\mathbf{g}; \boldsymbol{\mu}+ \Lambda \mathbf{y}, \Phi)N (\mathbf{y}; \mathbf{0}, \mathbf{I}), (1)$$

where Φ constitutes the non-uniform image noise, i.e., the variability not captured in the subspace model. Λ is an $n \times k$ matrix used to expand from the k-dimensional subspace into a full n-dimensional one, where n is the number of pixels in the image $\mathbf{g}$. The parameters Λ, Φ, and $\boldsymbol{\mu}$ can be learned by maximizing the likelihood of a set of images $\{\mathbf{g}_t\}$,

$$\log p(\{\mathbf{g}_t\} \log \sum_t \int_{yt} p(\mathbf{g}_t, \mathbf{y}_t), (2)$$

and a good low-dimensional representation of the image tends to be $E[\mathbf{y}|\mathbf{g}]$. The above probability model, called factor analysis (FA), also allows for the design of the optimal encoding strategy for the factors $\mathbf{y}$. A realted method, principal component analysis, was used by Moghaddam and Pentland for face recognition and compression [32]. By limiting their representation to the central part of the face they were able to represent each image in a carefully manually preprocessed database, with only 85 bytes describing 100 face factors y. In our case, we need a more robust coding scheme that does not require precise manual registration of images, and can encode more than just the central region of the face. We also include hair and the face shape, in order to lower the probability of false positive matches.

Recently, an extension of the subspace models that takes into account the possible transformation of the facial image, such as translations, rotations and scale has been proposed in [21]. In this model, called transformed component analysis (TCA), an additional random transformation variable T is applied to the image expanded from $\mathbf{y}$, and a new image $\mathbf{h}$ is observed:

$$p(\mathbf{h}, \mathbf{g}, \mathbf{y})= N(\mathbf{h}; \mathbf{Tg}, \mathbf{\Psi})N(\mathbf{g}; \mu+ \Lambda\mathbf{y}, \mathbf{\Phi})N(\mathbf{y}; \mathbf{0}, \mathbf{I})p(\mathbf{T}).$$

Such a model, when trained on an image set tends to automatically align all images to create the most compact subspace representation. The regular subspace models, in presence of tranformational variability in the training data will tend to create blurry models, while TCA creates sharper components.

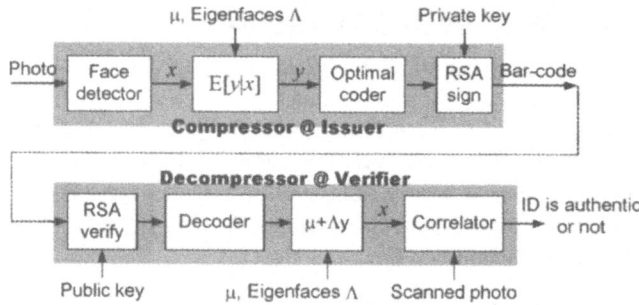

Figure 2: Block diagram of the face compression and decompression algorithm encapsulated within the FaceCert issuing and verification system. The Λ-subspace model $\mathbf{y}$ follows a Gaussian distribution and thus can be encoded close to its rate-distortion limit.

A hierarchical generative model like this is naturally suited for efficient compression, as it decomposes the variability in the data. To develop the coder, the model is first trained on a large number of face images, i.e., the subspace origin μ and subspace vectors Λ are estimated together with the pixel noise levels $\mathbf{\Phi}$ and distribution over the used transformations (rotations, scales, shifts and deformations) $p(\mathbf{T})$. Then, for a particular image to be encoded, the hidden variables are inferred and each of the conditional probability distributions, i.e., $p(\mathbf{T})$, $p(\mathbf{y})$, $p(\mathbf{g}|\mathbf{y})$, $p(\mathbf{h}|\mathbf{g}, \mathbf{T})$, is used in an appropriate entropy coder to create codewords for describing the geometric position and deformation of the image, as well as its subspace coordinates. As the model distributions are either multinomial or Gaussian, this procedure is straightforward. For example, for a Gaussian source a non-uniform quantization is used that is fine close to the mean of the Gaussian and coarse in the unlikely areas of the subspace.

The transformation information is then combined with the face cropping information needed to capture the face from the scanned ID and encoded in the barcode, while the subspace encoding is illustrated in Figure 2. First, given an ID photograph, we identify the facial structure to be modeled $\mathbf{x} = N(\Lambda\mathbf{y} + \mu, \mathbf{\Phi})$ with eigenfaces using a face detection algorithm [33], [34]. Vector μ denotes the first order statistics of the input image $\mathbf{x}$. As the posterior $p(\mathbf{y}|\mathbf{x})$ can be computed using the Bayesian rule, hence we compute:

$$\log p(\mathbf{y} \mid \mathbf{x}) = -\log p(\mathbf{x}) - \frac{1}{2}\mathbf{y}\mathbf{y}' - \frac{1}{2}\log(2\pi\mathbf{I})$$

$$-\frac{1}{2}(\mathbf{x} - \Lambda\mathbf{y} - \mu)'\Phi^{-1}(\mathbf{x} - \Lambda\mathbf{y} - \mu) - \frac{1}{2}\log(2\pi\Phi) \quad (3)$$

which points to: $E[\mathbf{y} \mid \mathbf{x}] = \hat{\mathbf{y}} = (\mathbf{I} + \Lambda'\Phi^{-1}\Lambda)^{-1}\Lambda'\Phi^{-1}(\mathbf{x} - \mu)$. Assuming $\Phi = \sigma^2 I, \sigma \to 0$, we conclude that $E[\mathbf{y} \mid \mathbf{x}] = \hat{\mathbf{y}} = (\Lambda'\Phi^{-1}\Lambda)^{-1}\Lambda'\Phi^{-1}(\mathbf{x} - \mu)$ which in the case when the basis vectors are orthogonal (e.g., Λ has been derived using PCA [20]) results in a simple least-squares approximation $\hat{\mathbf{y}}$ follows a Gaussian distribution, $\hat{\mathbf{y}} = (\Lambda'\Lambda)^{-1}\Lambda'(\mathbf{x} - \mu)$. In the Λ-subspace, $\hat{\mathbf{y}}$ and thus can be efficiently encoded using codes with long block lengths (for analysis see [35], [36]), so as to approach the theoretical rate-distortion limit for the distribution illustrated in Figure 4.

3.1 Face Compression Illustration

We conducted several experiments in order to evaluate system performance. We trained Λ using 400 images of 64x64 faces extracted from personal photo collections of our colleagues employees using a face detection algorithm that follows the work of Viola et al. [34]. The resulting dataset contains alignment errors that were dealt with automatically by the transformed component analysis. We tested the coding performance on the Yale and Rockefeller face databases. Later in the paper we also report a separate field test of the entire creation and verification process by issued over 4000 IDs in two days and estimating the false positive and negative verification rates.

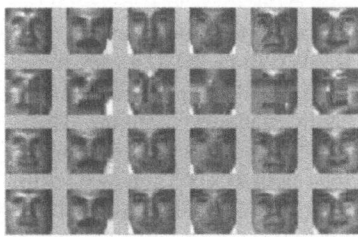

Figure 3: Five faces extracted from the Yale face database and the compressed images using JPEG (second row), PCA (third) and TCA (fourth). TCA achieved an RMSE of about ten intensity levels, considerably bellow the difference between any two images in the set. Both TCA and PCA were trained on a separate unrelated database of 400 images derived from personal digital photo collections.

In Figure 3 we show comparison between the JPEG, PCA and TCA coders on several faces in the test set. On average, at low bitrates, we were able to make JPEG encode the gray level images with 255 levels with 360 bytes and a root mean square error *rmseJPEG*= 36, while both PCA and TCA performed better, with *rmsePCA*= 17, *rmseTCA*= 10, and with significantly lower bit rates of about 200 bytes for a 200-dimensional representation of images. TCA models used only shifts as the set of possible transformations **T**. The *rmse* differences among the images in the test set were between 35 and 65, even for images of the same people with slightly different expressions. Thus, the TCA result is well beyond the error of random photo replacement.

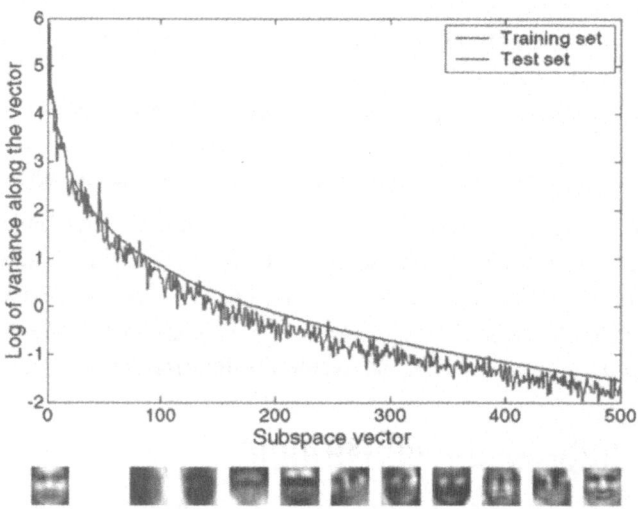

Figure 4: The distribution over the coordinates (strengths of the subspace vectors, or principal components) for the training set (blue), and a test set (red). According to the rate-distortion analysis of the blue distribution computed on the training set of 10000 images, for errors of roughly one intensity level out of 255, the image code would be only about 500 bits long. Bellow, we show the mean and the first ten subspace vectors.

Figure 4 shows the distribution of component strengths over the coordinates in the subspace. For this distribution, the optimal rate-distortion function indicates that for the error of standard deviation of 0.5 intensity levels (out of the 255), the number of bits needed to encode the image is about 500[3]. In other words, at 500 bits per face image, the coding error is expected to be smaller than 0.5% of the dynamic range of the image. This value is far bellow the scanning error of the system. On the same plot, we plot the distribution over the subspace coordinates of images in a separate small face dataset (165 images), using the derived subspace vectors (first ten of which are shown at the bottom of the figure). Note again that this results depends on fine alignment that TCA algorithm provides. In practice, it is possible that to reduce the cost of ID creation, a coarser alignment would be performed. In the field test we describe later, for example, we used the face code that was 1000 bits long.

4 FaceCerts – Verification

FaceCert verification consists of simple template matching. To be in accordance with the models in the previous section, a likelihood over the windows in the image can be used as a cost metric instead of template differences. For example, to use the likelihood as the similarity measure, one would take the message **f**, extract the window size and detection threshold *thr* as well as the subspace parameters y to compute:

$$\log p(\mathbf{h} \mid \mathbf{y}) = \int_{\mathbf{T},\mathbf{g}} \log p(\mathbf{h}, \mathbf{g}, \mathbf{T} \mid \mathbf{y})$$

---

[3] Result reported for Yale database. Images in the Rockefeller database required about 1600 bits for similar performance.

for all windows of appropriate size. If $\max_\mathbf{h} \log p(\mathbf{h}) > thr$, then the ID does contain the face encoded in the bar code. If the position of the isolated face is stored in the barcode, the integration over transformation $\mathbf{T}$ is not necessary.

The detection threshold *thr* depends on the compression-print-scan error which FaceCerts-must tolerate. This error can be used by the adversary to minimally modify the facial features on an image from a given collection of valid FaceCert IDs in order to create another image possibly as close as possible to adversary's facial features. In the next section of the paper, we show that the combined compression and scanning error can be made so low that such an attack becomes futile – it leads to the altered face that is virtually indistinguishable from the original.

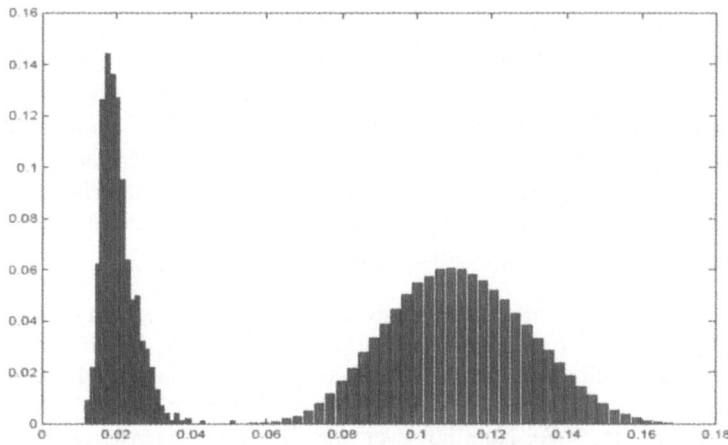

Figure 5: The distribution of the compression errors vs. the distribution over the pairwise distances on the set of 4239 faces we collected in our field test. The abscissa denotes the normalized Euclidean distance between two images, whereas the ordinate quantifies the distributions of interest.

5 Experiments: A Field Test

To test the entire solution, we developed and installed fully automated ID creation centers at a technology exhibition visited by thousands of people. The visitors created their own IDs by scanning their existing smartcard badges to provide personal information and then standing in front of the camera which took a snapshot of their face. Then, the face detection software localized the face allowing both proper framing of the photograph and the speedup in the face compression algorithm described above by reducing the search space for the transformation variable. The proper FaceCert ID was then printed on an inexpensive business card paper and issued to the user, who could then scan it at various stations equipped with business card readers and scattered across the exhibit floor. The entire print and scan test was thus performed without any manual intervention.

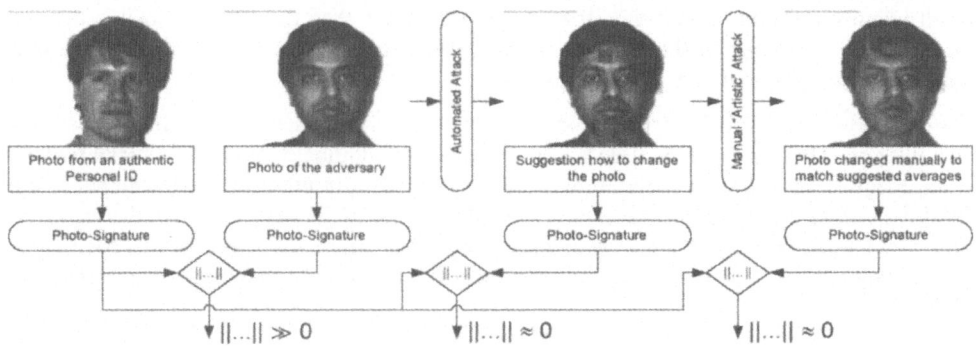

Figure 6: An example of the attack on the O'Gorman-Rabinovich Personal ID System. A photo from an authentic ID card (first photo) is obtained by the adversary (second photo) who does not resemble the person on the authentic ID card. Therefore, his photo has a different photosignature. After applying the automated attack, the adversary obtains the set of guidelines on how the first order statistics of his photo must be changed (third photo) and finally, the adversary artistically edits his photo so that the suggested changes in the first order statistics are fulfilled while having a realistic visual appearance (fourth photo).

In this way we collected 4239 faces and corresponding FaceCerts. Before the test, we had estimated the best generative model parameters for the code length of 1000 bits using EM optimization on a database with only 1000 faces. The compression error typically achieved using this face model and data allocation, was within 2-3% of the dynamic range. The scanning error was about 1% of the range. Note however that the scanning error can be reduced by printer/scanner combo calibration to be virtually nonexistent. Also, the compression error can be reduced to sub-2% levels by increasing the code to 2000 bits.

For our target code length of 100 bits and the inexpensive combination of an off-the-shelf printer and a business card reader, we had set up the detection threshold to 5% of the dynamic range of the images. We anticipated that such a threshold was high enough not to expect any false negatives (failed scans of valid IDs), and so none of the FaceCerts that were properly created failed the verification step.

To get a sense of the probability of false positives (IDs with photograph replaced that still passed the verification), we computed all pairwise distances on the set of collected faces as well as all compression errors (see Figure 5) and plotted the probability distributions on a single graph. In our event with 4239 distinct people, the probability of face substitution passing the verification step, i.e., that one of the computed pairwise distances was bellow the threshold of 5% was in the order 10^{-6}. Note that this probability is significantly lower than the probability that one finds a look-a-like (estimated between $10^{-4} - 10^{-3}$). As we have stressed in Subsection 1.1, by using other biometric features within the FaceCert system, one can rectify the deficiency of using only person's face for identification. Finally, we looked at the handful image pairs that could be interchanged on the IDs based upon our threshold selection;

they indeed looked sufficiently similar that a human verifier would not make the difference between them.[4]

Note that data allocation of 1000 bits leads to a barcode of the size equal to roughly one fifth of the size of the image on the ID. While our particular implementation only targeted a particular price/security ratio, there is plenty of ways to improve the rates depending on the application requirements. Techniques such as increasing in the barcode size, calibrating the scanner/printer combo, retraining the compressor on a larger database can be used to set the error rate to practically an arbitrary level without any significant change in the core technologies described in the paper.

6 Cryptanalysis of the O'Gorman-Rabinovich ID Card System

In order to demonstrate the effectiveness of our approach with respect to an existing technology, in this section, we briefly overview the key ingredient of the O'Gorman and Rabinovich personal ID system and then present a simple polynomial attack that guides an adversary to edit her photograph such that it has the same digital signature as a given photograph that is imprinted on an authentic ID card.

The ID card technology presented by O'Gorman and Rabinovich in [23] relies on a specific image digest function the authors call a photo signature method (PSM). PSM is a digest of the photographic content on a certified license. The objectives in PSM design are four-fold: (*i*) it must be a unique (or very close to a unique) identifier of the photograph; (*ii*) PSM must be concise (320 bits for a DSA signature); (*iii*) PSM must be invariant to noise, so that a PSM that has been subject to fading, dirt, nonuniform contrast change, and other common card noise still yields the same as or very close to the original PSM; (*iv*) the photograph must be difficult to modify, so as to match its PSM with that of a different photograph. As oppose to FaceCerts, both the original PSM as well as its cryptographic signature are printed on an ID card. Verification of the ID card is governed by deployed crypto-protocols.

The authors propose the following PSM: 1) Transform the original image into lower resolution images by performing low-pass filtering and subsampling by successive powers of two. These images are of sizes: level $l_0 \to N \times N$; level $l1 \to N/2 \times N/2$; level $l_2 \to N/4 \times N/4$; etc. 2) Choose all or some of these multiresolution levels, $l_{L1} \le l \le l_{L2}$, and place a grid of size $I \times J$ on each. At each grid intersection location, determine the average of pixels in $k \times k$-sized pixel neighborhoods, $G^l(i,j), 0 \le i < I, 0 \le j < J$. 3) For each grid point, a feature is determined. This feature represents the relative intensities of the neighboring grid points. The feature $S^l(i,j)$ is contained in 8 bits, where each bit corresponds to the eight grid neighbors and where a bit is one if the neighbor is greater than the grid value and zero otherwise. 4) For PSM elements at grid intersection points of each level, l, represented as $S^l(i,j)$, each PSM element is the next grid intersection value from the next level. For instance, if $L1=1$ and $L2 = 4$, then the PSM elements are:

$$S(i,j) = \{S^1(1,1), S^2(1,2), S^3(1,3), S^4(1,4),$$
$$S^1(1,5), S^2(1,6), ...\} \quad (5)$$

---

[4] Unfortunately, due to privacy reasons we cannot show any photographs from the face database in the paper.

In general, for a total number of chosen levels, L, lowest chosen level, $L1$, and a grid size of $I \times J$, the sequence of levels is, $l(i,j)=[L1+(i+jJ)]_L$.

Given a valid photo ID card and a photograph of the adversary, the goal of the attack is to edit adversary's photo such that its digital signature equals the one presented on the valid ID card. In that case, the adversary can replace the original photo on the ID card with her own. In this manuscript, we present an attack that achieves this goal by relying on two separate procedures: a) an automated phase – which creates a guidance for the next step, and b) artistic follow-up editing – which manipulates a photograph to satisfy the constraints posed by the automated step a). The steps of the attack and their effect on the corresponding photographs is illustrated in Figure 6.

The goal of the automated step of the attack is to create a set of guidelines for artistic editing. The idea behind the guidelines is based upon the fact that the important statistic collected for a given image is based upon the averages (first order statistics) of certain image regions $G^l(i,j)$ and most importantly, not their values but relations between them (e.g., whether $G^l(i,j) < G^l(i +1,j)$). Therefore, the attack is aiming to change the first order statistics of adversary's image such that its image regions obey the same relations as the relations of the image on an authentic ID card, while inducing minimal change to the adversarial image. An example of such changes, marked as darkened or enlightened rectangles on the adversarial image after the automated attack (see Figure 6), would guide the artistic editor of the image on what has to be changed on the image such that it is semantically appealing but still satisfies the suggested first order statistics. An example in Figure 6 shows that only slight edit of person's hair, an enlightened chin, and darkened right ear, is sufficient to equalize the PSMs of photos of two persons who do not resemble each other[5].

The algorithm that creates the guidelines for artistic editing is presented using the following pseudo-code:

Lets denote the first order statistics of adversary's photo as $G_A^L(i,j)$, the authentic photo as $G_o^L(i,j)$, and the resulting photo as $G_R^L(i,j)$ for all considered levels $L1 \leq L \leq L2$.

---

for all $L1 \leq L \leq L2$, $0 \leq i < I$, and $0 \leq j < J$
  set $G_R^L(i,j) = G_o^L(i,j)$.
repeat $I \times J \times L$ times
  for each $L1 \leq L \leq L2$
   for each $0 \leq i < I$
    for each $0 \leq j < J$
     set $G_R^L(i,j)$ to a value as close as possible to
     $G_A^L(i,j)$ such that the relations of $G_R^L(i,j)$ with
     respect to its neighbors in the resulting image
     are the same as the relations of $G_o^L(i,j)$ and
     its neighbors in the original authentic image.
     update all $G_R^l(i',j')$ that intersect with $G_R^L(i,j)$.

The attack first sets the first order statistics of the resulting image G_R to the ones exhibited by the authentic image G_O. Then, it iteratively reduces the distances between individual components of G_R and G_A such that for each alteration in G_R, the $\gtrless$ relations between the altered grid component $G_R^l(i,j)$ and its neighbors stay the same as the relations between the corre-

---

[5] Note that the quality of edits is poor on the example image.

sponding $G_O^L(i,j)$ and its neighbors in the authentic image. By construction, this algorithm leads to a set of first order statistics G_R which is at minimal linear distance with respect to G_A and still satisfies all the constraints imposed by the photo-signature of G_O. The worst-case run-time of the algorithm is $O(I^2 J^2 L^2)$; however, in all empirical runs of this attack, we have achieved the desired result in $O(IJL)$. The outermost loop of the attack is aborted if no G_R component is changed throughout a single run of that loop. An example of how adversary's photograph looks like after it is updated for corresponding distances between the final G_R and G_A, is presented as second from the right in Figure 6. Finally, the adversary encounters a trivial and only artistically challenging task to edit his photograph so that the changes in the first order statistics have visually realistic semantics as presented in the rightmost photo in Figure 6.

7 Conclusion

In this manuscript, we propose FaceCerts, a system for creating and verifying secure identity certificates. FaceCerts prevent tempering with the photograph or associated text by encoding the cryptographic signature of the face and text in a compact barcode readable by ordinary scanners.

Today, in a typical scenario, the verifier of the ID needs to connect to a remote database and retrieve a stored photograph for the comparison with the ID. In our system, all the necessary data for verification is securely stored on the ID itself, in a form of a barcode. The system does not depend on face recognition technology, but rather on the much more reliable face compression. We show that 100x66 pixel color face images can be compressed to about 1000 bits, while the color barcodes can reliably carry two to three thousand bits. A potential issuer of FaceCerts, such as a government agency, for example, may have a significantly larger database of facial images to train even better compression systems, using one of the methods we described.

References

[1]   R.L. Van Renesse. Optical Document Security. Artech House, 1998.

[2]   LaserCard Systems Corp. Details available from: http://www.lasercard.com.

[3]   R.L. Rivest, A. Shamir, and L.A. Adleman. A method for obtaining digital signatures and public-key cryptosystems. *Communications of the ACM*, vol.21, no.2, pp.120–6, 1978.

[4]   A. Freier, P. Karlton, and P. Kocher. The SSL protocol Version 3. December 1995.

[5]   T. Wang. Issues In Brief: The Debate over a National Identification Card. The Century Foundation, 2002.

[6]   CASIA Iris Image Database. On-line presence at: http://www.sinobiometrics.com.

[7]   A.J. Menezes, P.C. Van Oorschot, and S.A. Vanstone. Handbook of Applied Cryptography. CRC Press, 1996.

[8]   D. Schonberg and D. Kirovski. Iris Compression for Cryptographically Secure Person Identification. *IEEE Data Compression Conference*, to appear, 2004.

[9]   P.Y. Simard, D. Steinkraus, and J. Platt. Best Practice for Convolutional Neural Networks Applied to Visual Document Analysis. *IEEE International Conference on Document Analysis and Recogntion*, pp.958– 962, 2003.

[10]   Adobe Inc. OCR fonts. On-line presence at: http://www.adobe.com/type/browser/P/P_058.html.

[11]   I.S. Reed and G. Solomon. Polynomial Codes over Certain Finite Fields. *SIAM Journal of Applied Mathematics*, pp.300–304, 1960.

[12]   Wilhelm Research. Technical report available on-line at: http://www.wilhelm-research.com.

[13]   Symbol Technologies Inc. The PDF417 Barcode. Details available from: http://www.pdf417.com.

[14]   Y. Desmedt and A. Odlyzko. A Chosen Text Attack on the RSA Cryptosystem and Some Discrete Logarithm Schemes. *CRYPTO*, Springer-Verlag, pp.516–522, 1985.

[15]   D. Bleichenbacher. Chosen Ciphertext Attacks Against Protocols Based on the RSA Encryption Standard PKCS #1. *CRYPTO*, Springer-Verlag, pp.1–12, 1998.

[16]   J.-S. Coron, D. Naccache, and J.P. Stern. A New Signature Forgery Strategy. *CRYPTO*, Springer-Verlag, pp.1–18, 1999.

[17]   M. Bellare and P. Rogaway. The exact security of digital signatures: how to sign with RSA and Rabin. *EUROCRYPT*, Springer-Verlag, pp.399–414, 1996.

[18]   M. Bellare and P. Rogaway. Optimal Asymmetric Encryption How to Encrypt with RSA. *EUROCRYPT*, Springer-Verlag, pp.92–111, 1994.

[19]   M.A. Turk and A.P. Pentland. Face Recognition Using Eigenfaces. *IEEE CVPR*, pp.586–91, 1991.

[20]   I.T. Jolliffe. Principal Component Analysis. Springer-Verlag, 1986.

[21]   B.J. Frey and N. Jojic. Transformed Component Analysis. *ICCV*, pp.1190–6, 1999.

[22]   L.A. Ray and R.N. Ellson. Method and Apparatus for Credit Card Verification. U.S. Patent 5,321,751, June 1994.

[23]   L. O'Gorman and I. Rabinovich. Secure identication documents via pattern recognition and public-key crypto. *PAMI*, pp.1097–102, 1998.

[24]   Biometric Consortium. On-line presence at: http://www.biometrics.org.

[25]   T. Matsumoto, H. Matsumoto, K. Yamada, and S. Hoshino. Impact of Artificial Gummy Fingers on Fingerprint Systems. *Optical Security and Counterfeit Deterrence Techniques IV*, SPIE, vol.4677, 2002.

[26]   A.J. Mansfield and J.L. Wayman. Best Practices in testing and reporting performance of Biometric Devices. National Physical Laboratory, technical report available at: http://www.cesg.gov.uk/technology/biometrics/media/Best%20Practice.pdf.

[27]   G.I. Davida, Y. Frankel, and B.J. Matt. On the relation of error correction and cryptography to an offline biometric based identication scheme. *Proceedings of the Workshop on Coding and Cryptography*, 1999.

[28]   R. Anderson and M. Kuhn. Low cost attacks on tamper resistant devices. *International Workshop on Security Protocols*, vol.1361, pp.125–136, 1997.

[29]   P.C. Kocher, J. Jaffe, and B. Jun. Differential Power Analysis. *CRYPTO*, Springer-Verlag, pp.388–397, 1999.

[30]   J.-F. Dhem, F. Koeune, P.-A. Leroux, P. Mestre, J.-J. Quisquater, and J.-L. Willems. A Practical Implementation of the Timing Attack. *CARDIS*, pp.167–182, 1998.

[31]   D. Kirovski, H. Malvar, and Y. Yacobi. A Dual Watermarking and Fingerprinting System. *ACM Multimedia*, 2002.

[32]   B. Moghaddam, A. Pentland. Probabilistic visual learning for object representation. *Early Visual Learning*, pp.99–130, 1996.

[33]   G.-D. Guo and H.-J. Zhang. Boosting for Fast Face Recognition. *Personal communication.*

[34]   P. Viola et al. A unified framework for face datection and recogntion. *Learning workshop, Snowbird*, 2002.

[35]   T.M. Cover and J.A. Thomas. Elements of Information Theory. John Wiley and Sons, Inc., 1991.

[36]   A. Gersho and R. Gray. Quantization and Signal Compression. Kluwer, 1992.

Application

Spam is Here to Stay

Andreas Mitrakas

Ubizen NV
andreas.mitrakas@ubizen.com

Abstract

Spam has emerged as a modern day threat to electronic communications networks. Spam affects governments, service providers, commercial and private users alike. Spamming constitutes a breach of privacy, consumer protection laws, cyber crime laws and can have severe consequences for the party apprehended. Law enforcement that currently remains a cross border issue has yet to be enhanced in order to allow for law enforcement. Cooperation among service providers and the implementation of technical methods is likely to also make an impact. Enhanced end-user awareness can alleviate the burden of managing the huge amounts of spam without, however, necessarily solving the problem. A significant break through can be sought in the direction of authentication mechanisms including electronic identities that protect privacy and allow for personalized services.

1 Introduction

Ever since it first emerged, spam has threatened the unfettered use and evolution of electronic services. The facility with which large volume of unsolicited commercial communications circulate on the Internet threatens the functionality of email that legitimate users seek. Spam threatens government, businesses and consumers alike in terms of wasted resources to manage spam and potential exposure to fraud that goes along with it. Riskier for all potential recipients of spam is the distribution of viruses. Recently, several legislative initiatives have attempted to check spam in a way that meets the expectations of the public and private users. Additionally, a number of self-regulatory initiatives and measures also aim at bringing spam under control. While the success of these initiatives has yet to be proven, spam has been on the rise with rates shunning the ones presented just a few years or even months ago. The remainder of this paper examines the background of spam, it presents legislative initiatives in the EU and US and it addresses future trends in an effort contain spam.

2 Background

On 12 April 1994, attorneys in Arizona launched a homemade marketing software program in the hope to attract extra business. A script that flooded online message boards with an advertisement pitching the legal services of a specific law firm has been singled out as the starting point of spam. Although less conspicuous spam attempts had already been recorded earlier intrusive online marketing has since then become almost an epidemic of massive proportions (See, www.templetons.com). While the recipients' response was immediate unsolicited mass email has persisted since then. According to a ZDnet report quoting a published estimation, almost 82% of all email traffic in the US and 50% worldwide is spam.

The definition of spam has sometimes relied on the term unsolicited commercial email. This definition poses some problems though due to the difficulty to define the meaning of the term commercial in this context. Since spam encompasses non-private communications of some-

S. Paulus, N. Pohlmann, H. Reimer (Editors): Securing Electronic Business Processes, Vieweg (2004), 179-185

times malicious intentions it can be argued that spam is not an exclusively business related phenomenon. The Data Protection Commission in France (Commission National Informatique et Libertés – CNIL) has defined Spam as: „The practice of sending unsolicited emails, most frequently of a commercial nature, in large numbers and repeatedly to individuals with whom the sender has no previous contact, and whose email address may be found in a public space on the Internet, such as newsgroups, mailing lists, directory or website". Spam is unwanted because it:

- Interferes with daily tasks and reduces the ability to work effectively.
- Clogs communications networks and uses up network bandwidth.
- Undermines consumer confidence.
- Poses risks for end users through the risky offerings that are associated with spam.
- Is equally threatening electronic as well as mobile communications.

The legal repercussions of spam are so severe that include breach of privacy, breach of confidentiality, computer crime, consumer law and personal data law violations etc. Taking action against spam has been considered a priority and several initiatives across both Europe and the US have attempted to bring spam under control. Spam for the infrastructure service providers, entails unauthorized user of capacity, increased costs for filtering, security costs and support for dismayed customers. Organizational users risk losing business, business opportunities, and risk productivity losses from within their own employees. Individuals lose their time, content and often fall prey to fraud instigated by unsolicited offers and identity fraud scams.

To their defense spammers claim that they influence the sales power of the end user away from big market players. Commercially speaking, spam's combination of anonymity, volume and low cost make it worthwhile for many to try reap the benefits by assuming the risk. The business of commercial spam is based on a customer base that seeks marketing its wares in an unsolicited manner. The list of recipients' addresses comes from agents that collect addresses from Web pages, newsgroups, chat rooms, and other online destinations. The spammer relies on Internet servers in places where there is weak or no legislation associated with spam and where they can relay their messages anonymously. Spammers' identity is typically covered behind a fake name. Dedicated mailing programs are also used to get spam messages out and are usually also equipped with stealth features that evade filtering and go unnoticed.

In an effort to detect and avert spam relayed through their infrastructure, internet service providers implement message filtering at a large scale. By using software that checks senders' Internet addresses against a database of known spammers and rejecting emails that contain predetermined keywords, ISPs strive to contain the amount of spam circulated. ISPs often prevent their services from being used as a spam springboard by limiting the number of recipients each message can be sent to. ISPs also set up reporting channels for their customers where they can forward spam emails for reporting and blacklisting.

Among the most widespread forms of spam the following top the ratings:

- Adult material sent out indiscriminately to adults and children alike has been singled out by the National Consumers League in the US as the most broadly used form of spam.
- An urgent and confidential letter claiming to originate from a former government official or a person in danger, typically from a troubled place in the world asks for the recipients banking details to transfer large amounts and to also benefit the recipient. Recipients who reply back are requested to send relatively small amounts of money for legal fees, etc., or their accounts are simply cleaned out.

- As online sales grow spammers propose items that might not exist, check from parties with dubious reputation. Paying by credit card could be a remedy against such scams.

- The practice of trying to lure Internet users into disclosing personal financial information such as credit card numbers through e-mail scams can cost financial institutions dearly. Identity theft or „phishing" involves sending bogus e-mails, set up to look like they are from online retailers or other businesses, asking consumers to send credit card numbers and other information [Mitrakas 2002]. Spam and phishing scams erode consumer confidence in electronic transactions.

In spite of the growing costs associated with spam and the increased suspiciousness of email users towards it the success of spam remains unfettered although:

- The interest in spam is next to zero.

- The content of spam does not appeal to end-users.

- Technological measures are implemented by ISPs.

- Legislation has been introduced in the EU, US and elsewhere.

3 Legislative initiatives

In 2002, to counterbalance the threats posed by spam the European Commission took action against it by adopting a Directive on Privacy and Electronic Communications. The Commission also works together with the data protection authorities from the Member States (Article 29 Working Party).

Directive 2002/58/EC of 12 July 2002 on Privacy and Electronic Communications aims at a pan-European „ban on spam" to individuals. With only a limited exception referring to existing customer relationships, e-mail marketing is permitted subject to prior consent of the end user (Article 13). Consent can be given by purchasing similar products in the past by the consumer. The definition of similar products and services as those originally bought by the customer is not addressed in the Directive [Reed 2000]. However, the same provision includes two supporting safeguards, namely that the data may only be used by the same company that has established the relationship with the customer in the first place and that each message must include an opt-out option. It is, therefore, expected that companies will have a strong interest not to abuse the notion of „similar products or services" and that in this case the customer is in a good position to stop marketing messages should such abuse occurs.

Interestingly and in stark contrast with other Directives that make a distinction between electronic and mobile communications, SMS messages and electronic messages received on any mobile or fixed terminal are equally sanctioned under 02/58/EC. However, fax is not included in this exception. This Directive sets an „opt-in" regime that end users can initiate. Member States can also ban unsolicited commercial e-mails to businesses, which do not fall within the initial objectives of the Directive.

The new rules introduced with Directive 02/58/EC, apply to the processing of personal data in relation with the provision of publicly available electronic communications services in public networks within the EU. An important distinction, therefore, is that article 13 that establishes the opt-in rule is applicable to all unsolicited commercial communications received on and sent from networks in the EU. Messages originating from third countries must also comply with the rules of the Directive. Obviously the same applies to any communications sent by an address within the EU to recipients elsewhere. As it can be expected, however the gravest difficulty is associated with the enforcement of the rule with regard to messages sent from addresses outside the EU. With most spam reaching EU based end users from addresses outside the EU, this is by far the most important matter for end users, which, however, the Directive does not necessarily address sufficiently.

Member States had until October 2003 to transpose a „ban on spam" into national legislation. Delays to meet this deadline have resulted in certain member states being brought by the European Commission before the European Court of Justice.

Directive 02/58/EC is not the first attempt of the EU Commission to check spamming. The data protection directive (1995/46/EC) grants protection to any personal identifiable information that might be abused. The 1995 Directive introduces an opt-out procedure to deal with spam. Certain types of personally identifiable information such as religion, ethnicity etc., are covered by more severe restrictions of processing. An opt-out register, however, could lead to abuse since it is a formidable source of email addresses.

The issue of „opt-in" or „opt-out" has been quite critical in the EU. Opt-in creates permission, which is not objectionable. The Data Protection Directive is relevant also because it establishes the right to claim damages as a result of spam. The Directive 95/46/EC sets out that penalties can be sanctioned for infringements of personal data. Beyond fines and possibly also criminal charges, other remedies for infringes of personal data currently include an injunction to cease unauthorised personal data processing. Additionally, spamming might result in breaching other obligations under the general data protection directive, such as the duty to notify for data processing etc.

The electronic commerce Directive (2000/31/EC) requires email to be clearly and unequivocally identifiable as such as soon as recipients receive it. Opt-out registers did not exist at the time of the Directive and were not forthcoming as a result of the legislation. Should, however, an end user contact a vendor to buy something online, that vendor can send additional information. With regard to business users the Directive stipulates that member states could require opt-out arrangements rather than opt-in. By contrast Directive 02/58/EC requires a soft opt-in with some exceptions. Finally consumer protection legislation in the EU also impacts spamming due to the requirements of transparency in communications and service offers emanating from Directive 97/7/EC on consumer protection in distance contracts [Hoernle et al. 2002].

Computer-related crimes are: „traditional crimes that can be, or have been, committed by using other means of perpetration which are now carried out through an Internet based computer-related venue (e.g. e-mail, newsgroups, other networks) or other technological computing advancement" [Trento 2002]. To investigate cyber-crime and crimes carried out with the help or by information technology, law enforcement agencies seek access to content of communications, data in transit, stored data and authentication data. The criminal law consequences of spamming might well qualify to be dealt with under the Cybercrime provisions. Article 15 of the Convention on Cybercrime of the Council of Europe stipulates that investigative powers and procedures are subject to conditions and safeguards provided for under its domestic law in a way that provides for adequate protection of human rights and liberties. The Convention on Cybercrime addresses computer-related offences that include computer-related fraud, which stands for „the causing of a loss of property to another by: any input, alteration, deletion or suppression of computer data, any interference with the functioning of a computer system".

In the US Federal Legislation entitled Controlling the Assault of Non-Solicited Pornography and Marketing Act (S.877) (CAN-SPAM) has been introduced to focus upon controlling unsolicited commercial electronic mail messages. CAN-SPAM has made illegal to send spam that has false or misleading heading or origin information. Having a functioning return message capability and a physical postal address is essential because CAN-SPAM makes it illegal to send additional unsolicited messages to anyone who has indicated that they do not want to receive future messages from the sender. CAN-SPAM is an opt-out system but is also allows senders to provide „opt-in" to receiving certain kinds of email. ISPs who have posted notices stating that the web site or ISP does not store or transfer email addresses to any other party for unsolicited email purposes can benefit from CAN-SPAM.

Neither in the EU nor in the US seems to have been sufficient experience in enforcing the opt-in or opt-out rules for communications originating outside their respective territorial boundaries. It is a known fact that in cases of cyber-crime, international cooperation is critical in order to ensure the reconstruction of context and the collection of evidence. In the case of spamming international cooperation is needed in order to support the investigation on the identity of senders.

4 Self-Regulatory initiatives

User action has been a viable remedy against spam. In May 2003, the US based ISP, Earthlink, won a motion and a permanent injunction against a Buffalo, N.Y.-based sender of junk e-mail. Among other Internet providers, America Online has also sued spammers in a US federal court. AOL has won 25 spam-related lawsuits against more than 100 companies and individuals.

In *Compuserve v. Cyber Promotions*, 962 F. Supp. 1015 (S.D. Ohio 1997), the plaintiff, being Compuserve sued to enforce its contractual prohibition against mass electronic mailings. The defendant continued to spam even after being warned not to. Plaintiff successful sued under the theory of trespass to personal property.

In the early days of commercial Internet spamming had been largely considered unethical and dealt with in practice by trying to undermine the computers of the spamming senders. However, netiquette rules have currently a very limited influence on the day-to-day practice of commercial communications. Filtering software gave the next stage in ISPs fighting spamming however a common criticism is that often wanted email is filtered out together with unwanted email. Besides repeating offenders, one-time spammers pose an equally difficult problem much as resurfacing ones do.

To meet the goal of containing spam, building awareness could be considered as a step in the right direction. Creating user awareness on how to avoid or contain spam could have an impact to reducing the actual number of spam circulated in communications networks. Specialized end user software for the client or the server side that is anyway broadly available might also support awareness activities.

In general awareness of spam rights must stay in touch with the enforcement of data protection rights, an issue that still requires additional attention by the member states. The efforts of the French Data Protection Authority (CNIL) which is the national data protection authority have focused not just on the protection of personal data but they have made consistent efforts to ensure that spamming is somehow addressed and dealt with. The French Data Protection Authority has therefore, put up a web site that contains a significant amount of information package on spam such as basic guidance on how to prevent spam, information on how to report spam, users groups and associations active in this area, etc. Further action undertaken by public authorities, user and industry groups is likely to contribute to containing spam.

International cooperation is expected to promote the adoption of effective legislation in third countries. An additional objective for international cooperation is to work together with third countries to ensure effective enforcement of legislation. A successful example of fruitful international cooperation can be noted in the area of electronic signatures that has resulted in significant convergence across the adopted regulations in various countries and regions. The UNCITRAL Model Law on electronic commerce of 1996 has largely been based on several Model Electronic Data Interchange (EDI) Agreements [UNCITRAL 1996]. Public authorities might ensure international cooperation so that cross border implications of spam do not get hindered by the absence of judicial or investigative cooperation or even legal provisions. Working towards the methodological aspects of containing spam could also produce some results. A methodology and cost model in investigating spam cases might ease up the current difficulty to predict the amount of effort required. An additional contribution of public authorities could be given by developing standard mechanisms for the reporting and management of spam attacks. Service providers could greatly benefit from a coordinated action to support their efforts in addressing spam.

Pro-active action by the industry is also likely to have a positive impact. In this regard, service providers can be encouraged or in certain circumstances of severe breaches even be obliged to report spamming. Cooperation within the industry might also lead to service providers sharing blacklisting mechanisms in order to fend off attacks on their systems that consequently impact large numbers of users. Pro-active industry groups have also contributed by drawing up best practices and guides to direct marketing for example in order to enhance knowledge and provide notice on the legal consequences among their members. Special attention must be given to emerging forms of communication such as through mobile networks. Enforcing security mechanisms in collecting user data, storing and communicating shall make an impact in reducing spam and attacking systems by spreading viruses etc. [Pfleeger 2000].

As there is no better alternative to reducing spam than the direct cooperation of the knowledgeable end user action is an essential success factor. Refusing to give out one's own address and personal details in marketing actions and newsgroups is likely to impact the end user perception of spam. While creating separate accounts solely for the purpose of communicating with one single group does not reduce the global amount of spam it definitely helps the administration of a personal email in a straightforward and inexpensive manner. Finally, improving authentication mechanisms and enhancing the use of electronic signatures is also likely to impact the unauthorized use of end user information. While standardization might further seek to ensure interoperability in the area of electronics signatures for authentication, end user awareness shall contribute to curbing spam. The Directive 99/93/EC on a common framework on electronic signatures has resulted in a number of standards that are readily available in order to ensure the interoperability of authentication mechanisms based on electronic signatures [ETSI 2001]. Large-scale identity schemes definitely contribute to the ubiquitous use of authentication mechanisms that enhances privacy and is likely to contribute to reducing spam [Deprest et al. 2003] [eEurope 2002].

5 Conclusions

Spam is here to stay due to the inherent features of open communications networks that can be easily exploited to reach large numbers of recipients of undesired commercial communications. Legislation is likely to contribute in dealing with some of the consequences of spam, especially in establishing acceptable practices on disclosures for user contact information. However, legislation cannot necessarily succeed unless coordinated international action is taken. Especially in those countries where spam originates in, intensive efforts and international cooperation are needed in order to produce some results. Cooperation within the industry is another way to ensure that spam does not reach the end user in the current scale. End user awareness and change of practices can also reduce the burden of spam at the end user level. While eliminating spam altogether seems a goal that is difficult to reach under present circumstances, there is significant space for improvement from the present day situation if only consistent management measures are adopted through law and practice.

References

[Deprest et al. 2003]   Deprest, J., Robben, F., E-Government: the approach of the Belgian federal government, FEDICT and CBBSS, 2003.

[eEurope 2002]   eEurope Smart Cards, Identification and Authentication in eGovernment, a policy report for eEurope Smart Card Charter Trailblazer 2, 2002.

[ETSI 2001]   ETSI TS 101 042, Policy requirements for certification authorities issuing public key certificates, 2001.

[Hoernle et al. 2002]   Hoernle, J., Sutter, G., Walden, I. Directivee 97/7/EC on the protection of consumers in respect of distance contracts, in Lodder, A., Kaspersen, H.W.K., eDirectives: Guide to European Union Law on e-commerce, Kluwer law International, 2002.

[Mitrakas 2002]   Mitrakas, A., Citizen Centric Identity Management: Chip Tricks?, Network Security, MCC International, 2002.

[Pfleeger 2000]   Pfleeger C., Security in Computing, Prentice Hall 2000.

[Reed 2000]   Reed, C., Internet Law: Text and Materials, Butterworths, 2000.

[Trento 2002]   Transcrime Research Centre, University of Trento, Transatlantic Agenda EU/US Co-operation for Preventing Computer Related Crime – Final Report, 2002.

[UNCITRAL 1996]   UNCITRAL, Model Law on electronic commerce, 1996.

The Key to My On-Line Security

Paul Meadowcroft

Thales e-Security Ltd
paul.meadowcroft@thales-esecurity.com

Abstract

The paper will explain the infrastructure behind a variety of multi-application smart card services and how the security is implemented in a consistent way end-to-end across the various networks regardless of the interface channel used to perform the transaction. A number of applications will be considered, namely: EMV debit and credit, physical and logical access control, government id and digital signature, e-commerce and the 3D security architecture.

The understanding of how all these services can be linked together through a single multi-application smart card and how the supporting infrastructures can be integrated to provide a seamless user experience is the topic of this paper.

1 Introduction

With the roll out of EMV smart cards beginning, chip debit and credit cards are here to stay. The smart card is becoming the de facto user authentication token, cryptographic key container and personal security module.

With the promise of multi-application smart cards it appears that we have more technology than we know what to do with. Certainly cards are capable of holding large amounts of data, numerous applications and performing complex cryptographic calculations, but how do you manage this complexity and variety on millions of cards?

Any IT manager knows how difficult it can be to manage a community of personal computer (PC) and laptop users with different operating systems and application suites and smart cards are beginning to present as complex a processing environment as the personal computing world. The benefit of a corporate PC is that it usually only has to link to a single network environment, the corporate LAN, but to realise the benefits presented by a multi-application smart card we need to use it in many different network environments, such as: ATM, PoS, corporate network, Internet and unconnected personal readers.

This paper presents a day in the life of Jo Smart and her multi-application SMART card. Jo uses her SMART card as a personal security module to provide security for her transactions and to authenticate her identity as she conducts her personal and business life on-line. Jo uses her SMART card to check her stock portfolio via her interactive television, access her office and logon to the network, buy securely on-line and in the physical world, sign and send her tax return to the government and submit the monthly salary run for her company on-line to BACS.

S. Paulus, N. Pohlmann, H. Reimer (Editors): Securing Electronic Business Processes, Vieweg (2004), 186-197

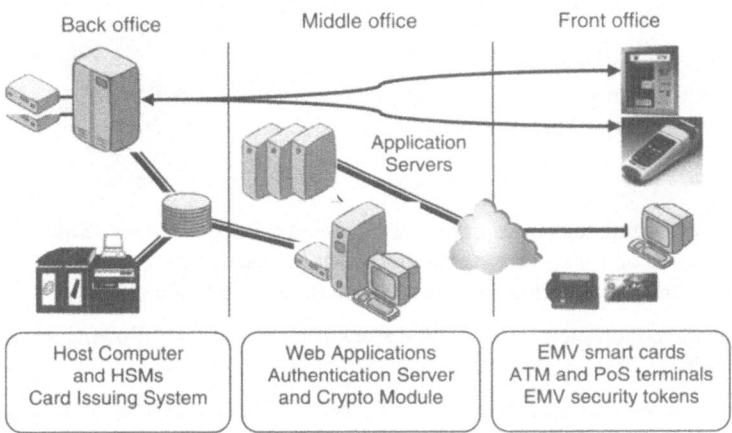

Figure1: EMV Authentication architecture

2 Smart card issuing

There are two types of multi-application smart cards available today:

1. Proprietary cards that can be issued with a number of applications on them
2. Open Standards cards, such as GlobalPlatform and MULTOS cards, that can be issued with one or more applications on them but can also have new applications added to them post issuance

The issue is not a technical one, smart cards can support multiple applications, but a business issue about who owns and controls the real estate on the cards and what brand appears on the surface of the card.

For the purposes of this illustration all the applications Jo needs are put on to her smart card when it is issued by her bank. The following applications are loaded on her smart card:

1. EMV credit
2. EMV debit
3. EMV authentication
4. Digital signature
5. Secure Open Data Storage
6. User and message authentication

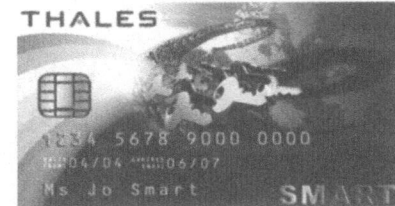

Fig 2: Jo's multi-application SMART card

3 On-line authentication

Jo subscribes to an on-line stocks and shares trading system provided by her bank. She has been given an unconnected, hand held smart card reader which she can use with her smart card to calculate a dynamic password to logon to the service. She can view her portfolio and issue buying and selling instructions. The service is provided over the Internet with a zero footprint on her PC, all she needs to access the service is a standard web browser.

The security requirements are:

1. Information confidentiality
2. Strong user authentication
3. Message integrity and proof of origin

The information confidentiality is provided by Secure Sockets Layer (SSL) as part of the standard web server and web browser applications. Jo can check that the little padlock appears in her web browser to tell her that her information will remain secret.

When Jo is prompted to logon to the bank's stock trading site the following security processing steps take place:

1. Jo enters her user id into the web browser and is then presented with a random challenge
2. Jo puts her smart card into her hand held reader and enters her PIN. The PIN is checked by the card and if it is correct Jo is presented with a menu of the available applications on the card
3. Jo selects the authentication application on the card which prompts her to enter the random challenge displayed by the web browser
4. When Jo has entered the challenge the smart card performs a cryptographic calculation to generate a unique response to the challenge. This is displayed by the hand held reader
5. Jo types the response into the web browser
6. The web server passes the response to an authentication server which, using Jo's key held on the access database, checks that the response is correct for the issued challenge (strong user authentication)
7. Once Jo has been authenticated then the application server retrieves Jo's information and presents it to her web browser via the web server

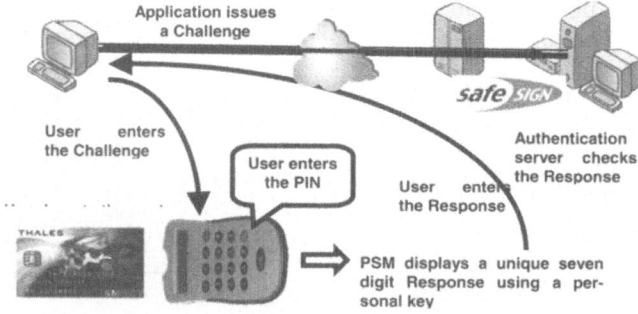

Figure 3: SafeSign PSM user authentication process

Jo wants to send an instruction to the bank to sell some shares if they reach a certain price. As she works through the screens to set up the transaction she is finally prompted for a Message Authentication Code (MAC) to confirm the transaction details.

1. Jo puts her smart card into her hand held reader and enters her PIN.
2. Jo selects the message authentication application on the card and following the prompts enters the critical transaction details, such as: stock code, number of shares, price, type of transaction, date, etc.

3. When all the fields have been completed the smart card calculates a MAC over the data and displays the result on the reader
4. Jo types the displayed MAC into the web browser
5. The web server passes the message together with the MAC to the authentication server which, using Jo's key held on the database, validates the MAC against the message (message integrity). The fact that the cryptographic key used to validate the MAC is unique to Jo is proof of origin of the message
6. If the MAC is valid then Jo's instruction is processed by the application server. The MAC will be stored on the audit trail together with the transaction details

4 ATM transaction

The ATM (Automatic Teller Machine) or cash point machine network is global. You can use your ATM card at an HSBC cash point machine in Hong Kong to withdraw money from a Barclays Bank in the UK. The transaction goes half way round the world and back again in a few seconds and even the currency is converted on the way. This is all possible because Visa and MasterCard have set international standards for interoperability and security and provided the necessary network infrastructure.

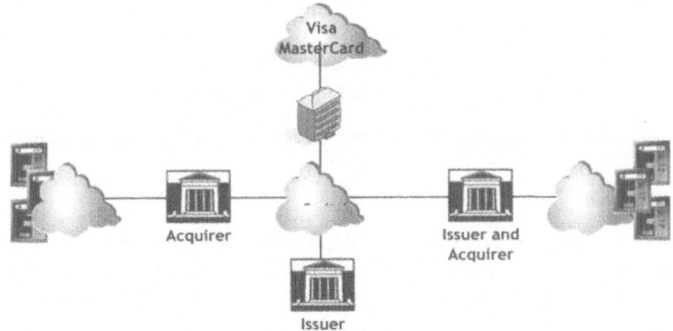

Figure 4: Typical ATM Network

The security requirement is to ensure that it is the valid cardholder with a valid card making the request to withdraw cash.

To do this the customer is issued with a card and a PIN (two factor authentication, something you have, the card, and something you know, the PIN). The card also contains a Card Verification Value (CVV) to ensure that the card details have not been tampered with.

For the system to remain secure it is essential that the only person to know the PIN is the valid cardholder. For this reason the PIN is never in clear outside the secure environment of tamper resistant hardware. The user entered PIN is encrypted by the ATM and remains encrypted until it reaches the issuing bank where it is compared to a stored value of the user's PIN and even this comparison takes place inside the secure confines of a tamper resistant hardware security module (HSM).

The security processing steps of an ATM transaction are:

1. Jo puts her card into the ATM
2. Jo enters her PIN using the ATM key pad
3. The tamper resistant key pad encrypts her PIN

4. The ATM sends the transaction details, containing the card data and the encrypted PIN to the acquiring bank
5. The acquiring bank looks at the transaction details to determine if Jo is one of its customers (an on-us transaction) or if Jo is the customer of another bank (a not on-us transaction)
6. If it is a not on-us transaction the acquiring bank sends the transaction, across the global network, to the issuing bank
7. If it is an on-us transaction, where the acquiring bank is also the issuing bank, then the CVV is checked (card authentication) and the PIN is checked (user authentication). Both these are cryptographic operations, performed inside the HSM, using the Data Encryption Standard (DES) algorithm and cryptographic keys known only to the card issuing bank (and possibly Visa or MasterCard if the bank wants them to offer a stand-in service)
8. If both the CVV and PIN are valid then a message is sent back to the ATM authorising the cash withdrawal

5 Physical and logical access control

Using Secure Open Data Storage (SODS) it is possible for a third party, in this case Jo's employer, to add information to her smart card after it has been issued. As long as the application adding, and subsequently using the data is SODS compliant, Jo's smart card can be used for applications that have nothing at all to do with the issuing bank.

In both the physical and logical access environments the security requirements are:
1. User authentication
2. User authorisation

Here Jo's employer has put her physical access identity code onto her card so that she can use it to enter the building and her user id and password so that she can logon to the corporate network using her card. In both cases Jo is required to enter her PIN, which is checked on the smart card, before her data is released to the access control application.

The combination of the card and the PIN provides user authentication and the user authorisation is provided by the access control applications once Jo's identity has been authenticated.

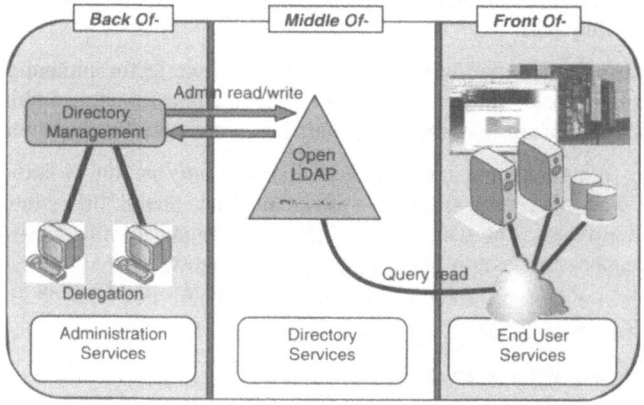

Figure 5: Physical and logical access control architecture

The central directory server holds the details of every employee in Jo's organisation and is the central directory server for both the physical access control and the network access control systems. The directory does not contain Jo's PIN as this is checked on the card itself. Unlike the ATM example the PIN is never transmitted across the network.

In this example the network is local to Jo's organisation and does not need to be connected with the issuing bank in any way. Her organisation is simply making use of data storage space on her smart card, made available through the SODS application, access to which is controlled by Jo's PIN.

Some physical access control systems use contactless technology with no PIN entry. This form of single factor authentication may be adequate for building access. The card technology exists to have both contact and contactless capability on the same card.

6 BACS payment

Jo has responsibility for submitting her company's payroll to BACS.

The security requirements are:

1. User authentication to ensure only authorised personnel can make BACS payments
2. Message authentication to ensure the message has not been tampered with
3. Non-repudiation to ensure that payments processed by BACS cannot be later denied by the sending organisation

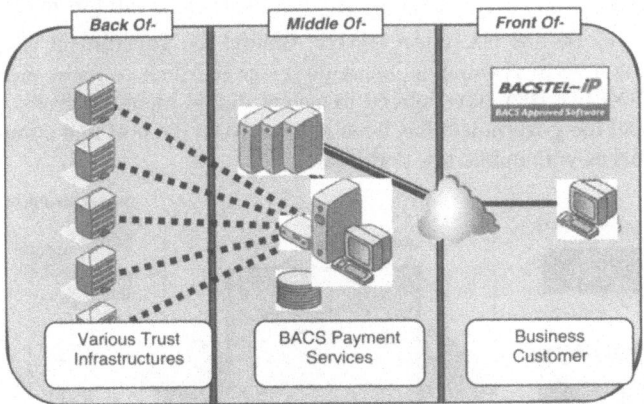

Figure 6: BACSTEL-IP architecture

Jo's bank has its own public key infrastructure and operates its own Certificate Authority (CA). When Jo's smart card was issued her bank put a private key and a public key certificate onto her card.

When Jo has checked that all the payroll data is correct she is prompted by the BACS application to digitally sign the transaction. She puts her smart card into the smart card reader, attached to her workstation, and enters her PIN.

The BACS application sends the hash value of the transaction to her smart card where it is signed using Jo's private key. The card returns the digital signature together with Jo's public key certificate to the BACS application.

In this example the network is the Internet connecting over 100,000 BACS participants. Jo's BACS application sends her signed payroll transaction to BACS where her digital certificate is checked against the issuing bank's PKI and her public key is then used to validate her signature on the payroll transaction. Again these cryptographic processes are carried out inside tamper resistant HSMs.

If her digital signature is valid then BACS can be confident that the transaction has not been changed since Jo sent it (message authentication), that it was Jo who sent the transaction (user authentication), and because her public key was sent in a certificate, that Jo works for a BACS participant and that she was authorised to make the payment (proof of origin). Also because the BACS authentication server keeps digitally signed audit trails of all transactions, if Jo's organisation later disputes the payment, they can prove that Jo submitted the transaction (non-repudiation).

7 On-line tax return

Jo has taken up the government's offer to submit her tax return on-line.

The security requirements are:

1. User authentication to ensure that it is Jo who has submitted the tax return
2. Document integrity to ensure that the content of the document does not change once it has been signed by Jo

The tax office has agreed to accept bank issued certificates as a valid form of identity and user authentication for its on-line tax return service. Behind the government web portal the government is running a multi-channel authentication server which contains the root CA keys of all the organisations that they have agreed to accept digital identities from. Using this federated identity model the government has been able to avoid the cost and complexity of having to issue all its citizens with public key certificates.

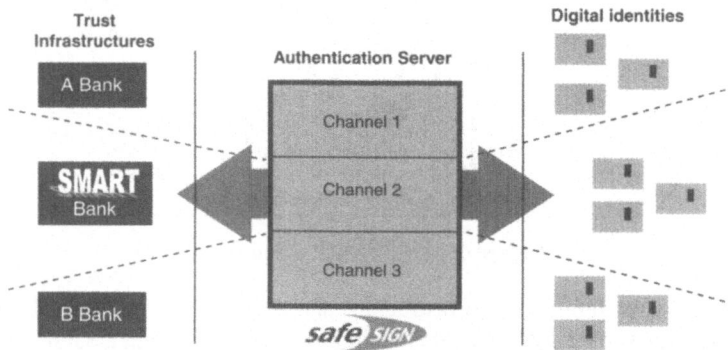

Figure 7: Integrating multiple trust domains

The processing steps to enable Jo to submit her on-line tax return are as follows:

1. Jo completes her tax return and when she is ready to send it she is prompted to digitally sign the form
2. She puts her smart card into the reader connected to her PC and enters her PIN. The PIN is checked locally by the smart card

3. Her on-line tax application calculates a hash on her tax form and sends the hash to her smart card which digitally signs it using the private key held securely on the card

4. The smart card returns the digital signature to the tax application which appends it to the tax form and submits it to the government gateway

The communications network is the Internet and the connection to the government gateway has been secured using SSL to ensure that the content of the messages between Jo and the gateway remain confidential.

The government gateway web server strips off the SSL encryption and passes the signed tax form to the government tax application server. The application server sends Jo's signed tax form and the public key certificate to the authentication server which can validate her public key against her bank's PKI and then uses her public key to check her digital signature. The authentication server keeps a signed audit of the transaction and passes the results of these cryptographic checks back to the tax application server. If all these checks are positive the tax application server processes Jo's tax form and stores it, together with her digital signature for legal recording purposes.

8 PoS transaction

The PoS (Point of Sale) network is global and controlled by international standards set by the card associations, Visa and MasterCard. The backbone network is the same as the ATM network linking the card issuing and card acquiring bank systems together across the Visa and MasterCard infrastructure.

Jo buys a dress at a high street store and uses her smart card to pay using the EMV credit application.

The security requirements are:

1. The merchant wants the transaction authorised to ensure that they will be paid for the goods

2. The bank wants to know that Jo's card is genuine and that Jo is the authentic user of the card

3. The bank wants to be able to control the card in the event that it has been reported lost or stolen

The security processing steps of a PoS transaction are:

1. Jo puts her card into the PoS terminal

2. The PoS terminal checks that Jo's smart card is genuine by performing Static Data Authentication (SDA) or Dynamic Data Authentication (DDA). The terminal contains the EMV root CA public key certificates for Visa and MasterCard.

3. The PoS terminal displays the amount to be authorised and prompts Jo to enter her PIN. Her PIN is checked locally on the card (two factor user authentication).

4. A number of terminal and card risk parameters are checked to determine if the transaction should be authorized on-line or not. For example, if the transaction value is below the merchant's floor limit and Jo's transaction limit has not been reached then no on-line transaction takes place at this time. The card generates a transaction certificate (transaction authorisation) and this together with the transaction details are stored by the PoS terminal and will be submitted as part of a batch of transactions later in the day. However, let us take a look at what happens if the transaction goes on-line for immediate authorisation

5. The smart card calculates an Authorisation Request Cryptogram (ARQC) based on the transaction and card details, but no PIN details, and sends it (via the PoS terminal) to the acquiring bank

6. The acquiring bank looks at the transaction details to determine if Jo is one of its customers (an on-us transaction) or if Jo is the customer of another bank (a not on-us transaction)

7. If it is a not on-us transaction the acquiring bank sends the transaction, across the global network, to the issuing bank

8. If it is an on-us transaction, where the acquiring bank is also the issuing bank, then the ARQC is checked (card authentication and transaction integrity) and Jo's account details and credit limit checked to see if she has enough funds available for the dress.

9. If all the details are correct and sufficient funds are available the host application uses its HSMs to calculate the Authorisation Response Cryptogram (ARPC) and sends an authorisation message back to the smart card, via the PoS terminal, authorising the transaction.

10. The smart card checks that the ARPC is correct, and from the card holder's bank. The card then generates a transaction certificate (transaction authorisation) and this together with the transaction details are stored by the PoS terminal

Typical HSM functions:
- Terminal key management
- PIN verification
- Authorisation ReQuest Cryptogram (ARQC) verification
- Authorisation ResPonse Cryptogram (ARPC) generation

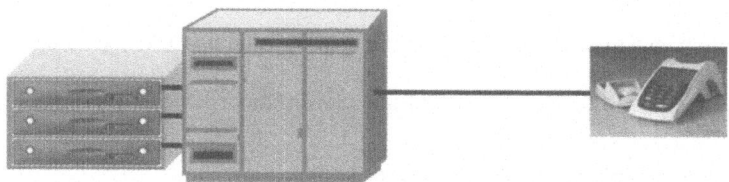

Figure 8: PoS transaction authentication and authorisation

Should Jo's card have been lost or stolen and is being used by someone else her bank can, during an on-line transaction, send a message to the card which effectively disables the card.

9 e-Commerce with strong authentication

Visa and MasterCard have agreed on the 3D Secure standard to provide additional security for card payment transactions over the Internet. This standard has been implemented as Verified by Visa and MasterCard SecureCode. At the moment the bulk of the 3D Secure implementations only use user ID and password as the user authentication mechanism. The weakness of passwords is well known and these systems are coming under additional pressure from phishing attacks, keyboard sniffing and other Trojan Horse applications. The drive from the card associations to increase the security of these e-commerce transactions is to combine 3D Secure with strong authentication using EMV smart cards.

To encourage this shift the card associations are introducing a liability shift so that the merchant and acquiring bank will no longer be liable for fraudulent or denied transactions if they were capable of performing a 3D Secure transaction.

The security requirements of these card based on-line transactions are:

1. The merchant wants the transaction authorised to ensure that they will be paid for the goods
2. The issuing bank wants to be confident that the valid card and cardholder combination initiated the transaction – strong two factor authentication using chip and PIN
3. The issuing bank also wants to be sure that the transaction details it receives for settlement are the same as the transaction details it authorised on-line
4. The acquirer wants to know that it will not be liable for any charge backs because the card holder later denies having taken part in the transaction

The network infrastructure is the Internet supported by the three domain infrastructure defined by 3D Secure (Issuer Domain, Interoperability Domain and Acquirer Domain) and Payment Network provided by the card associations.

Jo has been browsing the Internet to find the best flight to Paris. When Jo is ready to purchase her ticket the following security processing takes place:

1. The merchant asks Jo how she would like to pay
2. Jo responds that she wants to pay using her smart card and credit card account
3. The merchant's system interrogates the directory in the Interoperability Domain, provided by Visa and MasterCard, to find out which bank issued Jo's smart card and whether it is participating in 3D Secure
4. The merchant's system redirects Jo's browser to the issuer to enable them to perform cardholder authentication
5. The issuer pops up a dialogue box on Jo's browser in a window provided by the merchant
6. The issuer's Access Control Server prompts Jo to provide an EMV authentication value (one-time password) using her smart card and EMV hand held card reader
7. Jo puts her smart card in her hand held EMV reader and enters her PIN in the keypad (user authentication)
8. The reader generates a dynamic one-time number using the EMV DES key held in the smart card together with other information held on the card (card authentication)
9. Jo keys this value into the dialogue box where it is sent back to the issuer
10. The Access Control Server checks that the dynamic password is correct and calculates an authorisation code which is sent back to the merchant and the transaction is recorded on the Authentication History Server
11. The merchant stores the authorisation code together with the transaction details and completes the sale with Jo
12. Sometime later the transaction details, together with the authorisation code, are submitted as part of a batch of transactions by the merchant to the acquirer
13. The acquirer will then settle the transaction with the issuer using the traditional payment network
14. The issuer can validate the transaction details by checking the authorisation code in their back office transaction processing system using hardware security modules

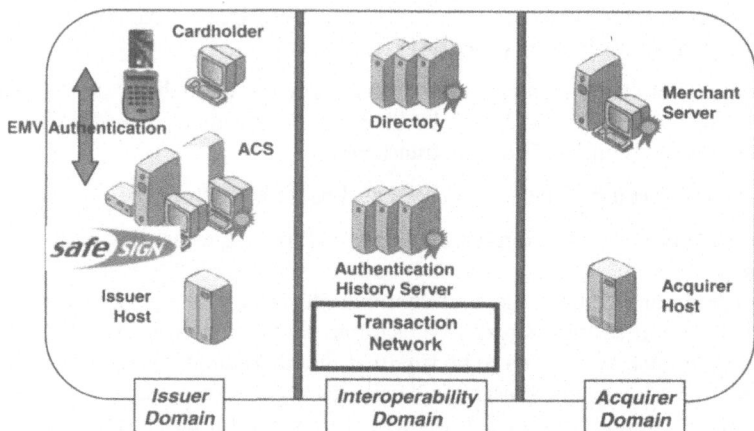

Figure 9: 3D-Secure with EMV authentication

10 Conclusion

As you have seen it is possible for Jo to use a single smart card to interact with a variety of different applications over different network infrastructures which can be completely independent of each other. Security can be implemented in a consistent way end-to-end across the various networks regardless of which interface channel Jo uses to perform her transaction. All these services can be linked together through a single multi-application smart card to provide Jo with a seamless user experience.

This future is only round the corner. The technology needed to implement these services is here now.

The challenge facing us is the business processes and agreements necessary for different organisations to trust each other's security implementation and processing systems to a level which is commensurate with the business risk. Standards such as the BS 7799 or ISO 17799 for Information Security Management can assist in this process, but it will be the realisation that it is not necessary to have issued a user's identity and security credentials to be able to make use of them.

Figure 10: The Key to on-line Security

References

[EMV]   EMV '96 Integrated Circuit Card Specification for payment Systems, Version
            3.1.1, May 31, 1998,
            http://www.emvco.com/documents/specification/view/Emvapp.pdf
            EMV 2000 Integrated Circuit Card Specification for Payment Systems, Book 1,
            Application independent to Terminal Interface requirements, Version 4.1, June
            2004, http://www.emvco.com/
            EMV 2000 Integrated Circuit Card Specification for Payment Systems, Book 2,
            Security and Key Management, Version 4.1, June 2004, http://www.emvco.com/
            EMV 2000 Integrated Circuit Card Specification for Payment Systems, Book 3,
            Application Specification, Version 4.1, June 2004, http://www.emvco.com/
            EMV 2000 Integrated Circuit Card Specification for Payment Systems, Book 4,
            Cardholder, Attendant, and Acquirer Interface Requirements, Version 4.1, June
            2004, http://www.emvco.com/

[GLPL]   GlobalPlatform, Card Specification, Version 2.1.1, March 2003,
            http://www.globalplatform.org/specificationview.asp?id=card
            GlobalPlatform, Card Security Requirements Specifications
            Version 1.0, May 2003,
            http://www.globalplatform.org/specificationview.asp?id=card
            GlobalPlatform, Key Management Requirements Systems Functional Require-
            ments Specification, November 2003,
            http://www.globalplatform.org/specificationview.asp?id=system

[SSL]   Alan O. Freier, Netscape Communications, Philip Karlton, Netscape Communi-
            cations, Paul C. Kocher, Independent Consultant, The SSL Protocol, Version
            3.0, November 18, 1996, http://wp.netscape.com/eng/ssl3/draft302.txt

[FIPS]   FIPS 46-2, Data Encryption Standard (DES), Federal Information
            Processing Standards, December 30, 1993,
            http://www.itl.nist.gov/fipspubs/fip46-2.htm
            FIPS 46-3, Data Encryption Standard (DES), Federal Information
            Processing Standards, October 25, 1999; includes specification for Triple Data
            Encryption Algorithm (TDEA), http://csrc.nist.gov/publications/fips/fips46-
            3/fips46-3.pdf
            FIPS PUB 113, Computer Data Authentication, Federal Information Processing
            Standards, May 30, 1985, http://www.itl.nist.gov/fipspubs/fip113.htm
            FIPS 180-1, Secure Hash Standard (SHA-1), Federal Information
            Processing Standards, April 17, 1995,
            http://www.itl.nist.gov/fippubs/fip180-1.htm

[PKCS]   PKCS #1, Version 2.1, RSA Cryptography Standard, RSA Laboratories, June
            14, 2002, http://www.rsasecurity.com/rsalabs/node.asp?id=2125

[3DSEC]   3D Secure System Overview, Visa International, Version 1.0.2, May 01, 2003,
            http://international.visa.com/fb/paytech/secure/main.jsp

[MDG]   MULTOS Developers Guide, MAOSCO Ltd., Version 1.30, 2000,
            http://www.multos.com/library/pdf/mao-doc-ref-
            005%20multos%20developers%20guide.pdf

[X.509]   R. Housley, RSA Laboratories, W. Polk, NIST, W. Ford, VeriSign, D. Solo,
            Citigroup, Internet X.509 Public Key Infrastructure Certificate and Certificate
            Revocation List (CRL) Profile, April 2002, http://www.ietf.org/rfc/rfc3280.txt

[ISO]   ISO 17799 – The Information Security Standard, Code of Practice for Informa-
            tion Security Management, 2000, http://www.iso17799.net/

Dealing with Privacy Obligations in Enterprises

Marco Casassa Mont

Hewlett-Packard Laboratories
Filton Road, Stoke Gifford, Bristol, UK
marco.casassa-mont@hp.com

Abstract

This paper focuses on the problem of dealing with privacy obligations in enterprises. Privacy obligations dictate expected behaviours, tasks and constraints that must be satisfied when handling personal and confidential data. This includes being compliant with data retention policies and satisfying constraints dictated by customers' opt-in and opt-out choices.

It is important for enterprises to address this problem to preserve their reputation and brand and be compliant with legislation and customers' requirements. This paper describes important related issues and requirements to be kept into account, including dealing with transactional, ongoing and long-term obligations.

Technical work has already been done for the management of obligations subordinated to authorization aspects and simple obligations for data retention: however, dealing with ongoing and long-term aspects of obligations is still a green field and open to research. We introduce and describe a trusted system, currently under research and development at HP Labs, dealing with the monitoring, enforcement and tracking of privacy obligations: this system will support the strong association of privacy obligations to data, accountability management and users' involvement.

1 Introduction

Enterprises store, manage and process large amounts of personal and confidential data related to their employees, customers and partners. On one hand, this information is fundamental to enable their business processes, interactions and transactions. On the other hand, personal data should be accessed and used only for the purposes for which it has been disclosed and with the consent of the data owners or data subjects. Enterprises increasingly recognise that dealing correctly and honestly with privacy matters can have a beneficial return in terms of branding, trust, customers' satisfaction and business opportunities.

When processing, using and transmitting confidential data, enterprises must be compliant with privacy laws. A lot of work has been done in terms of privacy legislation often driven by local or geographical needs. This includes European Community data protection privacy laws, various US privacy laws and more specific national privacy initiatives [Laur03]. Guidelines are also available on the protection of privacy and flows of personal data, including OECD guidelines [Oecd80], that describe concepts such as collection limitation, data quality and purpose specification principles and online privacy policies [Priv04]. Large enterprises that are geographically distributed across different nations might need to comply with different privacy laws.

Privacy policies can be used to represent and describe privacy laws, guidelines and privacy statements. Privacy policies, at the very base, express rights, permissions and obligations, usually in natural language that needs to be interpreted and understood by people.

This paper focuses on technical aspects related to the management and enforcement of privacy obligations as part of the wider problem of dealing with privacy policies.

In general privacy policies can be hard to enforce via IT solutions. The enforcement of privacy rights, permissions and obligations related to confidential and personal data requires the mapping of these concepts (that are most of the time abstract and based on high-level principles) into rules, constraints and access control, the meaning of which must be unambiguous so that it can be deployed and enforced by software solutions. Dealing with this still requires that the entities involved in the management of confidential and personal data follow best practices and good behaviours. However, being able to automate aspects of the enforcement of privacy policies and reduce the involved costs is important for enterprises.

Advancements in this direction have already been made when dealing with the (technological) enforcement of privacy permissions. Extended access control and authorization mechanisms have been built to check privacy permissions against users' rights, the purpose of the confidential information (that needs to be accessed) and the declared intents. This is the case, for example, of web transactions and interactions or applications/services within organizations that need to access and manipulate confidential data for business reasons.

More complex is the case of dealing with privacy obligations. They might include the deletion of confidential data after a predefined (potentially very long) period of time, periodic notifications and request for authorization to data owners or data subjects, fulfilment of opt-in/opt-out choices made by data owners, ongoing compliance with laws' obligations and internal guidelines. The events that trigger the fulfilment of privacy obligations can be completely orthogonal to the ones relevant for privacy permissions. Privacy obligations can have ongoing aspects that need to be monitored and satisfied over a long period of time. These tasks are challenging for enterprises because of the need for specific IT infrastructures and processes able to manipulate confidential data as dictated by privacy obligations.

The management and enforcement of privacy obligations, as first class citizens, is still a green field and open to research. In this paper we analyse some of the related issues, describe possible technical approaches to move towards a more explicit management and enforcement of privacy obligations and introduce a trusted system, dealing with obligations, that is currently under research at HP Labs.

2 Privacy Obligations

Privacy obligations define and describe expected behaviours and constraints to be satisfied by enterprises when dealing with confidential and personal data. Enterprises need to put in place underlying IT infrastructures, processes and mechanisms to be compliant with these obligations. This can be a challenging task due to the fact that privacy obligations can differ quite substantially depending on:

- **Level of refinement**: abstract vs. refined;
- **Enforcement timeframe**: short-term vs. long-term;
- **Expected enforcement actions**: one time vs. ongoing actions.

Privacy obligations can be very abstract, for example: „every financial institution has an affirmative and continuing obligation to respect customer privacy and protect the security and confidentiality of customer information" – Gramm-Leach-Bliley Act (1999). More refined privacy obligations can be expressed in terms of notice requirements, opt-out options, limits on reuse of information and information sharing for marketing purposes. At the other extreme, privacy obligations can dictate very specific requirements. This is the case where data retention has to be enforced for a long period of time or data is temporarily stored by organisations: privacy obligations can require that personal data must be deleted after a predefined number of years, e.g. 30 years (i.e. long-term commitment) – or in a few days if user's consent is not granted (i.e. short-term commitment).

The topic related to „privacy obligations" is complex: exploring all the possible implications and involved aspects goes far beyond the purpose of this paper. In this paper we focus on enforceable privacy obligations for personal and confidential data stored and managed by enterprises. In general different aspects need to be kept in account when dealing with these obligations:

- **The period of validity of obligations;**
- **The degree of enforceability of obligations;**
- **The events that trigger the need to fulfil obligations;**
- **The target (involved data) of an obligation;**
- **The actions that need to be executed to enforce an obligations;**
- **The entities that are responsible for enforcing obligations;**
- **Accountability criteria;**
- **Exceptions.**

It is important to clearly specify who is accountable for managing and enforcing privacy obligations. Exceptions need to be handled and criteria introduced (such as imposing strong auditing) to avoid abuses. In this paper we specifically explore the requirements and issues related to the management and enforcement of three core categories of privacy obligations: (1) long-term privacy obligations, (2) short-term privacy obligations, (3) ongoing privacy obligations. Table 1 shows examples of these types of obligations along with related events and actions.

Table 1: Types of privacy obligations and examples of related events and actions.

Long-term Privacy Obligations			
Events Triggering Obligations		Actions Dictated by Obligations	
Time-driven	1. at a specific date and time (e.g. 1:00am 01-Jan-2005) 2. after a certain period of time (e.g. 1 hour, 3 days, 5 minutes) 3. after the data has being used for a certain number of times (e.g. after being used twice) in a specific time-frame	Delete/ Update	1. delete all confidential data of a given data subject 2. partially delete data (e.g. delete only the credit card number) 3. replace data with an updated set of data (e.g. update subject's address)
Driven by Usage and Counters		Hide/ Unhide	1. hide (encrypt) all data of a subject from any access 2. hide a part of this data from any access 3. unhide all data 4. unhide a part of the data

Ongoing Privacy Obligations				
Events Triggering Obligations			**Actions Dictated by Obligations**	
Time-driven	1. periodically (e.g. every month)		1. send a report to a subject containing the status of their data and their opt-in/opt-out options (e.g. number of times being used, who has tried to access) 2. tell the subject what data he/she has provided 3. get updated data from subject 4. audit the logs, report any improper use of the data	
Driven by Contextual Events	1. when the data being used 2. when the data being transferred 3. when the data being deleted 4. a particular party/parties try to access 5. data is being used for certain purpose (e.g. send advertisement) 6. a set of data is going to be retrieved together 7. any action predefined by the data subject	Notify	1. notify the subject	
		Log	1. take logs	
		Access	1. default allow/disallow all access 2. allow 3. disallow	
		Consult	1. get authorization from data subject 2. get authorization from third party 3. check according to certain condition made by the user	
Others	1. when the privacy policies changed		1. Stop access to the data 2. update obligation	
Short-term and Transactional Privacy Obligations				
Obligations might need to be dictated by a transaction or an interaction. The actions specified by these obligations might need to be immediately fulfilled. These actions can be the same as the ones specified by long-term and on-going obligations.				

3 Important Issues and Requirements

Important issues and requirements need to be considered when dealing with the management and enforcement of privacy obligations:

- **Representation of privacy obligations**: privacy obligations need to be represented with an appropriate language to describe which data is affected by an obligation, the events and conditions that trigger the fulfilment of the obligation, actions to be carried on, which entities are responsible and accountable for their enforcement;

- **Association of obligations to data**: the association of privacy obligations to the targeted confidential data must not be easy to be broken. This aspect is particularly challenging in dynamic environments where confidential data can be moved around or sent to other parties;

- **Mapping obligations into actions**: when possible, actions dictated by obligations must be expressed in a way that can be programmatically enforced; otherwise, they should trigger related processes and workflows involving the human intervention and clearly state responsibilities;

- **Compliance of refined obligations to high-level policies**: the mapping of high level policies to refined privacy obligations (and the affected data) should be managed explicitly and tools built to spot potential inconsistencies and dependencies;

- **Tracking the evolutions of obligation policies**: obligation policies can be carried on over long periods of time and are subject to changes. Changes need to be tracked and obligations versioned, for accountability reasons and to deal with the evolution of the contexts and frameworks where these obligations apply;

- **Dealing with long-term obligation aspects**: long-term obligations have implications on the longevity and survivability of related processes and the involved data. Solutions needs to be build to last over a long period of time;

- **Accountability management**: as anticipated before, accountability management is fundamental to ensure that the enforcement of privacy obligations is carried on with clear responsibilities of the involved parties. This introduces requirements in terms of auditing, tracking of obligations and their monitoring;

- **Monitoring obligations**: the fulfilment of obligations must be monitored and checked against expected situations and behaviours. Despite good intents and enforcement mechanisms, it can always happen that the fulfilment of obligations is omitted. Monitoring mechanisms must be orthogonal to the enforcement mechanisms. Problems need to be notified to the responsible entities;

- **User involvement and awareness**: Users should have visibility of which obligations an organisation has with them. Tools should be provided to uses to allow them to monitor their fulfilment and directly manage their privacy obligations;

- **Complexity and cost of instrumenting applications and services**: the enforcement and monitoring of obligation policies can have an impact on the involved applications and services, both in terms of their instrumentation and development costs. A privacy obligation framework should reduce to the minimum this impact.

The management and enforcement of privacy obligations can be reasonably easy when the events that trigger them are well defined and easy to capture, for example they depend on time or known transactions or interactions. More complex is the case of privacy obligations related to ongoing obligations, triggered by the occurrence of events and conditions non-necessarily related to time or known transactions (for example dictated by laws, user's requests, etc.).

4 Addressed Problems

In this paper we address the problem of dealing with the explicit management of privacy obligations, on an ongoing basis, including short-term and long-term privacy obligations. This includes dealing with the monitoring, enforcement, and tracking of privacy obligations. We also want to address the related problems of managing the strong association of privacy obligations to data, enforce accountability and provide more transparency to users.

We believe that the reliable and verifiable management of personal data, in accordance with legal requirements and the policies of the data subjects/owners, is more easily achieved if it is controlled by privacy specific middleware rather than by application-level code. After all, the driving force behind any application solution is the set of business processes for which it is designed, not the privacy management aspects of the personal data it processes. The use of privacy management middleware allows a common (as supposed to piecemeal) approach to privacy issues to be taken, thereby creating trusted systems.

Work has already been done to address some of these issues, in particular related to the representation of privacy policies (and obligations), their enforcement in transactional and interaction-driven contexts and the management of simple long-term aspects of obligations for data retention. In many cases, though, obligation policies are considered as second-class entities the enforcement of which is subordinated to other aspects of privacy policies, such as privacy permissions.

A more explicit and comprehensive approach to privacy obligations is required. We aim at researching and building a trusted system where privacy obligations are considered as first-class „citizens" and can be managed without their subordination to other aspects such the management of privacy permissions or access control/authorization.

5 Related Work

Relevant work in the space of privacy management for enterprises is described in [KaSc02, KaSW02a, ScAs02, KaSW02b]. Enterprise Privacy Architecture is introduced and described in [KaSW02b], encompassing a policy management system, a privacy enforcement system and an audit console. Paper [ScAs02] introduces more architectural details along with an interpretation of the concept of privacy obligations. This concept is framed in the context of privacy rules defined for authorization purposes. This approach is further refined and described in the Enterprise Privacy Authorization Language (EPAL) specification [Epal04].

The above work makes important advancements in exploring and addressing the problem of privacy management in enterprises but it only considers the authorization and access control perspective as the driver for their representation, management and enforcement. It has still to be fully demonstrated that privacy obligations can be managed at their best from an authorization-based perspective. Privacy obligations can include aspects that are not really driven by authorization aspects, such as dealing with the deletion of confidential data at a specific date/event, periodically providing notifications to subjects about stored confidential data, dealing with ongoing requests dictated by subjects or laws. We believe that the representation, management and enforcement of privacy rights, obligations and permissions should be addressed without imposing any specific or dominant perspective.

In our proposed approach (described in the next sections) obligation policies are first-class „citizens" that are explicitly managed. Even if our architecture has high-level commonalities with the architecture described in [KaSc02, KaSW02a, ScAs02, KaSW02b] we further refine the concept of obligations and we introduce the concept of obligation versioning and tracking. We also split the enforcement mechanisms in two parts by including a scheduling mechanisms and an obligation enforcer where the obligations actions are carried out by flexible workflow processes that allows both automation and the involvement of people.

Mechanisms to deal with (privacy) obligations have already been implemented in products, in particular for data retention [Ibmt04] and in a variety of document management systems. Nevertheless, these approaches are very specific; they are focused on particular domains and handle simple obligation policies. Our work wants to push the barrier even further to create an obligation management framework that can be leveraged in multiple contexts, for different purposes.

A lot of work has been done in representing privacy policies, including obligations such as [Epal04, BJSW02, DDLS01]. Work describing the monitoring of obligations in policy management is described in [DDLS01]. Relevant work on mechanisms to associate policies to data is described in [KaSc02, KaSW02a, ScAs02, KaSW02b, CaPB03, AKSX02]. Each mechanism has pros and cons in terms of the implications for existing enterprise applications, services and data repositories. We can leverage aspects of this work, in particular [CaPB03] to provide a stronger association of obligation policies to confidential data.

6 Technical Details

This section provides technical details about the approaches and solutions under exploration at HP Labs to address the problems stated in section 4. Figure 1 shows a high-level architecture of a trusted system providing an explicit management of privacy obligations:

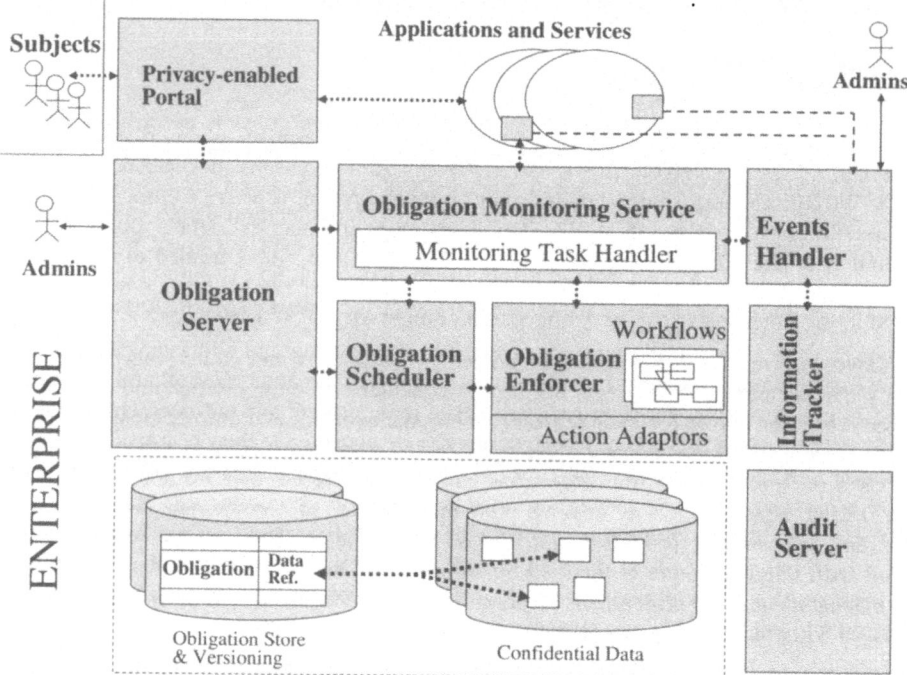

Figure 1: High-level Architecture

The obligation management system consists of:

- **Obligation Server**: it deals with the authoring, management and storage of obligations. It explicitly manages the association of privacy obligations to confidential data and their tracking and versioning. It pushes active obligations (i.e. obligations to be fulfilled) to the „obligation scheduler". One or more obligation servers can be deployed (and synchronised), depending on needs;

- **Obligation Store and Versioning**: it stores obligations and their mapping to confidential data. Multiple versions of obligations are also stored in this system;

- **Obligation Scheduler**: it is the component that knows which obligations are active, ongoing obligation deadlines, relevant events and their association to obligations. When events/conditions trigger the fulfilment of one or more obligations, this component activate the correspondent „workflow processes" of the „obligation enforcer" that will deal with the enforcement of the obligation.

- **Obligation Enforcer**: it is a workflow system containing workflow processes describing how to enforce one or more obligations. The enforcement can be automatic and/or could require human intervention, depending on the nature of the obligation;

- **Events Handler**: it is the component in charge of monitoring and detecting relevant events for privacy obligations and sending them to the obligation scheduler. The detection of events can happen via instrumented application/services. They can also be directly generated by users, administrators, the „obligation monitoring service" and the information tracker;

- **Obligation Monitoring Service**: it is the component, orthogonal to the scheduling and enforcement systems that monitors active obligations and if they have been enforced by analysing and checking for the effects of their actions;

- **Information tracker**: it is a component that focuses on intercepting events generated by data repositories, databases and file systems containing confidential data and providing this information to the event handler. It is aware of the location of confidential data (as described by the obligation policies) and checks for movements and changes happening to this data;

- **Audit Server**: it audits the relevant events and information generated by the overall system components and involved applications/services.

In our model, privacy obligations contain the description of relevant events/conditions, actions, targeted data (i.e. links to related confidential data) and accountable/responsible entities.

Issues arise when the overall environment is dynamic and data can be moved around: in this case the association of data to obligations policies can be broken or be left in an inconsistent state.

To address this issue we are exploring a variant of the architecture shown in figure 1, where stronger mechanisms are introduces to manage the association of obligations to data. Confidential data is obfuscated and strongly associated to privacy obligations by using cryptographic and enveloping techniques. A key management system is introduced to deal with this task as a subsystem of the Obligation Server.

Data envelopes are encrypted with the public key [HFPS99] of the key management system. The triple consisting of *<obligation policy, encrypted envelope, obfuscated data>* is stored as a replacement of the original data. The obligation policy must contain a reference to the competent Obligation Server but it can omit the reference to confidential data, as the policy is now directly associated to this data. In this way, the encrypted confidential data can be moved around and transmitted to other parties without an upfront control. The receiving party has to interact with the Obligation Server to decrypt the data: this allows the system to track and audit where the data is, check for relevant obligations and update its obligation store. The basic principles and additional details on how this approach can be implemented are described in [CaPB03, Casa04].

7 Discussion

Because of its nature, the system described in this paper has to be considered as a trusted system. It must be deployed by keeping in mind good security practices, especially for the platforms that will host our system components. Its core components are critical hence they require to be secured accordingly. Additional trust and accountability can be added by hardening the audit server and involving trusted third parties in the monitoring of the enforcement of obligation policies.

This system centralises the storage of privacy obligations along with their management. It can support the management of versions of privacy obligations over time and enable the tracking of their changes (and related applicability contexts) for auditing and accountability reasons. We are exploring how these aspects can be distributed to avoid potential bottlenecks and central points of failure, without compromising the overall security and integrity of the system.

The approach described in figure 1 is almost transparent to the data affected by privacy obligations. The second approach, involving cryptographic mechanisms, requires changes to data repositories to accommodate encrypted data. In both cases, applications and services might require some instrumentation, if applications/service-based events need to be detected. We are currently investigating how a hybrid solution can be used to accommodate different needs and requirements.

Our system explicitly focuses on the management and enforcement of obligations: this does not imply that it has to happen independently by other privacy aspects, such as permissions. It should be considered as a sub-system of a more comprehensive privacy management framework.

When dealing with long-term privacy obligations it is also important to ensure the reliability and longevity of the platforms running our system components and the survivability of the involved data and obligations. Work has already been done in this space, including [Ande96, EFL+98, KBC+00, Neum99, WBS+00], and can be leveraged.

8 Current and Future Work

An initial prototype has been implemented, consisting of four core components – obligation server, obligation scheduler, obligation enforcer and obligation monitor – and deployed within an enterprise environment. Figure 2 shows the architecture of the implemented prototype.

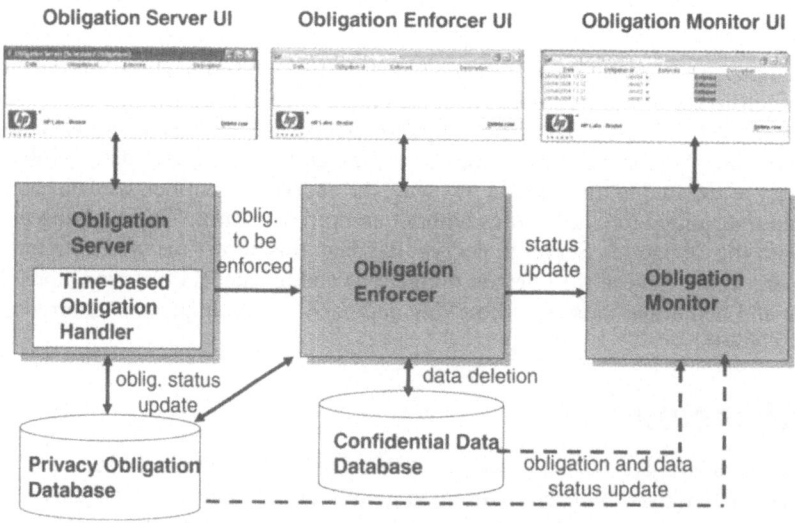

Figure 2: Architecture of Current Prototype

Privacy obligation policies have been represented by using an XML format to allow their future extensions. At the moment two categories of obligations are supported: long-term and short-term/transactional obligations. Modules to support ongoing obligations are under development. Current privacy obligations can be used to describe time-based events and actions requiring deletion or partial deletion of personal data stored in relational databases. The goal of this prototype is to show the feasibility of our ideas: the functionalities described in section 6 will be incrementally implemented in the next few months.

Our work and research is definitely in progress: technical aspects need to be further refined and investigated, especially the ones related to the life-cycle management of privacy obligations and events. The overall implications on enterprise applications and services need to be fully understood. Tools and mechanisms to address the compliance of refined obligations to high-level policies are also under investigation.

9 Conclusion

The management of privacy obligations is important for enterprises to preserve their reputation and brand, be compliant with legislation and customers' requirements and increase business opportunities. This paper describes important issues that need to be kept into account by enterprises when dealing with privacy obligations. In our vision privacy obligations (as well as for other privacy aspects, including rights and permissions) need to be considered as first-class „citizens" within privacy management frameworks.

We introduce a technical approach to deal with the explicit management of privacy obligations including transactional/short-term, long-term and ongoing privacy obligations. We provide a high-level description of a trusted system and its components dealing with the monitoring, enforcement, and tracking of privacy obligations. We discuss the problem of strongly associating privacy obligations to confidential data in dynamic environment and dealing with accountability management.

Our research and work is in progress. A prototype has been developed to test our ideas. Additional functionalities will be added in the next months.

References

[Laur03]   Laurant, C., Privacy International: Privacy and Human Rights 2003: an International Survey of Privacy Laws and Developments, Electronic Privacy Information Center (EPIC), Privacy International.
http://www.privacyinternational.org/survey/phr2003/, 2003

[Oecd80]   OECD: OECD Guidelines on the Protection of Privacy and Transborder Flows of Personal Data. http://www1.oecd.org/publications/e-book/9302011E.PDF, 1980

[Priv04]   Online Privacy Alliance: Guidelines for Online Privacy Policies.
http://www.privacyalliance.org/, Online Privacy Alliance, 2004

[KaSc02]   Karjoth, G., Schunter, M.: A Privacy Policy Model for Enterprises. IBM Research, Zurich. 15th IEEE Computer Foundations Workshop, 2002

[KaSW02a]   Karjoth, G., Schunter, M., Waidner, M.: Platform for Enterprise Privacy Practices: Privacy-enabled Management of Customer Data. 2nd Workshop on Privacy Enhancing Technologies, Lecture Notes in Computer Science, Springer Verlang, 2002

[ScAs02]   Schunter, M., Ashley, P.: The Platform for Enterprise Privacy Practices. IBM Zurich Research Laboratory, 2002

[KaSW02b] Karjoth, G., Schunter, M., Waidner, M.: Privacy-enabled Services for Enterprises. IBM Zurich Research Laboratory, TrustBus 2002, 2002

[Epal04]   IBM: The Enterprise Privacy Authorization Language (EPAL), EPAL 1.1 specification. http://www.zurich.ibm.com/security/enterprise-privacy/epal/, IBM, 2004

[CaPB03]   Casassa Mont, M., Pearson, S., Bramhall, P.: Towards Accountable Management of Privacy and Identity Information, ESORICS 2003, 2003

[Ibmt04]   IBM Tivoli: IBM Tivoli Storage Manager for Data Retention, 2004

[BJSW02]   Bettini, C., Jajodia, S., Sean Wang, X., Wijesekera, D.: Obligation Monitoring in Policy Management, 2002

[DDLS01]   Damianou, N., Dulay, N., Lupu, E., Sloman, M.: The Ponder Policy Specification Language, 2001

[HFPS99]   Housley, R., Ford, W., Polk, W., Solo, D.: RFC2459: Internet X.509 Public Key Infrastructure Certificate and CRL profile. IETF, 1999

[AKSX02]   Agrawal, R., Kiernan, J., Srikant, R., Xu, Y.: Hippocratic Databases. IBM Almaden Research Center, 2002

[Ande96]   Anderson, R. J.: The Eternity Service. Proc. PRAGO-CRYPT 96, CTU Publishing House, Prague, 1996

[EFL+98]   Ellison, R.J., Fisher, D.A., Linger, R.C., Lipson, H.F., Longstaff, T.A., Mead, N.R.: Survivability: Protecting your Critical Systems. Proceeding of the International Conference of Requirements Engineering, 1998

[KBC+00]   Kubiatowicz, J., Bibdel, D., Chen, Y., Czerwinski, S., Eaton, P., Geels D., Gummadi, R., Rhea, D., Weatherspoon, H. , Weimer, W., Wells, C., Zao, B.: OceanStore: An Architecture for Global Scale Persistent Storage. University of California, Berkeley, ASPLOS 2000, 2000

[Neum99]   Neumann, P.G.: Practical Architectures for Survivable Systems and Networks. SRI International, Army Research Lab, 1999

[WBS+00]   Wylie, J.J., Bigrigg, M. W., Strunk, J. D., Ganger, G. R., Kiliccote, H., Khosia, P.K.: Survivable Information Storage Systems. IEEE Computer, 2000

[Casa04]   Casassa Mont, M: Dealing with Privacy Obligations: Important Aspects and Technical Approaches. To appear in proceeding of the 1st International Conference TrustBus 2004, Springer Verlag, LNCS, 2004

Trusted Computing: From Theory to Practice in the Real World

Dipl. Math. Alexander W. Koehler

Utimaco Safeware AG, Hohemarkstraße 22, D-61440 Oberursel,
Fed. Republic of Germany
alexander.koehler@utimaco.de

Abstract

Trusted Computing technology is now able to provide solutions to today's enterprise IT security issues. There is a need to increase control over the corporate network. Mobility increases productivity, but with new risks, which have to be handled by technology that is able to ensure security with acceptable costs. Creating security needs well-thought-out concepts, technology, infrastructures, and people who develop, communicate with, and use security products. This paper is intended to deliver one full line of a picture of Trusted Computing, starting with the objectives, looking at the status of Trusted Computing today, and some existing applications, and ending with a view of what will come next.

Broadly-accepted standards are an important prerequisite for any new concept or technology. The Trusted Computing Group (TCG) is the industry-accepted standards body which combines the IT security expertise in Mobile Security of vendors such as Utimaco Safeware AG. Case studies help integrate the views of customers in the presentation on products and vision

Disclaimer

The intention of this paper is to build the bridge between theory and reality. In consequence there is a need to use real products to relate to, and explain, Trusted Computing. This should not be considered as surreptitious product promotion.

1 Why Trusted Computing?

Trusted Computing is a highly-complex matter, and so is the TCG. There are no doubt many definitions of trusted computing. I have chosen this one: It is an IT environment, or an area within it, in which a user, IT administrator or business partner can have „trust". The term „trust" should be considered as a general term that incorporate other concepts such as „system integrity", „reliability", and „predictability". These concepts can be defined as those concepts on which well-known threats such as malicious code, badly-written code, or hardware design weaknesses, could have an influence, as soon as somebody tries to exploit them. This paper, which is simply intended to provide the reader with an introduction to Trusted Computing, does not define the terminology involved in any more detail. There are plenty of technical details, abbreviations and assumptions. Before we begin describing the technology and other details, it is important to agree on some basics. It will then be much easier to understand the TCG and all its ramifications. I would like to begin by classifying these assumptions.

S. Paulus, N. Pohlmann, H. Reimer (Editors): Securing Electronic Business Processes, Vieweg (2004), 209-218

1.1 Assumption 1:

The use of additional hardware components increases security dramatically

If you store a secret, such as a key, on your PC's hard drive, then there is a good chance that somebody else can read it. Several tools are available for detecting key patterns on the hard drive or in RAM. To avoid exposing the key to such attacks it is better way to store the key in a separate location that no malicious software can access. This does not solve the problem that the key has to be transferred to RAM to be processed by the CPU. The solution to that is to have a separate processor at the location where the key is stored. The key will be processed there, and will never leave it. That's secure. This kind of storage and dedicated processing unit package is implemented as smart card, if a removable hardware component is required, or as a Trusted Platform Module, in which case it is integrated with the processor board.

1.2 Assumption 2:

Ultimate protection for data is only given by encryption.

Access control mechanisms may work, but past experience has shown that access control is a barrier that can be overcome without great effort. Usually access control means nothing else than an attribute for a set of data. If the managing software, be it the operating system itself or an application, respects this attribute, the access control mechanism is secure. If other software or operating system is used to access the data, then the access control mechanism no longer provides protection. Improvements in access control system programming does not improve the level of security: there is a need to change technology. The solution to this security task is encryption. Encryption can be considered as the ultimate level of data protection. Encryption does not protect against destroying the content by erasing a file. This is still in the scope of access control. We have seen that the content is well-protected against being read, as it is encrypted. What we need to protect with the ultimate level of security are the keys used for encryption and decryption. Here we refer back to assumption 1, and we can then conclude: Encryption keys need to be stored and processed in dedicated hardware such as smart cards or the TPM (Trusted Platform Module). The TPM is described in detail in chapter 2. TPM (Trusted Platform Module).

To summarize: Ultimate data protection has two prerequisites: 1. Use of encryption technology 2. Use of dedicated hardware for key storage and processing, such as smart cards or a TPM.

So far we have discussed how to provide data with the best-possible protection. But what about the software, the operating system? How do we know that the PC platform is not being manipulated by malicious code? For example, if a thief with a stolen identity tries to use another PC device to penetrate a corporate network. How does the network server knows that the PC device which is trying to connect to it is the one it claims to be? The answer to all that is given by the TPM (Trusted Platform Module) which is described in the next chapter.

2 TPM (Trusted Platform Module)

The TPM is a fairly simple, mass-produced silicon chip. It consists of a silicon print similar to the one used on a smart card, such as the Random Number Generator, Key Generation and RSA Engine, Non-Volatile Storage, Program Code and Execution Engine.

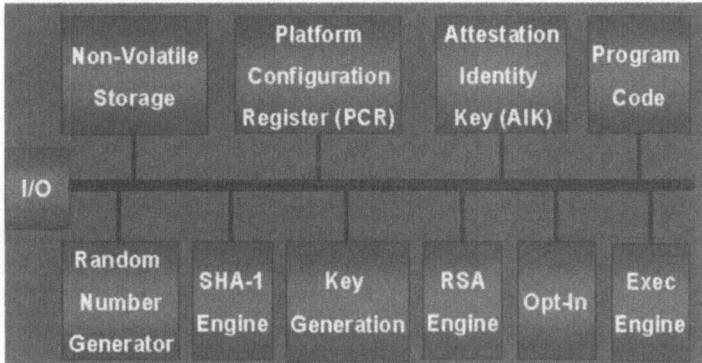

Figure 1: Trusted Platform Module (TPM)

This means that the user use the TPM to perform the same tasks as a smart card, apart from the fact that the TPM „smart card" does not live in a smart card reader, from which it can be removed. The TPM is attached to the motherboard of the PC or other platform. The TPM is much more than a smart card. We will first look at how its additional features will help the user or the IT administrator. The TPM offers two fundamental values to the device:

2.1 „Who am I?"

The TPM can be used to pass on a unique identity to the larger computing device. This identity is based on the ability of a TPM to store an asymmetric private key and perform basic RSA operations using that key. The TPM stores a private key or digital certificate that is associated with a private key stored in the TPM. Using this approach, TPMs can be used to assert identity.

2.2 „Can I be trusted?"

The TPM can be used to evaluate the integrity of software running on a PC or any other computing device. A TPM can be used to store measured integrity information about software for future reference. It does so using so-called HASH functions (algorithms). This creates a way to test whether the software in use is exactly the same as the software installed by the administrator. The assertion is that if the software is the same, the device can be trusted. If the software has been modified, perhaps the device can no longer be trusted. One way to determine if a unit of data has been modified is to hash the original version, preserve the hash value, and use that value as a reference in the future. If the hash value of the unit of data changes, the reason is that the data has been changed. Another capability of the TPM is that it contains Platform Configuration Registers (PCRs) to provide persistent and protected storage for hash values. When an authorized individual configures the device, that person can hash critical components of the software suite in the device and store those values in PCRs. Later, when the device is in use, these critical software components can be hashed in real time and the calculated values can be compared to the stored values. If they match, those components have not been modified since last accessed by the administrator. If they do not match, an unauthorized agent has changed a critical element of the software suite. In this case, it may be prudent for the corporate network security staff to treat the device as compromised.

The tasks of the TPM are:

- Keeping secret information such as passwords and keys out of the reach of software attacks
- Generating high-quality keys, using a hardware random number generator
- Processing private keys inside the unit
- Storing measured data

We have seen before that there are some similarities between the TPM and a smart card. I think everybody agrees that a smart card inserted in the PCMCIA slot of a notebook would neither replace nor control the main CPU (Pentium etc.). Nevertheless, it is sometimes claimed that the TPM controls the PC. This is incorrect. The need for the TPM to store data passed to it from the CPU is based on a simple physical rule: If the data which is measured from an object is stored in the object itself, then the measured data would be exposed to the same kind of attack as the object itself. It would be easy for an attacker to manipulate the measured data in the same way that they manipulated the object's data, and it would be impossible to detect. Hence, any kind of measurement would be worthless. This is the reason why the TPM and CPU need to be two physically-separate units.

The TPM is the most tangible element of the Trusted Computing Group concept. The Trusted Computing Group has defined the standard to which TPMs chips are to be designed. Leading chip vendors already offer TPMs and the most important PC desktop and Notebook vendors already offer multiple product lines that include the TPM chip. However, to create security, much more is needed than this piece of hardware.

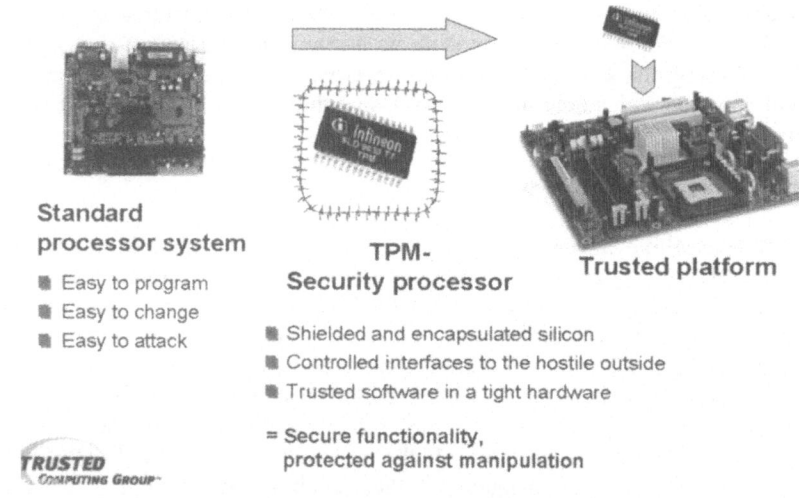

Figure 2: Standard Processor vs. Dedicated Security Controller

3 TCG: Trusted Computing Group

Security in a networked world is a task of worldwide partners. There are many interfaces: from software engineers to special interest groups, government and legal bodies, from industry analysts to the press, and so on. To organize security, there is a need for a central body. The Trusted Computing Group is this body.

The Trusted Computing Group, which was launched on April 8, 2003, is incorporated as a not for profit corporation with international membership and broad industrial participation. The purpose of the TCG is to develop, define, and promote open industry standard specifications for embedded hardware-enabled trusted computing and security technologies, including hardware building blocks and software interfaces, across multiple platforms, peripherals, and devices. By using the building blocks and software interfaces defined by the TCG specifications, the industry can address a range of security needs without compromising functional integrity, privacy, or individual rights.

TCG was created with an organization structure and governance model, as defined by the TCG bylaws, which is similar to many other computing industry standards bodies. These include the following:

- An open membership model with multiple membership levels
- A Board of Directors consisting of Promoters and elected Contributors
- Multiple Work Groups that are open to Promoter and Contributor members, and seek active participation by these members
- A reciprocal reasonable and non-discriminatory (RAND) patent licensing policy between the members
- Supermajority voting at Board and Work Group level to facilitate progress.This structure is designed to enable the rapid development of open, industry standard specifications with broad industry participation, and to foster widespread adoption of the organization's specifications.

The key deliverables of TCG will be hardware and software interface specifications, white papers and other materials that facilitate understanding and adoption of the specifications, and marketing programs that promote awareness and customer adoption.

For more information about TCG, please visit www.trustedcomputinggroup.org

4 TCG, operating systems and hardware platforms

The TPM provides tremendous improvements to IT security when it is integrated into, for example, application software solutions. The TPM could do even more if it could be used by the operating system. During February 2004 Microsoft announced that the TPM will be part of the successor to the Windows XP operating system, code named Longhorn. The secured operating system component has been named NGSCB (Next Generation Secure Computing Base). Developing an NGSCB for Longhorn is still on-going and subject to major changes during the lifetime of this paper. For this reason, this paper will not describe the NGSCB.

If an operating system used the TPM, the real benefit would only come together with redesigned hardware platforms. To get the full picture for Trusted Computing, I propose to examine Intel's announcement in February 2004 of a new project, code-named LT for LaGrande Technology.

Remember that today's PC (micro)processor design goes back to the 1980s. At that time, these microprocessors were designed to do their job despite the limitations inherent in their hardware design. This hardware design was quite different to the one used for minicomputers or even mainframes. For instance, protected execution is a classic must in computer science. It prevents DoS (Denial of Service)-type attacks from being successful.

Today we need to bring back the benefits of a fully-featured hardware design. Improvements to the hardware design need to be compatible with the most common platform in the world, which is the PC platform, so backwards compatibility is mandatory. For this reason Intel is enhancing the PC platform not only with this functionality, but even more. The additional functionality, such as protected graphics, arises from today's threats and needs. (20 years ago, graphics were not an issue on most client devices). This is LT:

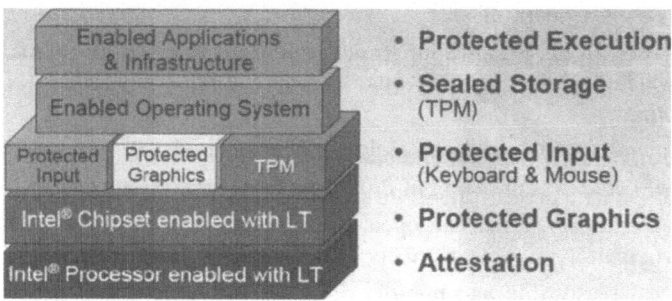

Figure 3: Summary of LT Capabilities

LT improvements over the standard PC platforms are implemented on functions, which are provided by the TPM.

LT provides a kind of „vault", which is a protected partition. Security-sensitive tasks are performed inside this protected partition. The vault has some limitations on its functionality. Software developers are requested to only use the vault for security-sensitive parts of their code. The main part of the code should be executed in the standard partition, as it is today.

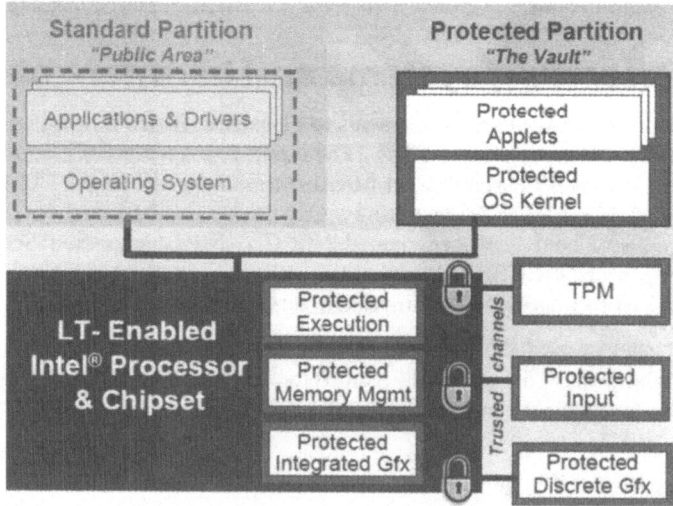

Figure 4: Protected LT Environment

Improvements in operating system design, coordinated with changes in the design of the PC hardware platform, are a great step forward – in theory. But in the real world it will take several years, as millions of today's PC platforms will continue to operate as stand-alone machines or, most of them, linked to a network. What we will see are several incremental steps by the hardware vendors and operating systems vendors to implement the next stages of IT security.

One advantage of the TCG concept is that there is no need to wait for a rosy future. Today, all major PC vendors already offer Notebooks and PCs with a TPM, so users can already benefit from increased security by using TCG technology today. The next chapter describes one real-life example of security software and shows how TCG technology is beneficial to today's security software.

5 Real-life security products: Increased benefit by using TCG technology

Notebooks are the preferred tool of corporate users. Usually Notebooks carry a large amount of important data. Notebooks are also at threat from several identifiable types of attack.

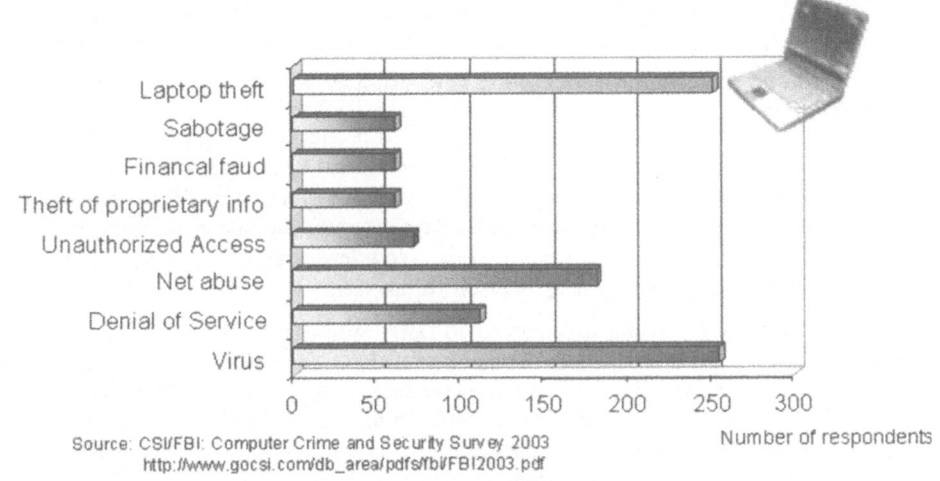

Source: CSI/FBI: Computer Crime and Security Survey 2003
http://www.gocsi.com/db_area/pdfs/fbi/FBI2003.pdf

Figure 5: Types of Attack on Mobile Devices

Number one is the same as for any other PC, it is a virus attack. It is essential for a networked device such as a Notebook to have antivirus software installed on it. But what is about the number 2 threat, theft? Theft means that you are no longer in possession of your property. Let me quote what Microsoft says about that. There are the ten immutable laws of security. Law number 3 says: If a bad guy has unrestricted physical access to your computer, it's not your computer anymore. Microsoft is synonymous with today's Windows operating system technology. Does this mean we have to live with the fact that notebooks represent a threat with which we are obliged to live ? Not at all. If we widen the scope beyond the operating system, there is an answer.

We classify the status of the notebook into two simple categories. The first is „power off". This is usually the case when the attackers gets hold of the Notebook. Let's have a look at power-off protection.

Imagine the Notebook is stolen, or just left in a taxi. It can be protected. The method is called Bulk Encryption. Bulk Encryption means that every sector on the hard drive is encrypted, which includes all operating system files. The individual encryption of selected files and folders requires a sophisticated security policy and disciplined users. A disciplined user is a user who is willing, and has the time, to care about where to save files, delete the ones which are no longer needed, and so on. This means the user must comply with some sort of security policy, point by point. Often this is not feasible in the real world. The solution is Bulk Encryption. It frees the user from such tasks and makes them more productive, and makes the system secure. Bulk Encryption runs in the background without any kind of user interaction.

Bulk Encryption means full protection on power-off. It protects both system files and the SAM (Security Account Manager) database in which password hashes are stored. An attacker could swap the SAM with a rogue version. Bulk Encryption protects the operating system, programs, data, etc.: it protects everything. It even prevents the thief from reading the hibernation file in which even individually-encrypted files would be stored as plain (unencrypted) text, if they were being used at the moment when hibernation started.

Bulk Encryption is a technology which is already in use on millions of clients around the world. It has never been cracked for more than 10 years. However, security is not static: threats and defense scenario evolve continuously. For this reason every vendor should go far beyond today's threats when considering modern security technology. They should for example include hardware protection for encryption keys. Another issue to consider is that, in theory, a dictionary attack is always possible against any software-only solution. It is extremely difficult if somebody wants to run it against a certified product. Nevertheless, dictionary attacks simply become impossible if they have to be run against hardware. This is the case with the TPM: if a TCG hardware component, the TPM, is added to a proven IT security software solution, this improves security even more at the present time, and makes security better prepared for future attacks, which are certain to come. Now let's consider what the TPM can do when the Notebook is „on", known as „power-on" protection.

As soon as the Notebook running it is subject to fairly similar threats to a desktop PC. The TPM hardware chip protects credentials such as private keys or secure passwords. Passwords could be generated automatically, and long and complex, as they would be handled internally within a machine. This will make it extremely difficult to crack them. Passwords protected by the TPM will enable Single-Sign-On to the operating system and applications, which means increased security combined with increased user productivity.

The TPM offers another benefit when it comes to insider attacks. Imagine somebody removes a hard disk drive from a corporate desktop and installs it somewhere else. As they know the passwords, they will be able to read the data. The TPM will prevent them from doing so. The password the user knows is only the one used to open the TPM to access other secret information about the operating system, programs or the network. If there is no TPM or if there is another TPM, the attempt to access this other secret information will fail. This concept is called Machine Binding. Data can be tied to the machine.

At the beginning of this paper the True Random Number Generator was described, as one component of the TPM. The application shown here uses this hardware key generator to increase the level of security, as described above.. An example of how these keys can be used in the product referred to here is that, not only is the client authenticated at the server, but vice versa: mutual authentication. This prevents rogue servers cheating an honest client. To end this part of the paper, I would like to quote a famous mathematician: „Anyone who considers arithmetic methods of producing random digits is, of course, in a state of sin", said John von Neumann.

SafeGuard Easy, combined with the TPM and IBM's ESS (Embedded Security Subsystem), is already in use in several European financial services companies. These companies typically use Notebooks as real fat clients. They use custom application software to provide their consulting services to their customers. It would reduce their competitive advantage if this software were available to anybody else. In addition, customer data is also processed on these clients. The service company is responsible for the privacy of this data. The consequence is that security has to be state-of-the-art, yet place no limitation on productivity. „SafeGuard Easy combined with IBM's ESS technology is the only acceptable solution for us," said one of the customers. Obviously the technology is of real benefit to customers.

We have seen here how a real-life high-quality security product can use the benefits of TCG technology. TCG technology means increased security, improvements in user-friendliness and productivity, or reduced costs, and in some cases even a combination of all of these factors. Obviously this matches TCG's declared design goals: Delivering robust security with user control and privacy. In the next chapter we will examine the prospects for the near future. It is another endorsement of the thesis that security is much more than just hardware and software. It is about concepts, infrastructures and so on: the mirrored picture of a networked world.

6 The Near Future of Trusted Computing:TNC (Trusted Network Connect)

So far this paper has focused on the PC platform and Trusted Computing as a sort of point solution. For the sake of completeness, it should be mentioned that Trusted Computing relates to every kind of device that has a certain level of data processing power, and is able to link to a network. This includes PDAs, smart phones, intelligent printers and whatever devices will be developed in the near future. If we look beyond devices, there is the network itself.

The networks, systems, software applications, and data of many enterprises and organizations form a critical foundation and essential structure for their daily operations. Without a reliable and functional network, the business is not secure.

The issue is that point solutions are simply not adequate, and that an end-to-end, comprehensive approach to the security problem is a good way to push security to a higher level. An industry standards-based solution for securing the endpoints of host connections is a critical step on the path to this comprehensive approach, and it is critical for an acceptable solution to our growing network security problem.

The Trusted Network Connect specification for multi-vendor networks will provide a common architecture for vendor solutions that will:

- Ensure endpoint integrity by establishing a level of „trust" in the state of an endpoint. Specifically, solutions based on the specification will ensure the presence, status, and upgrade level of mandated applications, revisions of signature libraries for anti-virus and intrusion detection and prevention system applications, and the patch level of the endpoints, operating system and applications.

- Maintain access policy by helping ensure that the endpoint machine and/or its user authenticate and establish a level of trust before connecting to the network.

- Provide quarantine measures for endpoint machines that do not meet the security policy requirements for „trust" and, if possible, apply appropriate remedial measures, such as upgrading software or virus signature libraries to enable the endpoint to comply with security policy. TCG is developing an open specification to improve network security and integrity.

The Trusted Network Connect specification, due to be available at the end of 2004, will assist in protecting networks from viruses, worms, denial of service attacks and host software vulnerabilities by allowing users to enforce security policies to prevent vulnerable or untrusted systems from connecting to the network.

7 Summary

IT security is not a static topic but an on-going process. The concept and content of Trusted Computing is an important building block to create robust security products which will provide substantial improvements to IT security. TCG concepts already reach to the future, and an additional strength is that Trusted Computing already works with today's products, infrastructures and business processes.

Abbreviations and References

TCG	The abbreviation has two meanings: Trusted Computing Group; the organization as a standards body www.trustedcomputinggroup.org Technology based on standards provided by TCG
TPM	Trusted Platform Module: a dedicated security chip bound to a PC or other hardware platform, manufactured by Infineon, for example. http://www.infineon.com/cgi/ecrm.dll/ecrm/scripts/prod_ov.jsp?oid=29049
TNC	Trusted Network Connect www.trustedcomputinggroup.org
SafeGuard Easy:	Bulk encryption product by Utimaco Safeware AG www.utimaco.com
ESS	Embedded Security Subsystem by IBM http://www.pc.ibm.com/us/think/thinkvantagetech/security.html
LT	LaGrande Technology by Intel http://www.intel.com/technology/security/
NGSCB	Next Generation Secure Computing Base by Microsoft http://www.microsoft.com/resources/ngscb/default.mspx

Acknowledgments:

First and foremost I would like to thank all the members of the TCG who provided inputs in several formats, from informally discussions to management presentations. Special credit goes to Stacy Cannady (IBM), David Grawrock and Monty Wiseman (Intel), Thomas Rosteck and Hans Brandl (Infineon). I also owe the mentioned gentlemen thanks for the contribution of diagrams as presented in this paper.

In this document names and brands are properties of their respective owners.

Electronic Signatures – Key for Effective e-Invoicing Processes

Stefan Hebler

TC TrustCenter AG
A Betrusted Company
Sonninstraße 24 – 28
20097 Hamburg
stefan.hebler@trustcenter.de

Abstract

The goal was to improve business processes and to save costs in a major intenational industrial corporate group by enabling the electronic exchange of invoices. An electronic mass signature solution, built on TC TrustCenter's digital certificates, was implemented as part of a large-scale pilot project. The signature complies with strict EU tax laws, meets technological, procedural, and legal demands, and can be easily integrated into the complex processes of electronic invoicing. The solution thus represents a significant added value for companies and is another innovation within the business sector of digital signatures.

1 Introduction

Trustworthy business processes are generally based on reliable information, such as sender identity (authenticity) and the correctness of a document's content (integrity). This is why in the paper-based world, documents are written on business stationery and carry a signature. Nowadays, electronic data processing and the automated generation of paper-based documents are gradually eliminating the need for hand-written signatures.

But not only are hand-written signatures being eliminated, even paper documents themselves are becoming increasingly redundant as more and more processes are now entirely electronic. For electronic documents, this development is causing electronic signatures to increasingly replace hand-written ones. The EU and several other countries have already implemented laws regulating the equalization of an electronic signature with a handwritten one (see EU Signature Guidelines, German Signature Act).

In addition, various laws, requiring a hand-written signature for documents to be legally recognized, have been modified in many countries (including Germany) to explicitly place an electronic signature on the same legal level as a hand-written signature. German tax and social laws are one example.

The expansion and modification of the German VAT law from January 1st 2002 now makes electronic invoices with qualified electronic signatures eligible for input tax deduction.

In addition, guidelines for data access and the verifiability of digital documents (GDPdU), as well as other directives, regulate processes of archiving and verifying electronic invoices.

These far-ranging legal changes greatly affect electronic invoicing and archiving and allow for a new degree of efficiency and cost reduction.

S. Paulus, N. Pohlmann, H. Reimer (Editors): Securing Electronic Business Processes, Vieweg (2004), 219-227

In contrast to the handwritten signature, its electronic counterpart can be generated automatically and can thus be fully integrated into an electronic workflow, which significantly reduces manual work investments. This automation is especially crucial for invoice generation and invoice receipt because of the large numbers of documents that are being exchanged and processed.

The electronic signature can digitalize the entire invoicing process for both the invoicing party and the invoice recipient, making paper-based bills a thing of the past.

E-invoicing also eliminates error-prone and thus inefficient and expensive media breaks[1]. Furthermore, the modified legal framework enables the replacement of paper-based archiving with simple and cost efficient electronic archiving.

Our project goal was to find the ideal way to implement these new opportunities for cost reduction and increased efficiency. We thereby faced two challenges: The observation of all legal regulations and the smooth realization of the sensitive and critical processes involved in invoicing and invoice receipt.

The following picture illustrates the advantages of electronic invoicing:

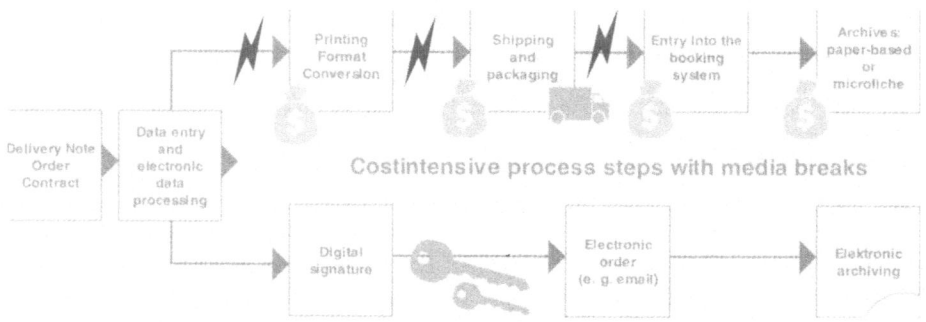

2 Requirements

The system that was to be developed faced a number of legal and procedural requirements. To prevent delays at an advanced project stage, the legal demands received our initial attention.

2.1 Legal Requirements

The legal requirements for tax-deductible electronic invoices are essentially derived from the following laws and regulations:

- VAT law
- VAT executive order
- Principles of data access and the verifiability of digital documents (GDPdU)
- Principles for proper DV-based accounting systems (GoBS)

---

[1] Media Breaks - interruptions that occur in a process when switching from a paper based medium to an electronic medium

- BMF (German Federal Ministry for Finances) letter from January 29th, 2004
- Signature Act
- Signature Ordinance

For project purposes, these demands were divided into four categories:

- generating and including the electronic signature
- mass signing by a third party
- processing and documenting the signature verification
- archiving the signed invoice

2.1.1 Generating and Including an Electronic Signature

Quality requirements for electronic signatures are derived from §14 of the German VAT law:

„An electronic account with a qualified electronic signature (with provider accreditation) is considered an invoice, according to § 15 Abs. 1 of the Signature Act." (Translated from German original)

The quality of an electronic signature is determined by two features: The verification of a person's identity in compliance with legal regulations and the assignment of this information to a key pair (digital certificate). Only the reliable validation of the data contained in the certificate equalizes the electronic signature with the handwritten one. In addition, the key pair generation on the signature card is relevant. This quality feature is provided by TC TrustCenter, part of the international Betrusted Group and an accredited certification provider. The procedure ensures that a certificate cannot be copied or be used by several people.

Naturally, the entire procedure of affixing signatures to massive numbers of invoice documents requires special measures to secure the system from unauthorized access.

Once it has been activated, the signature card automatically signs all documents with a legally binding signature, which makes it especially important to secure all system components.

The solution developed during this project only uses hardware components that are relevant for the signature function as well as self-developed software components preventing electronic attacks using SSL encryption for all communication channels. In addition, system manipulation is prevented by protecting individual components. The entire system can only be administered by a superordinate role concept. All components are physically located in TC TrustCenter's high security data processing center, which ensures the highest-possible degree of protection and control.

2.1.2 Mass Signature by a Third Party

The mass signature procedure developed for this project raised two crucial questions:

6. Is it admissible that a natural person as the signature card owner signs invoice documents on behalf of an invoicing party?

7. Is it admissible to use automated mass signature procedures that do not require the signatory to check the document content?

In a letter from January 29th, 2004, the German Federal Ministry for Finances responded positively to these questions:

Concerning question 1:

Section 1.1: „Invoice"

„An invoice can be issued by the invoicing party itself or by a commissioned third party at the expense of the invoicing party." (§ 14 Abs. 2 Satz 5 UstG) (Translated from the German original)

Section 2.2.1 „Qualified Electronic Signature"

„15 According to § 2 Nr. 7 SigG, this certificate can only be issued to natural persons. It is admissible that one or more company members are authorized to sign in the name of the enterprise. In this case, tax obligations of the company or the authorized third party remain untouched." (Translated from the German original)

Concerning question 2:

Section 2.2.1: „Qualified Electronic Signature"

„18 For the generation of qualified electronic signatures, all technological procedures (e.g. smartcard, kryptobox) are admissible as long as they comply with the Signature Act. The company must provide proof of the compliance upon request. The invoicing party may also make use of an automated mass signing procedure to sign invoices." (Translated from the German original)

2.1.3 Processing and Documenting the Signature Verification

In the „principles of data access and the verifiability of digital documents" (GDPdU), defined in a letter from the BMF, the VAT law regulates the access of financial authorities to electronic invoices and signature verification processes.

The GDPdU distinguishes between 3 types of access, which are at the discretion of the verifying person:

- immediate access to the data processing system of the party liable for taxation in read-only mode.
- indirect access in read-only mode
- delivery of the data carrier to the financial authority

The essential requirement for all three access types is that the party liable for taxation provides the verifying authority with all necessary auxiliary means. For this purpose, a software tool was developed during the project, which is used to display electronically signed invoices. This so-called „TC Cryptographic Message Viewer" is distributed to all verifying authorities at no cost.

The signature verification process is regulated in section 2, part 1 of the GDPdU:

„The qualified electronic signature with provider accreditation, according to § 15 Abs. 1 of the Signature Act, is part of the electronic account. The original state of the transferred and possibly still encrypted documents must be verifiable at all times. This requires, in addition to the demands of section VII letter b) number 2 of the GoBS (a.a.O.), that prior to a further processing of the electronic account, the qualified electronic signature must be verified with regards to the integrity of the data and the signature authorization. It furthermore requires that the results are documented." (Translated from the German original)

To meet these demands, the functions of the TC Cryptographic Message Viewer were expanded: The validation of the certificate used for signing and the verification of the signature's integrity were realized. Another function is the result documentation, which stores the results of all validations and integration verifications.

Upon realization of the project, it was decided to provide users and interested parties with the TC Cryptographic Message Viewer free of charge.

The following picture shows the TC Cryptographic Message Viewer, a signed document, and the result documentation required by the GDPdU:

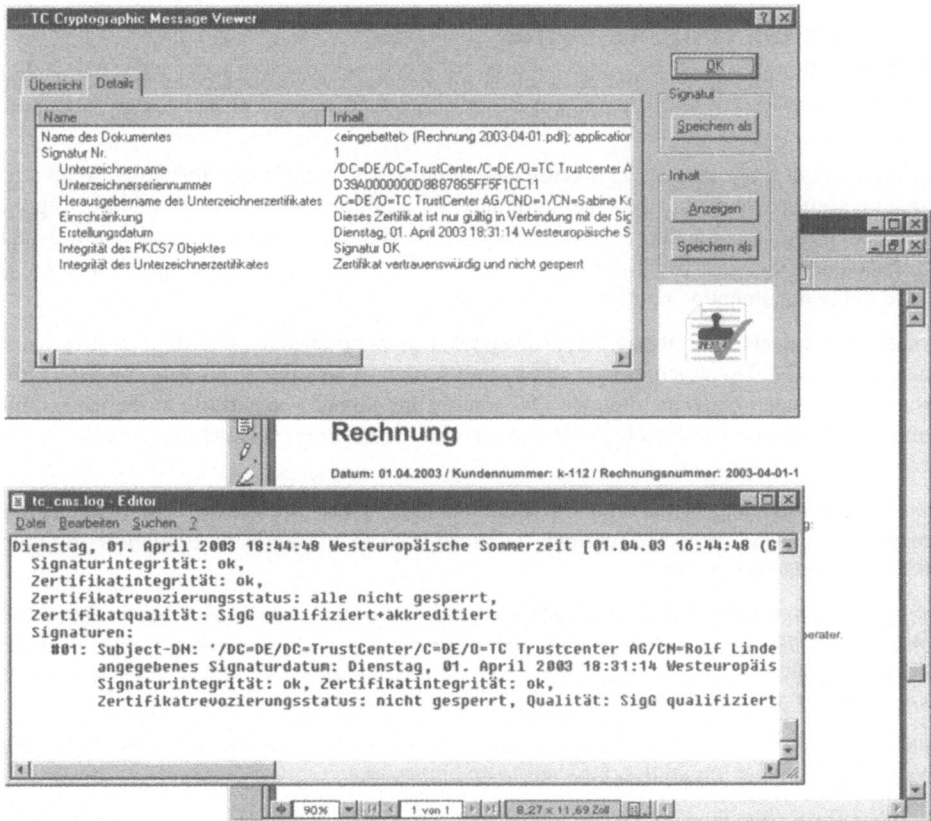

2.1.4 Archiving the Signed Invoice

At the basis of the GDPdU (explained in 2.1.3), are the „principles for proper DV-based accounting systems" (GoBS), BMF letter from November 11th, 1995.

The GoBS regulate the electronic archiving of documents that must be kept to comply with the general fiscal law.

In section VIII. „reproduction of documents available on data carriers" (Tz. 8 of the GoBS), it is stated that:

„a) The party obligated to keep records who can only provide documents on data carriers, is required at his/her own expense to provide the auxiliary means needed to make the documents readable. Upon request of the financial authority, s/he is required to immediately print out the documents in whole or in part or to provide other readable reproductions (compare II)." (Translated from the German original)

Since the GoBS do not prescribe the type of data carrier used for archiving, TC TrustCenter's mass signature solution features a database to archive signed invoices.

It was therefore particularly important to provide financial authorities with the means to view archived invoices, in this case the TC Cryptographic Messenger described under 2.1.3.

2.2 Process Requirements

The introduction of a mass signature solution for electronic invoices faced a special challenge because all processes involving invoicing and invoice receipt are highly sensitive and company-critical.

During many of these processes, documents are already generated automatically. With a mass signature solution, they can now be automatically equipped with a legally binding signature as needed. The mass signature solution developed during the course of this project was named „TC Document Server." With the help of flexible interfaces, the system can be directly connected to the document generation system of the invoicing party.

Incoming documents are administered through a queuing system according to priority. The concept of the TC Document Server allows any format to be signed and thus simplifies its integration into heterogeneous systems. Documents are signed – according to demand– immediately after they are received (synchronal) or with a time delay (asynchronal) before they are made available for download.

The further processing of the signed invoice has been made flexible because of the different demands within the project. They can be transferred to the invoice recipient as download, batch processing or via e-mail.

The special prerequisites that an accredited certification provider must meet in terms of the technological, physical, and organizational security of its data processing center lead to the decision to make long-term archiving a part of this solution. All signed documents can be stored in TC TrustCenter's data base archive in encrypted form for twelve years.

Another feature of the TC Document Server is high availability, which is especially significant for the complete integration into automated processes.

For this purpose, the mass signature solution TC Document Server is operated in parallel master mode, in which all system components are operated redundantly. Furthermore, this form of operation is optimized for the processing of peak demands during automated load distribution.

The signature card is a so-called SigG unlimited card. The German Signature Act requires that the signatures are generated by specially protected components (chip cards). The SigG unlimited card is a high-performance SigG-compliant chip card, which has been specially approved for server operation.

2.2.1 Architecture Overview

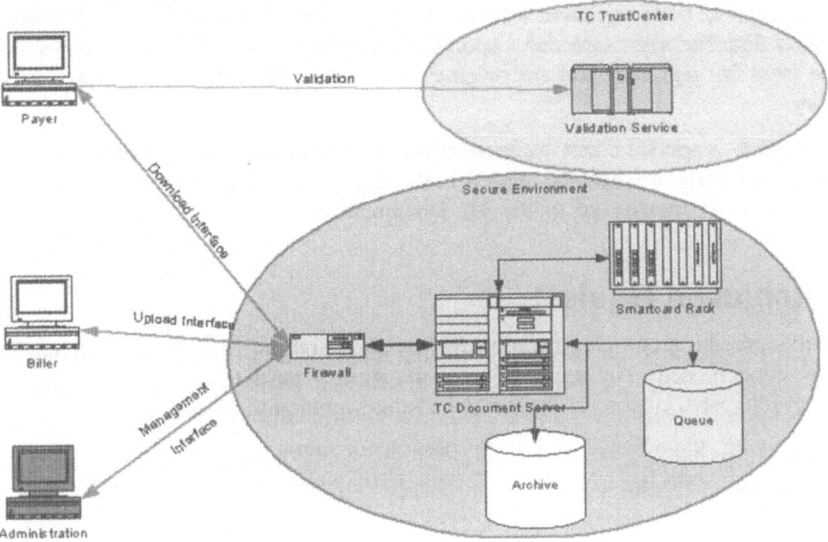

2.2.2 Data Communication

Data communication to and from a TC Document Server takes place over Intranet or Internet and HTTPS protocols are used. The accompanying encryption ensures that sensitive documents cannot be accessed or modified by unauthorized third parties. The use of firewalls and client certificates successfully restricts access to authorized personnel.

2.2.3 Protocol for Document Upload

An important project requirement was the possibility of manual and automated use of this signature service. With this solution, documents to be signed can be uploaded using standard web browsers via HTML forms. Script-controlled and thus automated upload is also possible.

In addition, the server can be reached via the SOAP protocol and can therefore be very simply integrated into e.g. Java (J2EE) and Microsoft NET environments. The SOAP protocol is also supported by mySAP. The SOAP interface is especially suitable for an integrated automated workflow.

The use of the TC Document Server interfaces takes place via secured HTTPS connections, preventing interception and manipulation. The simultaneous use of HTTPS client certificates prevents unauthorized access.

2.2.4 Signature Formats: Encapsulated or Detached Signatures

Signatures are generated in the standardized PKCS#7 format. Two characteristics exist here: The encapsulated format (pkcs7 message), in which the document that is to be signed is contained in the signature file. The other is the detached format (pkcs7 signature), in which the unchanged document is present alongside the signature.

2.2.4.1 Conversion of the Signature Format: Detached to Encapsulated

The advantages of both signature formats can be combined in that the TC Document Server generates a detached signature and a special client component creates an encapsulated signature file from this signature and the original documents. An additional signing process is not necessary.

To achieve this, a special client component for the remote hashing procedure was developed. During remote hashing, only the digital hash value relevant for the generation of the electronic signature is transferred to the TC Document Server. This significantly reduces data volume.

2.3 Achieved Goals

During this project, a complex solution for the mass signing of electronic invoices was successfully implemented. The experience of the project participants and numerous inquiries from other interested customers illustrate the future-orientation of this solution.

In the following, the advantages of the solution for invoicing parties and invoice recipients are summarized under the headings cost reduction, quality of service, security, and return on investment.

2.3.1 Cost Reduction

- Incoming electronic invoices from different contractors can be signed centrally and are thus eligible for input tax deduction in accordance with § 14 Abs. 4 Satz 2 of the VAT law.
- Complete substitution of paper-based invoices due to a consistently electronic invoicing process without cost-intensive media breaks[2]
- Elimination of costs for printing, packaging, and postage due to electronic mailing or possibility of download
- Paper-based archiving is replaced by simple and cost-efficient electronic archiving
- The automated processing of incoming electronic invoices eliminates manual process steps such as receiving controls and entrance into the accounting system
- With the automated invoice processing, payment goals and discounts can be optimally exploited

2.3.2 Quality of Service

- The consistently electronic invoice processes are far less prone to errors and can be easily administered
- The customer's electronic invoice data offers a successful and flexible marketing instrument and contributes to an increase of customer retention
- The use of the TC SigG unlimited card is the prerequisite for the mass dispatch of electronic invoices without time delays

---

[2] Media Breaks - interruptions that occur in a process when switching from a paper based medium to an electronic medium

2.3.3 Security

- As an accredited certification provider, TC TrustCenter offers the highest-possible degree of legal security for the recognition of electronic invoices by the financial authorities

- The electronic invoice sending process can be separately protected by optional data encryption

- The TC Cryptographic Message Viewer enables the automated and legally-compliant signature verification and documentation, allowing for mass numbers of invoices to be processed at once

- TC TrustCenter as an accredited provider ensures the verification of signatures for the long term (30 years)

2.3.4 Return on Investment

- In most cases, investments for the electronic invoice signature are amortized within the first year, even for small invoice volumes

- Because of the scalability, modularity, and standardized interfaces of the TC Document Server, investments for the electronic invoice signature remain transparent at all times

- Particularly the complete substitution of paper-based archives with electronic ones leads to a quick ROI

Legally Binding Cross Boarder Electronic Invoicing

Georg Lindsberger[1] · Gerold Pinter[2] · Alexander Egger[3]

[1]XiCrypt Technologies GmbH
georg.lindsberger@XiCrypt.com

[2]PricewaterhouseCoopers
gerold.pinter@at.pwc.com

[3]Campus02 – University of Applied Science
alexander.egger@campus02.at

Abstract

With the implementation of electronic invoicing the European Union is expecting an increase of electronic trade. According to legal requirements in the EU, invoices with deductible input VAT have the status of an official document. In most member states digital signatures have to be used in order to issue an official electronic invoice. This article is about the legal aspects and technical requirements for electronic cross boarder invoicing within the European Union. The award winning project „Legally Binding electronic invoicing" (e-Business board of the Austrian government) will be presented. The focus of this project was to implement a legally binding electronic invoicing solution in Austria. Additionally a survey is summarized which investigated the attitude of the Styrian people towards electronic invoicing.

3 Legal situation of electronic invoicing

Electronic invoicing has been touted as a 'killer application' of the Internet. Electronic invoicing involves a multitude of advantages, such as lower cost, higher efficiency or faster transactions. Every single step of the process takes place within the same medium. Up to now invoices have gone through computerized accounting systems, have been printed, enveloped and sent to the recipient via conventional mail. Then the recipient had to enter the hardcopy-invoice into his accounting system in order to complete the procedure.

With electronic invoicing it is no longer necessary to print, envelope and send invoices per mail and store them. That means you can reduce costs and accelerate proceedings. Consequently electronically delivered invoices will cut printing, packaging and postage costs. Electronic invoicing can assist companies in reducing the inefficiencies and costs associated with traditional paper-based billing. Therefore, the European Council Directive (2001/115/EC) which is concerned with invoicing requirements obligated the Member States to approve electronic invoicing as of January 2004. [EK03]

S. Paulus, N. Pohlmann, H. Reimer (Editors): Securing Electronic Business Processes, Vieweg (2004), 228-236

3.1 Legal situation in Austria and Germany

According to legal requirements in Austria until recently invoices had to be exchanged as hard copy to enable the recipient to deduct VAT. Only telecopies had been equally accepted so far. According to law electronic invoices as well as electronic vouchers were not legally approved as invoices in the conventional sense.

Section 11 of the Austrian Tax Act has been changed in that way, that electronic invoices have to be accepted by the tax administration. Unfortunately the legislator did not stipulate in detail which requirements electronic invoices have to fulfill to enable VAT deduction for the recipient. The precise definition of the authenticity and integrity of the electronic invoice was left open to a decree. After discussions about which security level should apply for electronic invoices the ministry of finance was in favor of qualified signatures while applicants were against electronic signatures. Finally, taking into account Germany's experience in this field the minister of finance decided that an electronic invoice must bear an advanced electronic signature. The advanced electronic signature must be based on a certificate issued by a registered certification authority but it does not have to be a qualified certificate. [Pin03]

In Austria the criteria for invoices and their obligatory record were expected to come into effect with the second Tax Act amendment, 2002. This second Tax Act amendment already passed the Council of Ministers and the financial committee and provides the amendment regarding the approval of electronic invoices. The amendment states that electronically transferred invoices are going to be tax deductible from profits tax if their source authenticity and their content's integrity can be guaranteed. Another precondition is that the recipient must agree to the electronic transmission.

Germany's counterpart to this directive came into effect on January 1st, 2002. According to this regulation electronically signed invoices have to be equally acknowledged and are deductible from input VAT. Under the terms of the German VAT Act, however, only authorized electronic signatures based on a qualified certificate are accepted.

3.2 Cross boarder invoicing

The strictest requirement a member state could impose is an advanced electronic signature within the meaning of Article 2 (2) of Directive 1999/93/EC based on a qualified certificate.

For the member states it is also possible to require no electronic signature for electronic invoicing. That means the requirements within the member states vary from advanced electronic signatures based on a qualified certificate to no signatures at all.

To enable cross boarder invoicing within the EU the legal requirement of that country applies in which the recipient wants to deduct VAT and the strictest requirement should be fulfilled. In other means if you are using advanced electronic signatures based on a qualified certificate you fulfill the strictest regulation possible in the European Union.

3.3 Storage liability

Electronically transmitted invoices have to be stored for several years as paper invoices. Over this period of time the authenticity and the integrity of the content of the electronically transmitted invoice must be guaranteed.

This regulation, however, is connected with some difficulties. Data carriers for the storage of invoices are subject to an ageing process. Floppy disks are only legible for two or three years, CD-ROMs five to seven years and hard disks can also only be read for some years, depending on how often they have been used. Another problem that arises when storing data is the renewal of software. Software programs are often replaced by new versions. This means that documents compiled with a certain version can probably not be read any more with a later version.

Another critical problem is the validity period of electronic signatures. Electronic signatures can lose their validity due to technological changes or because of the revocation of certificates. The European Telecom Standards Institute (ETSI) elaborated the standards for long-time validity of electronic signatures. From the technical point of view it is advisable to store the electronic invoices in a trusted digital repository which supports long-term signatures.

4 Technical solution

To realize secure and legally binding cross boarder invoicing within the EU you should have a system which supports advanced electronic signatures based on a qualified certificate for signing your invoices. The electronic invoices have to be stored in an archive guaranteeing the authenticity of the origin and integrity of the content of the invoices throughout the storage period.

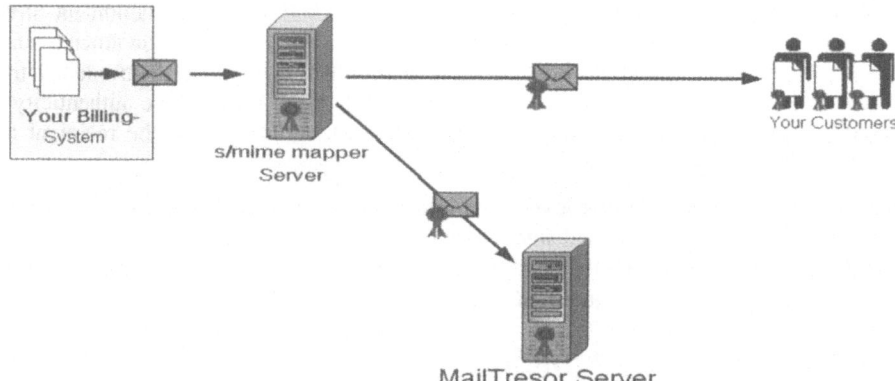

Figure 1: S/Mime Mapper and System MailTresor used to sign and store invoices

To fulfill the requirements described above, XiCrypt Technologies GmbH, an Austrian company, has introduced System MailTresor together with the signature server S/Mime Mapper, which provides both transmission and secure storage of electronically signed documents supporting advanced electronic signatures. The solution of XiCrypt supports all kinds of signatures in both sending and storing documents. As it is based on the Mime Standard, it can be used with any software supporting email and the recipient of an invoice has only to have access to a standard email client. The solution of XiCrypt is divided into two parts:

- S/Mime Mapper: The S/Mime Mapper is an application that transparently signs, verifies, encrypts and decrypts electronic messages (email) according to the S/Mime standard [DHR+98].

- System MailTresor: The System MailTresor is an archive and electronic signature preservation solution for storing the electronically signed emails.

These two solutions form the basis for a legally binding electronic invoicing solution. S/Mime Mapper and MailTresor are described in detail in the next two sections.

4.1 Signing electronic invoices using S/Mime Mapper

Most invoicing applications are using email to transfer invoices from one business partner to another. To use this kind of invoicing system the application only has to be able to generate electronic invoices as emails. The rest is handled by the S/Mime Enhancement Server and the System MailTresor.

The S/Mime Enhancement Server (S/Mime Mapper) allows sending S/Mime-secured emails. It supports all algorithms and message formats defined in the S/MIME Version 2 specification, thus guaranteeing inter-operability with other S/MIME-compliant products of the customers.

The cryptographic functionality of the program remains transparent to the invoicing system. The invoicing system of the company only needs to generate emails including the electronic invoice. S/Mime Mapper also supports hardware security modules (smart cards etc.) [DGP03]

Sending electronic invoices

1. The electronic invoice is generated by the billing system of the company. The company only has to be able to generate email invoices.

2. The billing system sends the message to the host where the S/Mime Mapper software is running

3. The S/Mime Mapper software receives the email (invoice) and electronically signs the message

4. S/Mime Mapper relays the processed message to the MailTresor server.

In order to support advanced electronic signatures S/Mime Mapper can be used together with a certified mass signature creation smart card via the supported PKCS#11 interface. The security environment of S/Mime Mapper, its relationship and boundary to other components, is described in more detail in the next section.

4.2 S/Mime Mapper – security environment

The S/Mime Mapper implements a proxy for electronic mail protocols that is capable of automatic on-the-fly handling of signatures and encryption. The S/Mime Mapper is configured to be placed in between standard email protocol communication of an invoicing application and an email server. The invoicing application and the server communicate using the standard protocols SMTP, POP3 and IMAP. Alternatively, the S/Mime Mapper can be placed between two email servers using the SMTP protocol to communicate. The S/Mime Mapper is controlled by a policy that specifies under what circumstances an email is to be signed or encrypted or when already signed email is to be verified or encrypted email is to be decrypted. Encryption and signing is only done when messages are sent using the SMTP protocol. Decryption and verification is done when messages are received using any of the other protocols. These tasks are done automatically and transparently to the user agent or the email server.

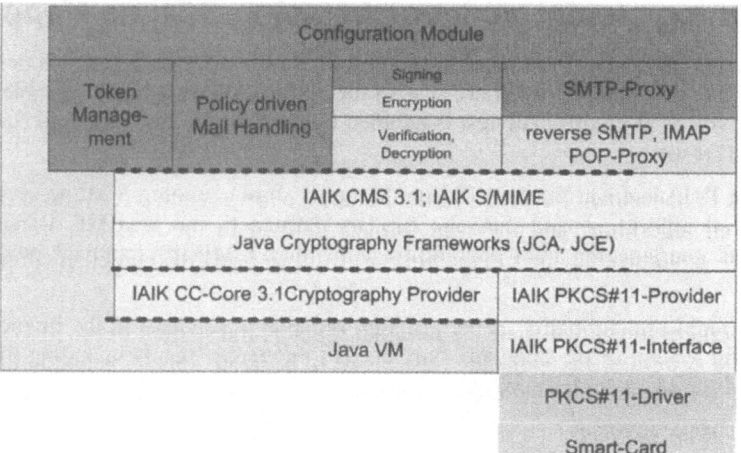

Figure 2: S/Mime Mapper and its environment

The S/Mime Mapper manages a set of security tokens for all email addresses it is configured to handle. Whenever a message is to be signed, the S/Mime Mapper picks the corresponding token to sign the message. It depends on the sender's email-address which token is chosen.

Signing itself is done by the IAIK CMS and S/Mime toolkit that is designed to handle cryptographic messages conforming to the S/Mime standard [DHR+98]. To create the signatures, the CMS toolkit again makes use of the IAIK JCE CC-Core 3.1 toolkit and of cryptographic hardware. In case of electronic invoicing, a certified mass signature creation device, that is accessed via the standard PKCS#11 interface can be used. The IAIK PKCS#11-wrapper and the IAIK PKCS#11-provider bridge the gap between the standard JAVA crypto interface and the PKCS#11 driver provided by the vendor of the cryptographic token used. Figure 1 shows a Java Virtual Machine VM running the S/Mime Mapper which again uses components to sign and verify email messages.

4.3 Archiving digitally signed emails

A problem that arises when using electronically signed emails for electronic invoicing is the method to archive emails in a way that the electronic signature stays verifiable over years. Email messages archiving systems need to take care of this problem. Archiving electronic data however is easily understood by most users. Even well trained users, who are saving signed emails in state of the art digital archives, could face problems validating an electronic signature that has been created seven years ago. They may well be able to retrieve the email properly including the signature but they may face the following difficulties:

- The signature does not verify, because the certificate was revoked or the required revocation information is no longer available.

- The signature does not verify, because the algorithm used was broken or the used key-length is too small.

The ETSI standard TS 101.903 defines a data format for that purpose. To ensure that electronic signatures are durable over years, this standard extends the signatures with additional security elements to meet the legal requirements for the storing of signed documents over a certain number of years.

Electronic signatures – as defined in the European Directive on Electronic Signatures – provide basic authentication and integrity protection and can be created without accessing any online services. However, without the addition of time-stamps and other relevant data, like revocation information, the electronic signature cannot be verifiable in the future. To address this issue, ETSI TS 101.903 [ETS01] defines the following signature formats:

- Support for Advanced Electronic Signatures including signed properties like Signing-Time, SigningCertificate, SignaturePolicyIdentifier or CommitmentTypeIndication.

- Advanced Electronic Signatures with Timestamp [ACPZ01], to take initial steps towards providing long-term validity.

- Advanced Electronic Signatures with complete validation data, which saves the references to the set of data supporting the validity of the electronic signature.

- Advanced Electronic Signatures with extended validation guarantees that any keys used in the certificate chain or the revocation status information can be compromised and the certification path data and revocation status data would not be stored anywhere else.

- Archive Validation Data provide protection against the case that keys or other cryptographic data would become weak and the cryptographic functions become vulnerable.

While the ETSI-standard explicitly aims at advanced electronic signatures as defined by the European Directive, the measures taken are equally applicable to signatures of a lower quality. Apart from the problem of keeping an electronic signature verifiable there is still the basic problem of keeping the data of the email readable. Storage technologies have more or less solved the problem of keeping the bit stream readable, nevertheless there is still no solution to ensure the readability of file formats. With emails the problem is especially important for attachments. We can assume, that trivial format of simple text emails will still be readable by future data processing machines. When using electronic signatures one has to keep in mind that a common approach in digital preservation, the conversion of the file to a newer file format, is not possible. This approach alters the file and therefore breaks the signature. MailTresor is simulating or preserving the system and capable of reading the file. No matter which technique is used to keep file formats readable a management process is used to monitor the danger of files becoming unreadable. If such file formats are detected measures have to be taken to preserve readability of the file. When dealing with electronically signed email MailTresor adds further functionality to state of the art archiving systems:

- Validating the electronic signature
- Generating enhanced electronic signatures
- Generating meta data
- Monitoring the stored files

MailTresor adds additional security to state of the art archives to guarantee authenticity and integrity all over the storage period.

5 Electronic invoicing in practice

In June 2003 the e-Business board of the Austrian government announced an open invitation to tender for projects supporting electronic signatures. The intention of this call was to push electronic signatures in practice. Campus02 University of Applied Science and XiCrypt Technologies won the call with the project „Legally Binding electronic invoicing". The focus of this project was to implement a legally binding electronic invoicing solution. Project partner for implementing the reference electronic invoicing solution has been WIFI Styria. With a market share of 20 percent, the Austrian Chamber of Commerce's Institute of Business Promotion (WIFI) is the top training and further education institute in Austria. More than 320,000 participants attend approx. 26,000 courses taught by 11,000 trainers. The WIFI institutes have an annual turnover of EUR 109,009,251.25. WIFI has an extensive national network of institutes with at least one main WIFI in each province and 80 branches which all offer WIFI courses.

WIFI Styria issues about 45.000 invoices per year to 25.000 customers. The aim of the project was to digitalize step by step the whole business process for sending the invoices in electronic form to the customers. As a matter of the rearrangement of the invoicing process concerning electronic invoicing, WIFI Styria is expecting an enormous cost reduction. Within the first year 10% of all invoices can be issued electronically. Consequently a cost reduction of at least € 20.000 can be realized in the first year.

Technically the integration of the electronic invoicing system was a straight forward process. The invoicing system of WIFI Styria was already able to generate invoices as emails. S/Mime Mapper has been integrated between the invoicing application and the outgoing email server. All emails using the sender email address *einvoicing@wifi.wkstmk.at* are digitally signed based on a qualified certificate. No cross boarder e-invoices are needed and therefore no qualified certificate is needed as well. Additionally the System MailTresor is used to archive the digitally signed invoices. A rule in S/Mime Mapper was defined that signed emails are also transmitted to System MailTresor. MailTresor preserves the email invoices over the legal storage period.

What else has to be taken into consideration is the recipient's attitude towards electronic invoicing. WIFI Styria has a conventional business to consumer relationship. There were almost no studies about the customer's attitude towards electronic invoicing available. That's why part of the project was a survey about electronic invoicing. The survey investigated the attitude of the Styrian people from the age of 15 with internet access towards electronic invoicing. The survey was conducted through face to face interviews in November 2003 by students of Campus02. 7 interviewers questioned 258 people. The survey included the following issues:

- Attitude toward email: How many email addresses are used by one customer? How often does a customer change his/her email address?
- Used software: What programs for checking email are used? Can the customer read PDF files?
- Internet use: How often is a customer accessing the internet? How often does the customer check his/her emails?
- Popularity of the term „e-Billing": What does the customer associate with the term „e-Billing"?
- Electronic invoicing – Yes or No: Does the customer accept his/her invoices per email?

The results of the survey were surprising. 96% of all interviewees hold at least one email address. 60% check their email account daily and 90 % check their emails at least once a week. 89% change their email address less than once a year. This leads to the conclusion that email is a reliable way to transmit the invoices to the customer.

87% of all interviewees are using email clients like MS Outlook, Outlook Express, Netscape or Lotus Notes. All these applications are supporting the S/Mime standard. In other words 87% percent have an application that can check the digital signature of the e-invoice without installation of additional software. This is a strong argument for signing the invoices using the S/Mime standard.

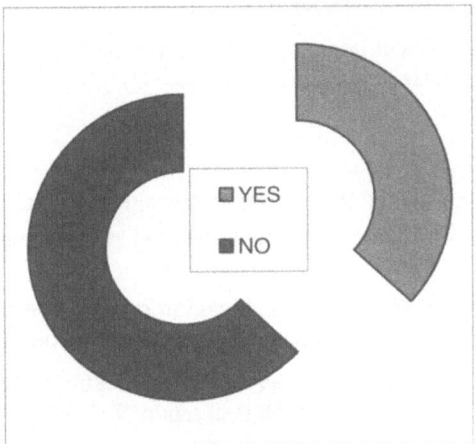

Figure 2: Do you want your invoices per email?

Only 12,5 percent of the interviewees use Acrobat Reader. Sending the invoice only as PDF will not be appropriate. Therefore, WIFI Styria is sending the email invoices as plain text. More than half of the interviewees already associate the transmitting of invoices via the internet with the term „e-Billing". The fact that 37% (**Figure 2**) would already accept their invoices per email – without marketing activities – is also surprising.

The survey has shown that issuing the invoices using email is the right decision. In order to guarantee a successful project, the introduction of the electronic invoicing system should be supported by marketing activities. The installation of the electronic invoicing system at WIFI Styria is now completed. Within the next month WIFI Styria will start issuing invoices per email.

6 Conclusion

The requirement for electronic invoicing within the European member states vary from advanced electronic signatures based on a qualified certificate to no signatures at all. To enable cross boarder invoicing within the EU the legal requirement of that country applies in which the recipient wants to deduct VAT and the strictest requirement should be fulfilled. In other means if you are using advanced electronic signatures based on a qualified certificate you fulfill the strictest regulation possible in the European Union.

One way to issue electronic invoices is to send them per email to the customers. Most accounting applications already support email invoices, but without electronic signatures and without a trusted digital repository which support long-term signatures. Therefore, the legal requirements cannot be fulfilled.

An easy way to extend the existing accounting system with the necessary features is to use the electronic signature server S/Mime Mapper for signing the email-invoices and the trusted digital repository MailTresor to archive the invoices over the legal storage period. S/Mime Mapper supports advanced electronic signatures based on a qualified certificate and can therefore be used for cross boarder invoicing.

The customer survey about electronic invoicing has shown that it is a good way to issue the electronic invoices using email. Email together with the S/Mime standard to support digital signatures will be the best way to issue legal compliant invoices to end customers.

Additionally the fast and efficient implementation of the electronic invoicing system at WIFI Styria has proved to be of great advantage in practice.

References

[ACPZ01]   C. Adams, P. Cain, D. Pinkas, and R. Zuccherato. RFC 3161: Internet x.509 public key infrastructure time-stamp protocol (TSP), aug 2001. Status: INFORMATIONAL.

[CCS01]   Reference model for an open archival information system (OAIS). Technical report, Consultative Committee for Space Data Systkoeems, July 2001.

[DGP03]   DI Georg Lindsberger DDr. Gerold Pinter. Elektronische Rechnungsstellung Ebilling Suite by XiCrypt. Technical report, XiCrypt, 2003. http://www.xicrypt.com/knowhow.php

[DHR+98]   S. Dusse, P. Hoffman, B. Ramsdell, L. Lundblade, and L. Repka. RFC 2311: S/MIME version 2 message specification, mar 1998. Status: INFORMATIONAL.

[DLF01]   Metadata encoding and transmission standard (METS).Technical report, Digital Library Federation, 2001. http://www.loc.gov/standards/mets/http://www.loc.gov/standards/mets/.

[EK03]   Mounir El-Khoury. Standards and Developments on electronic invoicing. Technical report, CEN/ISSS eInvoicing Focus Group, bruessel, Germany, june 2003.

[ETS01]   Etsi ts 101 903 xml advanced electronic signatures (xades). Technical report, European Telecommunications Standards Institute, 2001.

[Pin03]   Gerold Pinter, Georg Lindsberger. Elektronische Rechnungstellung – Vorschläge für eine Verordnung zu § 11 Abs. 2 UStG, Steuer und Wirtschaftskartei 11/2003

SecMGW – An Open-Source Enterprise Gateway for Secure E-Mail

Tobias Straub[1] · Matthias Fleck · Ralf Grewe · Oliver Lenze

Computer Science Department
Technische Universität Darmstadt
{tstraub I mfleck I grewe I lenze}@cdc.informatik.tu-darmstadt.de

Abstract

Securing e-mail with cryptography and PKI is an effective countermeasure against common threats like SPAM, malware, or industrial espionage. Compared to the troublesome handling of PKI-enabled applications by end-users, the idea of a centralized gateway managing all cryptographic tasks seems very attractive.

However, such a gateway represents a single point of attack as it stores a lot of keys. We show how to address this issue by means of threshold cryptography and describe the SecMGW concept which easily integrates in existing environments. SecMGW was implemented solely using open-source products making it a cost-effective solution, well-suited for small and medium enterprises.

1 Introduction

From the beginning of the Internet era until today, e-mail was and still is one of the most important applications on the net. While its usage has massively grown over the last two decades to currently more than 15 billion daily messages[2], present technology is pretty much the same as it was in the early days. In particular, security was not a design criterion in RFC 821 [Post82] and 822 [Croc82], which is the reason why users are exposed to numerous threats today. As opposed to RFC 822-mail, X.400 or proprietary solutions (used e.g. in the military), in fact have built-in security features, but these standards have only little relevance in practice [Oppl01].

The standard e-mail protocol (RFC 822) has no means to provide data origin authentication, integrity protection, or message confidentiality. Without additional protection mechanisms, users are thus exposed to unsolicited commercial e-mail (a.k.a. SPAM), the risk of being impersonated or to attackers that may eavesdrop on messages in transition. Indeed, e-mail can be secured with cryptography if a public key infrastructure (PKI) involving the end-users is at hand. This is an effective countermeasure against violations of confidentiality and authenticity, as well as against spammers since digital signatures would allow a more efficient and reliable filtering. Most commercial off-the-shelf e-mail clients originally support encryption and digital signatures according to the S/MIME standard, PGP/OpenPGP plug-ins are also available free of charge for all major operating systems.

---

[1] The author's work was supported by the German National Research Foundation (DFG) as part of the PhD program "Enabling Technologies for Electronic Commerce" at Technische Universität Darmstadt.

[2] As estimated by an IDC study [IDC02] for the year 2002. This number is expected to double until 2006.

S. Paulus, N. Pohlmann, H. Reimer (Editors): Securing Electronic Business Processes, Vieweg (2004), 237-249

However, as experience has shown, these features are hardly used in practice. End-users are often deterred by the complexity and abstractness of security mechanisms on the one hand and the insufficient usability of the corresponding applications on the other hand. A number of studies have shown that users already encounter problems when they are asked to apply passwords properly (see [SaBW01, Sass03] for a survey), not to mention conceptually more complex techniques like SSL connections [FHH+02].

Kaufman et al. [KaPS02] state that „humans are incapable of securely storing high-quality keys, and they have unacceptably slow speed and accuracy when performing cryptographic operations." But this is exactly the case with end-to-end e-mail security: Users have to pay a certain price for the benefits of public key compared to symmetric key cryptography [Davi96]. Due to their intrinsic complexity, public key systems transfer responsibilities to the users that are otherwise being centrally handled by a server or administrator. Among these burdens are the management of keys, certificates, and status information. Whitten and Tygar [WhTy99] emphasize that security is usually a secondary goal and has an abstract nature. Their empirical evaluation of a PGP-capable e-mail client confirmed the hypothesis that users have a hard time applying security tools accurately in practice. Usability deficiencies of the software are an important reason why security mechanisms fail.

It is a common belief that risks in security software are very often due to human error [VoVo02]. This leads to the conclusion that security mechanisms either require a careful software design combined with profound end-user training or a technological re-design and a switch to another paradigm. Delegating difficult cryptographic tasks from the client side to a central, trusted authority is a typical approach in the latter direction. Applying these ideas to the e-mail scenario in an enterprise environment, the idea of centralizing cryptographic tasks is an apparent way to facilitate end-users' task and to reduce the complexity visible to them. Due to the way how e-mails are processed and stored by a central server, such a service could be put into practice without affecting the flow of information. A common criticism however to such a crypto e-mail gateway is the fact that it naturally represents a single point of attack as it stores a lot of plaintext messages and – what is even worse – private keys.

In this paper, we show how the issues of usability and security can be addressed by an e-mail gateway using threshold cryptography. The objectives and our concept of the Secure Mail Gateway (SecMGW) are described in the following section postponing technical details of our prototype to Section 3. Related work is reviewed in Section 4 before a discussion and an outlook to further work concludes the paper.

2 Objectives and Design

As pointed out before, facing end-users with e-mail security is often problematic. In this section we first list a number of design objectives and feature requirements for a centralized secure e-mail gateway. This leads us to deployment and policy/processing considerations in Section 2.2 and 2.3. Using threshold cryptography in order to enhance security is an essential idea of SecMGW. It is described in detail in Section 2.4. A security analysis is given in Section 2.5.

2.1 Scenario and Requirements

The scenario we have in mind is a small or medium enterprise with an existing e-mail infrastructure. This may include an Internet provider offering appropriate service to the enterprise or the company's own mail server, possibly augmented with groupware functionality. We take into account that there are different groups of users each having specific security requirements. The general user, which we refer to as *common user*, is not expected to use end-to-end secure e-mail, i.e. members of this group implicitly delegate all cryptographic operations to a central service, the so-called *secure mail gateway*. Common users are assisted by an administrator who sets up the gateway and sometimes intervenes when human action is necessary. Besides common users, there may be a minority of employees with higher security needs, e.g. members of a resource or personnel department. These people can not always delegate all operations to the gateway since they are handling sensitive data and have to preserve confidentiality on the whole way to and from their desktop. As a consequence, they have to be educated accordingly concerning the usage of secure e-mail. We refer to them as *sophisticated users*.

In the following, we list a number of requirements towards and properties of SecMGW which have a significant impact on realization:

- Common users' contact with technical terms and details should be reduced to a minimum. This however does not exclude means to perceive and express individual security goals on a higher level e.g. in the form of declaring the content of a particular e-mail as „sensitive". At the same time, the solution should comply with current e-mail clients requiring no or only minor configuration changes on the client-side.

- From the viewpoint of common users, encrypting and signing outgoing e-mail should happen seamlessly. This also applies to the possible decryption and verification of incoming e-mail. Since the certificate of a communication partner outside the enterprise may be unknown to the gateway or this particular user may not even have a key pair, there are limitations to this concept as instant encryption of outgoing and signature verification of incoming e-mail are impossible. This is a typical situation where administrator interaction is required.

- From the viewpoint of sophisticated users, the gateway should not interfere with already encrypted or signed e-mail and just pass through such messages. The gateway should permit sophisticated users to configure the behaviour of the gateway (to a certain extent which is governed by an overall policy).

- To ease deployment, we seek a solution which flexibly integrates in an existing e-mail environment without the need for major changes on the server side. This is an important issue since companies may already use a groupware server like Microsoft Exchange or Lotus Notes with suitable user clients. In order to build cost-effective and platform-independent software, we favour open-source components written in Java.

2.2 Modes of Operation

There are basically three ways how SecMGW can be integrated in the network infrastructure. This section lists these variants together with their pros and cons.

Differences mainly arise from the question whether SecMGW is deployed as a supplementary or as an exclusive server. In the former case, SecMGW's functionality is limited to the pure cryptographic and PKI tasks, whereas it works as a perfect mail server in the latter case. We call this the *single host* mode as e-mail clients communicate directly with the gateway. This is an attractive all-in one solution for companies without a pre-existing individual e-mail infrastructure.

However, companies that already run their own mail server would not want to alter their configuration significantly. SecMGW may nevertheless cooperate with a groupware server or a primary mail server easily. There are two possibilities since SecMGW may be either placed on the internal network behind the other server or in front of it with a direct connection to the Internet. We refer to these variants as *inner* and *outer host* mode. Both are transparent to the existing server as well as to the clients.

The outer host configuration is a must in groupware environments where client and server are tightly integrated to provide functionality exceeding that of a standard mail server (e.g. scheduling resources and meetings). Since they are following a proprietary protocol, SecMGW does not have the ability to mediate their communication. However, SecMGW may sign and encrypt e-mail that leaves the groupware server. Cryptographic envelopes and digital signatures of incoming e-mail messages are automatically opened and verified respectively and then removed from the e-mail. The result of signature verification and the information whether the data was transported confidentially, is incorporated in the e-mail header and/or body. An important shortcoming of an outer host SecMGW is the fact that e-mails are stored in the clear on the groupware (or primary mail) server. To avoid this problem, SecMGW can operate as an inner host which is similar to the single host mode in that the clients directly communicate with SecMGW. In this situation, incoming e-mail is forwarded to SecMGW where it is stored and encrypted only when the client authenticates itself and connects to its mailbox[3]. Consequently this requires the setup and management of user accounts at SecMGW and precludes proprietary protocols (see above).

2.3 Mail Processing and Security Policy

In this section, we discuss different security policies that can be enforced by the gateway. Disregarding the fact that e-mail may be stored unprotected on a network server in the outer host configuration (see the previous section), policy issues are independent of the mode of operation. In the following, we distinguish between common and sophisticated users since the gateway's action depends on the type of user. It may also be reasonable to make an even finer distinction and assign each user to a group with its own policy.

Let us first consider the case of a common user receiving an e-mail from a person outside the company. The gateway looks up the user's private key in its key store and decrypts the ciphertext if the e-mail is encrypted. In any case, the gateway can easily check the integrity of a signed e-mail. Verifying sender authenticity is more difficult, since the gateway has to construct a certificate chain from a known trust anchor to the sender's certificate. Besides, a stricter policy may claim that the revocation status of all certificates in the chain has to be validated which introduces another level of complexity. The gateway embeds the security status (e.g. „private message", „sender verified") in the e-mail itself, either in the subject line or at the beginning of the body in a well-marked section[4]. SecMGW stores further information in proprietary header fields which are transparent to the user. Depending on particular security needs, an e-mail with an unknown sender certificate may either be delivered at once with a „sender not verified" flag or held back until an administrator has established the necessary trust relationship. All certificates and trust anchors are managed centrally by the gateway. This has the advantage that trust decisions have to be made only the first time an external entity sends e-mail to someone in the company.

---

[3] An alternative is to leave mails on the existing mail server, e.g. for archiving purposes, and retrieving them in the moment when a client connects to SecMGW.

[4] Obviously, precautions have to be taken as to prevent senders from imitating this status information.

Outgoing e-mail is always signed by the gateway on behalf of the sender if it is a common user. The use of encryption has to be specified in detail. Following a strict policy, all e-mail that leaves the company has to be encrypted which requires all recipients to have a key pair and a valid certificate. SecMGW may need to generate a key pair and corresponding certificate for users that do not have one on-the-fly (see Section 2.5 for the issue of key distribution). If SecMGW detects that an external user who has been issued a key pair and certificate by SecMGW uses another certificate in a subsequent mail sent to the company, the latter replaces the former one in SecMGW's certificate store. According to a lax policy, outgoing e-mail is encrypted when possible, i.e. when a certificate matching the recipient's e-mail address is known to the gateway. The gateway may be configured to otherwise add a trailer to the e-mail telling the recipient that message confidentiality was not assured and how he could get a certificate. A compromise between both extremes is to let the sender decide which level of security is appropriate for a particular message. As long as he requests confidentiality (via a flag in the subject line), the e-mail is treated according to the strict, otherwise according to the lax policy. SecMGW offers the possibility to compress the message before applying the cryptographic operations. Reducing redundancy is useful both to save bandwidth and from a security point of view.

E-mail that comes from or is addressed to a sophisticated user is handled by the gateway in the following way: Incoming e-mail that is encrypted is not processed any further. However, if it is unencrypted and signed, the sender's certificate (if included in the mail) can be added to the certificate database. Similarly, outgoing e-mail that is unencrypted may be encrypted by the gateway if it knows the recipient's certificate (the gateway notices the sender about this action and supplies him with the certificate for later use). Another idea is to let the gateway wrap a signature around each outgoing message even if it is already encrypted by the sophisticated user. As a consequence, the signature may help the receiving end detecting the authenticity of the mail (the fact that it comes from a known company). If this feature is activated by default, sophisticated users may want a possibility to switch it off (e.g. by an „anonymity" label in the subject line).

The current design allows users to individually override the default policy on a per-mail basis by passing commands via the subject line. SecMGW strips off these commands before delivering the message.

2.4 Threshold Cryptography

In the scenario presented above, cryptographic operations are delegated to a central authority which we called SecMGW. For technical reasons, such an authority requires a direct connection to the Internet and has to store all decryption and signing keys, thus making it vulnerable and attractive to internal or external attacks. From the users' viewpoint, the gateway has to be trusted to a large extent since it has the capability to impersonate them or steal their decryption keys. As a practical consequence, the administrator of the corresponding computer has to be fully trusted or the system has to be made robust against tampering. The former is a quite unsatisfactory and often unrealistic condition whereas the latter is a complicated task since administrators (must) usually have extensive capabilities on the operating system level.

To prevent unauthorized access to the central key store, either by a fraudulent administrator or an intruder, SecMGW enforces a four-eye principle with the help of threshold cryptography. For the sake of simplicity, in this section we assume that SecMGW works as single host. An adaptation to the other modes of operation is straight-forward.

The basic idea of threshold cryptography is to split a private key into several pieces which are kept secret by different parties. Common public key algorithms like RSA, DSA, or ElGamal (the latter is used in PGP) even allow *threshold function sharing* which means that the parties can apply the private key without reconstructing it. We sketch the mathematics of two party RSA, an idea due to Boyd [Boyd89]. As usual, the cryptosystem consists of a modulus N being the product of two prime numbers and a pair of exponents e and d satisfying $e \cdot d \equiv 1 \bmod \varphi(N)$. Encryption is done by raising the plaintext to the e-th power modulo N; this mapping is denoted ε. The private exponent $d \equiv d_1 \cdot d_2 \bmod \varphi(N)$ is *shared multiplicatively*[5] between the two parties who only know their respective share d_i. To decrypt a ciphertext $c = \varepsilon(m)$, the parties compute $\delta_2(\delta_1(c)) = \delta_1(\delta_2(c)) = m$ where $\delta_i : c \mapsto c^{d_i} \bmod N$ resembles the standard decryption operation (except for the exponent). The computation of a digital signature is similar for RSA, whereas DSA (or the ElGamal signature scheme) requires another round of communication between the parties [Stra04a]. Like RSA, distributed ElGamal decryption requires only a single message exchange between the shareholders.

Figure 1 illustrates how threshold cryptography works in the e-mail gateway setting: An encrypted message is delivered to the company's mail server connected to the Internet. This server uses its share d_1 to compute δ_1 and forwards the partially decrypted message to its counterpart. Note that this partially decrypted message is unintelligible to a potential eavesdropper on the internal network. When the recipient connects to her mailbox to download the message, the respective server applies δ_2 and returns the plaintext (via a secure channel).

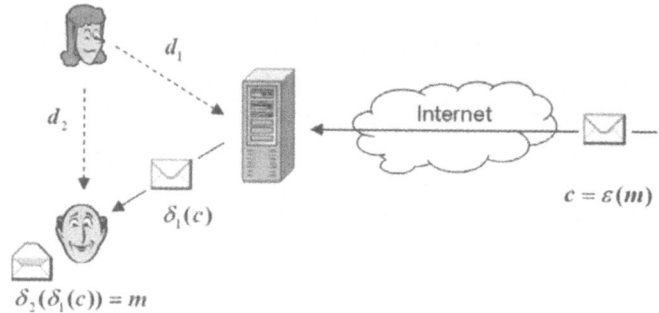

Figure 1: Delegation with end-to-end security.

It can be shown that a single share does not provide any information about the private key or any advantage in order to decrypt the ciphertext. If all end-user keys are shared between two computers (that are administered by different persons) according to Figure 1, even compromising one subsystem would not harm overall security. The extra costs for implementing this four-eye principle are tolerable since both systems operate in nearly the same way. Initial key generation may take place on the client at the moment when a new user registers or even in a distributed manner with the two subsystems involved (see [Stra04b] for details). We emphasize that the four-eye principle can be generalized to a k-out-of-n secret sharing. This means that each private key is split into n pieces requiring the cooperation of an arbitrary subset of k shareholders for each private key operation. For instance, 2-out-of-n schemes can be used for load-balancing since cryptographic computations are time-consuming.

---

[5]An alternative is to use an *additive sharing*, i.e. $d = d_1 + d_2 \bmod \varphi(N)$ which yields a quite similar scheme.

Figure 2 shows another application of threshold cryptography. Consider the situation where Alice, a sophisticated user, goes on holiday and wants her e-mail to be redirected to her vacation replacement Bob. Passing the private key to the gateway or to Bob is a trivial solution, but this would violate the policy of end-to-end security. A way to overcome this problem is to let Alice split her private key and pass one share to Bob and store the other one on the gateway. When receiving an encrypted message for Alice, the gateway will apply its half of the key and Bob will do the same to obtain the plaintext. Note that in this delegation scenario, it is necessary that Bob is also a sophisticated user.

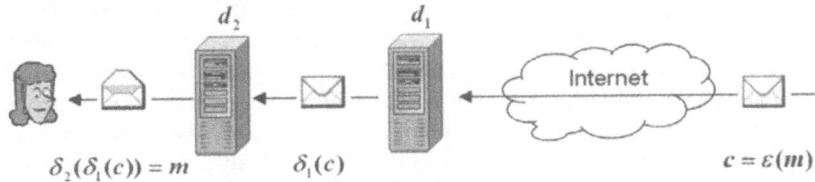

Figure 2: Decrypting e-mail using threshold cryptography.

2.5 Security Considerations

One may argue that a centralized gateway managing all cryptographic tasks offers less security compared to a perfect end-to-end solution. But this leaves out of account the users being the most important link in the security chain. For good reason, end-to-end e-mail security is hardly found in practice, but centralized solutions are gaining importance.

There are two general security criticisms towards a gateway from the cryptographic point of view: Firstly, the stretch between client and gateway is the weakest segment of the e-mail's route. Secondly, the central key storage on the gateway may attract attackers or become a bottleneck and single point of failure. The first issue can be addressed by transport layer security mechanism like SSL/TLS with certificate-based server authentication. This thwarts eavesdropping attacks on the internal network. However, it is crucial to also avoid impersonation attacks because of their severity. Possible countermeasures are authenticating the sender using SMTP-AUTH with a strong password, restricting access to a certain IP address, and a lockout mechanism to face password-guessing attacks. We presented a way to solve the second problem in the previous section, so we do not go into detail here.

In Section 3, we outline the distributed software architecture of the SecMGW prototype. Implementation-specific security aspects are postponed to this section. It goes without saying that general (non-cryptographic) system security measures have to be taken, both concerning the servers running one or more SecMGW components and the clients as well. The definition of appropriate administrative procedures goes hand in hand with these precautions.

We conclude this section by looking more closely at the cryptographic layer. Consider the case where an e-mail is encrypted and digitally signed at the same time. These two operations can be performed in different order; both have their pros and cons. An e-mail that is first signed and then encrypted, does not reveal the identity of the sender indicated in his certificate. The „From" entry in the e-mail header can be easily obscured to provide anonymity in transit. If the content is encrypted prior to signing, this exposes the sender's identity which is helps the recipient to check the origin before opening the mail. However, in the latter case, an active attacker may detach the original signature and replace it with his own. It is a good practice to use different key pairs for signing and encryption, since a backup copy of a decryption key should be kept in a safe place to avoid data loss. This is neither advisable nor necessary for signing keys. We note that this practice however has the drawback that an encryption key cannot be inferred from a certificate used for signing (cf. Section 2.3). In order to unambiguously indicate that an e-mail was processed by a central gateway and to avoid negative legal implications, X.509 certificates issued by the gateway should include an appropriate policy extension.

Key distribution is a major issue in all public key infrastructures. Applied to our setting, the question of how to securely deliver a softtoken to the intended person arises when the gateway generates a key pair for an external user. A softtoken is typically encrypted under a symmetric key which is derived from a password, so the problem reduces to conveying the password. The most secure method is to transmit this information *out-of-band* which means over a communication channel other than e-mail (e.g. ordinary mail, fax, telephone, short messaging service). However, this is usually not practicable, since these processes are hard to automate and necessary contact information is often not available. A reasonable comprise is to send two e-mails (perhaps with a certain delay) to the recipient containing the softtokenand the password. A more secure alternative, which requires a public accessibly SSL web site, is to send the respective link instead of the softtoken itself. The user is told to retrieve the softtoken from the web server authenticating himself with the password. The server allows only a single access to the softtoken and triggers an alarm otherwise. In case the legitimate recipient is locked out, this indicates that an attack has taken place.

3 Technical Details

We have implemented a prototype of SecMGW using the Java Apache Mail Enterprise Server version 2.2 (JAMES[6]). To illustrate our concept, further technical details are given in this section.

3.1 Overview

An overview of the components and their interaction in the inner or single host mode is depicted in Figure 3. In the outer host mode, e-mail clients do not communicate directly with JAMES.

SecMGW consists of four core components, namely JAMES which is used as an e-mail processing framework, the SecMGW mailet which comprises most of the program logic, the Tomcat[7] web server (version 5.0) which provides a HTTP-based administration interface, and our own certificate and key manager (CKM). The software is pure Java technology, thus guaranteeing platform independence. JAMES and Tomcat are open-source products distributed under the Apache Software License.

Tomcat, JAMES and the CKM communicate via Java Remote Method Invocation (RMI). This permits a distributed infrastructure with these modules are placed in different environments, e.g. in a DMZ (demilitarized zone) or a trusted network, respectively. All RMI channels are secured using SSL/TLS with mutual authentication. Establishing a connection to the configuration interface also requires a mutually authenticated connection to the Tomcat web server. SecMGW administrators are issued particular X.509 certificates for this purpose.

---

[6] http://james.apache.org

[7] http://jakarta.apache.org/tomcat/

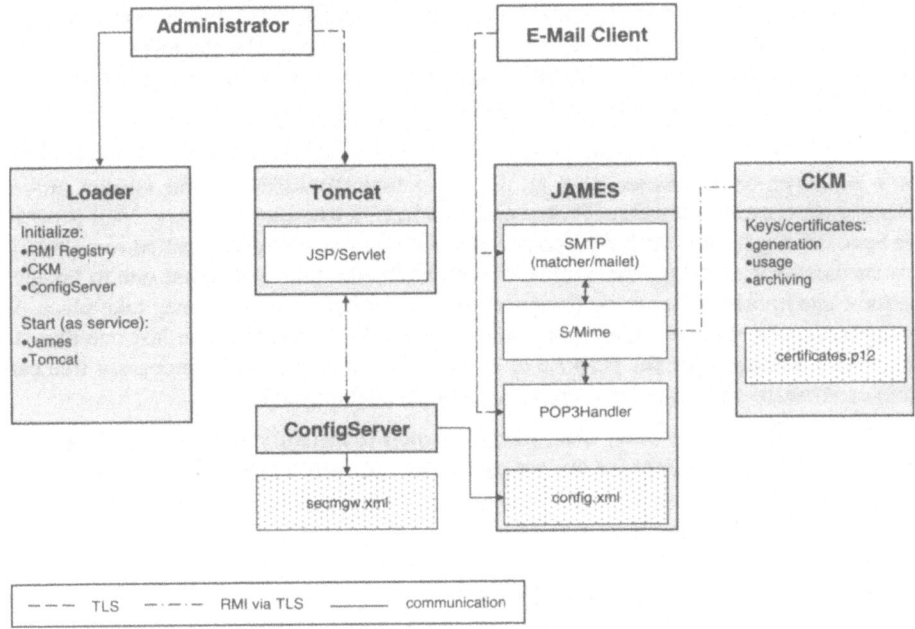

Figure 3: Overall architecture of SecMGW.

For security reasons, the whole communication between e-mail clients and JAMES is also tunnelled through SSL/TLS. However, client authentication is not compulsory in this case. Besides the core components, SecMGW includes a loader that uses the Java Service Wrapper[8] to start SecMGW as a service (on Windows operating systems) or a as Unix/Linux daemon.

3.2 Supported Technologies

The present version of SecMGW supports the Simple Mail Transfer Protocol (SMTP) and the Post Office Protocol version 3 (POP3) allowing the gateway to operate in any of the modes described in Section 2.2. An Internet Message Access Protocol (IMAP) implementation is available in JAMES, but it is still considered experimental. SecMGW supports S/MIME[9] with the following cryptographic algorithms: The block ciphers AES (with 128, 192, and 256 bit keys), CAST5, IDEA, RC2 (each with 128 bit keys), and 3DES (192 bit), the message digests MD5 and SHA-1, and the asymmetric algorithms RSA and DSA.

3.3 JAMES and SecMGW Mailet

JAMES relies on the Phoenix Avalon Framework container[10], a micro kernel which facilitates the handling of server-specific tasks like logging, thread management, or security. The core of JAMES is its *SpoolManager*. This is a mail processing engine that carries out operations by means of so-called *matchers* and *mailets*. Matchers and mailets appear in pairs. A matcher is basically a filter that checks e-mails for a certain condition, for instance a particular address,

---

[8] http://wrapper.tanukisoftware.org

[9] S/MIME version 3 is specified in RFCs 2630 to 2634.

[10] http://avalon.apache.org/phoenix/

content or a header field value. If a matching e-mail is found, it is handed over to the corresponding mailet. While matchers have only read access to e-mails, mailets may alter messages in any fashion. Content/SPAM filters, sender notification, or time-stamping services, to name only a few, can be implemented this way.

Matcher/mailet pairs can be organized sequentially in a so-called *processor* which applies the pairs in the given order. Mailets may initiate premature termination of the current processor and hand over control to another. Processors thus form a tree-like structure. Mail processing in the SpoolManager starts with the uppermost node in the tree which is called root processor. If it is an incoming message, the SecMGW matcher/mailet pair is the first one to be applied since the e-mail possibly has to be decrypted before further processing may take place. With outgoing messages, it is the other way round: the SecMGW mailet is the last one that is applied to these messages for the purpose of encryption and signing. The processor tree can be flexibly customized and extended on request to fit particular needs.

If JAMES is configured as outer host, incoming mail is instantly decrypted and verified. In the other cases, the mail messages are not decrypted and verified until a POP3 request occurs so that information is kept encrypted on the server. We have modified JAMES' POP3 handler to provide this functionality.

3.4 Tomcat and ConfigServer

SecMGW is entirely configurable via a web interface build with Java Server Pages (JSP). JSPs are dynamically compiled to servlets which are executed in Tomcat's servlet container. Since servlets run exclusively in a Java Virtual Machine, this minimizes the risk of security holes on the web server, e.g. due to buffer overflows.

Currently, the configuration menu is arranged in four sections. The first one allows the administration of server settings, like specifying local domains, changing relay settings, ports, etc. The second section deals with policy issues. This comprises the default algorithms for encryption and signing, the order in which they are applied and whether outgoing e-mails should be compressed by default (cf. Section 2.3). The syntax of the commands passed via the subject line of an e-mail can also be configured here. The purpose of the third section is to manage user accounts and passwords; the fourth provides real-time information about the server status.

Configuration changes made via the web interface are handed over by Tomcat to a ConfigServer which in its turn modifies the XML configuration files of JAMES and SecMGW and restarts the components if necessary.

3.5 CKM

The certificate and key manager carries out all cryptographic computations where private or public keys are involved. Key pairs and certificates are kept in a central database which is currently realized as PCKS#12 key store. PKCS#12 provides integrity protection and confidentiality by means of a password. CKM also handles the tasks of certificate archiving and validation. The latter functionality is not fully supported yet, as for instance, certificate revocation list (CRL) or validation according to the online certificate status protocol (OCSP) are not implemented. CKM has its own small certification authority (CA) which generates RSA key pairs and issues the corresponding certificates. At the moment, the same key pair is used for encryption and signing. Key pairs that were generated for external users and the corresponding passwords are automatically sent out to the respective person.

CKM is built on the Java Cryptographic Architecture (JCA), which introduces an abstraction layer concerning the classes that provide cryptographic functionality. This allows interchanging cryptographic providers and algorithms flexibly. The current version relies on the BouncyCastle[11] S/MIME package and the BouncyCastle provider. Functionality for threshold cryptography is still experimental and kept in a separate library. An existing RSA or DSA key can be split into two additive and multiplicative shares respectively. There are also classes that implement distributed signing and decryption. A distributed key generation algorithm is available for DSA.

4 Related Work

The main idea of server-based cryptography is either to relieve clients with restricted computational power (which is the case e.g. with mobile phones[12]) or to reduce the logical complexity and mental workload of their users [HuFi02, JaEb02]. Perrin et al. recommend a far-reaching delegation of PKI tasks to enterprise users [PBMO02]. The use of asymmetric cryptography would then be restricted to inter-domain communication with enterprises acting as end-entities.

The idea of crypto e-mail gateways is described in [Seem03, Pohl03]; [GeKe04] gives an overview over existing products. Most of them are commercial. An open-source implementation for Linux is provided by GEAM[13] (GEAM Encrypts All Mail). It extends an existing mail server with the PGP functionality of the GnuPG package providing message confidentiality, but no digital signatures. SecurE-mail Gateway[14] and CryptoEx Business Gateway Classic[15] work as outer host only. Both use a subject line-based mechanism to pass commands to the server like SecMGW does. PGP Universal[16] is the only solution which comes with an optional client-side component operating as a local proxy (running under Windows or MacOS). If the intended recipient of a confidential e-mail does not have a key pair yet, she is offered a download page or a web-based access to the e-mail protected by a password. By means of its own client, PGP Universal offers the possibility to enforce security policies even beyond a company's borders. It is equipped with a built-in virus scanner and SPAM filter.

None of the realizations so far makes use of threshold cryptography. However, threshold cryptography is already used in several other applications: Examples include a „virtual smartcard" realized by splitting a private key into two halves, one derived from a user password and the other one stored on a central server [MaRe03]. Such a virtual smartcard allows instant key revocation similar to the online semi-trusted party which uses „mediated RSA" described in [BoDT01]. The Apache web server and a Certification Authority are protected with threshold cryptography as part of the ITTC project (Intrusion Tolerance via Threshold Cryptography, see [WuMB99]). Distributed RSA signing (in conjunction with distributed key generation) was also used in the context of a time stamping service [ABF+00]. [Stra04] describes a protocol to enhance the security of certificate enrollment using two-party RSA or DSA signatures.

---

[11] http://www.bouncycastle.org

[12] http://www.a1.net/CDA/navigation/nav_frame/0,2756,286-1693-html-de,00.html

[13] http://www.g10code.de/en/p-geam.html

[14] http://www.utimaco.de

[15] http://www.cryptoex.com/cryptoexclassic/gateway.aspx?lang=en, requires Windows 2000 server.

[16] http://www.pgp.com/products/universal/index.html

5 Conclusion

In this paper, we addressed the issue of securing e-mail with cryptography. Our work was motivated by the hypothesis that end-to-end security is not likely to catch on due to its inherent complexity. The concept of a central gateway for secure e-mail was presented; furthermore threshold cryptography was applied to avoid the existence of a single point of failure.

We built a prototype of which technical details were given. It is based on widely accepted open-source components. Experiences show that our approach is feasible since the overhead for cryptographic computations is tolerable in practice. If necessary, a speed-up can be achieved by dedicated crypto hardware and/or the load-balancing approach outlined in Section 2.4. Not all of the described features are implemented yet. PGP integration and functionality to handle fine-grained policies is underway.

References

[ABF+00]   H. Appel, I. Biehl, A. Fuhrmann, M. Ruppert, T. Takagi, A. Takura, and C. Valentin. Ein sicherer, robuster Zeitstempeldienst auf der Basis verteilter RSA-Signaturen, DuD Fachbeiträge, vieweg, 2000. (in German)

[Boyd89]   C. Boyd. Digital multisignatures. Cryptography and Coding, Clarendon Press, 1989.

[BoDT01]   D. Boneh, X. Ding, and G. Tsudik. A method for fast revocation of public key certificates and security capabilities. Proc. 10th USENIX Security Symposium, Washington DC, USA, 2001.

[Croc82]   D. Crocker. Standard for the Format of ARPA Internet Text Messages. RFC 822, 1982.

[Davi96]   D. Davis. Compliance defects in public-key cryptography. Proc. 5th USENIX Security Symposium, San Jose, USA, 1996.

[JaEb02]   M. Jalali-Sohi and P. Ebinger. Towards Efficient PKIs for Restricted Mobile Devices. Proc. IASTED International Conference Communications and Computer Networks, Cambridge MA, USA, 2002.

[FHH+02]   B. Friedmann, D. Hurley, D.C. Howe, E. Felten, and H. Nissenbaum. Users' Conception of Web Security: A Comparative Study. Proc. Conference on Human Factors in Computing Systems, Minneapolis, USA, 2002.

[GeKe04]   R.W. Gerling and S. Kelm. E-Mail-Verschlüsselungsproxies in der Praxis. Proc. 11th DFN-CERT/PCA Workshop, Hamburg, Germany, 2004. (in German)

[HuFi02]   B. Hunter and B. Filipovic. Enabling PKI Services for Thin-Clients. Datenschutz und Datensicherheit (26), 2002.

[IDC02]   International Data Corporation (IDC): Worldwide Email Usage Forecast, 2002-2006: Know What's Coming Your Way. 2002.

[KaPS02]   C. Kaufman, R. Perlman, Radia, and M. Speciner. Network Security: Private Communication in a Public World. Prentice Hall, 2002.

[MaRe03]   P. MacKenzie and M.K. Reiter. Networked Cryptographic Devices Resilient to Capture. International Journal of Information Security 2 (1), 2003.

[Oppl01]   R. Oppliger. Secure Messaging with PGP and S/MIME, Artech House, 2001.

[PBMO02] T. Perrin, L. Bruns, J. Moreh and T. Olkin. Delegated Cryptography, Online
          Trusted Third Parties, and PKI. Proc. 1st Annual PKI Research Workshop,
          Gaithersburg MD, USA, 2002.

[Pohl03] N. Pohlmann. Die virtuelle Poststelle. IT-Sicherheit im verteilten Chaos, Secu-
          Media Verlag, 2003. (in German)

[Post82] J.B. Postel. Simple Mail Transfer Protocol, RFC 821, 1982

[SaBW01] M.A. Sasse, S. Brostoff, D. Weirich. Transforming the 'weakest link'. BT Tech-
          nology Journal 19 (3), 2001.

[Sass03] M.A. Sasse. Computer Security: Anatomy of a Usability Disaster, and a Plan for
          Recovery. Proc. Conference on Human Factors in Computing Systems, Fort
          Lauderdale, USA, 2003.

[Seem03] Seemann, Henning: Pragmatic Solutions to Make E-Mail Security Work. Proc.
          Information Security Solutions Europe, Vienna, Austria, 2003.

[Stra04a] T. Straub. Zur Absicherung von PKI-Outsourcing mit Hilfe verteilter digitaler
          Signaturen. Proc. DACH Security, Basel, Switzerland, 2004. (in German)

[Stra04b] T. Straub. How to strengthen certificate enrolment. Proc. WartaCrypt, Bedlewo,
          Poland, 2004. (to appear)

[VoVo02] J. Voßbein and R. Voßbein. KES/KPMG-Sicherheitsstudie: Lagebericht zur IT-
          Sicherheit. kes 3 and 4, 2002, available online http://www.kes.info. (in German)

[WhTy99] A. Whitten and J.D. Tygar. Why Johnny Can't Encrpyt: A Usability Evaluation
          of PGP 5.0. Proc. 8th USENIX Security Symposium, Washington DC, USA,
          1999.

[WuMB99] T. Wu, M. Malkin, and D. Boneh. Building Intrusion Tolerant Applications.
          Proc. 8th USENIX Security Symposium Washington DC, USA, 1999.

Web Service Security – XKMS (TrustPoint)

Daniel Baer[1] · Andreas Philipp[2] · Norbert Pohlmann[1]

[1]Gelsenkirchen University of Applied Sciences
Department of Computer Science
Distributed Systems and Information Security
Neidenburger Str. 43, D – 45877 Gelsenkirchen
{daniel.baer | norbert.pohlmann}@informatik.fh-gelsenkirchen.de

[2]Utimaco Safeware AG
Transaction Security
Germanusstrasse 4, D – 52080 Aachen
andreas.philipp@aachen.utimaco.de

Abstract

Web services have grown up and developed a considerable potential: They are based on an open, dynamic exchange of data. Their openness is their greatest plus and contributed to their wide acceptance. This openness, however, and the resulting lack of security is at the same time the barrier that prevents web services from being used on a broad basis. Web services have to become safe if they are to transmit sensitive data securely.

The prerequisites for the secure electronic exchange of data and information are confidentiality, integrity, and reliability. The adequate means to meet these demands are encryption and the digital signature on the basis of cryptographic methods. A Public Key Infrastructure (PKI) provides the adequate software, protocols, and standards. If web services are to be protected comprehensively and on the long run, a PKI is needed. Establishing and operating a PKI, however, is a complex task requiring different protocols on the client side – and not all application programs respectively application terminals are able to meet these requirements.

New approaches enable the easy communication with a PKI. Web services and the Simple Object Access Protocol (SOAP are easy means to make use of remote services within a Service Orientated Architecture (SOA). The XML Key Management Specification (XKMS defines a protocol with which keys can be validated and managed on the basis of XML via web services. The resulting advantages make using a PKI easier and leaner. In this work, the XKMS specification is introduced, its functional principle is explained, its advantages and disadvantages are described, and an insight is provided into the realization of a SKMS responder in the framework of the TrustPoint project.

1 Web services and IT security

Web Services respond to the call for interoperable heterogeneous systems – independently of platforms and manufacturers. They enable what was until a few years ago only possible in limited ways or by performing complicated mechanisms (e.g. Electronic Data Interchange, EDI): the unlimited exchange of IT applications and services by means of standardized procedures for the joint use and processing of data.

S. Paulus, N. Pohlmann, H. Reimer (Editors): Securing Electronic Business Processes, Vieweg (2004), 250-258

Sounds great? If only there wasn't the other side of the coin: The data exchange methods used by web services – such as the HTTP protocol – are open by necessity and nature. This leads to a multitude of security problems from the network to the application layer.

Web services consist of a variety of protocols and methods for the exchange of information. These include standards such as Universal Description, Discovery and Integration (UDDI), a registration and directory service with the corresponding Extensible Markup Language interfaces (XML), or the Web Services Description Language (WSDL), a language for the description of a web service's functions. However, the protocol most widely used by web services for the exchange of messages is the Simple Object Access Protocol (SOAP) which is transported via HTTP or the Simple Mail Transfer Protocol (SMTP). The classical SOAP provides no such security functionalities as the protection of integrity or confidentiality. This is where security in the framework of web services steps in. By means of the method call provided by SOAP, procedures for the protection against the non-authorized request of methods as well as procedures for the protection of confidentiality, integrity, and authenticity are defined. The following figure demonstrates once again the dilemma – the difficulty of securing the web service itself on the one hand (which is not dealt with in this article), and the necessity to secure the intercommunication relations on the other hand.

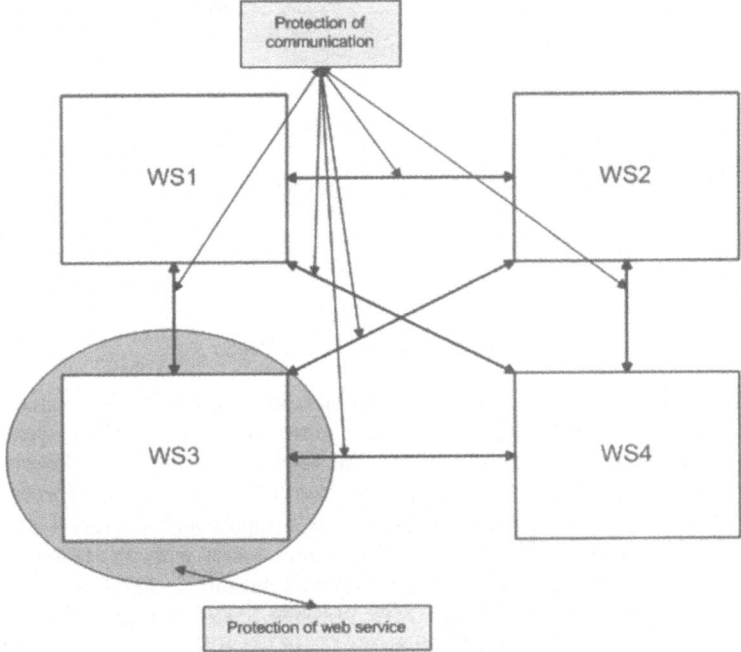

Figure 1: Securing a web service and establishing trustworthiness

The WS-Security standard makes a specification available with which it is possible to realize the consistent security of SOAP messages on the basis of tokens, X.509 certificates, and the use of encryption methods. WS-Security defines in a first step the frame where within an XML document the security information is embedded in a SOAP message. The security standards XML-Encryption and XML-Signature stand for the preservation of integrity and confidentiality. This means that there are now two methods to guarantee the integrity of data, the origin of data, and the confidentiality of data.

2 Problems with PKIs

Establishing and operating a PKI structure is a complex task. High costs of investment and integration also have to be considered. If a PKI furthermore is not only to be used within an enterprise, it has to be capable to communicate and operate with external PKIs. The following figure shows the most vital aspects regarding the diversity of communication and protocols.

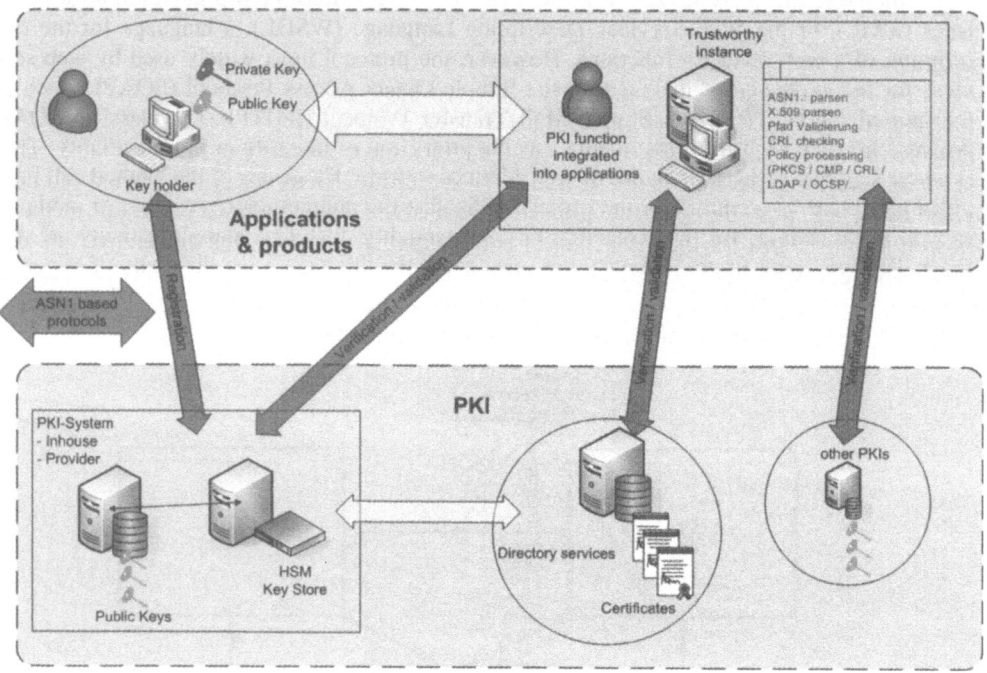

Figure 2: Overview of a PKI

So far, the main focus of PKIs has been the administration of certificates – not the software which makes use of the certificates. The infrastructure was there, but there were only a few applications. This situation has changed today, but what is still missing is the urgent need to use a PKI: there is no such thing as a „killer application" for everybody. Moreover, the integration of PKI standards into application software is complex and requires a lot of development work. This is where the XKMS protocol becomes useful with its approach to delegate the complex task of certificate validation and administration to a central agent. Based on the processes and mechanisms of PKIX and Web Services Security, business applications can now make full use of the advantages of certificate-based security.

3 XKMS Services

The idea behind the XKMS specification is to provide an enlarged number of XML definitions in order to realize a complete interface to common PKIs internally or to third-party suppliers. The following figure demonstrates the XKMS approach following the PKIX model (compare figure 2).

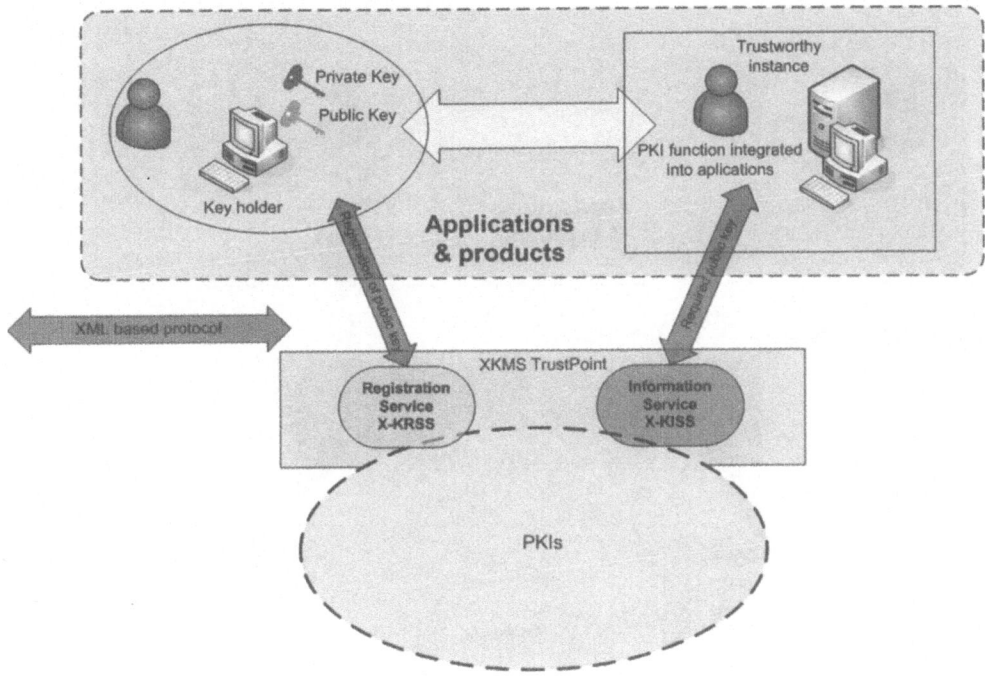

Figure 3: XKMS model

XKMS generally makes two services available:

- XML Key Registration Service Specification (X-KRSS); specifies the life cycle of keys (registration, revocation, renewal) and, if necessary, the retrieval of the corresponding private keys.

- XML Key Information Service Specification (X-KISS); specifies the request operations in connection with the verification of public keys and the corresponding certificates.

The core of these services is the XKMS protocol which implements a request/response process on the basis of SOAP.

(Note: In version 2.0, XKMS enables so-called compound requests, i.e. requests with several operations resp. certificates by one client, as well as the asynchronous processing of requests.)

So what would the typical case look like where XKMS is needed? A web service or an application generate X-KISS/XKRSS requests and pass them to a trustworthy intermediate instance (in the following called „TrustPoint") for further processing. The TrustPoint, a web service itself, constitutes the interface to existing Public Key Infrastructures. It interprets the XML tags specified by XKMS and can thus e.g. localize a requested public key and send it back as certificate, or interpret and validate a received certificate. The functional principle is illustrated below, with the European Bridge CA already being integrated according to the objectives of the project to realize a TrustPoint.

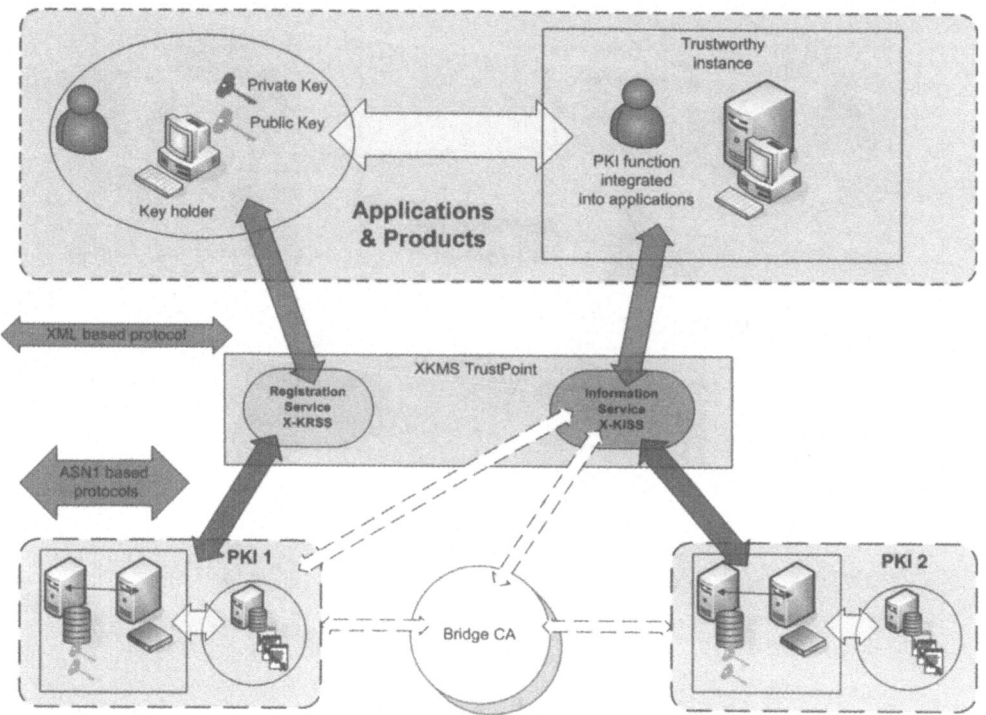

Figure 4: Overview of XKMS

3.1   Pros and Cons of XKMS Services

This chapter provides an overview of the advantages and disadvantages of XKMS services. The authors wish to state explicitly that the cited disadvantages solely refer to problems in association with the general securing of web services.

Advantages:

- Reduced complexity at client side
  A wide range of applications and devices can thus use the PKI functionalities. For instance, pocket PCs or embedded systems with their low processor performance and comparably small working memory can be supplied with the complete scope of functions.

- Easier implementations
  Different operating systems no longer require individual implementations. All functionalities are made available centrally.

- Easy roll-out
  With the real work being performed on the server side, new functions can be provided „on the fly" for all users without modifications on the client side.

- Central trust management
  A central trust policy can be defined and easily realized.

- Open standards
  The XKMS specification is based on open XML standards which can be used by any operating system and programming language.

- Security for the future
  XKMS services are provided centrally by open standards. New developments can thus be implemented fast and centrally, applications only have to be adapted a little bit or not at all.

Disadvantages:

- DOS attacks
  As all web services that are to be freely available, XKMS services are prone to DOS attacks. These can only be prevented by means of web service firewalls and SOAP firewalls.

- Single point of failure
  Due to the centralization of trust services, the availability and fail-safe operation of the system are a top priority. This should already be considered and realized by means of adequate measures in the conceptual phase of the system's design and operation.

4 The TrustPoint project

It is the aim of the TrustPoint project to establish and operate an XKMS responder. The TrustPoint is established completely by open-source components. The free availability of and insight into source texts are vital characteristics in the development of security-relevant software.

The TrustPoint project is split into two phases according to the actual state of planning.

The objectives of the individual phases are briefly described in the following.

Phase I:

In a first step, the architecture and the system design of the XKMS responder are defined. Apart from the choice of hardware and software components, the infrastructures to be implemented are in the main focus of the first planning phase, as well as the integration of the European Bridge CA (EBCA). The scope of functions to be realized in the XKMS responder in project phase I is restricted to the functions locate and validate of X-KISS.

Phase II:

In project phase II, the scope of functions of the TrustPoint is extended by the X-KRSS functions. Besides this, the outsourcing possibilities are considered.

4.1 TrustPoint phase I: Architecture and specification

Project phase I is restricted to the X-KISS functions locate and validate. In a first step, the transmission of SOAP messages and the evaluation of XKMS functions is realized. The certificates are then sent to a local PKI and checked there. Due to the connection of the Trust-Point to the European Bridge-CA, the central bridge directory services and bridge control services can be used.

The architecture of the XKMS responder is divided into four logical modules:

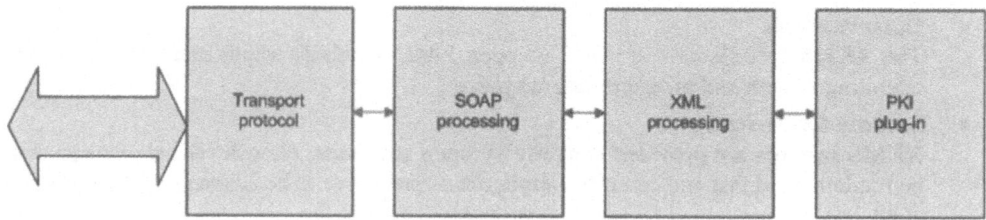

Figure 5: Modules of the TrustPoint

Transport protocol

This module provides the necessary transport protocols for the communication with the XKMS responder. In project phase I, only HTTP resp. HTTPS are realized.

For the transmission of messages via the HTTP protocol, Apache Tomcat is used. Tomcat enables among others the connection via HTTP and HTTPS by means of various so-called connectors.

SOAP processing

In the framework of the SOAP processing, based on SOAP V1.2 all functions are made available which are needed to process the embedded XML messages further.

For the processing of SOAP requests and responses, Apache AXIS is used. SOAP embeds the XML messages into the SOAP body element within the SOAP envelope. The optional SOAP header is not used. With SOAP-Faults, SOAP makes appropriate error messages and descriptions available. Apache AXIS represents an elaborate implementation of the Simple Object Access Protocol V.1.2. It provides a framework for the development of clients and servers and is independent of the used transport protocol. In the TrustPoint project, AXIS is run as servlet within the servlet container of Apache Tomcat, with AXIS realizing the packing and depacking of SOAP messages and providing a WDSL for every web service.

XML processing

For the further processing of the XML messages, the XKMS function is extracted by means of correspondingly realized instances of the X-KISS classes. The X-KISS classes also make the function available which is needed for the generation of the response message. The XML security API of the Apache XML project is used for the optional signing of messages, enabling the optional signing of XKMS responses.

PKI plug-in

By means of the different PKI plug-ins, the certificates contained in the X-KISS messages are passed on for control purposes. For this purpose, the common PKI protocols and messages as specified according to PKIX are used.

The following figure provides an overview of the TrustPoint software architecture realized in phase I.

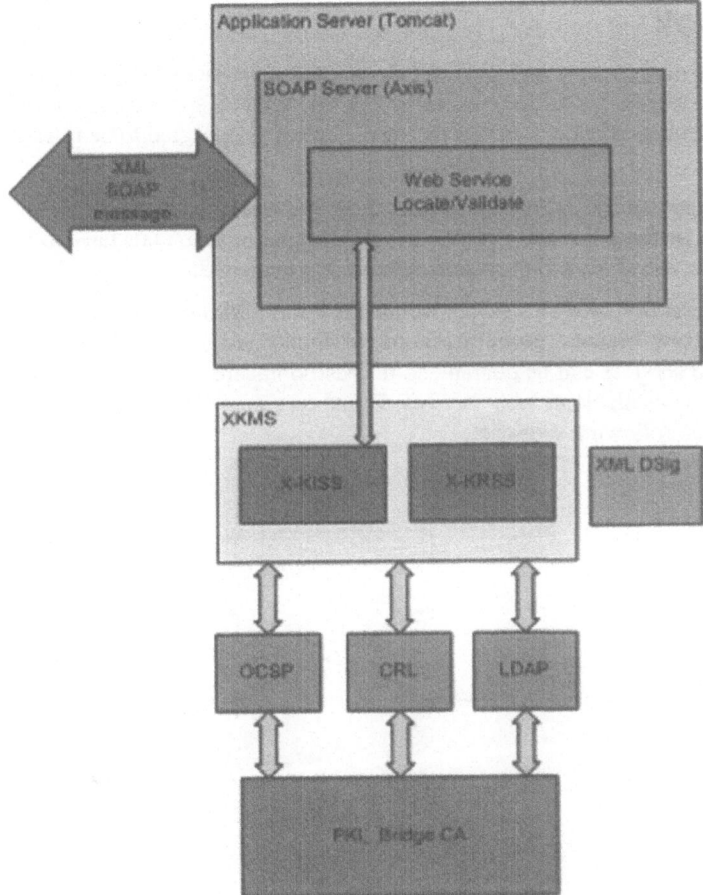

Figure 6: TrustPoint software architecture in phase I

4.2 TrustPoint phase II: Extension of functions

After completion of phase I, the XKMS responder is ready to work. Certificates can be found and validated by the TrustPoint.

In phase II, the TrustPoint is to be extended by the functionalities of the X-KRSS specification. X-KRSS defines functions for the registration, issuing and revocation of keys. It is to be possible that either the client or the TrustPoint generate a pair of keys. If the key is generated by the TrustPoint, the private key has to be transmitted securely. This is guaranteed by using XML encryption.

Apart from the functional extension of the TrustPoint, project phase II is focused on the integration and realization of different policies. For this purpose, in a first step models and possibilities are to be evaluated which enable the standardized concentration of different requirements, mechanism strengths and procedures.

5 Outlook

Regarding the expectations and applications of central services for the security of electronic business processes, it has to be considered that the XKMS specification is still in the status Candidate Recommendation, and that the specification is expected to be released at the end of 2004.

A variety of applications and fields of operations is already being discussed today. However, the increasing performance rates of the next generations of terminals have to be taken into account when the use of XKMS in mobile devices is considered.

With the introduction of web services within ERP and DMS systems, the path has now been cleared to perform business processes more efficiently and in a modular way. The trustworthiness of web services can be guaranteed if TrustPoints are used which in turn make all necessary functions available as web services. Based on figure 1 at the beginning, these assumptions lead to the following scenario.

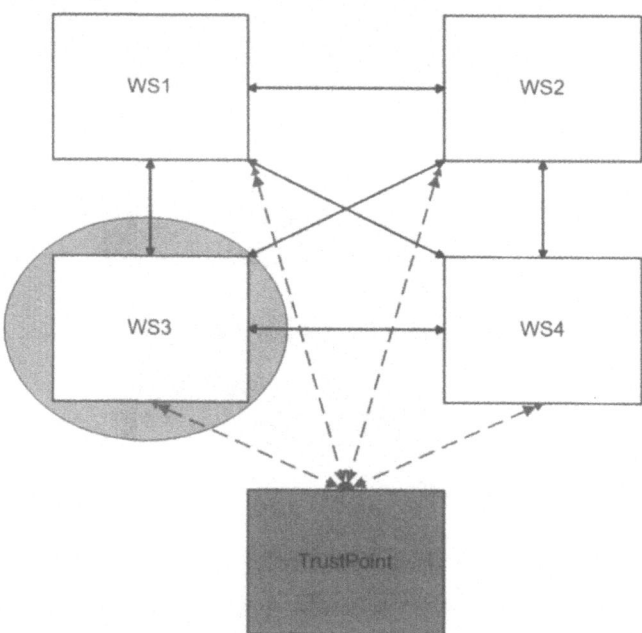

Figure 7: Web services scenario with TrustPoint

References

[W3C04]   W3C: XML Key Management Specification (XKMS 2.0), Candidate Recommendation 5 April 2004, http://www.w3.org/TR/xkms2/

[Neil03]   M. O` Neill: Web Services Security, Osborne (2003)

[Nash02]   A. Nash, W. Duane, C. Joseph, D. Brink: PKI E-security implementieren, mitp (2002)

[Snell02] J.Snell, D. Tidwell, P.Kulchenko: Webservice-Programmierung mit SOAP, O`Reilly (2002)

EPM: Tech, Biz and Postal Services Meeting Point

José Pina Miranda[1] · João Melo[2]

[1]MULTICERT – Serviços de Certificação Electrónica, S.A.
jose.miranda@multicert.com

[2]CTT – Correios de Portugal, S.A.
joao.m.melo@ctt.pt

Abstract

Market forces have combined to form the intensely competitive postal environment we see today. While posts are struggling with declining volumes and increasing costs, Posts have to redefine the way they do business to compete and achieve high performance in this difficult environment.

The investment in secure infrastructures for e-services is under way by major Posts, confident that customers will one day adopt the new electronic means of communication that are designed to be user-friendly and, above all, trusted and secure – two features delivered by the physical Post, that will be carried over to the future secure electronic infrastructures offered by the Post.

The Portuguese Post (CTT), UPU (Universal Postal Union) and other major Posts are exploring areas where technology, business and postal services meet, especially in the area of e-Business: special attention is being given to the development of the Electronic PostMark (EPM), the newest secret weapon that Posts hope that will earn them, their customers' trust in the electronic World.

Moreover, major software houses, including Microsoft, are taking an interest in the electronic postmark, and want to include it in future editions of their software suites.

The little imprint that always had a special place in the top right-hand corner of postal items is beginning to find a new role in the electronic World.

1 EPM – trust and security through digital imprints

With EPM (Electronic PostMark) growing in importance in Europe and North America, UPU (Universal Postal Union) has developed a worldwide standard for electronic postmarks [UPUn03] so that all the digital imprints exchanged by Posts in the future can be recognized and accepted everywhere in the same way as traditional postmarks are today. Moreover, the European Committee for Standardization (CEN) and the Organization for the Advancement of Structured Information Standards (OASIS) in the United States are studying the UPU standard with the purpose of its adoption and publication.

1.1 What is an Electronic Postmark[1]?

The EPM is fundamentally a **non-repudiation service** of perceived value that postal customers can subscribe to.

---

[1] A small overview will be given in this section, based on the UPU standard specification [UPUn03].

S. Paulus, N. Pohlmann, H. Reimer (Editors): Securing Electronic Business Processes, Vieweg (2004), 259-267

Non-repudiation is important in e-commerce to prevent parties of a transaction from disputing or denying the transaction after the fact. The fact that electronic data can be easily tampered compels the usage of a system (or infrastructure) by which parties can trust the information they share and use in everyday transactions. This requirement for trust is referred to in both the legal and crypto-technical worlds as non-repudiation. The primary goal of a non repudiation system is to prove WHO did WHAT and WHEN, and maintain evidence of such information to resolve disputes, or for auditing and compliance. For organizations that need to automate business processes and transactions, EPM is a suite of services that provides a trusted digital equivalent to paper-based signed documents.

Technically speaking, the purpose of **non-repudiation** is to provide verifiable proof or evidence recording of data, based on cryptographic check values of all the following: approval, sending, submission, transport, receipt and knowledge.

A **non-repudiation service** supports the capture and reproduction of evidence data attesting to the fact that a business transaction was conducted and completed in an environment of integrity and trustworthiness with respect to:

- **Who** originated and participated in the transaction/document;
- **When** the transaction/document was sent and received by each participating party;
- **What** transaction/document was sent and if the content was intact throughout transmission at each step;
- **Why** the transaction/document was signed (declaration of intent).

Time stamping services are an aspect of non-repudiation services which provide „...a strong and verifiable cryptographic statement that a specific digital record existed at a specific moment in time. Time stamping a digital record provides the relevant parties with a verifiable statement of when the digital record was known to exist. Time stamping a digitally-signed record can further provide the relevant parties with a verifiable statement that the digital record was signed while the signing certificate was valid [...] time-stamping services thus provide the technical basis for general non-repudiation services, and for both Common Law – and Latin-derived notorial services." [ABAs91].

The EPM can be applied to various types of transactions/documents and adds to their significance in business use. Although the EPM solution provides all the benefits, security, and trust of PKI (Public Key Infrastructure), it does not show the complexities of PKI to the end user but hides them in a comprehensive „stamp" appearance. It is visual and comprehensive leaving the complexities to the experts. In simple terms: It is an easy user experience ... overseen by trusted, international, regulated authorities – The Posts.

1.2 EPM core business services

The **EPM service** involves most or all of the following key services in order to ensure end-to-end transaction integrity and evidence collection in a confidential environment [UPUn03]:

- **Digital signature verification services:** ensures that the electronic content of all messages can be verified for both content and signer integrity as well as ensuring that all input is maintained as evidence and can be re-verified at any point in the future;
- **Time stamping services:** all signature verification services are time stamped with a unique EPM attesting to the fact that the Post providing the EPM Service stands behind the evidence gathered during the signing ceremony, as well as the subsequent verification status;

- **Confidentiality Services:** encryption at origin and decryption at destination guarantees absolute security and privacy for business transaction stakeholders and provides a high degree of confidence that sensitive business information is hidden from all but the intended recipients;

- **Non-Repudiation Services:** retains all customer-required tracking and evidence records of significance within the business transaction life cycle. Combined with user-authentication, timestamping, and message integrity, these tracking records ensure an extremely trustworthy end-to-end business transaction process. It is intended that the EPM Service, through the implementation of jurisdiction-specific legislative requirements, can act as a legally binding transaction notarization service both within and across Postal domains;

- **Event Logging Services:** physical storage of the evidence (i.e. escrow) data associated with EPM-logged and verified business transaction data is a core capability of the Electronic PostMarking service – these electronic records are maintained by the EPM Service provider for as many years as required by the customer and the postal service;

- **Non-Repudiation Challenge Support Services:** Postal Administration provides the individual or organization any and all required evidence of the existence, integrity, and logged time of any business transaction tracked by the service. This information can be re-produced digitally or physically and can be sent to any required arbitrating party for their assessment.

1.3   Business applications

We can think on thousands of electronic business applications where EPM becomes a key issue. The following two cross-state/cross-border applications and the examples of the applications that are driving the adoption of EPM in six countries, described in the next section, are more than enough to foresee the potential of this technology.

1.3.1   E-Gov

Government agencies are seeking ways to reduce the burden on citizens and businesses [USPS03], the EPM provides a service by which organizations can implement a receipting process to facilitate a basic system of records of all electronic transactions for a customer of that agency. A standard manifest will save countless hours of organizational and retrieval activities for organizations and individual customers alike.

Offering of the EPM has the ability to stimulate electronic contracting and transactions by encouraging people who may be reluctant to use the Internet or technology to do business electronically. By stimulating widespread use of electronic systems, the EPM has enormous potential to significantly increase government and commercial adoption of such systems. In turn, increased adoption of electronic systems facilitated by the EPM will enhance national productivity by stimulating the technology industry and eliminating the costs associated with preparing, shipping, and storing paperwork.

1.3.2   Automated Validation of Electronic Trade Documents

The validation of trade document is a frequent and very important task in the functioning of the international supply chain [UPUn03]. Documents are validated at practically any point where supply chain processing switches from one supply chain operator to the next. Documentary checks are needed to obtain insurance cover, for customs clearance, for ordering and delivery and for to obtain trade finance. An important component in the validation of documents is the verification of the authenticity of the trade document itself, the identity of the issuer, the time when the document was issued and whether the document has been changed after it.

An automation of the document validation procedure would significantly reduce costs and delays in international supply chain operations. In addition, the use of electronic tools and access to centralize trusted databases will increase the security for supply chains and help to combat fraud and crime.

2 The proof (and business) is in the postmark

When the Internet revolution started in the early 1990s, many felt that email and Internet technologies would replace traditional paper-based communication, rendering posts irrelevant. This narrow vision didn't take into account that

1. the postal service is a 2.000 year old business that has reinvented itself for several times to respond to economic and social changes and meet customers' needs, and

2. posts could take advantage of the possibilities of the new information society, to expand the range of services they offer to customers and develop innovative services to anticipate customers' needs in the electronic World.

In the digital World, the EPM allows a person or business to apply a trusted time-and-date „stamp" to an electronic document or file, and store and archive all non-repudiation data needed to support a potential court challenge.

2.1 EPM – Posts new business in the electronic World?

The increasing substitution of letter-post exchanges by its electronic counterparts (fax and e-mail) poses a serious challenge to Posts that face the inexorable decrease of revenue in their traditional business. Posts are fighting back and exploring areas where technology, business and postal services meet, especially areas where trust and security become key issues, since these are the two major assets of the physical Post, and Posts are keen to carry them over to electronic services, hoping to earn/regain their customers' trust in the electronic World.

The investment in secure infrastructures for e-services is under way by major Posts, confident that customers who adopt the new electronic means of communication will soon feel the need of a neutral Trusted Third Party (TTP) that delivers electronic trust and security services, especially in the area of e-Business. Posts believe that if they are able to deliver such TTP e-services, due to the trust relationship that they have established with their customers in the physical World, Posts will be citizens and companies first choice for securing and trusting all the electronic transactions in the digital World, especially those transactions that need non-repudiation data to support a potential court challenge.

Major Posts in industrialized countries are giving special attention to the development of the Electronic PostMark (EPM), and six Posts are far ahead, driving the adoption of EPM in their countries.

2.1.1 United States Postal Service

In the United States, Authentidate, an authentication technology specialist, carries out electronic postmark operations on behalf of the USPS. At present, **financial services** and the **legal sector** are the main users of digital imprints, but **government agencies** are beginning to take an interest, too. The Social Security Administration is currently the main user; the EPM, combined with **electronic archiving**, has been incorporated into numerous applications forming part of its Secure Transport Service. An EPM add-on is also available for **Microsoft Office XP** and 2003, enabling users of these software packages to add a digital signature to a document, time-stamp the contents and verify the authenticity, validity and integrity of a document. [UnPo04]

2.1.2 La Poste (Belgium)

The Belgian Post offers its range of electronic services through Certipost, in close collaboration with Belgacom. These services range from simple mail certified with an electronic postmark, guaranteeing the date and time of dispatch, the identity of the sender and the integrity of the message, through **electronic registered mail** and **billing**, using time-stamping and digital notarization, providing irrefutable proof and long-term archiving capabilities in case of dispute. Since the introduction in 2003 of its electronic communications services, which enable businesses to send bills, payslips or other confidential documents to customers, suppliers or employees, the Belgian Post has processed more than 55.000 transactions; this figure is set to top half a million by the end of 2004. [UnPo04]

2.1.3 Canada Post

Canada Post was the first Post to have brought its electronic postmark into line with the UPU standard. As the Canada Post Corporation Act gives a **legal standing to all messages** – whether physical or electronic – that bear a postmark, the EPM is an integral element of a **government project to put all federal services online**. Some 70 services will be joining the two already online, on whose behalf the Post handles up to 40.000 transactions a month. Canada Post is also using the service to postmark **physical mail address changes** made from its website. An EPM add-on has also been created for use with **Microsoft Office**. [UnPo04]

2.1.4 La Poste (France)

The French Post, keen to give the electronic postmark the same values as its traditional counterpart, has retained the familiar appearance of a physical postmark. But for La Poste, the priority is to establish the EPM's credibility by conducting an experiment based on a new flagship service, the **electronic registered letter** service, currently under development. [UnPo04]

2.1.5 Poste Italiane (Italy)

Pioneered in 2000, the Italian Post's digital postmark is still being developed. In 2003, Poste Italiane piloted its electronic postmark with a group of users made up of 200 businesses both large and small. It is currently analyzing the results of these tests in order to decide on the future direction of the project. Postecom, a subsidiary of Poste Italiane providing Internet services, acts as the issuing authority for electronic postmarks. [UnPo04].

2.1.6 CTT Correios – Detailing the Portuguese EPM service

As traffic on the information highway becomes heavier, people and businesses expect to deal with a trusted party that protects their messages (and transactions) and their right to privacy. For years, CTT has been the most trusted company in Portugal and, regulations on employees conduct as well as legal guarantees enhance customer confidence and trust for secure and confidential delivery of information. In fulfilling its obligation to provide universal postal service, CTT has a reputation as neutral Third Party, and want to continue to honour that role through innovative and secure services and products.

The MDDE (*Marca do Dia Electrónica*) Electronic Postmark (EPM) service launched on the 15th September 2003 – the first EPM paid service worldwide that is being used on a daily basis by Portuguese lawyers –, protects the integrity of electronic mail (or data), through the use of auditable time stamps, digital signatures and hash codes. These postmark allow relevant parties to verify the authenticity of e-mail messages content and provide evidence to support non repudiation of electronic transactions.

The initial version of the MDDE electronic postmark, is targeted at lawyers, members of the Portuguese Lawyers Association, who already sent documents to the courts by secure e-mail, and have started to use the MDDE service in order to add non-repudiation evidence of the date and time the electronic mail left their computers. The MDDE EPM service:

- digitally signs and adds an electronic stamp on electronic transactions such as e-mail messages,

- adds non-repudiation evidence of the time and date when it was sent (following IETF/PKIX RFC 3161 [ACPZ01] and the European Electronic Signature Standardization Initiative (EESSI) „Time Stamping profile" [ETSI02]) – the MDDE EPM employs a secure time stamping clock, synchronized to the Observatório Astronómico de Lisboa (OAL), the official Portuguese source of time.

- assures relevant parties of the integrity of the contents,

- provides irrefutable proof that the message was really sent (since the MDDE postmark is append to the original e-mail message at CTT's SMTP gateway, only after the e-mail message has really left the sender's computer – this is an unique feature of CTT's electronic postmark), and

- works with every e-mail client software.

CTT expanded its portfolio of electronic offerings with the launch of an electronic postmark (EPM) service (marketing and selling it as the electronic counterpart of the physical registered letter service) on the 15th September 2003, and by the end of June 2004, 2244 lawyers were using the service and over 60.000 postmarked e-mail messages have been sent. Around 500 messages a day are postmarked (each postmark costs 0.25 €), and 8 to 10 new users are signing up daily for the service (25 € yearly service fee). This figure is set to rise significantly from September 2004 onwards, when lawyers will be obliged to send digitally signed and postmarked e-mail to courts, and courts will have to answer in the same way.

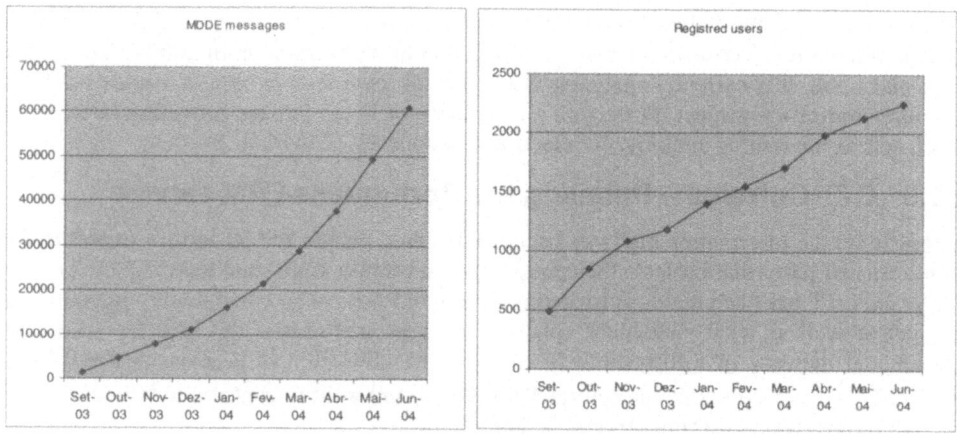

Figure 1: MDDE messages and registered users in the service

A subsequent upgrade will provide senders with electronic return receipts.

Putting it all together – How MDDE Works ?

Security services provider Multicert, a joint venture of the Portuguese Post along with Portugal Telecom, Portugal Mint and SIBS, developed the MDDE EPM and is operating the service for the Portuguese Post. The solution is backed by a PKI infrastructure (that supports PKCS#7 digital signatures, timestamp and OCSP – Online Certificate Status Protocol – validation) that assures authentication, integrity and non-repudiation for all the parties involved.

Subscription –user fills online form at the MDDE service site (sce.ctt.pt) and downloads and installs the MDDE plug-in;

Sending email – The user/lawyer composes a mail message in his usual e-mail software client. When the „send" button is pressed, the MDDE plug-in window appears and the client selects if the email is sent with or without MDDE EPM;

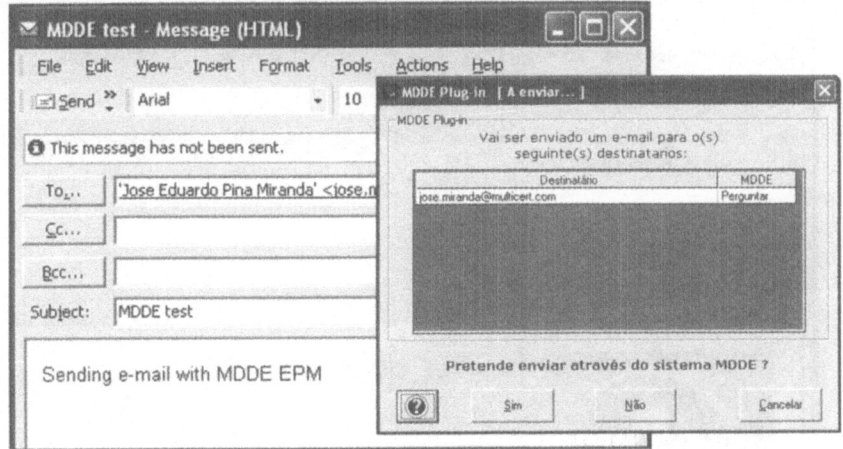

Figure 2: Sending e-mail with MDDE

Receiving MDDE email messages – The receiver opens the MDDE email message and faces the following information:

- familiar „stamp" appearance, with non-repudiable legal date and time the message was sent,
- MDDE ID, Senders' MDDE plug-in license and two attachments:
  - Original message (appended by the MDDE Proxy),
  - MDDE EPM.

For reading the original message the receiver has only to open the attachment with the original e-mail message.

Notice that the sender also receives a „copy" of the MDDE email message, which can be used as a non-repudiation proof of the time, date and content of the e-mail message sent.

Validating MDDE email messages – All email messages that have been electronically postmarked by the MDDE service include the MDDE digital signature and a signed date/time stamp. If needed, the relevant parties (sender and receivers of the e-mail) can access the

MDDE service web page and validate online the MDDE email message, retrieving the following information, amongst other:

- The content of the email message has not been modified in any way since the MDDE was applied.

- The MDDE service signature has not been modified or tampered with since it was signed.

- The certificate used to sign the MDDE EPM was not expired or revoked at the time the MDDE date/time stamp was issued.

- The MDDE date/time stamp denotes the exact time and date at which the EPM was issued by the MDDE EPM Service.

- The EPM date/time stamp has not been modified or tampered with.

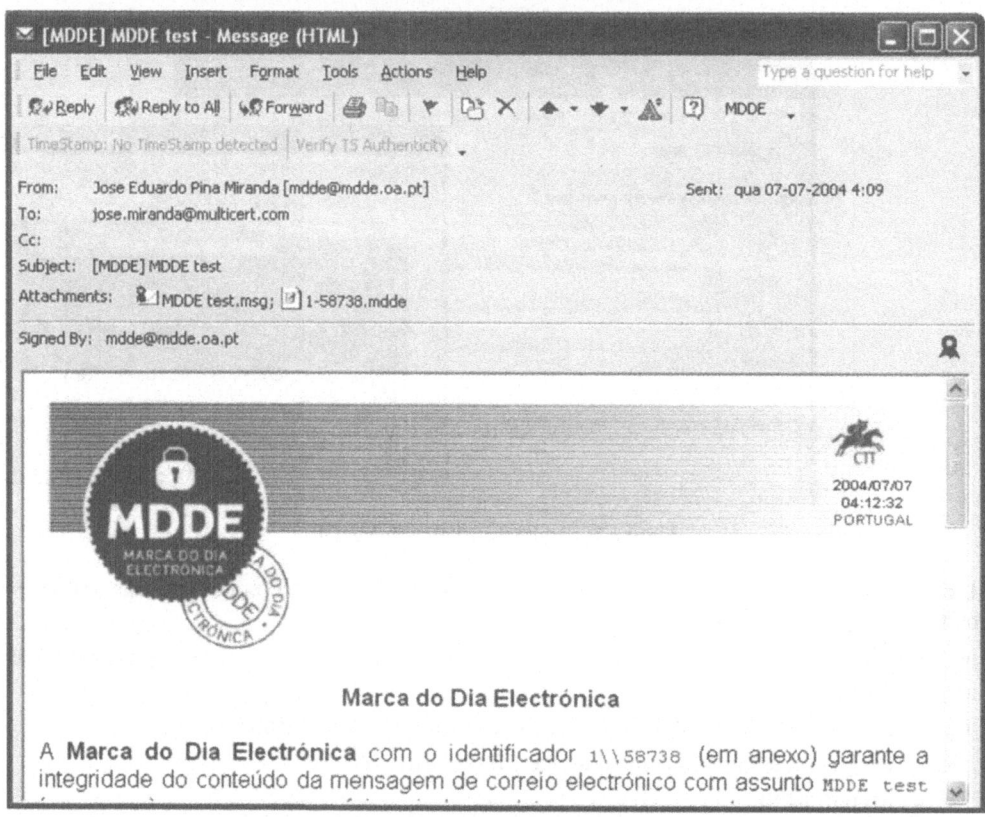

Figure 3: Receiving an e-mail message with MDDE

3 Conclusions

Posts have centuries of experience in the role of a trusted third party and are moving aggressively to establish the strategic partnerships required to enable the services that will facilitate more and more digital commerce and the adoption of new digital services which improve efficiency.

The business applications where Electronic Post Mark (EPM) becomes a key issue are endless. However the potential of this technology will only be realized if digital imprints exchanged by Posts in the future can be recognized and accepted everywhere in the same way as traditional postmarks are today. The development of the UPU EPM worldwide standard [UPUn03] and the adoption and publication of the standard by the CEN and OASIS is the first step in the long journey of digital imprint acceptance. The second step can be quickly reached if major software houses, like Microsoft, Adobe and Sun take enough interest in the electronic post-mark, and include it in future editions of their software suites. After these two steps have taken effect, the usual services, skills and capabilities of the postal industry in the Information Society – Posts facilitate international and domestic trade; Posts assist in building economies; Posts are the hub for the three principal economic flows in the world: information, goods and money; Posts bridge the digital divide; Posts provide a universal communication service to the whole world; Posts manage addresses; Posts are trusted – will be added by a surprising and important role: Posts build the digital trusted services required, for many years, by the Information Society and, fill the gap between the policy and legal framework for digital commerce (already in place, in most countries) and the technological platforms built to facilitate digital commerce.

The little imprint that always had a special place in the top right-hand corner of postal items can play an exciting new role in the electronic World.

References

[UnPo04]   *Confiance et sécurité dans les TIC – Le cacher de la poste faisant foi.* In: Revue de l'Union Postale Universelle. Editor: Journal, UPU, 2004 – n° 1, p. 18-21.

[Leav04]   Leavey, Thomas: *Universal Service facilitates Access to Information.* In: Pushing the Envelope – Volume 1. Editor: Journal, Montgomery Research, Inc, 2004, p. 16-18.

[UPUn03]   Universal Postal Union: *Electronic Postmark – EPM Interface Standard.* 2003.

[ABAs91]   American Bar Association: *ABA PKI Assessment Guidelines.* 1991.

[UPUn03a] Universal Postal Union: *Trade Facilitation, Security Concerns and the role of the Postal Industry for the Global Economy in the Information Society.* 2003.

[USPS03]   United States Postal Service: *USPS Electronic Postmark® (USPS EPM®) White Paper.* 2003.

[ACPZ01]   Adams C., Cain P., Pinkas D., Zuccherato R.: *RFC 3161 – Internet X.509 Public Key Infrastructure Time-Stamp Protocol (TSP).* IETF, 2001.

[ETSI02]   ETSI: *Time stamping profile.* TS 101 861, 2002.

Practice

Managing Trust in Critical Infrastructure Protection Information Sharing Systems

John T. Sabo

2291 Wood Oak Drive
Herndon, Virginia 21401
USA
Computer Associates International
john.t.sabo@ca.com

Abstract

In North America and Asia Pacific countries, private sector companies, non-profit organizations and governments are developing partnerships to protect national critical infrastructures, such as electricity, energy, financial services, healthcare, information technology, telecommunications, transportation, and water systems. This paper discusses the operation in the United States of Information Sharing and Analysis Centers (ISACs), trusted information sharing systems which communicate alerts, vulnerabilities, and best practices and ensure coordinated incident response in critical infrastructure sectors. It describes operational and policy requirements and issues identified by the Council of Information Sharing and Analysis Centers (ISAC Council) for successful and trusted deployment of such information sharing systems, including the operational relationship of ISACs to U.S. government systems. It also discusses security and privacy issues which these systems must address to ensure widespread adoption and effectiveness.

1 Background

Globally, it has become increasingly evident that private sector companies, non-profit organizations and governments must develop partnerships to ensure national critical infrastructure protection (CIP) in such sectors as electricity, energy, financial services, healthcare, information technology, telecommunications, transportation, and water. Protection is needed from both cyber security and physical threats.

With upwards of 85% of such critical infrastructures owned an operated by private sector companies in the United States, Information Sharing and Analysis Centers (ISACs) have been established to provide 24 by 7 operational capabilities to communicate alerts, vulnerabilities, best practices, and threat information to members, to provide a coordinated incident response capability for their respective sectors, and to interface with government monitoring and analysis centers. ISACs were formally defined by then President William Clinton, in his 1998 Presidential Decision Directive 63 (20 May 1998) following recommendations of a Presidential commission studying critical infrastructure protection issues. In the current administration, President Bush's Homeland Security Presidential Directive-7 (HSPD-7), the emphasis on public-private sector information sharing continues:

S. Paulus, N. Pohlmann, H. Reimer (Editors): Securing Electronic Business Processes, Vieweg (2004), 271-280

> *„The Department and the Sector-Specific Agencies will collaborate with appropriate private sector entities and continue to encourage the development of information sharing and analysis mechanisms. Additionally, the Department and Sector-Specific Agencies shall ... identify, prioritize, and coordinate the protection of critical infrastructure and key resources; and ... facilitate sharing of information about physical and cyber threats, vulnerabilities, incidents, potential protective measures, and best practices."*
> [HSPD03]

With a number of ISACs now operational in the United States, the security, privacy, and trust issues they have begun to identify can provide valuable lessons as the ISAC model is explored internationally.

Because they are private-sector based, ISACs have very different organizational, funding and trust models, reflecting differences in their sectors. For example, certain ISACs are operated and managed by existing industry organizations (such as the Electricity ISAC), some are independent non-profit corporations (such as the Information Technology ISAC), and some are organized in partnership with government (Telecommunications ISAC). This diversity has prevented the development of a consistent ISAC operational model. Nevertheless, there are common issues affecting ISAC operations and their ability to interoperate effectively with one another and with government, particularly the Department of Homeland Security, which holds primary responsibility for critical infrastructure protection for the United States government.

Representative ISACs and their primary sponsoring organizations are shown in the following table:

Sector	Principal Organizers
Chemical	American Chemistry Council and other industry associations
Electricity	North American Electric Reliability Council (NERC)
Energy	American Gas Association and American Petroleum Institute
Emergency Management and Response	U.S. Federal Emergency Management Agency (FEMA)
Financial Services	The banking, securities and insurance industries
Highway	American Trucking Associations
Information Technology	Leading information technology companies, including Computer Associates, CSC, General Dynamics, Microsoft
Public Transit	American Public Transportation Association
State Government	Multi-State ISAC, New York State
Surface Transportation	Association of American Railroads
Telecommunications	National Coordinating Center for Telecommunications (NCC) with industry participation
Water	Association of Metropolitan Water Agencies

2 ISAC Council

To provide a forum for cooperation, 14 ISACs have come together as an ISAC Council. Members are Chemical, Electricity, Emergency Management and Response, Energy, Financial Services, Healthcare, Highway, Information Technology, Multi-State, Public Transit, Research and Educational Network, Surface Transportation, Telecommunications, and Water. More detailed information is available at www.isaccouncil.org. The mission of the ISAC Council is to „advance the physical and cyber security of the critical infrastructures of North America by establishing and maintaining a framework for valuable interaction between and among the ISACs and with governments."

In addressing this broad mission, the Council has undertaken a number of efforts: to identify and resolve ISAC community issues, especially ISAC operations and operational policy; maintain and enhance inter-ISAC coordination; establish and maintain a dialogue with the governmental agencies that deal with ISACs; develop a practical data and information sharing protocol; develop analytical methods to assist the ISACs to support their own sectors and the other sectors with which there are interdependencies; and identify and disseminate knowledge and best practices.

The ISAC Council has had significant success in working across sector lines and with the department of Homeland Security. One of its key tasks has been to formulate a working definition of an ISAC as a starting point for understanding the private sector's responsibilities for CIP. Key components of that definition establish an ISAC as a trusted, sector specific, entity which:

- provides a 24-hour/7-day secure operating capability that establishes the sector's specific information and intelligence requirements for incidents, threats and vulnerabilities
- collects, analyzes, and disseminates alerts and incident reports to its membership based on its sector focused subject matter analytical expertise
- helps the government understand impacts for its sector;
- provides an electronic, trusted capability for the membership to exchange and share information on cyber, physical, and all threats in order to defend the critical infrastructure, and
- provides analytical support to government and other ISACs regarding technical sector details and in mutual information sharing and assistance during actual or potential sector disruptions whether caused by intentional, accidental or natural events.

Sector focus, analytical capability, secure, trusted 24x7 operations, and collection and dissemination capabilities are the key components of this definition, and help distinguish ISACs from other organizations having a different role to play in critical infrastructure protection. For example, some organizations do not have staff capable of analyzing vulnerability and threat information against a specific sector's operational environment, or do not have the capability of generating new, sector focused information for distribution to their members, other ISACs and government. Such organizations, however valuable, would not meet the ISAC Council definition.

Given these characteristics, the importance of ISACs as a trust community cannot be underestimated. Their success, both in private sector terms and from the government perspective, will be based on their capability of ensuring adherence to information sharing policies, identifying and authenticating participants in their networks, reaching broadly into their sectors, and providing value to members. However, such a public-private trust community with such a broad national security mission has not existed before, and a number of issues need to be understood and addressed if it is to be successful. The ISAC Council has begun to undertake this effort.

3 Trusted Information Sharing: White Papers

The ISAC Council has established regular meetings for issue resolution, provided a central contact point and mechanism for interaction with the Department of Homeland Security, worked with DHS to establish an Emergency Notification System for crisis response, and identified trusted information sharing mechanisms and networks that will work in private sector environments. With respect to this last area of focus, a key initiative has been the identification of barriers to trusted information sharing among ISACs and government and the preparation of eight issue papers (white papers) to identify barriers and where possible propose solutions.

As a principal co-author of one white paper, and as contributor and reviewer for the others, I believe it is important to understand the policy and operational trust issues raised in the papers. I recommend reading the papers directly (available at www.isaccouncil.org. It is important to note that the papers reflect the collective analysis of members of the ISAC Council in addressing issues of concern to ISAC operations and do not necessarily reflect all the operational structures used for CIP by the sectors (in some instances sectors have other protection mechanisms in addition to ISACs).

The private sector emphasis is important in the U.S. environment. However, many of the white papers identify issue and suggest approaches to problems that would be relevant in many countries which have de-regulated critical infrastructure industries and where government cannot implement solutions without private sector cooperation.

Taken together, the papers are beginning steps in tackling serious policy and process issues challenging the implementation of an effective private sector and government information sharing and analysis partnership and in fact are a catalyst for additional work to resolve the critical issues they identify.

4 The ISAC Council White Papers

The white papers are listed below, along with a short abstract describing the key issues which they address [ISAC04].

4.1 Government-Private Sector Relations

This paper addresses coordination and communication between the government and sectors, coordination and communication among the ISACs, incident data sharing, analytical information sharing, communications including mechanics and protocols, physical and cyber interdependencies between sectors, and research and development requirements.

4.2 Homeland Security Presidential Directive 7 (HSPD-7) Issues and Metrics

Homeland Security Presidential Directive-7 (HSPD-7) establishes a national policy for Federal departments and agencies to identify and prioritize United States critical infrastructure and key resources and to protect them from terrorist attacks. Although primarily focused on Federal agency responsibilities for critical infrastructure protection, it also establishes expectations related to government interaction with the private sector. The ISAC Council has examined the current status of privately owned and managed critical infrastructure protection in the United States and identified a number of areas in which collaborative work with the private sector is necessary if the broad expectations raised by HSPD-7 are to be realized.

4.3   Reach of the Major ISACs

This paper describes the degree of penetration or reach into the United States economy and infrastructure for each ISAC. It is designed to assist provide an understanding of the value of the ISACs in currently reaching into approximately 65% of the infrastructures of the United States economy held in private hands. The potential goal for the ISAC communities, as they mature, is to reach nearly 95% of those U.S. private infrastructures.

4.4   Information Sharing and Analysis

This paper is an effort to establish a path forward and future vision for information sharing and analysis and to provide a functional model for Critical Infrastructure Information Sharing and Analysis. Based on various government and critical infrastructure meetings during the fall of 2003, it addresses a number of objectives, including increased information sharing and analysis, security efforts to support the broadest possible reach both within and outside critical infrastructures so that no entity is excluded and to ensure long-term viability, realize cost efficiencies, and reduce redundancy, where possible.

4.5   Integration of ISACs into Exercises

The United States government has been planning and conducting exercises to test the readiness of CIP and Homeland Security systems and stakeholders. However, there has been little to no integration of active private industry infrastructure into these exercises. In certain instances, private industry participation in the scenario was simulated. There has been no ISAC involvement in these national level exercises. The ISACs and private infrastructure must become fully integrated into these exercises. Private industry must become a critical element of these training exercises, which are a key element of both homeland security and homeland defense training.

4.6   ISAC Analytical Efforts

ISAC analysis should consider both physical and cyber security, and should address immediate, mid, and long-term information and intelligence requirements. The current and planned analytical capabilities of the various ISACs must be understood as a baseline for further inter-ISAC coordination and interaction, with the analytical strengths of the ISACs providing the basis for further inter-ISAC cooperation. Government sponsorship and support of these analysis efforts must be considered and encouraged. A model that integrates private industry into the government intelligence cycle should be adopted.

4.7   Vetting and Trust

Efficient and effective processes for sharing critical infrastructure and security information on a timely basis must be developed. These processes must address the flow of information within an ISAC, among individual ISACs and between ISACs and government agencies. The processes must ensure that the information is available to the appropriate people, while providing reasonable assurance that the information cannot be used for malicious purposes and is not indiscriminately re-distributed so as to become essentially public information. The ultimate effectiveness of these processes will be determined by the trust relationships that are established among the organizations participating in the information sharing.

4.8 Policy Framework for the ISAC Community

The policy areas discussed in this paper are those that directly relate to fundamental ISAC functions and that cross ISAC and government boundaries: to report and exchange information concerning incidents, threats, vulnerabilities, solutions and countermeasures, best security practices and other protective measures, in accordance with national critical infrastructure protection policy, and to establish a mechanism for systematic and protected exchange and coordination of such information. To make information sharing real, it is essential to lower the practical risks of sharing information through both technical means and policies and to develop internal systems capable of supporting operational requirements without interfering with core business. Consequently, the technical means used must be simple, inexpensive, secure, and easily built into business processes. The policy framework must reduce perceived risks and build trust among participants

5 A Common Theme: Trust

Despite their focus on different issues, a common theme addressed in the papers is how to establish – from the private sector perspective – a trusted, information sharing network among private sector companies and government to manage and coordinate vulnerability, threat, alerts, response, remediation and risk mitigation and analytical information affecting the common national good and do so in a way that actually provides a measurable level of protection.

A fundamental issue running through many of the papers is that of trust – what is needed to build trusted, secure information sharing systems among ISACs and with government. This is not an in considerable issue, since the effectiveness of information sharing for CIP purposes must depend on the timelines and accuracy of sensitive vulnerability, remediation and threat information *and* the ability to provide that information to the right organizations for appropriate action. In effect this requires establishing strong operational security and privacy policies and auditable controls.

5.1 Three ISAC Information Sharing Issues

Three fundamental issues are now emerging and being examined by ISACs with respect to information sharing within sectors, across sectors and with the government:

- **What information is needed** for sharing within ISACs, across ISACs and with the government, and how should this information be collected, stored, processed and communicated? -- *For example, when is it appropriate to share „raw" data and to whom, versus sharing aggregated data or analysis? Is classified information needed by ISAC operations centers?*

- **What kind of analysis and reporting** is needed and how is this shared with participating organizations (ISACs, U.S. governments, member companies, international governments) and with their members and employees? -- *For example, who should have access to the most sensitive analysis? Should there be „executive" and other role-based views of information, in addition to the network/security operations center view?*

- **What controls** must be put into place to protect the shared information – both in terms of personal and business privacy as well as information security? *-- For example, how are cross-jurisdictional authentication policies, data classification rules, privacy management and technical security and audit controls to be systematically addressed?*

All three issues are critical for building trusted CIP systems and are being addressed by ISACs and government. However, even as work is underway to answer the first two sets of questions, we must begin understanding the personal and business information security and privacy risks inherent in building CIP information sharing and analysis systems, develop appropriate policies to mitigate those risks, and identify appropriate procedural and technical controls to implement those policies.

5.2 Security and Privacy Trust Components

The following discussion of security and privacy risk management in information sharing systems is adapted from [Sabo04], p. 4-8.

5.2.1 Managing Security Risk

In the information security field, there exists a generally accepted body of knowledge available to practitioners to address most security requirements, including general policies; codes of security practices and lifecycle security models; security technologies, tools, products, and services; and audit instruments and technologies. While all of this capability will be critical to effective implementations, it is useful to examine four specific areas of security to guide initial thinking about how to build a trusted information sharing infrastructure.

Generally, information security controls in the ISAC context must include threat management, identity management, access management, and a security management capability (the latter to provide a comprehensive view of the network, systems and applications from a security perspective and enable effective security management). Given the distributed nature of the systems interacting in a national CIP system (companies, intra-ISAC, inter-ISAC systems, ISAC-government systems, and government-government systems), all of the following components must be used to build a trusted foundation for information sharing.

Threat Management controls protect networks and systems against external and internal threats, assess vulnerabilities, and they identify and mitigate physical- and systems-based risks and attacks – in effect, protecting the CIP infrastructure itself.

Identity Management controls provide a foundation for provisioning users and for role-based access, enabling role-based and portal views of information and applications. Uniform policy development will be necessary given the number of different organizations involved in the various ISAC and government organizations.

Access Management protects classified, regulated and business-sensitive resources; controls how resources are accessed and used; and ensures authorized availability across networks, systems and platforms. For ISAC purposes, „tiered" controls will be needed to reflect roles, information classification requirements, and particular organizational rules for information and for participants throughout the web of participating organizations and users. This is an important consideration, given the move toward defining one or more new classification categories for sensitive, „critical infrastructure information" falling outside the scope of Secret, Top Secret and other established national security classification levels.

Security Management capability is needed to effectively manage the security of the networked infrastructures. Included in this capability are resource management, impact correlation, secure collaboration, intelligent visualization, and predictive analysis tools.

Although further work is clearly necessary to improve our understanding of security risks and controls in the ISAC- government information sharing environment, the technologies, tools, practices and other components for addressing information security requirements are understood and available in the marketplace. However, to date, very little cross-sector and government-private sector work has been done to develop necessary policies.

5.2.2 Managing Privacy Risk

Understanding business and personal privacy risks, and then using appropriate and available policies and technical controls to mitigate them, are another important issue. For purposes of this paper, privacy is used as a broad technical term to include essential privacy principles such as those required under the U.S. Privacy Act of 1974:

- Identify and publish systems of records

- Inform individuals about the purpose the data was collected, their rights, the benefits of having the data, the obligations of the agency to protect the information

- Provide reasonable safeguards regarding disclosures and protections against security and integrity threats

- Maintain accounting of all disclosures of information except Freedom of Information Act and agency personnel who have need to know

- Assure records are accurate, relevant, timely, complete

- Permit individuals to access and amend their records

Information privacy management, as a technical discipline has, to date, achieved very little formal structure. In addition, aside from attempts to develop narrow technologies to address very specific privacy requirements (such as W3C's P3P standard [P3P] for expressing „notice" requirements), there are, as yet, no generally accepted and open standards-based architectures, protocols, languages, or schemas to ensure that privacy rules and policies can be embodied in IT systems or interoperate across networks that manage the lifecycle collection and processing of information. And yet both personal privacy as well as business privacy requirements must be engineered into the new cyber security architecture in order to enable the deployment of trusted systems.

An example of business privacy requirements in the ISAC environment is the formal IT-ISAC membership agreement (see www.it-isac.org). This agreement, signed by all members of the IT-ISAC, includes a number of rules for processing information, defined in a set of categories that the ISAC members must honor. Instantiating such business privacy requirements in networked information sharing systems will require an infrastructure capable of ensuring that data and information moving within and across ISACs and government systems are collected, processed, stored and communicated in accordance with defined business privacy processing rules. Additionally, it is important to note that the security controls noted in the prior section are necessary to support the security requirements of privacy policies. However, many privacy requirements exist outside the realm of information security, and include such things as „notice," „policy enforcement," „collection limitations," „re-disclosure constraints," and „individual access."

Considering the additional complexity of business privacy rules established by individual IS-ACs, their member companies, and governmental agencies (including State and local governments), it becomes obvious that building a scalable information-sharing infrastructure must address the automated management of differing (and perhaps at times conflicting) privacy rules and agreements.

Because currently available technologies can support it, an effective starting point may be the application of a broad privacy management framework, such as the Privacy Services Framework (v.1.1) developed by the International Security Trust and Privacy Alliance [ISTPA], a non-profit business alliance addressing privacy from a technology perspective.

Using the ISTPA Framework, cross boundary policies and operational requirements can be addressed by policymakers and system architects through a number of defined services and capabilities:

- *control and data usage* functionality, to ensure that policies drive business rules processing
- *certification* of system credentials
- *validation* of data
- *interaction* of data subjects, systems and processes
- individual and business *access* to data as well as *audit* capability
- use of *agents*
- *negotiation* where appropriate.
- *enforcement* of policy violations

Many of these Framework services can be supported by currently available technologies in business intelligence, data management, enterprise management, and storage management, particularly when applied to enterprise implementations of data sharing systems.

However, in cross-sector and government-ISAC networked systems, these technologies should be utilized within an interoperable privacy architecture. In this context, the ISTPA Privacy Framework can serve as a tool for developing a model for the IT-based automation of privacy rules across the full lifecycle of information and across multiple jurisdictional (government, ISAC, corporate) boundaries. It can be used as a foundation for the collaborative development of architecture of privacy management.

6 Conclusion

If we accept the importance of critical infrastructure protection as a national security priority, and also accept that both private sector companies and governments have mutually dependent roles in building such protection systems, then the work of the ISAC Council in the United States can be seen, however incomplete, as a valuable beginning. The ISAC Council white papers provide an understanding of key information sharing issues and address the mutual roles and responsibilities of government and the private sector in establishing CIP systems.

Central to those systems is trust. Without trust among all participants, CIP systems will not be able to achieve their potential and will not effectively support national security and private sector goals. And without careful attention to security and privacy risk issues, including development of appropriate policies and implementation of adequate operational controls, trusted public-private sector information sharing systems will not be possible on a national scale.

Today, as ISACs expand operations, and as, for example, the United States Department of Homeland Security begins implementation of its new Homeland Security Information Network (HSIN), understanding and managing security and privacy information sharing risks is an even more vital concern. This concern takes on a global character as information sharing across international boundaries is discussed among government and private sector companies. We must now begin to address these issues. Where possible, as in the area of information security, we must move quickly to establish acceptable policies and make use of available tools and practices to manage security risk in CIP systems. In less mature areas such as business and personal privacy management, we must begin to turn serious attention to developing standards-based, risk management practices, architectures and tools.

Together, they are needed to ensure that CIP information sharing systems are both trusted by participants, trusted by citizens, and are effective.

References

[HSPD03]   Homeland Security Presidential Directive 7
            http://www.whitehouse.gov/news/releases/2003/12/20031217-5.html

[ISAC04]   White Papers, www.isaccouncil.org, 2004

[ISTPA]   ISTPA Privacy Framework 1.1, www.istpa.org

[P3P]   Platform for Privacy Preferences, w3.org/P3P

[Sabo04]   Addressing a Critical Aspect of Homeland Security: Managing Security and Privacy, www.ca.com/Federal

Legal Status of Qualified Electronic Signatures in Europe

Jos Dumortier

Professor of Law – K.U.Leuven
Lawfort – Of Counsel – Bar of Brussels
jos.dumortier@lawfort.be

Abstract

It is a common misunderstanding that, in Europe, in order to have a legally valid electronic signature, you need a „qualified" electronic signature. The European Electronic Signatures Directive is very clear in this respect, though: it is forbidden to deny any legal effectiveness to an electronic signature solely on the ground that it is not qualified, for instance, because it is not based on a qualified certificate or because it was not created with a secure signature-creation device. The only consequence of using a „qualified" electronic signature is the „automatic" application of existing legal rules which are still referring to the handwritten signature. These rules are progressively disappearing because modern legislation no longer exclusively refers to information processing in paper format. The „qualified" electronic signature is therefore only a temporary concept, mainly useful for bridging a transition period. It can, on a longer term, be useful to have a standardized secure electronic signature for all kinds of applications, but such a standard should preferably not be dictated by the legal rules on the „qualified" electronic signature.

1 Looking Backwards: How Did It All Start?

To understand the objectives of the European Electronic Signatures Directive and in particular the purpose of the concept of „qualified electronic signatures", it is useful to recall the antecedents of the European regulatory framework.

1.1 First Digital Signature Laws in the US

The first legislative texts regulating electronic signatures were issued at State level in the US between 1995 and 1997. The Utah Digital Signature Act, which was enacted in 1995 and amended twice in 1996, is often cited as the chronologically first example of this kind of legislation. The Utah Act was the first to authorize commercial use of digital signatures. It governed the use of public-private key pair encryption and certification authorities. Certification authorities had to be licensed by the Utah Department of Commerce. During the following years and particularly in 1997-1998, similar laws were issued in several other States in the US, for example in Washington, Missouri and Mississippi. Only in a second wave, new State laws on this subject adopted a more technology-neutral approach and no longer referred to asymmetric encryption and certificates.

S. Paulus, N. Pohlmann, H. Reimer (Editors): Securing Electronic Business Processes, Vieweg (2004), 281-289

1.2 The German 1997 Digital Signature Law

The State legislation in the US inspired some of the national legislators in Europe, particularly in Germany and Italy. The German Parliament approved on 22 July 1997 a „Digital Signature Law". This law stated in its first paragraph that it was its purpose to „create general conditions under which digital signatures are deemed secure and forgeries of digital signatures or manipulation of signed data can be reliably ascertained". The law defined a „digital signature" as „a seal affixed to digital data which is generated by a private signature key and establishes the owner of the signature key and the integrity of the data with the help of an associated public key provided with a signature key certificate of a certification authority". The German 1997 law established a very detailed framework, which was further developed in the Ordinance of 8 October 1997. Licenses were to be granted to certification authorities wishing to operate under the legal framework, after examination of their application file which had to include a security concept in accordance with the security requirements of the law and after a check of the implementation of that security concept by a body recognized by the supervisory authority. From a European perspective, the crucial provision of the German law was § 15: „Digital signatures capable of being verified by a public signature key certified in another Member State of the European Union or in another State party to the Agreement on the European Economic Area shall be deemed equivalent to digital signatures under this Act insofar as they show the same level of security".

1.3 The 1997 Digital Signature Legislation in Italy

The German example was soon followed by the Italian government, in an implementation decree of the Law n° 59 of 15 March 1997. It provided that anyone intending to use a system of asymmetric encryption keys for authenticating a legally valid electronic document must obtain an appropriate pair of keys and make one of these keys public by means of the certification procedure carried out by a certifying authority. This certifying authority needed an official accreditation prior to the commencement of its activities.

The certification authorities had to be registered in an official public list kept by the public administration. Following art. 8 of the Italian decree, the certification procedures could also be carried out „by a certifying authority operating under a license or authorization issued by another Member State of the European Union or the European Economic Area on the basis of equivalent requirements".

1.4 From „Digital" to „Electronic" Signatures

Inspired by the State legislation in the US, the laws introduced in Germany and Italy focused exclusively on „digital signatures" in the technical sense. The Italian implementation decree of 1997, for example, defined a digital signature as „the result of the computerized validation procedure based on a system of paired asymmetric keys, one public and one private, allowing the signatory, by means of the private key, and the recipient by means of the public key, to demonstrate and verify the origin and integrity of a computer document or of a set of computer documents".

Later on, this terminology was changed in the European Directive, in order to adopt a more „technology-neutral" approach. The Directive introduced a very broad definition of the term „electronic signatures", including not only signatures created on the basis of „digital signature technology" but all „data in electronic form which are attached to or logically associated with other electronic data and which serve as a method of authentication". The relationship between digital signatures – a specific technology based on asymmetric encryption aimed at securing the origin and the integrity of computer data – and electronic signatures – a legal concept referring to all kinds of data authentication – is schematically represented in Figure 1.

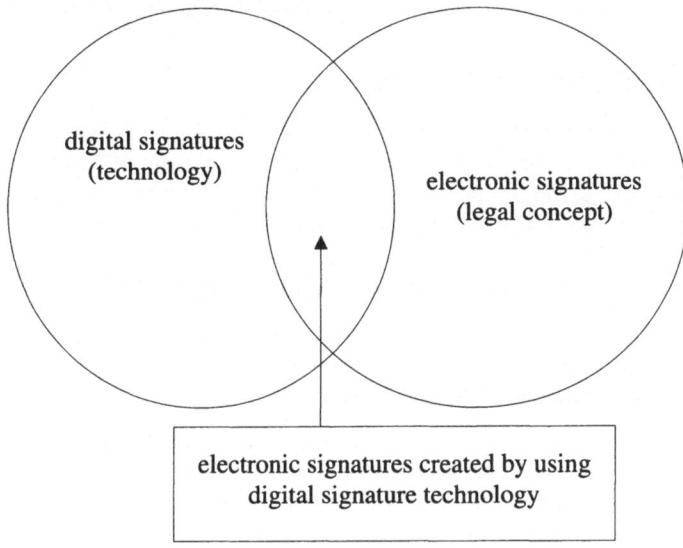

Figure 1: Relationship between „digital" and „electronic" signatures

The exclusive focus on one particular technology was, however, not the main reason why the European Commission reacted against the national legislation issued in Germany and Italy. It was primarily the requirement to subject certification services to national licensing schemes, which led to the European Commission's reaction.

1.5 No National Licensing Schemes, Please!

The introduction of national licensing schemes for certification authorities in Germany and Italy was a thorn in the eye of the European Commission. The internal market had to be restored quickly. If every Member State were to submit the provision of certification services to a prior authorization by authorities of that Member State and adopt their own technical rules for electronic signature products, it would evidently be impossible – or at least very cumbersome – for a service provider to develop European-wide certification services or for vendors to sell their products throughout the European market.

In a Communication to the Member States, published in 1997, the European Commission stated: „Divergent legal and technical approaches would constitute a serious obstacle to the Internal Market and would hinder the development of new economic activities linked to electronic commerce. An EU policy framework for ensuring security and trust in electronic communication and safeguarding the functioning of the Internal Market is therefore urgently needed. The European Union simply cannot afford a divided regulatory landscape in a field so vital for the economy and society".

The prohibition to subject certification services to prior authorization therefore became one of the core provisions of the European Directive. The access to this market should remain free and without any obstacle. This rule not only applies to certification authorities but to all categories of certification services, including time stamping services, trusted archival services, electronic notaries or even consultancy services in the area of electronic signatures.

2 Legal Recognition of Electronic Signatures

In its reaction against the initiatives in some of the Member States, the European Commission evidently had to propose a positive alternative in this area. Instead of leaving the recognition of electronic signatures to the Member States, the European Directive introduced a European-wide legal recognition for all kinds of electronic signatures.

2.1 What Does „Legal Recognition" Mean?

Recital (21) of the Directive specifies that „in order to contribute to the general acceptance of electronic authentication methods it has to be ensured that electronic signatures can be used as evidence in legal proceedings in all Member States."

In the same Recital one can also read: „National law governs the legal spheres in which electronic documents and electronic signatures may be used". In other words, Member States can freely decide for which circumstances electronic documents can be used, but once the use of electronic documents is accepted, the electronic signature should no longer be denied legal effectiveness.

It has to be added that the freedom of the Member States to allow or disallow the use of electronic media has been considerably restricted in a later Directive of 2002 (the European Electronic Commerce Directive). This Directive requires the Member States to remove all legal obstacles for the conclusion of contracts in electronic form.

2.2 Qualified Electronic Signatures

Article 5.1 states in its first paragraph that „Member States shall ensure that advanced electronic signatures which are based on a qualified certificate and which are created by a secure-signature-creation device „satisfy the legal requirements of a signature in relation to data in electronic form in the same manner as a hand-written signature satisfies those requirements in relation to paper-based data".

An „advanced electronic signature" is an electronic signature meeting the following four requirements: 1) uniquely linked to the signatory; 2) capable of identifying the signatory; 3) created using means that the signatory can maintain under his sole control; and 4) linked to the data to which it relates in such a manner that any subsequent change of the data is detectable. A qualified certificate is a certificate which is compliant with the format described in Annex 1 of the Directive and which has been issued by a provider who meets the requirements of Annex 2. A secure signature-creation device is a device which fulfills the security requirements of Annex 3 of the Directive.

2.3 Equivalence with Penned Signatures

The Directive attributes to qualified electronic signatures, in relation to electronic data, the same status as hand-written signatures have in relation to paper documents. It is nevertheless not contrary to Article 5.1 to replace current legislation requiring hand-written signatures by new legislation in which the use of electronic data is permitted without the use of qualified electronic signatures. It is also not the objective of the Directive to require the use of qualified electronic signatures in every situation in which, up to now, the use of hand-written signatures has been obligatory. On the contrary, such a requirement would often be an infringement of Article 5.2 of the Directive (see infra).

On the other hand, Member States can introduce new legislation requiring additional security guarantees, above the level of qualified electronic signatures. In relation to paper documents, hand-written signatures aren't the exclusive security measure either. In all cases, however, where in relation to paper documents a hand-written signature is estimated to be sufficient, Member States have to give an equivalent status to qualified electronic signatures when they start to allow the use of electronic data processing as a substitute for the paper documents. The status of the hand-written signature in its relation to paper documents determines, in other words, the status of the qualified electronic signature in relation to electronic data.

2.4 Prohibition to discriminate

Article 5.2 of the Directive states that electronic signatures may not be denied legal effectiveness and admissibility as evidence in legal proceedings solely on the grounds that it is in electronic form or that the signature is not a qualified signature. The effect of Article 5.2 is that Member States may not draft or maintain regulation, or endorse or authorize private rules with a view to condemn the use of an electronic authentication tool solely by virtue of its electronic format or its non-qualified nature.

This is, for example, relevant in a court proceeding: a judge could not refuse an electronic signature on the sole ground that it is not a „qualified electronic signature". He is, however, not obliged to give that signature the same legal effect that a hand-written signature would receive. Suffice it to say that the provision of Article 5.2 touches Member States' legislators as well. Laws denying legal effectiveness of electronic signatures solely on the grounds that they are not „qualified electronic signatures" would not be in line with Article 5.2.

2.5 Why Do We Need Qualified e-Signatures?

The label of „qualified electronic signature" is only meant to be used for testing the equivalence of an electronic authentication method with the handwritten signature in the paper-based environment. Using the label for other purposes is in principle not allowed.

For the European legislator, it was clear that „national law lays down different requirements for the legal validity of handwritten signatures". The objective was clearly not to harmonize the requirements for the legal validity of electronic signatures but instead to establish in every Member State the equivalence between the legal status of handwritten signatures in the paper-based environment and the legal status of electronic signatures in the electronic environment. In other words, the European legislator tried to determine a type of electronic signature, which should consequently be considered by every Member State as the equivalent of a handwritten signature.

It should be clear that, as a consequence of this choice, the legal status of qualified electronic signatures has not been harmonized between the Member States. The legal requirements for handwritten signatures differ from Member State to Member State. Qualified electronic signatures have the same status as handwritten signatures. Therefore the legal requirements for qualified electronic signatures are also different in each of the Member States.

3 Problems Regarding Qualified e-Signatures

European legislation has opted for a solution in which the legal regime for qualified electronic signatures „follows" the national legal regime for handwritten signatures. If a Member State has, for example, very strict rules for the legal validity of a handwritten signature on a certain type of contract, this Member State will apply the same strict rules to qualified electronic signatures for this same type of contract. If another Member State has very flexible rules for handwritten signatures for that type of contract, the rules for the use of qualified electronic signatures on that same type of contract will also be very flexible.

3.1 Qualified e-Signatures Refer to the Paper World

The legal regime for handwritten signatures is, in other words, the *reference point*, the principle being to award qualified electronic signatures in the electronic environment the same legal status as handwritten signatures in a paper-based context.

During the transposition of the Directive, some Member States, such as the UK, discovered that their legal system has no legal provisions for handwritten signatures. In the absence of national legislation for the use of handwritten signatures, it follows that there can be no legal status for the use of qualified electronic signatures either. If national law doesn't use the „handwritten signature" as a legal concept, it is impossible to use this concept as a reference point for electronic signatures.

More and more, specific rules are being addressed to the electronic environment, without any reference to the paper-based context. It is not hard to imagine that, ten or twenty years from now, many applications will only use communications in an electronic form and that the rules applicable to those applications will no longer refer to handwritten signatures. In other words, the handwritten signature will, bit by bit, loose its value as a reference point. It is therefore doubtful whether the concept of the qualified electronic signature as an „electronic equivalent" to the handwritten signature will survive in the longer run.

3.2 Divergences Make Qualified e-Signatures Useless

For the time being, and for most of the Member States' legal systems, linking the qualified electronic signature to a handwritten signature can perhaps be useful. Whether or not this will actually be the case, largely depends on how clear the concept of a „qualified electronic signature" actually is. It does not make much sense to require a Member State to award electronic signatures the same legal status as a handwritten signature on condition that it is a „qualified electronic signature", if this concept is not uniformly understood. A Belgian citizen, for example, wishing to make an electronic commercial transaction with a Greek company by using a qualified electronic signature should be certain that his/her signature will have the same legal status under Greek law as a handwritten signature. What I, as a Belgian, consider a „qualified electronic signature" should therefore be equally recognized as such by Greek authorities. The whole system adopted by European legislation is, in other words, only useful on the condition that there is one common European concept of „qualified electronic signature".

Unfortunately there remain a large number of divergences between Member States about the requirements for qualified electronic signatures. The requirements have been listed in general terms in the annexes of the Directive and further specified in EESSI standardization deliverables. In practice however, these efforts did not lead to a unique, interoperable qualified electronic signature that can be used across the whole European Union.

3.3 Qualified e-Signatures and Standards

Legislation can contain rules but should preferably not describe *how* people have to implement these rules. The „how" is the object of standards, which by definition have a voluntary character. As long as people comply with the rule, they should remain free to decide how they do this. It is true that, sometimes, legislation refers explicitly to standards, but only insofar that this is strictly necessary and the reference to a particular standard is mostly interpreted in a restrictive manner.

These elementary principles should be borne in mind when interpreting the Directive and, having regard to these principles, the reference to „qualified electronic signature" should not be extended. Meeting the requirements of a qualified electronic signature merely results in equivalence with the handwritten signature. The non-discrimination rule in Art. 5.2 explicitly prohibits going beyond this restriction and using the concept for other purposes.

One could call Article 5.2 for this reason a „long-term" provision. European legislation has not sought to use the concept of „qualified electronic signature" beyond the context of Article 5.1. As soon as it is no longer necessary to search for an „automatic" electronic substitute for the handwritten signature, the concept should be abandoned. Every kind of electronic signature should, from that moment onwards, be judged only with regard to its objective adequacy in the specific context.

3.4 Why Supervise Qualified Certification Authorities?

Various Member States have established supervision schemes for certification service providers which are very close to prior authorization. Article 3.1 is however very clear. Making the provision of certification services – qualified, accredited, or other – subject to prior authorization or taking other measures that have the same effect, is strictly prohibited by the Directive.

Fortunately the supervision of certification services by the Member States' authorities only affects providers established on their own national territory. One could have expected that Member States would keep the supervision regime for the providers established on their own territory as limited and as flexible as possible in order not to affect negatively the competitive position of their „own" service providers in comparison with providers established elsewhere.

Nevertheless many European countries have followed a completely different strategy. Some of the national supervision schemes put heavy burdens on the local certification service providers before these can begin to provide qualified services. Apparently Member States are still convinced that most of the qualified certificates issued to the public on their own territory will be provided by providers established on that territory. Another reason could be that some Member States use the supervision schemes to raise the security level of the providers established on their territory in order to improve their quality and hence their competitiveness on the European and international market.

In any case and as long as they avoid prior authorization, according to the Directive, Member States are largely free to organize the supervision of the certification service providers established on their territory themselves. Recital (13) states „Member States may decide how they ensure the supervision of compliance with the provisions laid down in this Directive". It was clearly not the objective of the Directive to have similar or harmonized supervision schemes in every Member State.

On the other hand, however, the establishment of heavy, bureaucratic supervision schemes for qualified certification service providers doesn't seem very useful. A supervision scheme should rather be considered as an element of consumer protection. In this perspective, it doesn't seem very logical to restrict the protection to certification authorities which issue qualified certificates to the public. A light-weight supervision of all kinds of certification services, in order to protect consumers, would seem more appropriate.

3.5   What about Voluntary Accreditation?

Recital (11) of the Directive states: „Voluntary accreditation schemes aiming at an enhanced level of service provision may offer certification-service-providers the appropriate framework for developing further their services towards the levels of trust, security and quality demanded by the evolving market; such schemes should encourage the development of best practices among certification-service-providers; certification-service-providers should be free to adhere to and benefit from such accreditation schemes." Therefore Article 3.2 of the Directive stipulates that Member States can maintain or even introduce voluntary accreditation schemes aiming at enhanced levels of certification-service provision.

The European legislator has estimated, very rightly, that voluntary accreditation schemes could be beneficial for the development of the market. It can give certification service providers operating in Europe the possibility of demonstrating their level of security and trustworthiness. Accreditation schemes could certify the adequacy of the security level of a particular certification service for being used in particular contexts or applications. For instance, specialized accreditation schemes could certify the adequacy of particular certification service for the health care sector.

Recital (11) also refers to the evolving market in this area. When new solutions are discovered and introduced into the market, accreditation schemes can help providers gain user trust. The accreditation schemes should mainly be created or maintained for the benefit of the providers themselves. They should encourage the development of best practices and remain up-to-date with state-of-the-art technology in the sector. They are a form of common quality control, organized at the level of a particular sector. Of course, setting up such accreditation schemes requires considerable resources, mainly in terms of expertise.

Consequently the aim of the Directive has never been to have a national accreditation scheme in every Member State. It is also fully incorrect to consider voluntary accreditation schemes as a means to control whether or not a certification service provider operates in compliance with the provisions of the Directive. The provision concerning voluntary accreditation schemes was intended mainly to prevent Member States from misinterpreting the prohibition of prior authorization. This prohibition should not be understood as incompatible with existing or future voluntary accreditation schemes. On the contrary, the Directive encourages the creation of such schemes, as long as the conditions related to those schemes are objective, transparent, proportionate and non-discriminatory. Moreover, as is stated in Recital (12): „Member States should not prohibit certification-service-providers from operating outside voluntary accreditation schemes; it should be ensured that such accreditation schemes do not reduce competition for certification services".

4   Conclusions

The concept of the „qualified electronic signature", referred to in Art. 5.1 of the European Directive, has been introduced in order to obtain more legal security on a short term. Our current laws have been conceived without taking into account digital information processing and electronic signatures. They have been drafted against the background of paper-based documents and handwritten signatures.

It would have been very cumbersome to modify all these current laws at once and to adapt them to the electronic environment. Moreover, it would not suffice to modify only the text of the laws. Legal rules are only effective if they are embedded in common practices and if they are well understood by public administrators, judges and by the society as a whole.

Art. 5.1 establishes therefore an equivalence between „qualified electronic signatures" and handwritten signatures. Whenever someone uses a qualified electronic signature in Europe, the same local rules will apply as those which apply to handwritten signatures. This creates some kind of European „passport" for online cross-border transactions: if a Belgian user orders a product on a website of a Greek vendor, he automatically knows that his (Belgian) qualified electronic signature will have the same legal status as a Greek *handwritten* signature.

This mechanism is only useful as long as Greek laws continue to refer to handwritten signatures. Little by little, laws in all the Member States are modernized and contain security requirements that take into account the context of digital information processing. The legal concept of „qualified electronic signatures", as a bridge to the laws of the „paper world", will therefore not survive in the longer run.

A completely different question is the one about the need for a standardized secure electronic signature that can be used for all kinds of transactions, preferably on a global scale. It is evident that such a standard would be highly beneficial for e-business.

The discussions that have been conducted and the specifications that have been drafted around the concept of „qualified electronic signatures" can certainly be used as one element in this standardization process. But it is important to free the minds and no longer consider the legal requirements of the Directive as a dictate in this perspective. A standard for secure electronic signatures should be conceived by the important stakeholders on the market, on the basis of technical, organizational and economical considerations, and should not be the result of a political compromise between European Member States.

The Finnish Ecosystem for Mobile Signatures

Werner Freystätter · Samu Konttinen

Valimo Wireless
Helsinki, Finland
www.valimo.com
{werner.freystatter | samu.konttinen}@valimo.com

Abstract

GSM and UMTS mobile phones provide a tamper resistant storage to store user credentials. The SIM card may take on other functions in addition to the management of end user for phone calls. The mobile phone is typically something very personal and something that you carry with you wherever you go and you'll notice if you lose it.

Based on these premises, all three Finnish mobile operators have chosen to built the infrastructure to enable authentication and other security-related and first services are being deployed now.

The aim of our presentation is to describe the use cases and business models on how various vendors co-operate and build an ecosystem that is beneficial to many actors (businesses and customers alike), both in terms of offering advanced security, as well as economies of scale for new services. In many ways this is unique and has not been seen in this magnitude in any other national environment previously. The co-operation between all mobile operators with Finnish Government to provide a digital identity for citizens and to employees as part of mobile operators value-added-service is creating new market opportunities for the industry.

The cases include a co-operation between mobile operator & public sector/ Retailing/Property management/Financial institutes etc.

1 Introduction

1.1 About Finland and a national electronic ID

In Finland the public sector has provided a major impetus in setting up a PKI (Public Key Infrastructure). In 1996 a common working group of three ministries issued a report stating that the electronic identification of a citizen is part of a state's core service infrastructure for an information society.

Then, a project called Finnish Electronic Identity (FINEID) was launched to specify a national PKI; and the Population Register Center (VRK) was nominated to act as a Certification Authority (CA).

Consequently, the first smartcards with the national ID layout and chip for storing the FINEID application, private/public key pair and user certificate were distributed in Dec. 1999.

S. Paulus, N. Pohlmann, H. Reimer (Editors): Securing Electronic Business Processes, Vieweg (2004), 290-298

1.2   About FINEID

The FINEID EID system is based on Swedish SEIS-standards (Swedish electronic ID), where the FINEID application specification is the same, but the certificate profiles have some minor changes compared to the SEIS standard.

The Finnish Smartcard vendor Setec is the only authorized manufacturer of the FINEID. The FINEID application has been implemented using Setec's smartcard operating system.

For a resident in Finland, the application procedure is similar to the practice when issuing conventional ID documents (e.g. passport); the citizen files an application at the local police office, where the officer identifies the applicant and checks the validity of the application. A couple of weeks later, the citizen needs to collect the ID card in person. The signing & authentication PINs are mailed in a sealed envelope to the citizen's mailing address. Before mailing, the police checks whether or not the address information in the population register database is the same as provided in the application form.

The FINEID card itself contains two private keys (and two certificates). One of the keys is used only for authentication and the other only for decrypting messages and generating digital signatures.

1.3   Problems

A bottleneck for the rapid increase in the number of FINEID cards has been the lack of services relying on the FINEID card and digital signatures

The private service providers seem to hesitate as long as the number of potential customers having the FINEID card is so small. Another barrier for the growth of the user number is the need of equipment i.e. the smartcard reader and the software necessary for utilising the reader in applications.

In addition, the other obstacles can be summarized as follows:

- Difficulty in managing the range of interoperable card readers and a relative „complex" setup when a citizen wants to use the FINEID with a home PC.
- Plenty of pilot schemes, but a lack of services with mass-market appeal.
- No strict legal requirement to use digital signatures for many transaction specific electronic services.
- Industry players confused about their roles

1.4   A new approach

The VRK continues to issue a smartcard with private / public key pair and certifies it i.e. FINEID. However, in addition, the VRK has agreed to issue certificates on behalf of service providers. Service providers implement the FINEID application on their platform of choice (for example, their own loyalty smartcard).

Thus, the VRK role has taken on a new dimension with an emphasis on controlling the RA process and certification process.

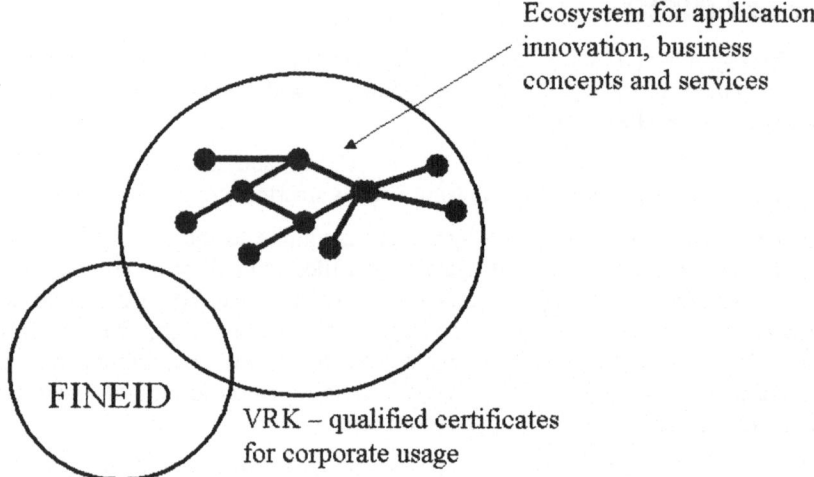

Ecosystem for application
innovation, business
concepts and services

FINEID

VRK – qualified certificates
for corporate usage

For issuing corporate usage certificates the VRK requires the user to be identified through either the FINEID card, or a vetted third party registration process. For example: OKO bank will be allowed to register their bankcard customers with their own process.

As a result of VRK's decision an exciting range of opportunities has emerged in Finland:

- Companies may consider to become trust service providers without investing into an expensive RA or CA-process
- The range of secure signature creation devices (SSCDs) can be expanded
- Qualified digital signatures can be deployed in scenarios that do not require the explicit use of the FINEID card and a card reader
- The use of digital signatures can be bundled with an existing range of services / service infrastructures.

2 Mobile Extension

Mobile and telecommunications is one of the key industry sectors that is now taking the opportunity to leverage the use of VRK's qualified certification service.

2.1 Salient features

- Mobile operators can offer non-qualified certificates with their own CA infrastructure in parallel with the qualified certificates where they rely on VRK. Both can co-exist in the same SIM card.
- The SIM card and mobile phone replace the smartcard / card reader combination
- The browsing channel and signing application are separated, offering a range of reselling opportunities to medium and large-sized IT service providers.

3 Business models for mobile signature service providers

At Valimo we have identified four business models:

- Validation Authority (VA)
- Mobile Signature Service Gateways (MSS-GW)
- Trust Service Providers (TSP)
- Identity Service Providers (based on the Liberty Alliance concept)
- Security Service Providers (SSP)

We describe each concept in turn.

3.1   Validation Authority (VA)

A VA provides a clearinghouse function for applications that require establishing the validity of a user and his digital certificate.

Aggregating revocation using OCSP-services, the VA is continuously accessible for PKI-based applications and able to compare certificates to all known and accessible sources of revoked certificates.

In a second instance, the VA provides services for verifying and validating signatures, which have been generated in the past.

3.2   Mobile Signature Service Gateways (MSS-GW)

The MSSP (Mobile Signature Service Provider) is a generic concept where a mobile operator equips its subscriber with the ability to generate digital signatures.

The mobile operator provides a web services interface to service providers allowing them to „order" digital signatures from an end user. Hereby it is important to note that the MSSP specification claims to be technology agnostic.

There are two approaches for implementing a mobile signature service.

1. server-side mobile signatures, where the signature is generated on behalf of a user in a central server

2. mobile-phone-originating signatures, where each user has a digital signing functionally incorporated into the phone

In addition to this, the MSSP specification allows for the use of symmetric „signatures" i.e. message authentication codes. Despite the choice of technology and design options, it has become clear that most vendors, mobile operators and indeed national digital signature laws require an implementation that features:

- the digital signing functionality in the mobile phone
- the use of public key cryptography,
- thus the use of digital certificates
- and finally the conformance evaluation for the whole infrastructure, where mobile phones and the embedded signing application are seen as a SSCD and SCA combination (SSCD = Secure Signature Creation Device and Signature Creation Application)

3.2.1 What is specified?

The MSSP specifications describe a web services interface that separates the technology infrastructure on the mobile operator and mobile phone user side from the back office systems of a group of service providers.

Service providers contact the MSSP via the web services interface and order a signature. The Mobile Operator then takes care of the rest. In that respect a mobile operator who wants to act as an MSSP not only needs to make the MSSP interface available, but also needs to implement the underlying infrastructure.

The following message calls are included:

- Signature Request / Response
- Status Request / Response
- Certification Request / Response
- Registration Request / Response
- Profile Request / Response
- Receipt Request / Response

The following diagram depicts the MSSP components, a generic set of mobile-signature-based services and their relation to the technology infrastructure.

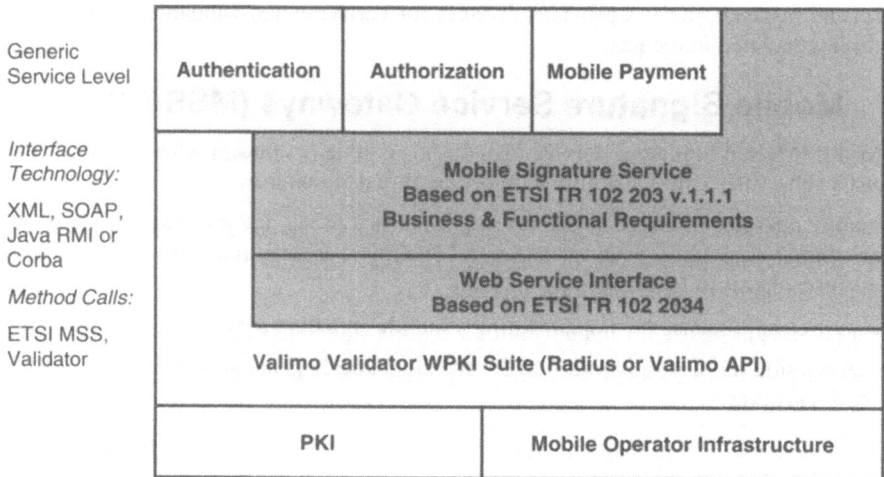

3.2.2 When does it make sense to offer an MSSP-compliant service interface?

Business-wise:

8. One or several service provider need to require the use of digital signatures
9. They are willing to trust a mobile operator to obtain the signatures on their behalf
10. A mobile operator has decided that equipping his subscribers with a mobile signing function is a worthwhile investment

Technology-wise:

1. Mobile Operator has worked out a logistics concept for equipping mobile subscribers

2. A public key infrastructure is either setup in-house or certification services are out-sourced

3. Mobile signature services are integrated into an on-line service interface for the end users (similar to a web-based e-mail account)

4. Mobile Operator assumes certain responsibilities in ensuring that the end users are able to use the service properly

5. MOs make sure that signing requests are only submitted from bonafide service providers

There is an option for trusted third party audits that ensure that both the service provider and mobile subscriber get a fair treatment when there is a dispute.

3.3   Trust Service Providers (TSP)

The following picture is used to describe a typical transaction. In this case, the three independent actors (user, service provider and trust service provider) interact in the following way:

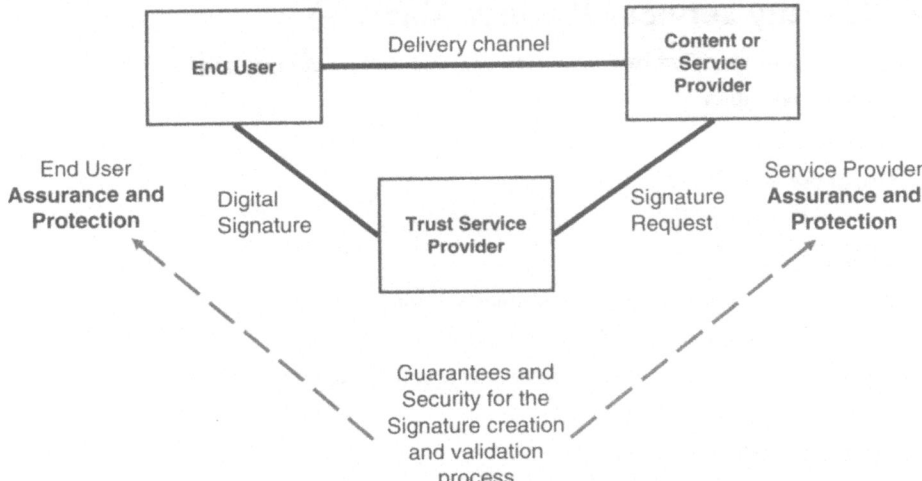

1. The end user triggers a service request that necessitates a validation requirement. The service provider's application server handles the service request.

2. The service provider sends a user authentication or transaction validation request to the Digital Signature Service System located in the premises of a trust service provider.

3. The trust service provider verifies the content provider's identity. This communication link is typically based on SSL processes to ensure the required security level.

4. The trust service provider sends a signature request to the user.

5. The user activates the personal trusted device's digital signature function by entering a signing PIN. A digitally signed message is returned to the Digital Signature Service System.

6. The trust service provider verifies the signature and validates the user's identity extracting information and the public key from the certificate issued by an appropriate Certification Authority (CA). The validation process includes several verification steps for both the user's certificate and the digital signature itself. For example, the Digital Sig-

nature Service System ensures that the policy constraints allocated to each certificate are respected.

7. Note, that certificates can be crosschecked with multiple CAs.
8. The trust service provider sends the transaction validation result to the service provider.
9. The service provider confirms the result to the user.

Each transaction validation or authentication request is appended with a time record and stored into the database. The database is accessible by the users and service providers.

Trust services include:

- Signature verification and certificate validation
- Signature archiving
- Time stamping
- Notary for signature requests and responses
- Vetting of service providers requesting signatures from a user

3.4   Identity services (Liberty Alliance)

Identity services as specified by the Liberty Alliance project compromise:

- Identity federation
- Authentication
- Use of pseudonyms
- Support for anonymity
- Global logout

Mobile operators are planning to offer an interface for:

- identity federation and defederation services
- supporting mobile-phone based authentication (PKI and non-PKI)
- Re-authentication services
- Identity provider brokering

Mobile operators are strong contenders for becoming a user's principal Identity Provider.

3.5   Security Service Providers (SSP)

Bundling mobile phone subscriptions with secure login and other authentication services.

Corporate customers i.e. companies that have purchased a number of mobile phone subscriptions for their employees have been singled out as one of the most important customer segments.

3.5.1   About a mobile operator's corporate customers

Corporate customers purchase bulk subscriptions for two reasons. First, they need to equip certain employees with a mobile phone, since their availability has become an integral requirement of how their business is conducted. In this group we can find individuals such as:

- Service engineers responsible for field work
- Sales people with a disproportionate amount of travelling

- Consultants and engineers working on customer sites
- Logistics personnel involved in the delivery process
- IT managers with mission-critical system responsibilities
- Manager to being available when necessary even 24 hours per day

Second, mobile phones have become a status symbol and a free mobile phone subscription (given a certain monthly spending limit) has emerged as a 'basic' company benefit for certain management groups.

3.5.2 Foundations for extending services to corporate customers

In this sense the mobile operator is already playing an important role in enabling a modern company to fulfil their mobile communications needs. In fact two critical aspects are facilitated: First, a mobile operator provides the tools to enable employees to communicate, being always available. Second, it enables an employer to maintain control over the communication costs.

As a result the following side effects are noteworthy: The MO knows the owner of the corporate account in terms of:

- Payment history – how regularly company pays its phone bills
- Number of employees that use a mobile phone
- Nature of communication needs (international, national, internal user group versus external communications)
- Changes in the company (employees with a subscription leaving or joining the company)

One can say that the corporate customer has taken up the mobile operator's offering to:

- Enable employees to be available to work outside office, to access and to communicate
- Control the usage of a work tool required by the employees (Measuring, billing, accounting)
- Centralize data collection and information processing (communication records) for further processing by the corporate customers' accountants

In the future – measuring employees working productivity and availability will also become an important issue.

4 Summary: What Valimo can offer

Valimo has specialized in developing solutions for mobile operators to start providing digital signature services. Our solution portfolio consists of gateway products to request and receive digital signatures from various signing device types. The service features include certificate validation and signature verification. A significant trend in our solution development has not only been to concentrate to wireless PKI, but to create bridge for several world leading business applications and identity management solution to utilise WPKI.

We teamed up with leading CA software/service providers, major handset and SIM card manufacturers, and several leading enterprise application providers.

We co-operate with all three mobile operators in Finland and are involved in several WPKI projects in Europe. Enabling transaction routing and to provide ETSI-compliant MSSP server with several enterprise add-on's has been our role in building the infrastructure of wireless

PKI. Professional services are provided to create requirements and to design dynamics in both technical and business perspective.

Our reference customers include several mobile operators, government ministries, Finnish gaming and gambling monopolies, large international enterprises and many others.

Providing state-of –the-art technology for several layers in the WPKI value chain has been a great challenge and Finland being very advanced in this field has been an attractive ecosystem all together to gain world-leading expertise. For more info please visit www.valimo.com.

References

Setec – www.setec.fi

VRK – www.vrk.fi

Liberty Alliance – www.projectliberty.org

ETSI specifications – www.etsi.org

Valimo Wireless – www.valimo.com

e-Transformation
Turkey Project

Aysegul Ibrisim · Rasim Yilmaz

Turkish Standards Institution
Computer and Information Department
TURKEY
{aibrisim I ryilmaz}@tse.gov.tr

Abstract

The objective of this paper is to share the action plan developed for the implementation of eEurope+ in Turkey. The paper will cover the new Telecommunication law, and other law orders in all segments of telecommunications services market like electronic signature law, information obtaining rights law, protection of personal data law, etc. in Turkey. The information security and security test standards and their implementation in Turkey are also going to be presented.

Turkey has participated in eEurope+ Initiative with other European Union (EU) candidate countries in June 2001. e-Transformation Turkey Project was launched as part of Turkey's commitment to join the European Union and, in particular, to leverage Turkey's potential to become an important player in the global arena.

In the scope of the objective declared above, new Telecommunication law, secondary telecommunication legislation, electronic signature law, information obtaining rights law, protection of personal data law, intellectual property rights law about protection of rights on electronic media, secondary legislation regarding consumers protection law, decree for adoption of European convention on conditional access will be covered as well as with the topics of: Implementation of security test standards, e-tariff project, responsible institutions for e-Transformation Turkey Project and their strucures and rolles.

1 Introduction

Turkey has participated in eEurope+ Initiative with other European Union (EU) candidate countries in June 2001. EU's ambitious Lisbon Strategy „to become the most còmpetitive and

dynamic knowledge-based economy in the world by 2010" is also well recognized by Turkey, and Turkish government is sharing the very same goal as a candidate country to an enlarged Union. Starting with Turkey's participation, an initiative has been launched to achieve the goals of eEurope+. As an evidence to Turkey's commitment to succeed in transforming Turkey into an information society in line with the Lisbon Strategy, e-Transformation Turkey Project is well underway and achieving its short term targets. e-Transformation Turkey Project was launched as part of Turkey's commitment to join the European Union and, in particular, o leverage Turkey's potential to become an important player in the global arena.

S. Paulus, N. Pohlmann, H. Reimer (Editors): Securing Electronic Business Processes, Vieweg (2004), 299-308

2 e-TRANSFORMATION TURKEY Project

The government took power in December 2002, and introduced the Urgent Action Plan (UAP) to help solve the problems on the most needed areas of interest. the first implementation period has been completed in December 2003. As a part of this Urgent Action Plan's Public Management Reform Section, e-Transformation Turkey Project was declared as a highpriority project. e-Transformation Turkey Project aims to foster the evolution and to co-ordinate information society activities with a coordination unit established solely for this aim.

Responsible institution for this specific project is identified as State Planning Organization (SPO), which is affiliated to the Prime Ministry. SPO is responsible for overall coordination of countrywide economic and social development programs, allocation of funds to public investment projects, and advising to the Government. Prime Ministry, NGOs, and all public institutions are identified as affiliated organizations for this project. To clarify the objectives and principles about the project, a Prime Minister's Circular, dated February 27, 2003 has been issued. According to this Circular, the objectives of e-Transformation Project are as follows:

- Policies, laws, and regulations regarding ICT will be re-examined and changed if necessary, with respect to the EU acquis; eEurope+ Action Plan, initiated for the candidate countries, will be adapted to Turkey.

- Mechanisms that facilitate the participation of citizens to decision-making process in the public domain via using ICT will be developed.

- Transparency and accountability for public management will be enhanced.

- Through increased usage of ICT, good governance principles will be put in place in government services.

- Spreading the usage of ICT.

- Public IT projects will be coordinated, monitored, evaluated and consolidated if necessary in order to avoid duplicating or overlapping investments.

- Private firms will be guided according to the above-mentioned principles.

In order to realize these objectives and to ensure the success of the project, a new coordination unit, Information Society Department, within SPO is established. This Department is responsible for the overall coordination of the project. Before this new project, lack of efficient coordination between institutions made the progress slow and ineffective. For the first time in Turkey, a separate division has been named as the coordinator of information society activities.

To increase the participation and the level of success, an Advisory Board with 41 members has been established. This consulting body consists of the representatives of public institutions, non-profit organizations, and universities. All Responsible institutions for ICT in e-Transformation Turkey Project and their rolles are given in the following table. (Table 1)

Table 1: Responsible institutions for ICT in e-Transformation Turkey Project.

Formulating the Information Society Strategy State Planning Organization All Public Institutions	Universities
Contemplating policies regarding the transformation of Turkey to a Center of Excellence in Software Development	State Planning Organization Ministry of Finance Undersecretaries of Treasury TUBITAK Universities
Investigating measures for widespread diffusion of Internet infrastructure and usage –including broadband access- all around the country	Ministry of Transportation Telecommunications Authority, Turk Telekom, NGOs, Ministry of National Education
Performing a preliminary study for license allocation in Third Generation (3G) telecommunication services	Telecommunication Authority Ministry of Transportation UMTS National Coordination Committee
Investigating Smart Card, Public Key Infrastructure and Security Testing standards	The Scientific and Technical Research Council of Turkey (TUBITAK) National Electronic and Cryptology Research Institute (UEKAE) Turkish Standards Institution
Developing pilot applications regarding the testing and Sustaining of Network Security	The Scientific and Technical Research Council of Turkey (TUBITAK) – National Electronic And Cryptology Research Institute (UEKAE) Telecommunication Authority Other related public institutions
Investigating economics and feasibility of Internet Data Center Applications	Ministry of Transportation Working Group for Technical Infrastructure and Information Security

In line with the government's schedule, the initial focal point in this project has been the Short Term Action Plan (STAP), which covers 2003-2004, for implementing specific tasks.

STAP puts 73 actions in force under 8 sections. These 8 sections are:

- Strategy
- e-Education and Human Resources
- e-Health
- e-Commerce
- Standardization
- Infrastructure and Information Security
- Legislation
- e-Government

3 Implemantation of eEUROPE+ In Turkey

3.1 Accelerate the putting in place of the basic building blocks for the Information Society

Turk Telekom, currently a 100% state-owned enterprise, is Turkey's biggest telecom operator. Along with full liberalization in the telecommunications market, Turk Telekom's privatization process is underway. As of April 2003, Council of Ministers has adopted a Principal Decree, which stipulates that the preparations as to the minimum %51 block sale and IPO of the company will be undertaken simultaneously. The decision pertaining to the selection of one of these two methods is to be made according to market conditions. In this respect, market analysis for Turk Telekom privatization has been completed and the Council of Ministers Decree for the new privatization strategy has been issued on November 13, 2003. According to this Decree, minimum %51 of Turk Telekom shares will be privatized through a block sale, while tender announcement for such sale will be launched by May 31, 2004 latest. Following the block sale, remaining shares will be offered to public in accordance with the process set by the Tender Committee.

For affordable communication services for all, the only way is to fortify the competition in the market. There would be more players that provide affordable and better services when a fullfledge competition is ensured in all segments of the market.

Turk Telekom had been a monopoly in the market for long years and has the most widespread infrastructure, which serves even to the most remote villages in the rural area. With liberalization, this infrastructure will be shared with new operators at the first step. It is expected that the new operators will invest in their own infrastructures in the mid-term and this will strengthen national infrastructure at large. Internet Access Providers (ISPs) were compelled to obtain services from Turk Telekom, as the owner of the nationwide infrastructure, for international connections, and this has appeared to be the most important concern for ISPs. Soon after liberalization, at the beginning of 2004, three other operators have been granted licenses for data transmission services over fixed lines. 4 These three operators are also the first group of companies to operate in the segments that has been held under monopoly before January 1, 2004.

The GSM market keeps on growing and the number of GSM subscribers has exceeded the number of PSTN subscribers in 2002 (25 million as of March 2003). Mobile telecommunications have proved that Turkish market provides investors with unpredictable growth opportunities that outperformed other markets with similar size and income. GSM operators are introducing their data services on GPRS networks, and mobile internet connection is believed to be a rival to traditional dial-up connections in the mid-term.

3.1.1 New Telecommunications Law

The need for a new Telecommunications Law has been recognized both in Urgent Action Plan and STAP. There are three institutions working on the draft version of the law, and it is going to be completed soon. The objective of this new law is to renovate the structure of old laws, namely Law No:406, Law No:2813, and some other amending laws, and to cover all needed areas of regulation for telecommunications market, such as interconnection, licensing, universal services and numbering, in line with the Acquis.

3.1.2 Secondary Telecommunications Legislation

Besides a new telecommunications law, TA is ordered in both Urgent Action Plan and STAP to complete the necessary legislation. In order to promote competition and regulate the market effectively, there are several important items, such as; licensing regarding VoIP, long distance telephone service, cable platform and network provision; rights of way; local loop unbundling; co-location and facilities sharing; numbering; personal data protection in telecoms sector; consumer rights and accounting separation needs to be completed as soon as possible.

Tariffs Directive is in force since August 28, 2001. Access and Interconnection Directive and Radio and Telecommunications Terminal Equipment (RTTE) Directive has been published on the Official Gazette in May 2003. There are two other Communiqués regarding the identification of and rules and regulation for the operators with dominant position or having significant market power.

Unfortunately, universal service obligations and the ways in which operators are going to be supported in under-served/commercially unviable areas are still missing parts of telecommunications regulation in Turkey. The universal service is defined in current telecommunications law (Law No: 406) as „minimum service"; but the rules, structure, and financial arrangements of this procedure remain to be introduced. Again, as part of STAP and government's program, Ministry of Transportation will prepare a Directive for Universal Service. After this Directive is introduced, incentives, financial grants, and other issues will have a legal basis.

3.1.3 Electronic Signature Law

The Electronic Signature Law (law no:5070) is published on the Official Gazette on January 23, 2004. The law legalized electronic signatures and declared Telecommunications Authority as the certification authority in Turkey. The law will be in force by July 23, 2004.

3.1.4 The Law regarding Right of Information

The Parliament approved the law and it has been published on the Official Gazette on October 24, 2003. The Law identifies the principles about the rights of citizens with regards to basis of transparency, openness, and equality of public management.

3.1.5 National Information Security Law

Turkish General Staff and the Ministry of Defense are coordinating a study for the draft law since 2000. Enactment of the law is envisaged in STAP in 2004.

3.1.6 Personal Data Protection Law

There is a commission under the Ministry of Justice working on the draft law since September 2000. It is a part of STAP and envisaged to be completed in 2004.

3.1.7 Secondary Legislation regarding Consumers Protection Law

A directive regarding the protection of consumers who are trading goods and services over electronic media has been published on the Official Gazette on June 13, 2003.

3.2 A cheaper, faster, secure Internet

Until late 2003, main type of internet access has been dial-up connection. But broadband access is slowly taking off with the help of recent developments. DSL infrastructure constitutes a significant portion of broadband access in Turkey. Turk Telekom has completed two important tenders for increasing DSL port capacity in 2003. 60,000 ports has been delivered in November 2003 and 200,000 ports will also be delivered in the second quarter of 2004.

UlakNet (National Academic Network) is connecting all state universities, several public institutions, and Armed Forces R&D departments since 1997. Starting from the mid-2002, a new project has been initiated to improve UlakNet infrastructure. In November 2002, the new improved infrastructure started to operate. With this project:

- International capacity increased 10 times, from 64 Mbps to 620 Mbps.

- All the university branches at rural areas are covered.

- The number of users reached 300,000.

- Domestic capacity between nodes increased to 2800 Mbps from 138 Mbps.

- An initial connection to European Academic Network (GEANT) with 155 Mbps is launched.

- The backbone speed is increased from 34 Mbps to 155 Mbps.

- Universities and R&D institutions are now connecting 4 to 75 times faster than before.

There are two actions in STAP related to the information security and smart cards. TUBITAK- National Research Institute of Electronics and Cryptography (UEKAE), in coordination with Turkish Standards Institute, is going to prepare a report about smart cards, PKI (Public Key Infrastructure), the security test standards and their implementation in public services.

Another action for TUBITAK-UEKAE is developing a pilot project for testing and provision of network security for public networks. Both of these actions are due December 2004.

3.3 Stimulate the use of the Internet

e-Commerce, e-Health, and e-Government are other three important topics in STAP. There are 6, 15, and 23 actions listed under these topics respectively.

For acceleration of e-Commerce, Undersecretariat of Foreign Trade, Ministry of Trade and Industry, KOSGEB (Small and Medium Industry Development Organization) are working together to develop pilot projects, to prepare reports and necessary changes in the legal infrastructure. These actions are composed of preparing a digital registry system for private firms, promotion of e-document and e-commerce by proper financial instruments, producing e-commerce statistics.

As to infrastructure development, connection of Small and Medium Size Enterprises to the internet is another project area for Turk Telekom. There are a number of Organized Industrial Zones (OIZ) projects, jointly conducted by Turk Telekom and OIZ administrations in order to provide broadband access to SMEs. Currently, there are 70 OIZs and 47 of them are connected to Turk Telekom's broadband infrastructure. Public administrations are also connecting to broadband. Especially, central organizations with rural offices across the country prefer broadband access for data transmission. With the introduction of central information systems and databases, and the emergence of massive transactions between central and rural offices in recent years, public administrations are seeking to use broadband. Besides, increased use of internet is another source of push for public administrations to switch to broadband access. Ministry of Agriculture and its affiliated offices, Ministry of Education, Istanbul Stock Exchange, Radio and Television Supreme Council are some of the examples of broadband users among public administrations.

To increase the number of online public services available, introduction of online services to citizens is stated as a priority in STAP strategy. Interoperability, common standards for the provision of services, funding models for e-government projects, e-teams at each public institutions and developing strategy and preparing implementation project for one-stop shop e-government portal are among the important topics covered in e-Government Section of STAP. These actions will provide a solid ground for e-government applications.

Most of the public institutions have web sites and some portion of them can offer interaction between the user and the government. Roughly, out of 200 public institutions 30 of them have the ability to interact with the users. Most of the rest are able to provide information only. e-Health Section in STAP has 15 actions, and for all actions the Ministry of Health is the responsible institution. Most of these actions are considered to be a part of Turkish Health Information System, which is underway since 2001. The aim of the actions is to establish the set of standards for classification and registry of information.

3.4 e-Tariff

First, it is aimed to spread and revise the Customs Automation Project (GİBOS), which was initiated in 1988 and implemented in five customs offices. It was necessary to change this project, which has a closed system structure due to rapid changes in the computer technologies (dependent on Computer Hardware and Operating System), especially because of amendments to harmonize our legislation with the Customs Union and European Customs Legislation. Financial support has been provided for this project comprising studies on modernization and automation of all C-customs offices from the World Bank; and the project has been included in „Public Financial Management Project" by the World Bank.

In studies carried out together with the World Bank, the SOFIX Customs software was offered by Douan Export, which French Customs Administration is also a partner through the provision of a loan.

The software named „BİLGE" has been adapted to include TIR-Transit Control, Incentives, Data Bank of Smuggling, Free Trade Zones, Passenger Transactions, Foreign Trade Statistics, according to Turkish Customs user demands. The implementation of BİLGE was initiated at the pilot site in July 1998.

BİLGE is a software developed using Relational Data Base Management System in a Client/Server architecture using object-oriented library in accordance with EU Customs Legislation.

With the advantage of Client/Server architecture, the following features are provided: Communication, data security, access facilitation, high processing performance, modularity and expandability. BİLGE comprises sub-systems for Summary Declaration, Warehouse Management, Tariff and Accounting.

Structure of the Customs Automation Project has three components: Headquarters, Regional and Local Customs Directorates. A pilot area has been selected from Istanbul Regional Directorates where 70 percent of export and import transactions are processed under this structure. An Electronic Data Processing Center founded within Atatürk Airport Customs Directorate has been linked to Customs Undersecretariat, Department of Communication and Data Processing as the regional center. The pilot application has been implemented successfully in Atatürk Airport Customs Directorate since July 1998. Totally 65 customs directorates and 16 customs regional directorates have been automated as of March 2003.

An international bidding for the deployment of the project throughout Turkey was opened; and the modernization deployment contract was awarded to a joint venture between KoçSistem and Sun Microsystems on 04.01.2000. Accordingly, Esenboğa Customs Directorate was computerized on 29.05.2000 under the project. The said project was successfully completed with the automation of Habur Customs Directorate at the end of October 2001.

The client/server based LANs have been connected one another to establish Wide Area Networks (WAN) or Customs Intranet in the customs sites to be automated. Servers will operate under SUN Solaris Operating System; and all applications, including BİLGE software will utilize Oracle RDBMS. When the project is completed, on-line and real-time transformations of more than 95 percent of export, import and transit transactions will be made.

Network has been widely operated interactively with external systems to store and process data, especially in export and import declarations of customs brokers. An X.400 network will be established for the customs partners to enter the Network system and to use EDI (in EDIFACT standards). Small partners having neither Customs nor EDI Translator software will be able to transfer the declaration data in EDIFACT standards to the Customs computer on www.customs-edi.gov.tr

BİLGE system system essentially consists of the following sub-modules:

- Detailed Declaration Module (Declarations for Entry-Exit and Transit and Warehouse, Follow and Completion formalities related with for the Procedures with Economic Impact)
- Shares, Payrolls
- Accounting Module (Procedures for Collection and Payment, Receipts for Cashier and Stocks and Shares, Payrolls for Collection, and Cash Procedures)
- Tariff (Duty and Fund Rates for Import Regime, Notifications of Import and Export, Free Trade Agreements, Notifications of Standardization, National and International Exemption Systems and Agreements)
- Reference Tables (Codes of Country and Foreign Currency, Customs Codes, Bank Codes, Document Codes, Measurement Units, etc)
- Follow up of Licenses and Quotas
- Risk Analysis and Selection Criteria

4 Implementation of IT Security Standards in Turkey and Turkish Standards Institiution

Turkish Standards Institution (TSE) is established in 1954 within the Turkish Union of Chambers of Industry and Commerce and Commodity Exchanges and the Standardization Law 132 granted TSE its current status in 1960.

TSE is the only organization in Turkey authorized to prepare national standards and represent Turkey in international standardization work.

TSE is responsible to:

- Prepare or ensure the preparation of all kinds of standards.
- Carry out all kinds of scientific and technical research and study on standards.
- Establish relations with international and foreign standardization bodies and to cooperate with them
- Establish laboratories for standardization research work and for the supervision of the standard implementation.
- Execute all kinds of work for promoting the high-quality production conformity to standards and to issue certificates.
- Perform research and development on metrology and calibration and to establish the laboratories necessary for this purpose

4.1 Common Criteria Evaluation

With the increase in the number of IT projects and applications in Turkey such as „e-government" and „e-commerce" , an international security standard to handle these IT projects' security aspects is required. In this persfective;

Turkey choose Common Criteria (CC) as a security standard because,

- CC is an ISO standard
- CC certificates are recognized in many nations,
- CC is easy to use, and both dealing with functional security and assurance in an object oriented method.Turkish Government has initiated a program to adopt Common Criteria(CC) standards in our information systems in December 2001. According to this program; IT Security Evaluation Laboratory settled in 2001. OKTEM, Information Technology Security Evaluation Facility, was settled under National Institute of Electronics and Cryptology. OKTEM will be able to evaluate IT products (between levels EAL1-EAL4) according to Common Criteria and Turkish Standards Institution (TSE) is assigned as the Certification Body. TSE has started to set up a national scheme in Turkey. Turkey signed Common Criteria Recognation Arrangement as a consuming nation in August 2003.

5 Conclusion

There are no more monopolies in the telecommunications sector in Turkey as of January 1, 2004. Turk Telekom's exclusive rights on voice transmission and infrastructure expired on this date. As stipulated by the law, other operators can operate in every segment of telecoms sector by obtaining a license from the Telecommunications Authority (TA). Main policy of the government in the telecommunications sector is to establish a competitive market structure in all segments in order to help increase service quality and number of innovative and valueadded services while reducing costs. Obviously, to achieve the goal of full liberalization is crucial, but the process will take time. Nevertheless, this beginning will bring along many opportunities for both companies and citizens. It is expected that full liberalization together with effective regulation will attract many other foreign investors too.

References

OECD Review of Regulatory Reform in Turkey, November 2002
http://www.oecd.org/dataoecd/40/7/1840741.pdf

State Planning Organization eEurope+ Progress Report–Turkey, June 2003
http://www.bilgitoplumu.gov.tr/yayinlar.asp

State Planning Organization e-Transformation Turkey Project Short-Term Action Plan , SPO-ISD, October 2003

State Planning Organization Information Society Department e-Government Projects, April 2004

Statistics Institude of the Government of Turkey
http://www.die.org.tr/TURKISH/ISTATIS/E56

TR. Prime Ministry Notice #2003/12

www.commoncriteria.org

www.iatf.org

Asia PKI Interoperability Guideline

InKyung Jeun · Jaeil Lee · SangHwan Park

Korea Information Security agency,
78, Garak-Dong, Songpa-Gu, Seoul, 138-803, Korea
{ikjeun I jilee I shpark}@kisa.or.kr

Abstract

PKI(Public Key Infrastructure) provides confidentiality, integrity, and non-repudiation services for e-transaction and various countries around the world offer a e-commerce service by using PKI. These PKI technologies can be used in e-transaction between countries like e-trade area. To do this, an inter-operability of PKI technology is necessary between different PKI domains. This paper introduces „Asia PKI Interoperability Guideline" that was developed by the pilot project between Asia countries for Asia PKI interoperability and intends to present the possibility of PKI interoperability between countries.

1 Introduction

PKI (Public Key Infrastructure) is an important enabling technology for secure online transactions, especially for cross border trade. PKI promotes secure transactions in terms of confidentiality and integrity protection, and provide a trust infrastructure to enable non-repudiation of transactions and messages in the Internet environment where business is conducted between business entities and individuals. The recent PKI initiatives in various countries in Asia, such as the establishment of certification framework, legislation of digital signature, and development of national PKI projects with different solutions and products, shape the national PKI structures at the domestic levels, and could potentially bring about economic impact across the region in varying degrees.

In terms of the promotion of global PKI framework, however, there is a need to ensure that parties in different PKI domains can interoperate. In this regard, it is necessary for cross border working initiatives to be formed to ensure that the different PKI structures and practices are examined and deliberated to develop a mutually agreed inter-working PKI framework at the regional and subsequently, international levels. Interoperability Working Group (IWG) of Asia PKI Forum (APKI-F) was conceived in March 2002 as a step towards achieving PKI interoperability in Asia. APKI-F, IWG started the discussion of how to design an interoperable PKI specification. We learned from various experiences in IWG member's countries and areas, and also learned from the experiences of the proof experiment for PKI interoperability. Especially two results of preceded experiments of PKI interoperability which are conducted by, Japan-Korea-Singapore-Chinese Taipei-Hong Kong, China and China-Chinese Taipei-Hong Kong, China.

The very purpose of this guideline is viewed in both functional and business aspects. From functional view, „PKI Interoperability" means the ability of separate PKI-enabled systems or services to be linked together and then work as well as operate as if they were a single entity. For electronic commerce, „PKI Interoperability" could be treated as „to be able to do secure and trusted business" without ad hoc and proprietary integrations. To maintain the neutrality and to ensure the usability, this guideline is only intended to provide a referential roadmap for

S. Paulus, N. Pohlmann, H. Reimer (Editors): Securing Electronic Business Processes, Vieweg (2004), 309-320

interested parties to achieve PKI interoperability within different scenarios and scales from Asian perspective.

Thinking of PKI interoperability as a set of levels, such as policy, legal framework, technology and application, makes itself a challenging but achievable endeavor and ambition. To realize the above purpose, the information contained in this guideline is to facilitate interested CAs to attain the objectives of mutually/multilaterally negotiating an understanding of and reaching the agreement on PKI trust model, component interfaces, certificate/CRL profiles, repository, certificate validation.

2 Trust Model

The PKI technology develops several CA-CA models in which the relying party can trust the information and digital certificates signed by other parties in multiple PKI domains. It is unlikely that end-entity transactions can be accomplished with the PKI applications without considering the PKI CA-CA model. After evaluating several possibilities, the IWG employs two major models, Cross Certification and Cross Recognition.

2.1 Cross Certification (CC)

The concept of Cross Certification is that a CA publishes a certificate to another CA. There are two kinds of Cross Certification. One is „Mutual Cross Certification". The other is „Unilateral Cross Certification". These are described below.

Mutual Cross-Certification   Unilateral Cross-Certification

Figure 1: Cross Certification (Mutual CC, Unilateral CC)

Mutual Cross Certification is the case where one CA publishes a certificate to the other, and vice versa. The relationship of „Cross Certification" is shown at the left of the Figure 1. Unilateral Cross Certification is the case where one CA publishes a certificate only to a remote CA. The model „Unilateral Cross Certification" is used when adopting a hybrid model and when a CA publishes a certificate to a subordinate CA. In multiple PKI domains environment, especially in international context, it is more suitable for each party to use the Mutual CC model when the Cross Certification model is employed.

2.2 Cross Recognition (CR)

Cross Recognition is a concept considered by APEC TEL WG, and is defined as follows:

> *An interoperability arrangement in which a relying party in one PKI domain can use authority information in another PKI domain to authenticate a subject in the other PKI domain, and vice-versa.*

An example of application for Cross Recognition is „Web browser model". Web browser has a lot of certificates as a trusted list. An example of the method to establish Cross Recognition is that a relying party stores the trust anchor certificates into application, decides whether to accept the sender's certificate or not, and validates the certificate based on the trust anchor information as user-acceptable trust point. The Cross Recognition covers a concept of the acceptance framework on how the relying party can decide to accept the trust anchor certificate of the other parties. However, this is out of scope in this document.

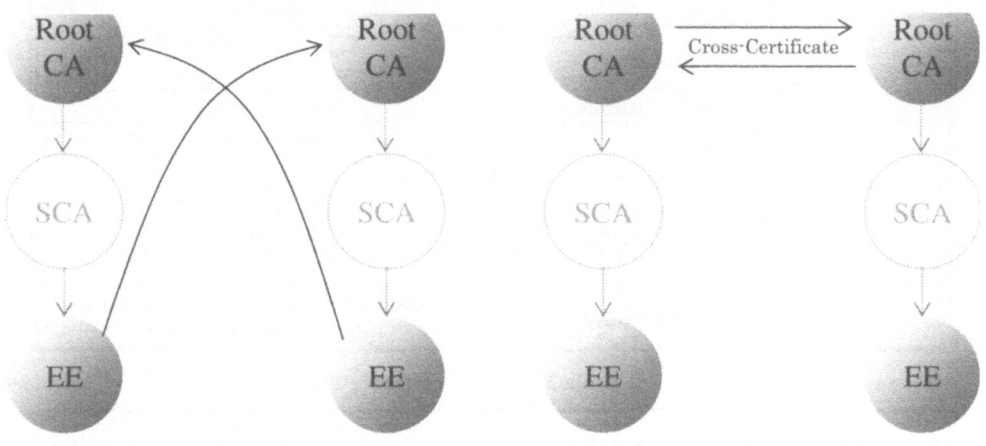

Figure 2: Cross Certificate   Cross Recognition

3 PKI Component Interface

The following figure shows the PKI components in the APKI-F, IWG architecture. There is a minimum set of the PKI components interfaces to be agreed upon between involved parties. Typically, the internal CA-RA-EE interfaces are not important for the multiple domains environment. Rather, the CA-CA interface and the EE-Repository interface are important and have to be agreed. The solid line is the interface to other domains, and the broken line is out of scope.

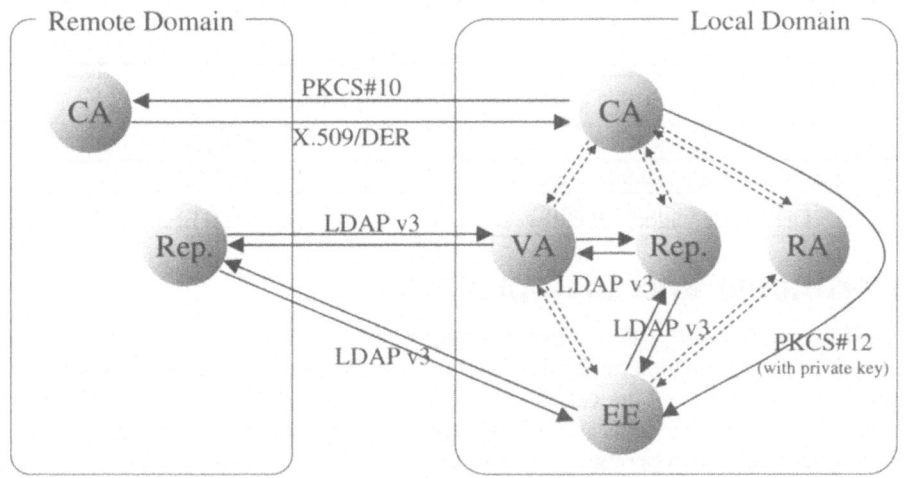

Figure 3: PKI Components

Here is the summary of the PKI components interfaces that be agreed. For the certificate profile, the detail will be described later.

Table 1: CA-CA interface

Content	Interface
Certificate profile	X.509(97) v3[x509], RFC3280[3280]
Certificate encoding format	DER[x690]
CRL profile	X.509(97) v3, RFC3280
CRL encoding format	DER
Cross-Cert request format	PKCS#10[p10]
Cross-Cert response format.	X.509/DER
The method to sends the fingerprint.	E-Mail
POP (proof of possession)	Verification of digital signature on certificate request format

Table 2: CA-EE interface

Content	Interface
EE Certificate response format	PKCS#12[p12] (Private-key included)

Table 3: End Entity-Repository interface and VA-Repository interface

Content	Interface
Repository access protocol(e.g., LDAPv2, LDAPv3, DAP)	LDAPv3[2251]

Table 4: End Entity-VA interface

Content	Interface
EE-VA access protocol	OPTIONAL
Role of VA	Certificate Validation Server (Path Construction, Path Validation)

Table 5: End Entity-End Entity interface

Content	Interface
Certificate path validation method	RFC3280
Certificate validation entity	VA, EE

4 Certificate and CRL profile

The certificate and crl/arl profile is based on the X.509 and RFC 3280 standards. The RFC 3280 provides the information on the details of the data fields and format and the guidance on the choices of the fields, and the values in each field. APKI-F, IWG creates a profile that is a great harmony with the standards and that is more specific to the choice of the data values and fields to maintain the interoperability in multiple PKI domains. The profile contains the basic and extension fields. The basic fields are needed to set the value in mandatory fashion. An extension can be non-critical or critical. If an extension is critical and an application does not recognize or cannot process that extension, the application must reject any transaction. The handling of the criticality follows the RFC 3280.

4.1 Policy of Designing Certificate/CRL Profiles

- Certificate/CRL profile is based on rfc3280 and X.509 (97).

- The profile is primarily designed for the digital signature usage for document exchange applications and for the secure email usage of EE.

- This profile includes the new fields of RFC3280, even not defined.

- The local encryption algorithm and private extensions of each country are not used. Currently APKI-F,IWG members agree upon only the SHA-1 for hash algorithm. Other choices can always be considered.

- The character set in Certificate/CRL must be within the range of PrintableString. (Multi-byte code is out of scope in this experiment.)

- xxxConstraint extensions MAY be used in the test environments. However in the real usage, complex xxxConstraint extensions are recommended not to use.

- Some parts are based on the present implementation and the limitations of the application such as Microsoft® Windows® operating systems and etc.

4.2 Root CA certificate Profile

The ROOT CA's self-signed certificate is used for signing other CA certificates, self-issued certificate, cross certificate, and its subordinate CA certificate. The ROOT CA certificate will be used to provide the public key of the trust anchor and the initial information of the certificate path processing.

1. Certificate Basic field

FIELD	NOTE
version(Mandatory)	Since extension field appears in this profile, the value MUST be set to 2 (v3).
serialNumber (Mandatory)	unique integer. Up to 20 octets.
Signature (Mandatory)	1.2.840.113549.1.1.5(sha1WithRSAEncryption)
issuer(Mandatory)	X.500 DN. Although DN is generally encoded by UTF8STRING, according to description of the X.520(2001), Country attribute is encoded by PrintableString.
Validity(Mandatory)	UTC TIME
Subject(Mandatory)	X.500 DN. And see issuer.
subjectPublicKeyInfo (Mandatory)	1.2.840.113549.1.1.1 (rsaEncryption), CA: 2,048bit
IssuerUnique`ID(not used)	
subjectUniqueID(not used)	

2.Certificate Extension field

FIELD	NOTE
authorityKeyIdentifier (optional, non-critical)	**keyID(Mandatory):** The hash value of Issuer's public key (SHA1 160bit). The 1st calculation method in RFC3280 ch.4.2.1.2. **authorityCertIssuer(optional):** DN · **authCertSerialNum(optional):** INTEGER When AuthCertIssuer is used, AuthCertSerialNum must be set as well. Vise versa.
subjectKeyIdentifier (Mandatory, non-critical)	The hash value of Issuer's pubic key (SHA1 160bit). The 1st calculation method in RFC3280 ch.4.2.1.2
keyUsage (optional, critical)	When used, keyCertSign and cRLSign should be included at least.
extKeyUsage (not used)	
privateKeyUsagePeriod (not used)	
certificatePolicies (optional, critical)	When used, policyID MUST be present.
policyMappings (not used)	
subjectAltName (optional, non-critical)	If the PKI domain wants to include email address or etc in the certificate, this field will be used.
issuerAltName (optional, non-critical)	If the PKI domain wants to include email address or etc in the certificate, this field will be used.
subjectDirectryAttributes (not used)	
basicConstraints (Mandatory, critical)	cA=TRUE pathLen=optional (INTEGER)
nameConstraints (not used)	
policyConstraints (not used)	
cRLDistributionPoints (optional, non-critical)	directoryName, URI
authorityInfoAccess (optional, non-critical)	If the PKI domain uses OCSP, this field will be used.
inhibitAnyPolicy (not used)	
freshestCRL (not used)	
subjectInfoAccessSyntax (not used)	

4.3 CC Certificate Profile

The CC certificate is a certificate, issued by the issuer domain to the subject domain. The CC certificate represents the subject domain policy is equivalent to the issuer domain policy. The certificate is allowed to use constraint-related extensions such as basic constraints, policy constraints, and name constraints. However, extreme cautions must be required in order to design such extensions in multiple PKI domains. The profile of this guideline currently requires only the basic constraint as a mandatory field in CA certificates.

1. Certificate Basic field

Same as ROOT CA Certificate

2. Certificate Extension field

About certificatePolicies, the critical-flag can be set as „non-critical", considering the implementation of the present application (e.g. Microsoft® Windows® 2000 operating system or earlier etc). However, it is necessary to check the policy in the path processing.

FIELD	NOTE
authorityKeyIdentifier (Mandatory, non-critical)	**keyId(Mandatory):** The hash value of Issuer's pubic key (SHA1 160bit). The 1st calculation method in RFC3280 ch.4.2.1.2 **authorityCertIssuer(optional):** DN **authCertSerialNum(optional):** INTEGER When AuthCertIssuer is used, AuthCertSerialNum must be set as well. Vise versa.
subjectKeyIdentifier (Mandatory, non-critical)	The hash value of Issuer's pubic key (SHA1 160bit). The 1st calculation method in RFC3280 ch.4.2.1.2
keyUsage (Mandatory, critical)	keyCertSign, cRLSign
extKeyUsage (not used)	
PrivateKeyUsagePeriod(not used)	
certificatePolicies(Mandatory, ether critical or non-critical[1])	policyID MUST be present.
policyMappings (Mandatory, non-critical)	
subjectAltName (optional, non-critical)	If the PKI domain wants to include email address or etc in the certificate, this field will be used.
issuerAltName (optional, non-critical)	If the PKI domain wants to include email address or etc in the certificate, this field will be used.
SubjectDirectryAttributes(not used)	
basicConstraints (Mandatory, critical)	cA=TRUE pathLen=optional (INTEGER)
NameConstraints(optional, critical)	
policyConstraints (optional, critical)	If the PKI domain wants to strictly validate of certificate policies, this field will be set as requireExplicitPolicy=0.
cRLDistributionPoints (Mandatory, non-critical)	„distPoint.fullname" must contain URI ldap://hostname[:portnumber]/dn?attr[;binary] (port number, attribute: Mandatory

---

[1] It must be verified of a policy by the case of non-critical as well as the case of critical.

	binary option: optional)
AuthorityInfoAccess(not used)	If the PKI domain uses OCSP, this field will be used.
inhibitAnyPolicy (not used)	
freshestCRL (not used)	
subjectInfoAccessSyntax(not used)	

4.4 EE Certificate Profile

The EE Certificate is used by individual or the electric ID to identify the entity for certain transactions. The issuer and subject name in the certificate is the DN for a corresponding entry in the directory.

1. Certificate Basic field

the same as ROOT CA Certificate

2. Certificate Extension field

About certificatePolicies, critical-flag can be set to non-critical in consideration of the present application implementation (e.g. windows2000 or earlier etc). However, it is necessary to validate of a policy also the same as the case of critical.

FIELD	NOTE
authorityKeyIdentifier (Mandatory, non-critical)	**keyId(Mandatory):** The hash value of Issuer's public key (SHA1 160bit). The 1st calculation method in RFC3280 ch.4.2.1.2 **authorityCertIssuer(optional):** DN **authCertSerialNum(optional):** INTEGER When AuthCertIssuer is used, AuthCertSerialNum must be set as well. Vise versa.
subjectKeyIdentifier (Mandatory, non-critical)	The hash value of Issuer's public key (SHA1 160bit). The 1st calculation method in RFC3280 ch.4.2.1.2
keyUsage (Mandatory, critical)	Please see 3.3.2**Fehler! Verweisquelle konnte nicht gefunden werden.** and 3.3.3 about a value.
ExtKeyUsage(not used)	
PrivateKeyUsagePeriod(not used)	
certificatePolicies(Mandatory, ether critical or non-critical [2])	policyID MUST be present.
PolicyMappings (not used)	
SubjectAltName (optional, non-critical)	If the PKI domain wants to include email address or etc in the certificate, this field will be used. And see 3.3.3.
issuerAltName (optional, non-critical)	If the PKI domain wants to include email address or etc in the certificate, this field will be used.
subjectDirectryAttributes(not used)	
basicConstraints	It recommends that CAs don't include a this field.

---

[2] It must be verified of a policy by the case of non-critical as well as the case of critical.

(optional, critical)	
nameConstraints (not used)	
policyConstraints (not used)	
cRLDistributionPoints (Mandatory, non-critical)	„distPoint.fullname" must contain URI ldap://hostname[:portnumber]/dn?attr[;binary] (port number, attribute: Mandatory binary option: optional)
AuthorityInfoAccess(not used)	If the PKI domain uses OCSP, this fieldwill be used.
inhibitAnyPolicy (not used)	
freshestCRL (not used)	
subjectInfoAccessSyntax(not used)	

4.5 ARL/CRL Profile

check whether a certificate in the certification path has not been revoked or not. This profile distinguishes the ARL and CRL in order for the CA to customize their revocation policy. This design policy suggests that the IWG profile accepts the CA revocation information in the CRL, which primarily includes the EE revocation information. In addition, the profile of this guideline accepts the separate/multiple CRL distribution policy based on the revocation reasons and serial number, for instance. This is up to the decision of the CA issuing policy. The application should handle the revocation policy of the CA.

4.5.1 ARL/CRL Basic field

FIELD	NOTE
Version (Mandatory)	Since extension field appears in this profile, the value MUST be set to 1 (v2).
signature (Mandatory)	1.2.840.113549.1.1.5 (sha1WithRSAEncryption)
issuer (Mandatory)	X.500 DN. Although DN is generally encoded by UTF8STRING, according to description of the X.520(2001), Country attribute is encoded by PrintableString.
thisUpdate (Mandatory)	UTCTIME
nextUpdate (Mandatory)	UTCTIME
revokedCertificates (Mandatory)	

4.5.2 ARL/CRL EntryExtensions

FIELD	NOTE
ReasonCode (Mandatory, non-critical)	
holdInstructionCode (not used)	
invalidityDate (optional, non-critical)	GeneralizedTime
CertificateIssuer (not used)	

4.5.3 ARL/CRL Extensions

FIELD	NOTE
authorityKeyIdentifier (Mandatory, non-critical)	**keyId(Mandatory):** The hash value of Issuer's pubic key (SHA1 160bit). The 1st calculation method in RFC3280 ch.4.2.1.2 **authorityCertIssuer(optional):** DN **authCertSerialNum(optional):** INTEGER When AuthCertIssuer is used, AuthCertSerialNum must be set as well. Vise versa.
issuerAltName (not-used)	
cRLNumber (Mandatory, non-critical)	unique integer. up to 20 octets.
deltaCRLIndicator (optional, critical)	If the PKI domain wants to use dCRL, this field will be used.
issuingDistributionPoint	Please see 3.4.4 about a value.
freshestCRL (optional, non-critical)	If the PKI domain wants to use dCRL, this field will be used.
crlScope (not-used)	

4.5.4 Value of cRLDistributionPoints andissuingDistributionPoints

The value of issuingDistributionPoints changes according to the CRL publication policy. This profile allows CA to have the partitioned CRL distribution policy. There are four types of publication policies of CRL that considered.

> (1) CA publishes one full CRL

> (2) CA publishes partitioned CRLs only

> (3) CA publishes one complete CRL and one complete ARL

> (4) CA publishes partitioned CRLs, and one complete ARL or partitioned ARLs

This profile defines the following three terms to avoid the confusion on the CRL distribution terms.

1. Full CRL is a CRL that lists all revoked certificate including the all EE and CA certificates

2. Complete CRL(ARL) is a CRL that lists all revoked certificates within two given scopes. One is the set of the certificates covered by the CRL that contains all the EE certificates only. The other is the set of the certificates covered by the CRL that contains all the CA certificates only.

3. Partitioned CRL is a partition of a full CRL or complete CRL(ARL), partition with some kinds of the criteria such as the range of the certificate serial number or some other ad hoc range. These criteria depend on the CA policy. The CA makes sure that the union of the full set of the partitioned CRL should be equivalent to a full CRL. This profile assumes that the partitioned CRL must be published at the locations of the cRLDistributionPoint.DistributionPoint.fullName and issuingDistributionPoint.distributionPoint.fullname fields.

The values of issuingDistributionPoints are as follows.

(1) CA publishes only one (FULL) CRL (no ARL)

```
iDP -- Optional (critical/non-critical)
   distPoint -- Optional
      fullName -- Optional
      nameRelativeToCRLIssuer -- not defined
   onlyContainsUserCerts -- forbidden to use
   onlyContainsCACerts -- forbidden to use
   onlySomeReasons -- forbidden to use
   indirectCRL -- not defined
```

(2) CA publishes separate CRLs (no ARL)

```
iDP -- Mandatory (critical)
   distPoint -- Mandatory
      fullName -- Mandatory
      nameRelativeToCRLIssuer -- not defined
   onlyContainsUserCerts -- forbidden to use
   onlyContainsCACerts -- forbidden to use
   onlySomeReasons -- forbidden to use
   indirectCRL -- not defined
```

(3) CA publishes one CRL and one ARL

```
iDP -- Mandatory (critical)
   distPoint -- Optional
      fullName -- Optional
      nameRelativeToCRLIssuer -- not defined
   onlyContainsUserCerts -- Mandatory in CRL
   onlyContainsCACerts -- Mandatory in ARL
   onlySomeReasons -- forbidden to use
   indirectCRL -- not defined
```

(4) CA publishes separate CRLs and ARL

```
iDP -- Mandatory (critical)
   distPoint -- Mandatory
      fullName -- Mandatory
      nameRelativeToCRLIssuer -- not defined
   onlyContainsUserCerts -- Mandatory in CRL
   onlyContainsCACerts -- Mandatory in ARL
   onlySomeReasons -- forbidden to use
   indirectCRL -- not defined
```

4.6 Repository Profile

To store the certificate and crl/arl information in repository, IWG profile employs the LDAP directory. IWG profile will use LDAP v3, primarily to use the referral function to fetch the certificates and crls/arls in multiple PKI domains enviroment. To simplify the directory operations, no replication and integrated-directory environments are considered. The profile suggests that the referral is a focal function in order to access to the information in other domains.

4.6.1 DIT

DIT structure in each country is not specified. This specification only mandates that the DN in a certificate should be corresponding to the structure of the DN in DIT.

A sample DIT is following.

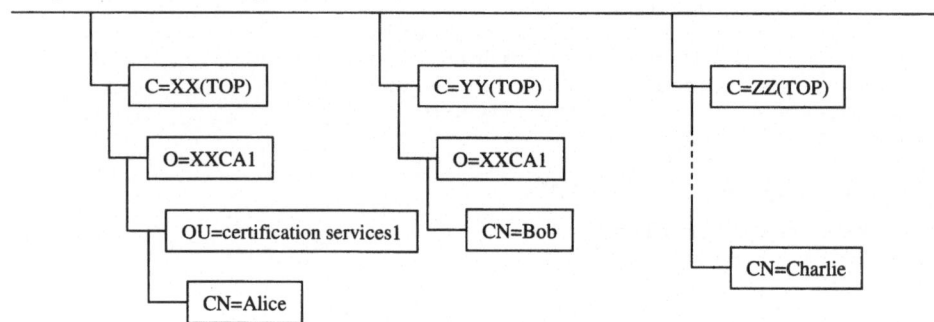

Figure 4: sample DIT Tree (3 parties) in one directory

In Figure 4, the „c=XX" entry, appropriate subordinate entry, and the referral should be defined. Note: in real usage, c=XX will not likely be used for the actual referral entry, since there is no such a representative directory server. The O or OU entry is the most likely.

References

[Hous02]   Russ Housle et al : Internet X.509 Public Key Infrastructure Certificate and Certificate Revocation Lisy(CRL) Profile, RFC3280, IETF, 2002

[APKI03]   APKIF : Asia PKI Interoperability Guideline v1.0, Asia PKI Forum, 2003

Recent PKI Experiences in Serbia

Dr Milan Marković

Delta banka a.d., IT Department
7b Milentija Popovića, 11070 Belgrade,
Serbia and Montenegro
milan.markovic@deltabanka.co.yu

Abstract

This is a survey paper about recent PKI experiences in Serbia. These PKI projects are briefly described in the paper and include PKI systems for: National Bank of Serbia, commercial banks – especially sophisticated PKI system in Delta bank, Serbian ID smart card project, Serbian Academic Institution network – NIOnet, etc. Also, the activities on these projects are followed by activities in preparing the Electronic signature Law and SubLaw acts, as well as for preparing the Data Protection Law in Electronic Communications. Besides, there were some educational activities in domain of electronic business security and computer network security in which the author is included.

1 Introduction

This is a survey paper about recent PKI (Public Key Infrastructure) experiences in Serbia. The survey period covers about four years from the mid 2000 year till now. In this period, there were several sophisticated PKI projects in Serbia, some of them are finished and some of them are still running, and the author was included in most of them. The paper gives some overview of the mentioned PKI projects, all activities that correspond to them, as well as an overview about legal and educational efforts in promoting PKI systems in Serbia.

The recent and current PKI projects that are briefly described in the paper include PKI systems for:

- National Bank of Serbia and its WEB based services: WEB based Registry of Securities and WEB based Registry of Rating and Solvency of Serbian companies,
- Belgrade Stock Exchange,
- Commercial banks – especially sophisticated PKI system in Delta bank; in this field, there are several PKI options which are related mainly to the electronic banking and home banking systems. Two PKI options are basic: in-house PKI solution in the particular bank and outsourced PKI solution to some Service center for electronic banking (there are currently 4 service centers in Serbia) or to some external Certification Service Provider (CSP),
- Serbian ID smart card project as a very sophisticated project with high quality security services implemented. Namely, next year in Serbia, it will be started issuing the four different citizen's smart cards: ID card, driver license, car registration license and weapon carrying license. Some of them will have holder's biometric features (color photo and fingerprint) and ID card will be enabled with two asymmetric keypairs for the future e-government systems.

S. Paulus, N. Pohlmann, H. Reimer (Editors): Securing Electronic Business Processes, Vieweg (2004), 321-332

- Serbian Academic Institution network – NIOnet. This is the project organized and funded by the Ministry of Sciences of Republic of Serbia and is intended for enabling the electronic communication between the scientific organizations and institutions, corresponding associating researchers, as well as with Ministry. The system will use WEB portals with strong user authentication procedure and secure e-mail systems based on central PKI system, established in the Ministry.

The activities on these projects are followed by appropriate activities in preparing the Electronic signature Law and Sub Law acts, as well as for preparing the Data Protection Law for Electronic Communications. The author of this paper was a member, and currently is a member, of the working groups for preparing all of these legal acts. Both mentioned legal activities are under the organization of the Ministry of Sciences of Republic of Serbia.

Besides, there are initiatives of Serbian Post Offices and Serbian Chamber of Commerce in promoting e-business and establishing public PKI systems in Serbia.

Also, there are some educational activities in domain of electronic business and computer network security that represents some background activities to the realization of the actual PKI projects. The author of this paper is involved in most of the PKI educational activities in Serbia. These include for example Computer network security and PKI systems courses at Military Academy and at Faculty for Business Informatics in Belgrade.

The paper is organized as follows. In Chapter 2, a brief description and general features of modern PKI systems are given, as well as some brief analysis of the Generic CA SW/HW system which was an approximate model for the most of the current PKI systems in Serbia. Chapter 3 is dedicated to the brief feature analysis of the current and most important PKI projects in Serbia. Legal activities in domain of Electronic signatures and PKI educational activities are elaborated in Chapters 4 and 5, respectively. Conclusions are given in Chapter 6.

2 PKI systems

Public-key cryptography uses a combination of public and private keys, digital signature, digital certificates, and trusted third party Certification Authorities (CA), to meet the major requirements of e-business security. Before applying the security mechanisms you need the answers for the following questions: Who is your CA? Where do you store your private key? How do you know that the private key of the person or server you want to talk to is secure? Where do you find certificates?

A public-key infrastructure (PKI) provides the answers to the above questions. In the sense of X.509 standard, the PKI system is defined as the set of hardware, software, people and procedures needed to create, manage, store, distribute and revoke certificates based on public-key cryptography [AbJo95, Schn96, Oppl98, FoBa01].

PKI system provides a reliable organizational, logical and technical security environment for realization of the four main security functions of the e-business systems:authenticity,

- data integrity protection,

- non-repudiationand data confidentiality protection. PKI systems are based on digital certificates as unique cryptographic based electronic IDs of relying parties in some computer networks. A content of digital certificate must be in compliance wit ITU-T X.509 recommendation.

PKI system consists of the following components:

- Certification Authority (CA) – responsible for issuing and revoking certificates, as well as for key management,
- Registration Authorities (RAs) – responsible for acquiring certificate requests and checking the identity of the certificate holders,
- systems for certificate distribution – responsible for delivering the certificates to their holders,
- certificate holders (subjects) – people, machines or software agents that have been issued with certificates,
- CP, CPS, user agreements and other basic CA documents,
- systems for publication of issued certificates and Certificate Revocation Lists (CRLs), and
- PKI applications (secure WEB transactions, secure E-mail, secure FTP, VPN, secure Internet payment, secure document management system – secure digital archives, access control system, working time control system).

The method defined in X.509 for revoking certificates involves the use of a certificate revocation list (CRL). This list identifies revoked certificates and is signed and timestamped by the CA. Normally, each certificate is identified by a unique serial number that is assigned when the CA issues it. The CA publishes the CRL, at regular intervals, into the same public repository (e.g. LDAP) as the certificate themselves. There are several types of CA:

- corporate CAs,
- closed user group (CUG) CAs,
- CAs of vertical industries, and
- public CAs.

Regarding the implementation approach, CAs could be divided to: outsourced CA – when some organization use certification services from the earlier established CA, and insourced CA – when some organization establishes its own CA services. In all cases, all CA organization mostly used the CA software-hardware technology from the established CA technology vendors, such as: Baltimore, Entrust, Utimaco, SmartTrust, RSA Data Security, NetSeT, etc.

In the following, a brief description is given of the Generic model of the Certification Authority software-hardware system which is realized as a web multitier architecture. The described system is similar to the most modern and most secure PKI systems today. Also, some possible variants of system realization depending on the set of the requests that should be fulfilled are discussed. This Generic CA represents a solution which could be fully customized to be adapted to the customer requirements.

2.1 Main features of Generic CA system

The Generic CA is a WEB-based Certification Authority system which could support both closed PKI systems with strictly defined users of usually only one or two different user profiles, as well as public PKI systems with more user profiles and more different ways of user registration. The Generic CA system represents the public CA system fully customizable to the particular requests of different users. Main features of the Generic CA system are:

- The system fulfils all worldwide PKI standards (X.509 and corresponding PKCS standards [RSAL02, RSAL93, RSAL00, RSAL01, RSAL99]) and cryptographic algorithms

[RiSA78, Schn96], and could be customized according to both adding new features and customizing the applied cryptographic algorithms.

- The Generic CA is WEB multitier CA application which is based on smart cards for end users.

- The Generic CA system supports different database servers, such as: MS SQL, Oracle or IBM DB2.

- The Generic CA supports a working system with one asymmetrical keypair, with two keypairs and combined system.

- The Generic CA supports a hierarchical PKI structure and has the off-line Root CA and more on-line Intermediate CAs. As a rule, each user profile should have its Intermediate CA server.

- The Generic CA supports different ways of the user registration, such as: through registration authorities (RA) and RAO operators, as well as directly (for specific user profiles) via WEB CA server.

- The Generic CA has implemented a procedure of distributed responsibilities (secret sharing, necessity of presence of number of specific users (k of n procedure)) in sense of creating the Root CA asymmetrical private key for generating the new Intermediate CA certificate.

- The Generic CA has a support for life cycle certificate management (renewal, suspension, revocation).

- The Generic CA has possibilities for electronic personalization of the smart cards and this could be done by client themselves, RAO or CAO.

- The Generic CA system has a support for printing PIN code (lettershop) for accessing the cards which should be sent to the user separately from the smart card.

- The Generic CA system provides the printing of different reports depending of the user needs.

2.2   Generic CA system's architecture

A system architecture of the described Generic CA system is given on Figure 1. What missing on the Figure 1 are application or WEB servers from different business processes which commonly use the Generic CA system. For example, WEB server in DMZ zone could be a business WEB server which will eventually realize strong authentication procedure of different users with smart cards, issued by the described Generic CA system. As it could be seen from the Figure 1, the Generic CA system consists of OnLine and OffLine parts. OffLine part represents RootCA which is used only in rare cases when the Root CA asymmetrical private key should be created for a purpose of generating a new Intermediate CA certificate in hierarchical structure shown on Figure 2, which is the most popular in the modern PKI systems. Root CA is located in totally separated room from the rest of the CA system where there exist a vault in which the Root CA asymmetrical private key's individual parts are securely stored. These parts are used according to the defined procedure of „distributed responsibilities" (or „secret sharing") in cases of generating new Intermediate CA certificates (this procedure is called „CA ceremony"). Eventually, the Root CA could be also in the same room (if necessary) as the OnLine CA but, as mandatory request, outside the LAN network and with mandatory vault for storing the Root CA private key parts. In the CA ceremony procedure, it must be present a corresponding minimal number of special CA employees who have access to the corresponding individual parts of the Root CA private key, stored on smart cards in special separated boxes of the vault. Namely, a corresponding pre-defined number of smart cards must be present in order to create the Root CA private key in HSM device of the Root CA server, fully in accordance with General public and Internal CA practises.

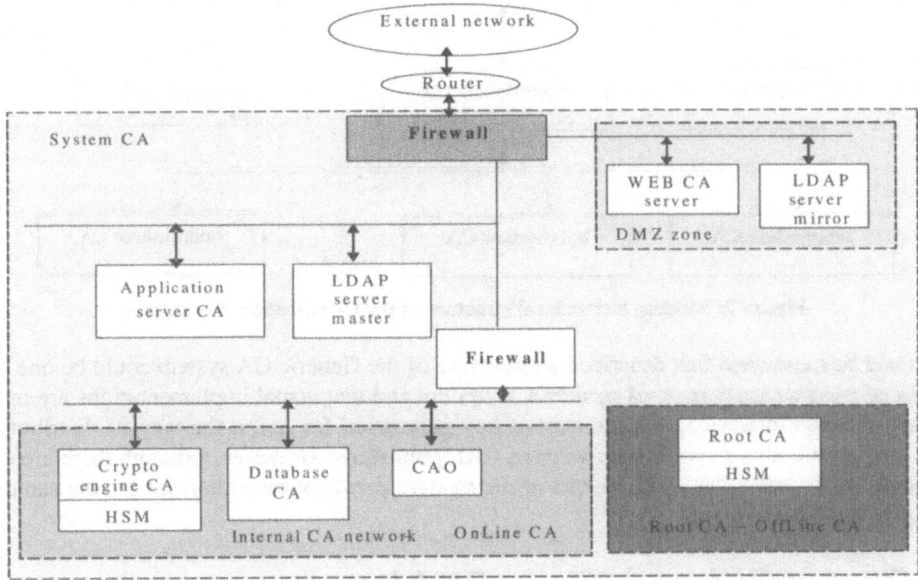

Figure 1: A simplified network configuration of the Generic CA system

After that, a new Intermediate CA asymmetrical keypair is generated in Root CA's HSM and the Intermediate CA certificate is created by a digital signature with applying the Root CA private key. The encrypted private key and certificate of the Intermediate CA will be programmed into the new smart card (Intermediate CA smart card) which will be installed into the HSM device of the new Crypto Engine server, intended for use as a OnLine CA for this Intermediate CA system. After that, Root CA private key will be deleted from the Root CA HSM device and the smart cards with Root CA private key parts will be returned to the vault.

As it could be concluded, it is possible that more Intermediate CA simultaneously work in OnLine working mode, i.e. that more Intermediate CA Crypto Engine servers are activated in the OnLine working mode for digital certificate generation (e.g. Intermediate CA for different kind of end users). OnLine and OffLine parts of the Generic CA system should support the using of the HSM modules, see Figure 1. These HSMs could be from different companies (e.g. Thales e-Security, nCipher, IBM, Baltimore, Chrysalis, Utimaco, etc). Also, the author was included in development of the proprietary HSM modul with some distinguished features and optimization capabilities [ĐoUM02, MaĐU02, MaĐU03, MaUĐ02, MSON01, UnMĐ01].

In DMZ zone, besides WEB CA server, there is LDAP mirror server which serves for publishing the CRL and ARL lists, as well as for eventual publication of issued digital certificates. This server is a copy of the master LDAP server which is located in the internal zone.

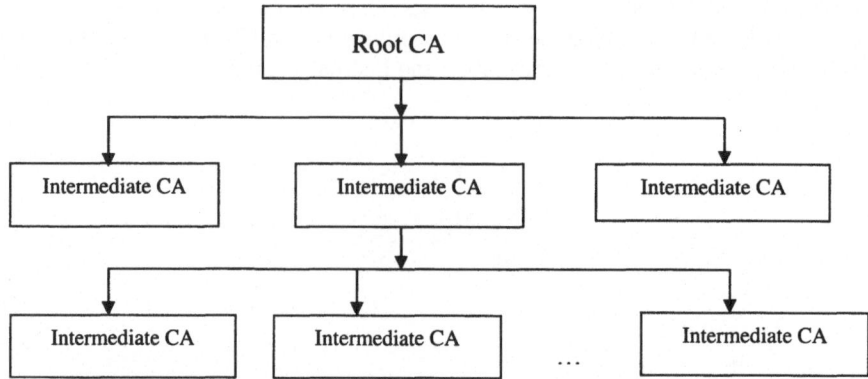

Figure 2: Modern hierarchical structure of the Certification Authorities

It should be mentioned that described architecture of the Generic CA system could be one example of possible realization of modern CA system and that actual implementations are more or less different depending on the way of key generation for users, the way of distribution keys and certificates, as well as on ways of CRL publishing. However, although there are differences, basic principles and concepts of the modern certification authorities are the same as in the described example.

3 Recent PKI projects in Serbia

As we said before, from the mid 2000 year till now, there were several sophisticated PKI projects in Serbia, some of them are finished and some of them are still running, and the author was included in realization of the most of these projects. In this Chapter, some overview of the mentioned PKI projects and all activities that correspond to them are given.

3.1 Financial sector

Starting from the year 2002 we have been faced with a number of secure financial web services established in Serbia. Almost all of them feature smart cards, digital certificates and digital signature technology. Most of them use the trusted WEB security model described in [SaMa03]. Particularly, security services offered by commercial banks, as well as by the National bank of Serbia have been applied for Serbian legal and private persons, mostly in the electronic payment applications. In fact, a financial sector was the driving force for development of PKI systems in Serbia since electronic banking transactions were the first electronic transactions in Serbia that needed applications of PKI systems and electronic signature technology. The first financial institution that was established a PKI system was a National bank of Yugoslavia (today National bank of Serbia) followed later by many commercial banks. Recently, Belgrade Stock Exchange and Serbian Bank Associations have also had some very important PKI projects. In a sequel, main features of the mentioned PKI projects are described.

3.1.1 National bank of Serbia

The National bank of Serbia was the first financial institution in Serbia that have operated a PKI system that issues X.509 digital certificates on PKI smart cards for its customers. It was for the national payment computer network, called PLATNET [SaNM01], started in the first half of the year 2000. After that, the National Bank of Serbia introduced and now fully operates RTGS (Real Time Gross Settlement) and Clearing systems that establish efficient countrywide interbanking payment infrastructure which is also based on specific PKI system.

The strategic change in payment system fostered a competitive banking environment and, as a result, several new institutions appeared and started to offer electronic financial services to their clients based on WEB technologies [FoBa01, Oppl00, SaMa03]. The most representative are Central Register and Depositary of Securities and Register of Solvency Information for legal entities. Both of the mentioned registers use the secure WEB services based on PKI smart cards for establishing secure communication channels between the users and the system. Also, both of the registers use the trusted web security model described in [SaMa03]. For the systems that are part of the National Bank of Serbia, the Information Security Department is responsible for overall PKI support. This is a special part of the National Bank of Serbia that provides Certification Authority service, key management and smart card personalization and management. CA system that operates in the National bank of Serbia represents an in-house CA solution and is based on the desktop offline version of the Generic CA that is described in the Chapter 2.

3.1.2 Belgrade Stock Exchange

The Belgrade Stock Exchange (BSE) is a financial institution that has operated few years. In the beginning, the BSE has operated in local computer environment inside the BSE's premises. Now, the BSE information system allows brokers to carry out their activities in the trading process from their locations (remote trading). This concept of remote trading fulfils all requirements of the modern stock exchange information systems. For the access to the BSE information system, brokers can use leased lines, ISDN and Frame Relay. The new remote system is based on Microsoft based remote VPN security solution based on PKI smart cards for brokers and digital certificates issued by an outsourced CA system.

3.1.3 Serbian Banking Association

The Serbian Banking Association (SBA) is an interbanking organization, constituted by the commercial banks representing their mutual interests. After some successful PKI projects that have been already in operation, the SBA now realizes a big project of Credit Bureau for citizens. This is also a PKI project that is based on PKI smart cards and digital certificates for citizens and bank employees. As in the case of the BSE, the SBA uses the outsourced PKI solution in its projects.

3.1.4 Commercial banks

The reason for such a fast development of security electronic banking services for Serbian legal persons, offered by the commercial banks, has been a structural change in payment system that happened last year. Instead of centralized Payment Bureau that was responsible for all payments in a country during last 40 years, starting from the year 2003, Serbian banks are found themselves in position that they are responsible for payment transactions for their clients, both legal and physical persons [SaMa03]. As a response to the new payment environment, the number of local banks started to offer Web based electronic payment services to their clients. These services have been assumed as a competitive advantage they use to attract the new customers. Now, practically all of the Serbian commercial banks that offer the secure web-based electronic banking service implement them on the basis of the PKI smart cards for their legal persons (legal persons that have accounts in this bank). In this way, legal person receives the e-banking packet from the bank consisting of the CD with client software (both application and security part), smart card reader and personalized smart card with X.509 digital certificate and asymmetrical private key. With this smart card and the software, legal persons are enabled to make secure financial transactions using Internet browser program and web site of the bank with a full set of secure functionalities (asymmetrical and symmetrical cryptographic algorithms, single-sign-on based on smart cards, etc.). Most of the Serbian commercial banks use secure web services based on the trusted web security solution, described in [SaMa03]. Also, there are several certification authority schemes (in-house and out-source) that banks use for issuing the digital certificates for their users. Besides, several banks joined their efforts and built Electronic Payment Bureau companies – Service centers. They act as a service provider to interconnect banks and their clients using open networks such as Internet. Usually, banks outsource complete web communication and legal persons connect directly to the service centers, not to the bank. The system also includes special security adapters to protect communication between the Service center and each of the banks. These companies are also responsible to provide adequate security support such as Certification authority and smart card personalization services. Most of the CA solutions (both in-house and out-sourced) are based on desktop offline version of the Generic CA solution, described in the Chapter 2.

Case study – Delta bank

Delta bank has advanced security solutions applied in its banking operations. As many other commercial banks, Delta bank has electronic banking solution for legal persons based on PKI smart cards and digital certificates issued by the in-house CA solution. Also, Delta bank has operated a secure home banking system for physical persons that is also based on the PKI system and mini CD for citizens for storage of private asymmetrical key and digital certificate. Besides the PKI system for external users, Delta bank has its own in-house PKI system for internal users (all employees) based on USB smart cards that store private key and digital certificate. These smart cards are integrated in the Windows domain and are used for Microsoft Windows Logon on the system, as well as for secure e-mail (based on S/MIME protocol) and secure internal core banking operations.

Besides these e-banking solutions, Delta bank is also a leader in payment card operations in Serbia. Last year, Delta bank issued a first EMV Visa chip card in Balkan area. Up to the end of this year there will be issued also an EMV MasterCard chip card. Future plans include establishing of multiapplicative smart payment cards for citizens that will include also 3D secure schemas (Verified by Visa and SecureCode) and PKI capabilities. Namely, in the first phase, these cards will include the following applications: EMV SDA (VSDC or M/Chip), OTP (one time password) for 3D secure and PKI for electronic signatures (eliminating mini CDs for citizens). In the second phase, citizens' chip cards of Delta bank will include: EMV DDA, OTP and PKI scheme that will enable multiple keypairs (at least keypairs for digital signature and digital envelope) and qualified electronic signature generation.

3.2 Serbian ID Card Project

As a currently most sophisticated and most complex system in Serbia that is based on PKI is a System for Issuing Smart Card Based ID Documents (ID Smart Card System). This system is the most up-to date system that produces high secured ID documents that will be also used in future Serbian e-government schemes. The System is intended for issuing ID documents but it will be used for all kind of personal documents based on smart cards: driving licenses, vehicle registration licenses and weapon carrying licenses. In other words, the System is mainly intended for issuing PKI smart card ID documents for storing personal data and appropriate keys for future e-governmental purposes but it could be used for issuing any of the personal cards, PKI or non-PKI, with or without chip, etc. Main elements of the Serbian ID Smart Card System are:

- Acquisition locations, which are territorially distributed in some governmental locations and which serve for citizen data acquisition for issuing ID documents,
- Private WAN Intranet network for secure links between remote sites and central governmental location (the System also could use the public Internet network if appropriate secure mechanisms are applied),
- Governmental WEB portal with secured and centralized user strong authentication (single sign-on), as an interface between the remote sites and central database. This authentication is used for secure access control of the system by the administrators of the acquisition locations,
- Application server that processes acquired alphanumeric and multimedia citizen data and store them in the central database,
- Central database which stores all necessary citizen data,
- Certification Authority which issue digital certificates for administrators of acquisition locations, citizens and for network resources,
- System for data preparation which realizes all cryptographic processes in the procedure for data preparation and produces the corresponding production files for smart card personalization,
- Central personalization system which process personalization data and results in completely personalized ID documents (visually and electronically),
- Card factory for producing cards that should be personalized which includes generating necessary security features for the card body.

PKI system of the Serbian ID Smart Card System is fully compliant with description of the Generic CA system, given in Chapter 2.

3.3 Serbian NIOnet Project

A project for establishing secure Serbian Academic Institution network – NIOnet started last year and it is currently in progress. This is the project organized and funded by the Ministry of Sciences of Republic of Serbia and is intended for enabling the electronic communication between the scientific organizations and institutions (NIOs), corresponding associating researchers, as well as for secure communication with and within the Ministry of Sciences of Republic Serbia. The system will use secure WEB portals with strong user authentication (by using strong challenge-response procedures and X.509 digital certificates) and secure e-mail systems based on central PKI system, established in the Ministry. This PKI system is, in the first phase of the NIOnet project, an offline desktop version of the Generic CA system, described in the Chapter 2.

4 Legal activities in domain of electronic signatures

Legal activities in domain of electronic signature and certification authorities in Serbia started in August 2000 by establishing a working group in domain of Yugoslavian Federal Ministry of Justice. Due to political reasons and problems in the country, the law proposal made by this working group was never adopted on the Federal level. After that, with shrinking the overall federal responsibilities, a new working group for Electronic signatures law preparation was established on the Serbian republic level by the end of 2002. A new updated proposal was given in the first half of 2003 when it was sent to the Serbian Assembly for adoption. Unfortunately, the law was not adopted before the Government changed and new elections happened by the end of 2003. Recently, the law proposal was additionally adjusted and backed to the government and we expect the adoption of the Electronic Signature Law very soon. The working group has tried to adjust the current proposal according to the latest findings and situation in EU and other European countries regarding the electronic signature legislative, best practices and development of PKI systems. In a meantime, the working group prepared corresponding sublaw acts regarding the application of qualified electronic signature technology, defining criteria for Secure Signature Creation Device (SSCD), as well as for criteria that Certification Authorities who issue qualified certificates need to fulfil. Author of this paper was, and currently is, a member of the working groups for electronic signature law preparation, from the August 2000 till now. Also, the author of this paper is a member of the working group for preparing Data Protection Law in Electronic Communications which is currently in running phase.

5 Educational activities

Besides all these technical and legal activities, there are also some educational activities in domain of electronic business and computer network security that represents some background activities to the actual PKI projects. The author of this paper is involved in most of the PKI educational activities in Serbia. These include for example Computer network security and PKI systems courses at Military Academy and at Faculty for Business Informatics in Belgrade. For example, the Faculty for Business Informatics in Belgrade started last year a specialistic study for Security in Information Systems which is really unique in our country and probably in wider environment of surrounding countries. The author of this paper holds two courses in this study: Computer Networks Security and PKI systems. Besides, the author of this paper has held short tutorials (one or two days – see description in [Mark02]) in Serbia and Montenegro and surrounding countries (e.g. Macedonia, etc.).

6 Conclusion

In this paper, a survey and an subjective analysis of recent PKI experiences in Serbia are given. These PKI projects are briefly described in the paper and include PKI systems for: financial institutions (National Bank of Serbia, Belgrade Stock Exchange, Serbian Bank Associations, commercial banks – with emphasis of PKI systems in Delta bank), Serbian ID smart card project and Serbian Academic Institution network – NIOnet. Also, the activities on these projects are followed by activities in preparing the Electronic signature Law and SubLaw acts, as well as for preparing the Data Protection Law in Electronic Communications. Also, there were some educational activities in domain of electronic business and computer network security, as well as PKI systems in which the author is included. Also, there are future plans for developing new large and mass systems based on smart cards and PKI (e.g. future Serbian healthcare information system based on citizens and doctors smart cards – see some ideas in [MaSK04]).

References

[AbJo95]   Abrams, M.D., Joyce, M.V.: Trusted system concepts, Computers and Security, VOL. 14, No. 1, Elsevier Science Ltd., 1995.

[ÐoUM02]   Đorđević, G., Unkašević, T., Marković, M.: Optimization of modular reduction procedure in RSA algorithm implementation on assembler of TMS320C54x signal processors, Proc. of DSP 2002, July, Santorini, Greece.

[FoBa01]   Ford, W., Baum, M.S.: Secure Electronic Commerce: Building the Infrastructure for Digital Signatures and Encryption, Second Edition, Prentice Hall PTR, Upper Saddle River, NJ 07458, 2001.

[MaÐU02]   Marković, M., Djorđević, G., Unkašević, T.: Influence of key length in possible optimization of RSA algorithm implementation on signal processor, in Proc. of ICEST 2002, Oct., 1-4, pp. 23-26, 2002.

[MaÐU03]   Marković, M., Đorđević, G., Unkašević, T.: On Optimizing RSA Algorithm Implementation on Signal Processor Regarding Asymmetric Private Key Length, in Proceedings of WISP 2003, Budapest, Sept. 2003, pp. 73-77, 2003.

[Mark02]   Marković, M.: Cryptographic Techniques and Security Protocols in Modern TCP/IP Computer Networks, Short-Tutorial, in Proc. of ICEST 2002, Oct., 1-4, 2002.

[MaSK04]   Marković, M., Savić, Z., Kovačević, B.: Secure Mobile Health Systems: Principles and Solutions, in M-Health: Emerging Mobile Health Systems, Robert H. Istepanian, Swamy Laxminarayan, Constantinos S. Pattichis, Editors, KLUWER ACADEMIC/PLENUM PUBLISHERS, to be published in 2004.

[MaUÐ02]   Marković, M., Unkašević, T., Đorđević, G.: RSA algorithm optimization on assembler of TI TMS320C54x signal processors, in Proc. of EUSIPCO 2002, Toulouse, France, Sept. 3-6, 2002.

[MSON01]   Marković, M., Savić, Z., Obrenović, Ž., Nikolić, A.: A PC Cryptographic Coprocessor Based on TI Signal Processor and Smart Card System, Communications and Multimedia Security Issues of the New Century, R. Steinmetz, J. Dittman, M. Steinebach, Eds., Kluwer Academic Publishers, 2001, pp. 383-393.

[Oppl98]   Oppliger, R.: Internet and Intranet Security, Artech House, 1998.

[Oppl00]   Oppliger, R.: Security Technologies for the World Wide Web, Artech House, ISBN 1-58053-045-1, 2000.

[RiSA78]   Rivest, R., Shamir, A., Adleman, L.: A Method for Obtaining Digital Signatures and Public-Key Cryptosystems, Commun. of the ACM, Vol. 21, No. 2, pp. 120-126, Feb. 1978.

[RSAL02]   RSA Laboratories, PKCS #1 v2.1: RSA Cryptography Standard, June 14, 2002.

[RSAL93]   RSA Laboratories, PKCS#7: Cryptographic Message Syntax Standard, Version 1.5, November 1993.

[RSAL00]   RSA Laboratories, PKCS#10 v1.7: Certification Request Syntax Standard, May 26, 2000.

[RSAL01]   RSA Laboratories, PKCS#11 v2.11: Cryptographic Token Interface Standard, Revision 1 – November 2001.

[RSAL99]   RSA Laboratories, PKCS#12 v1.0: Personal Information Exchange Syntax, June 24, 1999.

[SaNM01]   Savić, Z., Nikolić, A., Marković, M.: Cryptographic Proxy Gateways in Securing TCP/IP Computer Networks, in Proc. of Information Security Solution Europe Conference, ISSE 2001, London, September 26-28, 2001.

[SaMa03]   Savić, Z., Marković, M.: Development of Secure Web Financial Services in Serbia, in Proceedings of ISSE 2003, October 7-10, 2003.

[Schn96]   Schneier, B.: Applied Cryptography, Second Edition, Protocols, Algorithms and Source Code in C, John Wiley & Sons, Inc., New York, Chichester, Brisbane, Toronto, Singapore, 1996.

[UnMĐ01]   Unkašević, T., Marković, M., Djordević, G.: Optimization of RSA algorithm implementation on TI TMS320C54x signal processors based on a modified Karatsuba-Offman's algorithm, in Proc. of ECMCS'2001, 11-13 September, Budapest, 2001.

CCTV and Workplace Privacy – Italy

Paolo Balboni

Centre for Liability Law, Tilburg University,
The Netherlands
p.balboni@uvt.nl

Abstract

Video surveillance has penetrated every day life. The data which are collected during video surveillance activities consist mainly of images and sounds which either identify or allow the identification of data subjects, directly or indirectly, in addition to monitoring their conduct. Thus, the implementation of closed circuit TV (CCTV) as a convenient means to achieve various security purposes raises issues as regards privacy and data protection. Moreover, the widespread use of surveillance also jeopardizes the citizens' freedom of movement and behaviour. The paper presents an analysis of how Italy strikes the balance between security and privacy requirements in relation to the phenomenon of video surveillance. To that end, the Italian Data Protection Authority's Generally Applicable Regulation of 29 April 2004 (Decalogue 2004) is dealt with. Particular attention is given to the use of close circuit TV (CCTV) in the workplace, which is an environment where the relationship between surveillance and personal rights was pointed out long ago. After an evaluation of the rules concerning video surveillance and the way the courts and the Data Protection Authority apply them, it is concluded that the interest in privacy has significantly increased in Italy since privacy legislation has been enacted.

1 Introduction

The ongoing increased use of close circuit TV (hence CCTV) and the increased use of other technologies that potentially reduce the privacy of citizens (e.g., e-mail monitoring) was one of the reasons for Tilburg University's Centre for Law, Public Administration and Informatization to initiate a research project titled 'The Reasonable Expectations of Privacy and the Reality of Data Protection', which is founded by the Netherlands Organization for Scientific Research (NWO). In this project several European researchers and researchers from outside Europe, like the United States and Canada, work together to answer the question how privacy is protected by law and what this protection actually means (by discussing relevant regulation and case law). Although the project covers a broad range of privacy and data protection issues, and includes the development of a case law database, a book is prepared, which focuses on two interrelated subjects: workplace privacy and video surveillance. In the fall 2004, the book will be published consisting of country reports from the United States, Canada, Belgium, Germany, Hungary, Italy, the Netherlands, and the United Kingdom. I co-authored the report on Italy. The title of the book is not available yet. Prof. Corien Prins, dr. Sjaak Nouwt, and Berend de Vries are the editors of the book, which will be published by T.M.C. Asser Press, The Hague (NL) in IT&Law Series. For more information see the website of the project available at: <www.privacynetwork.info>.

1.1 Topic and aim

In the present paper, a short version of the Italian report is presented. The aim is to provide the reader with an idea of how Italy deals with security and privacy requirements in relation to the phenomenon of video surveillance. Particular attention is paid to issues related to the use of CCTV in the workplace. Furthermore, some highlights of the other country reports are given in order to stress the different ways of regulating and approaching the same issue.

1.2 Structure and argument

The fundamental rights and freedoms jeopardised by the use of CCTV cameras such as the right to respect for privacy and freedom of movement and behaviour will be dealt with in Section 2. The freedom of movement is not only considered in a physical sense, but also in a more fundamental sense as the freedom to move without having inevitably to leave continued and/or frequent traces of one's movements for the benefit of permanent 'optic informers'. subsection 2.1 is about the way in which Italy has dealt so far with the privacy and data protection issues which are related to video surveillance. In Section 3 the Italian Data Protection Authority's Generally Applicable Regulation of 29 April 2004 (hence Decalogue 2004) will be discussed. This regulation updates and specifies principles, duties, and obligations related to the processing of data by means of video surveillance which were set out in the Italian Data Protection Authority's Generally Applicable Regulation of 29 November 2000 called the 'Italian Decalogue' (hence Decalogue 2000). The rules concerning the use of CCTV in the workplace will be specifically dealt with in Section 4. Section 5 contains some conclusion on the Italian system. Finally, highlights of other country reports are in Section 6.

2 Video surveillance and related issues

The data which are collected during video surveillance activities consist mainly of images and sounds which either identify or allow the identification of data subjects, directly or indirectly, in addition to monitoring their conduct. Thus, the implementation of CCTV as a convenient means to achieve various security purposes raises issues as regards privacy and data protection. Therefore, the right to respect for privacy, as established in Articles 5, 6, and 8 of Council of Europe Convention No. 108/1981 for the Protection of Individuals with Regard to Automatic Processing of Personal Data and Article 8 of the Convention of Human Rights and Fundamental Freedoms (hence ECHR) is jeopardized by the use of video surveillance systems. However, in addition to consider the extent to which the surveillance causes a breach of privacy, one should evaluate the effects resulting from the widespread use of surveillance as regards citizens' freedom of movement and behaviour."

Bentham's ideas of the Panopticon (1787) can help understand the effects of video surveillance on citizens' freedom of movement and behaviour. The Panopticon consisted of a central inspection tower surrounded by a ring-shaped building which is composed of cells, each housing an inmate. Control was maintained by the constant sense that prisoners were watched by unseen eyes. Not knowing whether or not they were under supervision, but obliged to assume that they were, conformity was the individual's only realistic option. In this respect, the architectural design of the Panopticon created a state of conscious and permanent visibility that assured the automatic functioning of self-control and self-discipline.

Nowadays, the same feeling of conscious and permanent visibility can be aroused by a massive use of video surveillance systems. Therefore, freedom of movement, which is referred to in many constitutional charters as well as in Article 2 of Additional Protocol No. 4 to the ECHR, intended not only in a physical sense, but also in a more fundamental sense – that is to say, the freedom to move without having inevitably to leave frequent, not to say continued, traces of one's movements for the benefit of permanent 'optic informers' – can be seriously jeopardised by the deployment of CCTV. Furthermore, 'being seen without seeing' may influence people's conduct and activities. On the one hand, hidden filming and/or control devices do not promote any openness for citizens. On the other hand, cameras and other devices which are known to have been installed at a given location might lead to 'submissive' behaviour of citizens. These hidden and very dangerous potential effects of widespread video surveillance should be borne in mind for the following analysis of the rules and the tendencies in case law related to the deployment of CCTV.

2.1 Italian law related to video surveillance

The right to privacy in Italy has gone through several phases as far as its legal basis is concerned. During the first phase, it was based on Article 8 of the ECHR. In the second phase, the right was based on Article 10 of the Civil Code which grants a person protection of his rights to his image, i.e., the right to prevent the use of visual images of a person and the dignity or reputation of this person's family. In the third phase, the basis was seen to lay in Article 2 of the Constitution, which protects a person, both as an individual and in the social group expressing his personality. In the fourth phase, the right is justified by reference to the general principle of protection of the person, as acknowledge and guaranteed by the Constitution as well as the European Union through the Directive which was implemented in Italy with Law 675/96. The last and present phase started on 1 January 2004 when the Data Protection Code (hence the Code) entered into force. The right to the protection of personal data was finally codified in Italy in Section 1 of the Code. Focusing the attention on video surveillance, Section 134 of the Code rules that the Italian Data Protection Authority, which is called Garante, shall encourage the adoption of a code of conduct and professional practice applying to the processing of personal data which is performed by means of an electronic image acquisition device – video surveillance. The Garante set out updated and specific principles, duties, and obligations in the Decalogue 2004 which must be complied with until the time this code of conduct is ready.

3 Italian Decalogue 2004

On 29 April 2004, the Italian Decalogue 2004 was published. Due to the entry into force of the Code and the many cases of misuse of video surveillance systems brought to the attention of the Garante during the past four years, it was clear that there was an urgent need to update and specify the principles set out in Decalogue 2000. Decalogue 2004 consists of two parts: a general part setting out the guiding principles, duties, and obligations which must be complied with for a lawful deployment of video surveillance systems, and a more specified part in which the Garante sets out some additional rules related to video surveillance activities which are carried out in specific environments: workplaces, hospitals, schools, places of worship, and burial places.

3.1 General principles

The lawfulness principle, the necessity or data minimization principle, the principle of proportionality, and the finality principle are the four general principles set out in Decalogue 2004 to be complied with when processing personal data by means of video surveillance.

3.1.1 Lawfulness

The processing of personal data by means of video surveillance is allowed only if it is carried out in compliance with the rules laid down in the Code. Different rules apply if the data are processed, on the one hand, by public bodies or, on the other hand, by private bodies or profit-seeking public bodies.

Rules applicable to public bodies

In Section 18 of the Code, the rules applying to all processing operations performed by public bodies are set out:

„(1) (…). (2) Public bodies shall only be permitted to process personal data in order to discharge their institutional tasks. (3) In processing the data, public bodies shall abide by the prerequisites and limitations set out in this Code, by having also regard to the different features of the data, as well as in laws and regulations. (4) Subject to the provisions of Part II as applying to health care professionals and public health care organizations, public bodies shall not be required to obtain the data subject's consent. (5) The provisions laid down in Section 25 as for communication and dissemination shall apply."

Data must be processed within the framework of institutional tasks. This is the *condition sine qua non* which the public bodies must comply with when processing personal data.

Rules applicable to private bodies and profit-seeking public bodies

When personal data are processed by private entities or profit-seeking public bodies, there are two conditions which must be alternatively fulfilled in order to make the process lawful. The data subject's express consent must be obtained as is set out in Section 23. If the subject does not consent, data processing is allowed if it is „necessary to pursue a legitimate interest of either the data controller or a third party recipient in the cases specified by the Garante on the basis of the principles set out under the law, also with regard to the activities of banking groups and subsidiaries or related companies, unless said interest is overridden by the data subject's rights and fundamental freedoms, dignity or legitimate interests, dissemination of the data being ruled out" (Section 24). The second way to make video surveillance lawful is called 'interests balancing'. The Garante has to weigh up the legitimate interests either of the data controller or of a third party recipient and the data subject's rights and fundamental freedoms, dignity, or legitimate interests in order to assess whether or not the processing of data is lawful. Moreover, the Garante has pointed out that the Code does not apply to the use of video surveillance which is carried out for individual security purposes (Section 5 (3)) – e.g., video cameras which survey the entrance of private dwellings. This type of surveillance must be strictly limited to the entrance, avoiding filming nearby areas and limiting in any way the freedoms of subjects other than the ones who live in the house under surveillance. According to Article 615 *bis* of the Penal Code (which governs the offence of 'invasion of privacy'), anyone who uses film or sound-recording equipment unlawfully to obtain information or pictures of private life in the dwelling of another person or in any other private residence is liable to a penalty of six months to four years' imprisonment. The Garante specified that if video surveillance systems are installed for the protection of common areas in a block of flats either by the flats' owners or by organizations which are in charge of the administrative management of the block of flats, the purposes of the video surveillance can no longer be defined as individual. Thus, the Code is applicable. Moreover, the communication and the dissemination of the images are forbidden.

3.1.2 The necessity or data minimization principle

The necessity or data minimization principle is set out in Section 3 of the Code: „Information systems and software shall be configured by minimising the use of personal data and identification data, in such a way as to rule out their processing if the purposes sought in the individual cases can be achieved by using either anonymous data or suitable arrangements to allow identifying data subjects only in cases of necessity, respectively." The data minimization principle together with the simplification principle, which is mentioned in Section 2 of the Code and specified further in Section 77, are the two pillars of the new Italian law on privacy and data protection as set forth in the Code. The necessity of the data minimization principle is specified further by the principle of proportionality, which will be dealt with below.

3.1.3 The principle of proportionality

The principle of proportionality come into play in two different phases: the phase before the installation, when it is decided to take recourse to video surveillance and the phase after the installation, when video surveillance is carried out.

The proportionality of recourse to video surveillance

Recourse to video surveillance systems complies with the principle of proportionality in the event of concrete dangers and related real needs of deterrence. Furthermore, video surveillance may only be deployed on a subsidiary basis. The proportionality principle entails that these systems may be deployed if other type of prevention, protections or security measures, requiring no image acquisition – e.g., the use of armoured doors to prevent vandalism, the installation of automatic gates and clearance devices, joint alarm systems, better and stronger lighting of streets at night, etc. – prove clearly insufficient and/or inapplicable with a view to the purposes.

The principle also applies to the selection of the appropriate technology, the criteria for using the equipment in concrete cases, and the specification of data processing arrangements as also related to access rules and retention period.

The Garante further specifies that the deployment of web cams or on line cameras for commercial purposes is not allowed if the data subjects are identifiable.

The deployment of fake video cameras is also forbidden. In fact, even if the processing of personal data does not take place, the feeling of being observed by 'optic informers' may influence people's movements and behaviour (as was already pointed out in Section 2 on the basis of the example of Bentham's Panopticon).

Proportionality in carrying out video surveillance activities

Turning the attention to the application of the principle of proportionality in the phase when the video surveillance activities are carried out, the personal data must be adequate, relevant and not excessive in relation to the purposes for which they are collected or further processed. To that end, the filming arrangements should also be taken into account. The visual angle, the location of the video cameras, and the modality of recording images must fit to the purposes. Furthermore, detailed images, magnifying, or zooming must be avoided when not necessary.

3.1.4 The finality principle

The finality principle is set out in Section (1) (b) of the Code: „Personal data undergoing processing shall be collected and recorded for specific, explicit and legitimate purposes and used in further processing operations in a way that is not inconsistent with said purposes." A corollary of this principle is the fact that the data controller is allowed to pursue only purposes which fit into its competence.

3.2 Duties and obligations

After stating the four general principles, the Garante sets out several duties and obligations to be fulfilled by the data controller when he processes personal data by means of video surveillance.

3.2.1 Duty to inform

Clear information regarding the presence of CCTV must be given to all the subjects who could be filmed. The information content is laid down in Section 13 of the Code. Information can be provided also in a summary fashion. To that end, the Garante provides a simplified standard model in Decalogue 2004.

3.2.2 Preliminary verification

The processing of personal data by means of video surveillance must be carried out in compliance with the rules prescribed by the Garante. Section 17 of the Code sets out the general rule: „(1) Processing of data other than sensitive and judicial data shall be allowed in accordance with such measures and precautions as are laid down to safeguard data subjects, if the processing is likely to present specific risks to data subjects' fundamental rights and freedoms and dignity on account of the nature of the data, the arrangements applying to the processing or the effects the latter may produce. (2) The measures and precautions referred to in paragraph 1 shall be laid down by the Garante on the basis of the principles set out in this Code within the framework of a check to be performed prior to the start of the processing as also related to specific categories of data controller or processing, following the request, if any, submitted by the data controller."

3.2.3 Authorization

In the case of sensitive or judicial data such as images of sick persons or prisoners, prior authorization of the Garante is needed according to Sections 26 and 27 of the Code. The authorization should not be confused with the preliminary verification. The authorization is the *conditio sine qua non* for the processing of sensitive or judicial data. The prior authorization on the basis of Section 17 of the Code is a possible action taken by the Garante on its own initiative or at the data controller's request in order to lay down some rules which help the latter in carrying out a lawful processing of data. It has to be stressed that the implicit authorization is not enough. Therefore, each request for authorization must be followed by an explicit answer from the Garante.

3.2.4 Notification

Section 37 of the Code sets out the specific grounds in which notification is needed. If the law requires notifying the Garante of the processing of personal data, it must be specified that the processing is carried out by means of video surveillance. The rules which are set out in Section 37 of the Code are further specified in the Garante's Generally Applicable Regulation of 31 March 2004. In this regulation, the Garante laid down specific exceptions to the grounds which are listed in Section 37 of the Code. In other words, the regulation lists specific situations in which processing of data that falls within the scope of Section 37 need not be notified. More precisely, in the Generally Applicable Regulation of 31 March 2004, the Garante specifies that notification is not needed when data which are processed for purposes of security or protection of individuals or properties are related to wrongful or fraudulent behaviour and the images or the sounds collected are only temporarily stored. Thus, when a subject decides to process data by means of video surveillance, it should check whether the processing falls with the scope of grounds listed in the Generally Applicable Regulation of 31 March 2004. If it does not, it must notify the Garante specifying the fact that the processing is carried out by means of video surveillance.

3.2.5 Written designation of the subjects involved in the data processing

Data processors and persons in charge of the processing (Sections 29 and 30 of the Code) who are allowed to use video surveillance systems and to access the recorded data must be listed. Furthermore, monitoring must take place so that they can access only the data which are necessary in order to perform their tasks. Access to the data is prohibited to other subjects with the exception of police or judicial authorities.

3.2.6 Security measures

The rules related to data and systems security are set out in Title V of the Code (Sections 31-36). The general rule concerning security requirements is laid down in Section 31: „Personal data undergoing processing shall be kept and controlled, also in consideration of technological innovations, of their nature and the specific features of the processing, in such a way as to minimize, by means of suitable preventative security measures, the risk of their destruction or loss, whether by accident or not, of unauthorized access to the data or of processing operations that are either unlawful or inconsistent with the purposes for which the data have been collected."

3.2.7 Retention of images

In application of the principle of proportionality, data may be kept no longer than is necessary for the purposes for which the data were collected or subsequently processed. It may be justified to record images for a few hours, not later than twenty-four hours after the moment of recording. An exception to this rule is the case in which an alert has been issued or else a request has been made deserving specific attention. In such cases, there are reasonable grounds to await the decision to be possibly taken by the police or judicial authorities.

3.2.8 Data subject's rights

The data controller must guarantee the effective exercise of the data subject's rights set out in Section 7 of the Code. It is also specified that if a request to access personal data is made, „the response provided to the data subject shall include all the personal data concerning him/her that are processed by the data controller" (Section 10). It shall include data which refers to third parties only complying with the limitations laid down in Section 10 (5) the Code: „The right to obtain communication of the data in intelligible form does not apply to personal data concerning third parties, unless breaking down the processed data or eliminating certain items from the latter prevents the data subject's personal data from being understandable."

3.3 Breach of rules and related sanctions

Data controllers must comply with the rules set out in the Decalogue 2004. If a breach of the rules occurs, the processing is either unlawful or incorrect. Non-compliance may give rise to the following consequence. Firstly, „any personal data that is processed in breach of the relevant provisions concerning the processing of personal data may not be used." (Section 11 (2)) Secondly, „the Garante shall block or prohibit the processing, in whole or in part, if the latter is found to be unlawful or unfair partly because of the failure to take the necessary measures as per letter b), or else if there is an actual risk that it may be considerably prejudicial to one or more of the data subjects by having regard to the nature of the data, the arrangements applying to the processing or the effects that may be produced by the processing" (Section 143 (1) (c)). Similar action can be taken also by the judiciary. Thirdly, administrative or criminal sanctions can be applied according to Sections 161 *et seq.* of the Code.

4 Video surveillance in the workplace

Due to the complexity of the employer-employee relationship, European countries have produced or are in the process of producing laws, codes, or recommendations addressing several data protection issues related to the workplace environment. Italy was been one of the first countries in Europe to produce specific legislation. All the principles which have been stated so far apply to the deployment of CCTV in the workplace.

4.1 Legal grounds for privacy protection

In Italy, the use of audiovisual and other devices for controlling employees in the workplace has been prohibited since 1970. In fact, Article 4 of Law No. 300/1970 (hence, Workers' Statute) protects employees from any concealed workplace monitoring which offends the employee's dignity and freedom. Article 4 states that the deployment of CCTV for the surveillance of employees is in principle forbidden. However, CCTV can be installed for productive or security reasons under the condition that a shop level agreement is concluded with the local unions or if there is no union, with special administrative authorization from the local labour office. Article 4 of the Workers' Statute is referred to both in Section 114 of the Code and in Decalogue 2004 as a rule to be complied with in order for video surveillance in the workplace to be lawful. Moreover, Article 41 of the Constitution rules the freedom of enterprise and it states in paragraph 2: „It may not be carried out against the common good or in a way that may harm public security, liberty, or human dignity." This provision strikes the balance between the interests of the two parties involved in the employment relationship: the employers and the employees. Employers are free to develop their business in the way they like as long as they do not impinge upon public security, liberty, or human dignity. The deployment of CCTV as a means of surveillance of the production cycle is indeed a way of developing the business. However, it can endanger the employees' liberty and human dignity.

4.2 The specific rules set out in Decalogue 2004

Video surveillance is forbidden when it is aimed at checking the individual performance of employees in the workplace. Furthermore, in order for surveillance in the workplace to be lawful, the data controller must comply with the conditions laid down in Article 4 of the Workers' Statute. The concept of 'workplace' has to be interpreted in a broad sense, meaning that it is the place where an employee carries out his job is carried out. Therefore, the rules concerning video surveillance apply whether the job is performed inside or outside the company's buildings. Moreover, the installation of systems of video surveillance is forbidden in areas exclusively reserved to employees' use or areas to be used for purposes other than working activities, i.e., bathrooms, dressing rooms, showers, locker rooms, and recreational areas. Finally, the Garante has specified that filming in workplaces for popular or for institutional or a company's communication purposes is comparable to „processing operations which are carried out on a temporary basis exclusively for the purposes of publication or occasional circulation of articles, essays and other intellectual works also in terms of artistic expression"(Section 136 (1) (c)). Therefore, the rules of the Code concerning journalism are applicable together with the limitations imposed on the freedom of the press in order to protect the right of confidentiality, with the rules set out in the code of conduct applying to journalistic activities, and with the employees' right to object on legitimate grounds to the dissemination of their personal data.

The *ratio* of the rules concerning video surveillance in the workplace which are set out in Decalogue 2004 and in Article 4 of the Workers' Statute is that video surveillance activities which are carried out in the workplace must respect the privacy and autonomy of the employees while they do their job.

The decision in *Banco di Sicilia v. Fiba* (Court of Cassation, 16 September 1997 No. 9211) was crucial because it stated both the scope of application of Article 4 and the necessity to comply with the procedure set out by this rule even though the employees were aware of the installation of the CCTV. The Courts pointed out that Article 4 applies when there is a risk that distance monitoring of employees could be carried out. There is no need to prove that the video cameras are actually in use. It has to be assumed that when CCTV cameras are installed there is always the chance of distance monitoring of the employees. Therefore, since the moment CCTV cameras are installed Article 4 is applicable. It is not relevant whether or not the CCTV cameras are working. In addition, the Court stressed that the agreement with the local unions must be concluded, irrespective of whether employees are aware of the installation of the CCTV. The reason given by the Court is that the right of not been monitored is considered to be a personal right, which is, therefore, an inalienable right. For the sake of completeness, it is worth mentioning that in the *Marini* case (Court of Milan, 23 July 1991) it was stated that there is no need to reach the agreement of all the members of the local union, the majority is considered enough for the lawful deployment of CCTV. Moreover, it is irrelevant whether any local unions existed at the time the CCTV cameras were installed; as soon as the unions are set up, their agreement must be sought on the fact that the CCTV system can be kept.

Concerning the object of the protection granted by Article 4 in *Cuda v. Azienda energetica municipale* (Court of Milan 29 September 1990) it was specified that Article 4 grants protection to employees against at distance monitoring concerning the quality and the quantity of their job performance and their behaviour in the workplace. Furthermore, the literature has pointed out that the video surveillance of employees is prohibited also when they are carrying out activities not related to their job, i.e., during lunch or coffee breaks.

In Article 38 of the Workers' Statute, it is set out that the violation of Article 4 is a criminal offence. This means that an agreement with the local unions must be reached before CCTV cameras are installed for productive or security reasons. In case there are no unions, a special authorization from the local labour office is needed. If this procedure is not complied with, the employer is subject to the criminal sanction as set out in Article 38.

Moreover, the case law agrees on the fact that employers are free to check the job performance of their employees for instance through staff in charge of taking care of the interests of the employer. In this case, Article 4 does not apply. Thus, neither particular purposes of security or productive reasons nor agreement with the local unions are needed.

In conclusion, in *Società la Carica Veronesi Carla e C. S.A.S. v. Ledda* (Court of Cassation, 17 June 2000 No. 8250) it was decided that the evidence obtained by mean of video surveillance by the owner of a bar which shows one of his employees stealing moneys from the cash desk does not have any probative value because they were unlawfully collected. The Court decided that the use of video surveillance was not the proportionate response by an employer to the risks he faced. Indeed, the Court pointed out that the use of CCTV must take into account the respect for human dignity even though it is carried out for business reasons. In fact, it means that the deployment of a constant surveillance of an employee on the basis of suspicion, although it was well-founded and later even confirmed by the images, is contrary to the general principle of proportionality. This decision is very significant because the Court was called to decide between the employer's interest related to the security and the conduct of his business and the employee's right to privacy. And it was decided in favour of the latter following the wording of Article 41 of the Constitution. Besides, the Court mentioned also the fact that the procedures laid down in Article 4 (2) of the Workers' Statute were not complied with.

5 Conclusion on the Italian system

Privacy and data protection is taken seriously in Italy. After an evaluation of the rules concerning video surveillance and the way the courts and the Data Protection Authority apply them, it can be affirmed that the interest in privacy has significantly increased in Italy since privacy legislation was enacted. Indeed it is possible to see the Garante and the courts' joint efforts in enforcing both the specific principles which are applicable to the privacy issues related to video surveillance and the rules of the Workers' Statute granting in this way the protection of the people's rights to privacy against very intrusive technologies such as CCTV.

Furthermore, compared to some other countries (see the example of the Netherlands and Belgium dealt with in Section 6.2) the Italian case law on violations of privacy by means of video surveillance is remarkably consistent. Apart from a few decisions, which are not even very recent, it is easy to notice a common approach to the cases and very similar criteria which have been applied in the decisions. This is crucial in citizens' feelings about privacy protection, and it also acts as a deterrent with regard to potential future misbehaviour concerning the deployment of video surveillance systems.

That Italy has an open eye for privacy issues is also borne out by the privacy legislation that has been adopted. The new Data Protection Code entered into force on 1 January 2004. Furthermore, codes of conduct regarding crucial topics such as investigations, video surveillance activities, the Internet, employer-employee relationships, and direct marketing are in preparation. Last but not least, the Decalogue 2004, which proves that the Garante is filling the legislative gap concerning video surveillance until the code of conduct is ready.

In conclusion, according to the results of the Eurobarometer survey on data protection awareness in the European Union which was carried out in the fall of 2003 Italian citizens are the best informed both on their privacy rights and on the existence of an independent Data Protection Authority.

6 Highlights of the other countries[1]

Highlights of the other country reports are given in order to emphasize the different ways of approaching and regulating the privacy and data protection issues related to the deployment of video surveillance.

---

[1] The highlights are based on the previews of the country reports draft. The case law mentioned is available at: <www.privacynetwork.info>. Last visited 22 June 2004.

6.1 Privacy and data protection is also a matter of culture

In the country report about the United Kingdom, it is concluded that a society gets the privacy that it wants. The idea is that people have to make the first step in order to defend their right to privacy denouncing its violations and then granting them protection is up to the 'system'.

Belgium, for example, is a country which has no culture of bringing issues of privacy before the court. Many conflicts on alleged unlawful use of technology by employers or by state officials never make it to the courts. In the areas of workers privacy, for instance, there is a tendency towards settling the matter amicably in order to avoid any negative publicity. This absence of consistency in jurisprudence echoes in the Belgian legislation. Privacy laws entered into force in the 1990s and a general law that provides adequate protection against illegal monitoring is still lacking.

In Hungary, the outcome is the same but the reasons are different. Employees are afraid to come forward with their complaints about data protection. They are reluctant to bring the complaints to the Data Protection Authority or a court. Due to their vulnerable position Hungarian employees are worried about loosing their job, about the possible retaliation of the employer, or about being unofficially (and illegally) black-listed, which would make their future prospects of finding a job very difficult. However, even in those rare instances when the courts apply the data protection rules, their interpretations of these rules are remarkably inconsistent.

6.2 Case law inconsistency: between pragmatism and judges' attempt to preserve their discretion in evaluating evidence

Case law inconsistency is one of the biggest issues related to the protection of privacy. It is frequently it is related to the judge's lack of knowledge on the topic or to some legislative gaps. However, sometimes the reasons have completely different nature. It seems that the Dutch case law is built up around notions of common sense and pragmatism, taking into account the specific circumstances and peculiarities of every case. Often in this sort of matters, the outcome depends on the circumstances. In the country report about Belgium the lack of case law consistency it is attributed to the unwillingness of the court to sacrifice its power to judge freely and to balance evidence. Clear example of this practice is the judgment of the Court of Appeal Ghent (28 March 2002). The court concludes that the retrieval and the use of surveillance camera images by the police, gathered by the registered office of the National Bank of Kortrijk, produces valid evidential material. In the opinion of the defendants, the whole operation violated the principle of finality laid down in the Law of 8 December 1992, implying that said images may not be used for other purposes incompatible with the initial purpose of the camera-surveillance. The judge could have easily responded to this argument by quoting Article 4 § 1 sub 2 of the same law. This provision states that personal data shall 'be collected for specified, explicit and legitimate purposes and not further processed *in a way incompatible* with those purposes' [own emphasis]. The use of the images by the police can be seen as compatible use. This is however not how the Court proceeds. What the Court does is recall its (familiar) principles of free evidence law, apply these principles in order to accept the evidence brought into Court and end its judgement with an unnecessary paragraph about the lack of precision of the Law of 8 December 1992 and the unwillingness of the Court to sacrifice its power to judge freely and to balance evidence in the framework of the law of criminal evidence, in favour of a strict application of the Law of 8 December 1992.

6.3 Suspicion as a condition for the lawful deployment of secret camera surveillance

The Italian case *Società la Carica Veronesi Carla e C. S.A.S. v. Ledda* (Court of Cassation, 17 June 2000 No. 8250) mentioned in Section 4.2 shows that in Italy the suspicion (although well-founded or even confirmed by the images) of a crime which has been committed by an employee is not a sufficient reason for the admission of evidences unlawfully collected by means of video surveillance.

However, in countries such as Belgium and Germany on the base of serious grounds for suspicion that a crime has been committed or will take place in the near future hidden cameras are allowed and the evidences collected are admissible.

In Belgium the owner of a shop installed a hidden camera and microphone to monitor the area around the cash register for he suspected one of the employees of stealing. By doing so, he recorded all the cashiers movements and conversations to gain evidence. The starting point of the judgement of the Court of Cassation (27 February 2001) is Article 8 of the European Convention of Fundamental Rights and Freedoms. The right to respect for one's private life is not an absolute right, interference is allowed when certain conditions are met. In this regard the Court remarks that the action of the employer is both legitimate and necessary. The Court of Cassation does not object to this kind of initiative as long as the employer has a legitimate suspicion of one of the employees committing a criminal offence.

In Germany, the Federal Labour Court (BAG) (27 March 2003) although acknowledging that an employee has the right of not being constantly monitored by means of hidden video surveillance systems and later admitted evidences collected in that way on the basis of a strong suspicion of the employer on an employee.

6.4 When the law enforcement is the problem

The United Kingdom is the only country among the reported ones which has specific regulation on video surveillance: the CCTV Code of Practice and a Data Protection Code on Monitoring at Work which refers expressly to video surveillance and to the CCTV code. However, the United Kingdom faces problems concerning enforcement: even where DP laws do operate, estimates from privacy activism groups are that perhaps as few as 10% of CCTV cameras are in fact DP-compliant. The lack of resources available to the UK Information Commissioner is the main constraint on enforcement of data protection generally.

6.5 Two different worlds

Although the differences between the European countries reported are remarkable, due to the implementation Directive 95/46/EC on Data Protection, these countries share the basic principle of privacy and data protection: the lawfulness principle, the necessity or data minimization principle, the principle of proportionality, and the finality principle. In contrast, the privacy and data protection pillars are completely different overseas. The United States and Canada refer to the concept of reasonable expectation of privacy which regarding video surveillance depends principally on an uneasy distinction between public and private places. Moreover, in United States whether the technology used to undertake the surveillance is in general public use also plays a role in the protection of the right to privacy.

References

[Butt00]   Buttarelli, G.: Protection of Personal Data with Regards to Surveillance (2000) and Guiding Principles for the protection of Individuals with Regard to the Collection and Processing of Data by Means of Video Surveillance, 2000. Available at <http://www.coe.int/T/E/Legal_affairs/Legal_co-operation/Data_protection/ Documents/Reports/G-Report%20Buttarelli.asp#TopOfPage>. Last visited 20 July 2004.

[Bent95]   Bentham, J.: The Panopticon Writings, Verso Books, 1995, p. 29-95.

[Alpa99]   Alpa, G.: The Protection of Privacy in Italian law. In: Markesinis, Basil S.: Protecting Privacy. Oxford University Press, 1999, p. 105-130.

[Ciri04]   Cirillo, G. P.: Il codice sulla protezione dei dati personali. Giuffrè, 2004.

[ElZa04]   Elli, G.: Il nuovo Codice della privacy [commento al d. lgs. 30 giugno 2003, n. 196]. Giappicheli, 2004.

[Fezz83]   Fezzi, M.: Calcolatori elettronici e controllo a distanza dell'attivita' dei lavoratori. In: Lavoro 80, II. 1983, p.569.

[Cuom98]   Cuomo, C.: Sull'applicabilita' dell' art. 4 Statuto dei lavoratori. In: La nouva giurisprudenza civile commentata. 1998, p.834-840.

[Gild96]   Gildre, G.: Innovazioni tecniche e art. 4 dello Statuto dei lavoratori. In: Il diritto del lavoro. 1996, p.478.

[Vera98]   Veraldi, S.: I limiti ai poteri di vigilanza del datore di lavoro: il divieto do controllo a distanza dei lavoratori. In: Rivista giuridica del lavoro e della previdenza sociale. 1998, p.61.

[Sara86]   Sarasella, W.: L'art. 4 Statuto dei lavoratori e l'impiego di elaboratori elettronici. In: Lavoro 80. 1986, p.343.

[Ichi79]   Ichino, P.: Diritto alla riservatezza e diritto al segreto nel rapporto del lavoro. La disciplina della circolazione delle informazioni in azienda. Giuffrè, 1979, p.120ff.

[Euro03]   European Commission: Data Protection. 2003, p.49. Available at <http://europa. eu.int/comm/public_opinion/archives/ebs/ebs_196_data_protection.pdf>. Last visited: 20 July 2004.

[Gara03]   Garante: Relazione. 2003, p.166-169. Available at <http://www.garanteprivacy. it/garante/navig/jsp/index.jsp?folderpath=Attivit%E0+dell%27Autorit%E0% 2FRelazioni+annuali+al+Parlamento%2F2003>. Last visited 20 July 2003.

[Cerc04]   Cerchi, A.: Rischio – tecnologia sulla privacy. In: Il sole 24 ore. Tuesday 28 April, p.27.

Enhancing Security of Computing Platforms with TC-Technology

Oliver Altmeyer, Ahmad-Reza Sadeghi,
Marcel Selhorst, Christian Stüble

Applied Data Security Group
European Centre for IT-Security (eurobits)
Ruhr-University Bochum
{altmeyer I sadeghi I selhorst I stueble} @crypto.rub.de

Abstract

We present an open security platform based on the specification of the Trusted Computing Group (TCG). The features provided by the proposed platform can be used to solve many existing security problems. The platform's main components are a conventional operating system, a security software layer (PERSEUS), and the hardware offered by the TCG. Exploiting the TCG functionalities, our security platform offers a variety of secure (trusted) services, e.g., secure booting, secure user interface, trusted GUI, and a trusted viewer, which are not offered by commonly used computing platforms. Together these services allow the implementation of security-critical applications, such as those generating digital signatures or enforcing a certain policy, while providing backward-compatibility to an existing operating system.

1 Motivation

The fast-growing e-commerce market which comes along with the rapid expansion of worldwide connectivity requires end-user systems that can fulfill a wide range of security requirements: authenticity, integrity, privacy, anonymity and availability. However, the experience of the past has shown that existing computing platforms, in particular operating systems, cannot guarantee these security requirements. Even with today's security technology such as cryptography, firewalls, or intrusion detection systems they cannot effectively protect individuals from executing malicious code. In particular, they neither provide appropriate mechanisms to enforce adequate security policies, nor can they be maintained by non-experts. The problems are caused by vulnerabilities in hardware and software due to architectural security problems and the inherent vulnerabilities resulting from complexity. This situation brings about the need for developing a new generation of secure computing platforms.

Trusted computing (TC) technology provides many useful functionalities and mechanisms giving us the opportunity to build secure IT systems. However, these functionalities can increase the security *only* in combination with a secure operating system. Only based on a secure operating system the computing environment can be trustworthy enough for security critical applications such as digital signatures or applications requiring policy enforcements. Using the functions provided by the TCG, we are developing a very small µ-kernel based open-source security platform. On top of this platform, an existing operating system (currently Linux) and security-critical applications can securely be executed in parallel. In particular, our platform offers all features required to establish a secure signature application.

S. Paulus, N. Pohlmann, H. Reimer (Editors): Securing Electronic Business Processes, Vieweg (2004), 346-361

2 Towards a Secure Signature Application

In the digital world of workflows and business models, the purpose of digital signature schemes is to adopt functionality that handwritten signatures have for documents on paper. In contrast to handwritten signatures that can (ideally) be created only by the identity assigned to the signature, digital signature schemes require complex mathematical computations which are performed by computing platforms. Moreover, digital signatures are created upon digital data which can be interpreted in different ways. For instance, by using different releases of rendering engines like Word or PDF, the resulting documents may look differently. To realize a signature system in the context of legal requirements, it is therefore important to focus on the transferred information (declaration of intention) rather than on the digital data (the bitstring) that encodes it.

Based on the TCG technology we are implementing a signature application that can be used to securely sign documents, i.e., it guarantees that the data viewed by the user is the same as the one the user signs. Here the platform establishes a trusted path between the user and the signature application whereby no other application can access the inputs/outputs of this application. More concretely, the signature application prevents the rendering component (e.g., PDF reader) from being manipulated[1]. In the following subsection, we will discuss the requirements of a secure signature application in more details.

2.1 Requirement Analysis

The (German) signature law [Gese01, Vero01] requires, beside the algorithmic security, the signature issuing components to ensure that the signed document is identical to the document verified by the signer. Moreover, to be able to securely verify a signature, an appropriate component must exist that correctly displays (i) which information of a document was signed and (ii) whether it has been modified.

Today's available signature applications attempt to fulfill these requirements by only allowing documents to be signed which are of a relatively fixed format, e.g., PNG or JPG. Ignoring the security problems following from the insecurity of the underlying operating systems, this approach has two main disadvantage: First, it is not really secure, since even a PNG or JPG document can be rendered in different ways. For instance, if the color depth of a computing platform is low, a signer may be unable distinguish light-written contents from the background color. Second, it is often, especially in the context of electronic workflows, desirable to be able to sign documents which will be edited in the future. If the document has to be converted into an image format like PNG, editing is not possible any more.

To ensure that signers can securely prove which document they have signed, a secure signing application providing a trusted viewer has not only to sign the document itself, but also the complete state (including hard- and software components) of the signer's computing platform. Unfortunately, this requirement cannot be fulfilled in practice, since it is, based on currently available open platforms, nearly impossible to provide the same platform configuration on the verifier's side that was used by the signer.

Therefore, to provide an environment that allows secure generation of digital signatures, the main idea of our approach is to ensure the following: Firstly, the components of the security-critical parts of the signature application that render signed data should only depend on a very

---

[1] It should be noted that we assume that the screen is not under the control of an adversary. This type of man-in-the-middle attacks cannot be prevented by any cryptographic means in software.

small software layer of reduced complexity. Secondly, this software layer should easily be reproducible on different hardware platforms. The in this context important security requirements to be fulfilled by such an environment are the following (for a more detailed analysis see, e.g., [PRS+01a]):

- *Abstraction:* The rendering engine must depend only on a very small software stack. Additionally, an abstraction layer has to ensure that these components do not depend on concrete hardware configurations.

- *Isolation:* Unauthorized components should not be able to manipulate the state of the trusted viewer and the underlying platform.

- *Algorithmic security*: One usually assumes the security of the underlying signature scheme, which is usually proven by the methods of modern cryptography, either using heuristics or standard proof based on reductions. However, these proofs may not be fully valid in the physical environment due to the information leakage, e.g., side-channel information (see also [MiRe04]). Here one should apply appropriate methods to prevent leakage of security critical information (e.g., on signing keys).

- *Configuration snapshots:* The signature application has to ensure that all state variables that are used by the rendering engine (to render the output) are measured.

- *Secure user interface*: A secure graphical user interface has to provide a *trusted path* such that rendered content cannot be manipulated, and that user input cannot be spoofed. Moreover, the secure user interface has to provide an *application authentication* mechanism that allows users to uniquely identify the application that receives user inputs or that displays the current information (faked dialogs [ADSW99], [TyWh96]). For instance, in case of a signature application the user should be ensured which window is controlled by the trusted signature application and which not (application authentication and labeling the application window).

- *Secure Booting*: It has to be prevented that unauthorized parties can manipulate the underlying operating system such that protection mechanisms can be bypassed.

2.2 Overview

In the following sections we will consider the building blocks required to fulfill the above mentioned requirements in practice. We consider a generic platform consisting of application, operating system and the hardware layer. The core components of our platform are a security software layer (PERSEUS) **[PRS+01a]**, **[PRS+01b]**, **[SaSt03]** acting as a security kernel on top of the functionalities offered by TCG. The security kernel provides a variety of the required security services such as abstraction and isolation and builds the basis for the secure user interface. The TCG specification offers useful functionalities particularly those provided by a Trusted Platform Module (TPM). We will recall the main aspects of the security kernel and the TCG specification in Sections 3 and 6.

To be able to deploy the features of the TPM, an appropriate driver is required. Beside developing such a module for our security kernel PERSEUS we have also developed a corresponding kernel module for Linux. This allows to implement certain security functionalities under Linux, making Linux more secure. This is considered in Section 3.2. A secure booting mechanism is provided using TCG functionalities for which we have developed a secure bootloader (tGRUB) based on TCG specifications. These aspects are subject of Section 4. In Section 5 we present our secure user interface implementation that is one of the core components of the trusted viewer explained in Section 6.

3 Trusted Computing

Trusted Computing (TC), as proposed, e.g., by TCG [**Pear03**], [**TCG03**] or Microsoft's Next-Generation Secure Computing Base (NGSCB) [**MVHC03**], defines new security functionalities under reduced tamper-resistant assumptions. Based on these functionalities secure IT-Systems can be built. Thus, one can design services for integrity checks of the underlying computing platform, called *attestation*, bind secret keys to a specific platform configuration, called *sealing*, generate secure random numbers, and securely store cryptographic keys. However, TC technology is not able to solve the present security problems *without* a secure operating system: The operating system is the only instance that controls all information flows above the hardware layer, and has therefore access to all security relevant data.

The main component of the trusted platform is called Trusted Platform Module (TPM) that can either be a separated chip or integrated in the underlying motherboard. The specialized hardware architecture of the TPM and its functions will be defined in the next section.

3.1 Trusted Platform Module (TPM)

The TPM architecture can be compared to an integrated smart card containing a CPU, some memory and special applications. The assumption is that the chip is tamper-resistant and mounted on (or integrated in) the motherboard. The main chip contains a special security controller with some internal, non-volatile ROM for the firmware, non-volatile EEPROM for the data, and RAM. Furthermore, it contains a cryptographic engine for accelerating encryption and decryption processes, a hash accelerator, and a random number generator (needed to generate secure cryptographic keys). Figure 1 shows the main architecture of the chip.

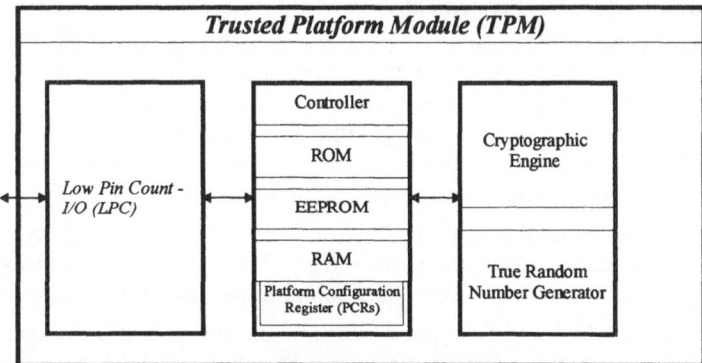

Figure 1: Architecture of the TPM.

The TPM uses the synchronous Low Pin Count-I/O-Interface (LPC-I/O) on the motherboard to communicate with the host PC. The data transmission is done through a FIFO inside the TPM LPC-I/O interface which can be accessed from both sides. The connection of the TPM to the motherboard is illustrated in Figure 2. The protocols defining the order of commands and transmissions between the host and the TPM are a challenge-and-response-dialogue, e.g., the host waits after every request for the corresponding response from the TPM before a new request is sent.

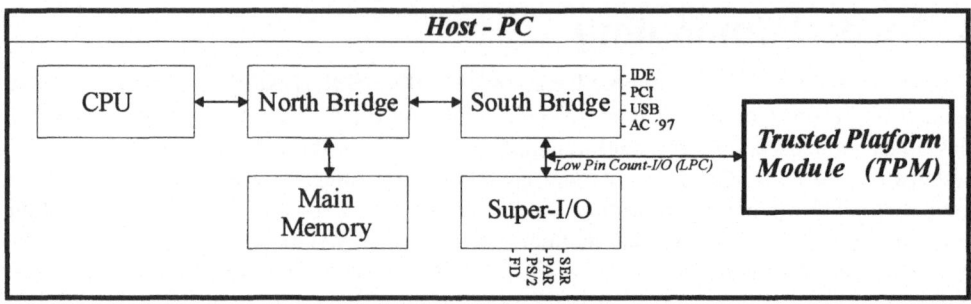

Figure 2: Host-PC with TPM.

Due to the properties of the LPC-interface, checksums for block-protection are not required. To configure the chip, configuration registers can be used to enable or disable functions of the TPM chip, and to configure the I/O-addresses for communicating with the chip. Data registers are used for transferring data between the host PC and the TPM chip, status and command registers are used to audit and control the performed operations. Depending on the used TPM chip different layers may exist above the hardware to transport control information, vendor specific information, or application data (e.g., data to be signed or commands to generate keys). The basic characteristics and functions of the TPM are as follows:

- Secure Identification: Every TPM contains a unique asymmetric encryption key pair, called *Endorsement Key* (EK), used to identify the TPM. The EK is certified by the vendor of the TPM. Since TCG specification version 1.2, the TPM owner can overwrite the initial EK by a newly created one.

- Key hierarchy: In order to use the TPM, a user takes ownership of the TPM by generating an asymmetric key pair called *Storage Root Key* (SRK) that is stored inside the TPM. The SRK encrypts sub-keys (for encryption and signatures) generated by the TPM that have to be stored outside the TPM. So-called key slots can be used to temporarily load keys into the TPM. The SRK is not migratable to another TPM, but sub-keys can be migrated, if specified during the generation process.

- Secure key generation: This feature allows a user to generate strong cryptographic signature and encryption keys based on the integrated random number generator. Note that weak cryptographic keys may completely compromise the underlying security goals.

- Asymmetric signature and encryption schemes: In the current TCG specification, the TPM contains signature and encryption schemes, which use RSA (up to a key length of 2048 Bit). Asymmetric cryptography is resource intensive (memory, CPU), but the TPM has specialized hardware functions to increase the speed of signing, encryption and decryption processes. The TPM can be integrated into embedded devices like cell phones or PDAs, which normally have limited resources.

- Hash algorithms: The TPM has integrated hash accelerators for the main standard hashing functions (e.g., SHA-1). These are widely used in order to check integrity and authenticity of data.

- Platform Configuration Register (PCR): These registers are used to store specific values of the system configuration inside the TPM. These can be read by users and applications in order to enforce or achieve security goals (see Section 4.1).

Using the above mentioned functionalities, one can realize a variety of security services. More precisely, many security weaknesses of the existing computing platforms can be solved combining TC with a security kernel as PERSUES (see Section 6). To realize the communication with the TPM, we have developed a TPM kernel module for PERSEUS and Linux.

3.2 Securing Linux

Although we mainly developed the TPM driver for the PERSEUS architecture, we explain in this section its general functionality based on a Linux port we also developed[2]. The reason for this is that the Linux driver architecture is more common than the PERSEUS development environment.

The TPM-related BIOS functions cover only a small subset of the functionality provided by a TPM. In order to use the whole TPM functionality (e.g., attestation, sealing, and random numbers), a TPM driver is thus necessary. IBM already has developed a GPL-based Linux driver for the TPM developed by Atmel[3]. Unfortunately, the TCG specification indeed defines the format of the commands to be send to a TPM, but misses to define the protocol to transmit the commands. Therefore, the IBM driver cannot be used in conjunction with TPM's of other manufacturers than Atmel, e.g., Infineon.

3.2.1 Linux TPM-Kernel-Module

One design goal of our TPM driver was to reuse as much as possible of the existing TPM driver developed by IBM, which consists of a three layer architecture (see Figure 3): The user interface is provided by different applications (UNIX commands) based on a library called libtcpa that converts the commands entered by the user into TPM commands according to the TCG specification. A Linux kernel module (tpm_infineon.ko) then sends them over the Low Pin Count I/O (LPC) bus to the TPM using a proprietary protocol. Both, user-level applications and kernel module communicate using the special character node device on the Linux file system /dev/tpm. Under the assumption that the libtcpa works according to the TCG specification, other TPM manufacturers can be supported by adapting the kernel module to the protocol of the TPM manufacturer.

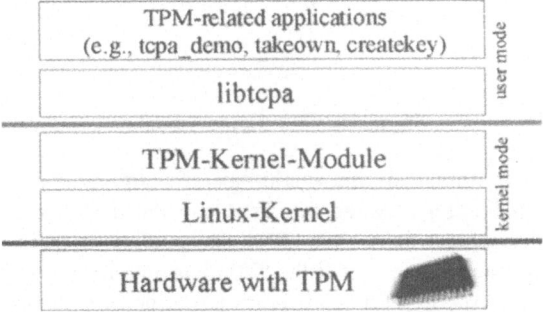

Figure 3: Layers of the Linux TPM driver

The communication with the TPM is unidirectional, so that either writing or reading is possible. The kernel module reads the data from /dev/tpm, transforms it into the TCG-specific

[2] http://www.prosec.rub.de

[3] http://www.research.bim.com/gsal/tcpa/

data format and sends it to the TPM-chip which stores it into its FIFO. The TPM will then perform the requested operation and send the data back to the kernel module, which writes it back to /dev/tpm. The detailed process of this communication, including kernel initialization and removal, is shown in Figure 4.

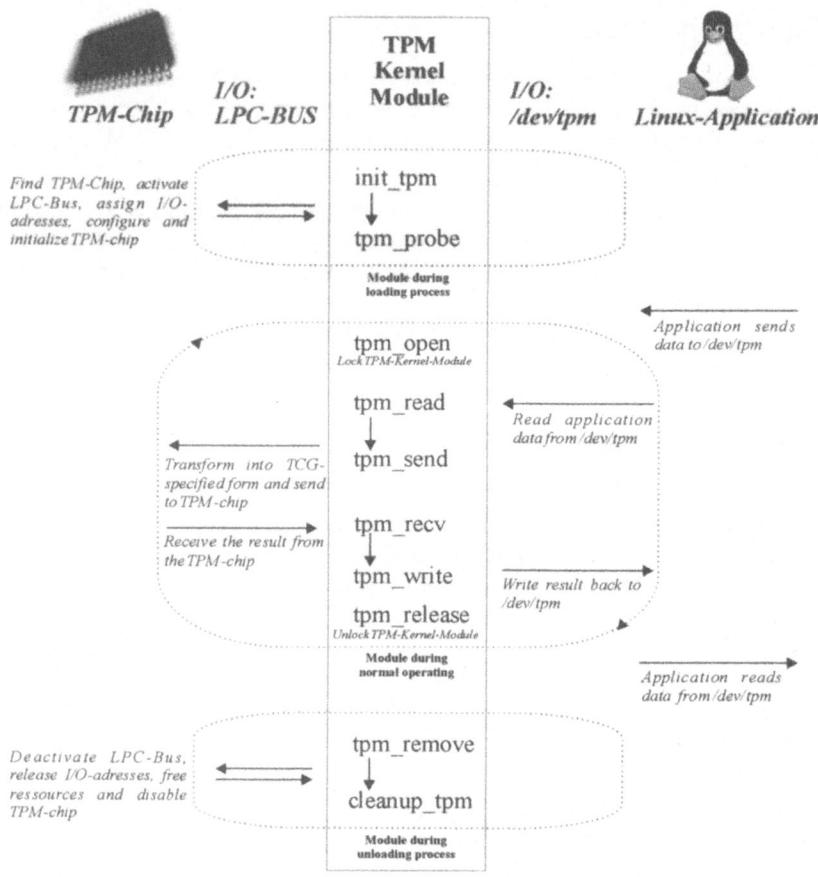

Figure 4: TPM Kernel Module.

The kernel module has to implement the vendor-specific communication protocols and has to ensure that the communication between the TPM and the host is correct. Furthermore, the kernel checks the status register inside the TPM. These allow to verify the state of the chip. For example special register bits are set if the TPM has data for the host or if the TPM FIFO is able to receive data. Error correction and abortion routines are also implemented in the kernel module. Since IRQ-handling is currently not implemented in the kernel module, it periodically checks the status of the TPM (polling). To interrupt the TPM in the case of an error a special polling timeout has been implemented in the kernel module. This prevents the system to hang during time-intensive processes like key generation.

4 Secure Booting resp. Trustworthy Booting

In order to prevent that malicious attackers or inexperienced users bypass security mechanisms by manipulating the operating system configuration, a secure boot process is required that ensures that only trusted operating systems are loaded as the basis for the secure signature application.

Informally speaking, booting is the process which is activated when a computer system is switched on. A boot process consists of three consecutive phases: At first, the hardware is initialized by the BIOS (Basic Input Output System). Secondly, a so-called bootloader loads and executes the vital components of an operating system (OS), and, thirdly, the OS starts its services needed to provide a fully functional system.

Commonly used computing platforms can neither give any guarantees that a specific operating system configuration is bootstrapped, nor do they provide mechanisms that allow users to verify the currently loaded configuration after bootstrapping. To prevent confusion, we hence name the latter form of booting *trusted booting*, while the former is called *secure booting*. The differences between both types may look minimal, but indeed they are very important: On the one hand, users can be sure that only trustworthy operating systems are loaded by a secure booting mechanism, while trusted booting requires an additional trusted platform (e.g., a handheld or another PC) to verify the configuration of the first one. On the other hand, trusted booting allows other parties than the user sitting in front of the computing platform to remotely verify the platform configuration.

4.1 Trusted Booting with TCG

First, it is necessary to secure the components involved in the boot process: BIOS, bootloader and operating system. It has to be guaranteed that they neither contain security-critical bugs enabling attacks, nor should they provide interfaces that are not considered by the boot process and which can be used to maliciously manipulate the platform state.[4] Moreover, the transitions between these components also have to be secured, because otherwise an adversary may be able to replace a correct element with a malicious (insecure) version.

The solution that was chosen by the Trusted Computing Group (TCG) is called chain of trust: Starting with a *root of trust*, every component measures the integrity of the succeeding one before transferring control to it. In practice, a pre-BIOS measures the configuration of the BIOS, the BIOS measures the bootloader, and the bootloader measures the operating system. To prevent manipulations of the root of trust and to securely store the measurement results, some tamper-resistant hardware is required.

The specifications presented by the TCG offer solutions for both problems: A trustworthy pre-BIOS and integrity checks. One component of TCG is the *Core Root of Trust and Measurement* (CRTM). This is an extension to the BIOS with the ability to check the integrity of the basic system hardware. Thus, the CRTM is adequate to be the root of the chain of trust. The other main component is the TPM, which provides some basic cryptographic functions and also secure memory (see Section 6). The required integrity measurements are performed by computing SHA-1 hash values of all components in the boot process. These values are stored in the protected PCR. Note, that the TPM does not decide whether the measured values

---

[4] Many bootloaders allow, for instance, to select the screen resolution and the color depth used by the operating system. If the user interfaces which select the properties of the screen are not adequately protected, attacks against trusted viewers for digital signatures are possible.

are trustworthy or not (which would be required to provide secure booting). Instead, the TPM provides a mechanism called *attestation* that informs a remote party about the measured values based on digital signatures.

4.2 Trusted GRUB (tGRUB)

Commonly used bootloaders are designed to be flexible in use and configuration, but they are not secure against (malicious or accidental) manipulation and therefore not suitable to be used in secure or trusted booting environments.

Our goal was the development of a TCG-enabled secure bootloader that closes the gap between secure hardware provided by the TCG and our PERSEUS security architecture (see Section 6). We decided to use the GRUB (*GRand Unified Bootloader*) as a basis for our security extensions, due to the following reasons: (i) It is published under the GPL, (ii) it has the ability to boot different operating systems including the μ-kernel used by PERSEUS, and (iii) it has a powerful interface that allows a very flexible configuration. Our improved bootloader, called tGRUB, is able to boot every operating system that can be booted by the original GRUB. It requires a computer system with extensions according to the TCG specifications (version 1.1b). tGRUB has been successfully tested on standard IBM PC and Thinkpad notebooks.

Commonly used bootloaders are too large to fit into the 512-byte bootsector of a standard PC. Therefore, they are themselves separated in different parts or *stages*. The GRUB, for instance, consists of two basic parts. The initial one is called stage1 and is located in the bootsector, which can either be the first sector of a floppy disk or a hard drive[5]. The only task of stage1 is to locate and load the second stage. Due to the limited size, stage1 is not even capable to load the complete second stage. Therefore, stage2 itself is also divided in two parts where the first one loads the rest. The functionality of GRUB (i.e., the ability to boot an operating system, together with the configuration interface) are all located in stage2 which doesn't suffer under a space limitation.

4.3 Design of tGRUB

By using the features of TCG, the original GRUB is extended in such a way that it is capable of checking the integrity of the basic operating system components (e.g., the kernel). Several modifications of the GRUB components were necessary:

- stage1 itself is already checked by the CRTM respectively by the extended BIOS. Since stage1 has to load the first part of stage2, additional code measures the integrity of these data before actually loading them.

- The first part of stage2 has been extended in such a way that it measures the integrity of the rest of stage2 before it is loaded and executed.

- The rest of stage2 measures the configuration of all operating system modules that will be loaded by GRUB. Using Linux, e.g., it measures the integrity of the kernel and the initial ramdisk.

- It is also necessary to guarantee that the configuration file and the command-line interface (GRUB shell) provided by GRUB cannot be used to maliciously change the system state. Otherwise, there may be the possibility for an adversary to undermine the additional security features. This problem is solved by measuring used parts of the GRUB

---

[5]On a hard drive, the bootsector is called Master Boot Record (MBR).

configuration file menu.1st as well as additional commands entered by the user using the GRUB shell.

All integrity checks are performed in the same way: At first, the data to be checked is loaded into the memory, hashed by the SHA-1 algorithm of the TPM, the resulting values are appended to the PCRs.

To increase the trustworthiness of operating systems which do not support TCG, we integrated a new functionality into the GRUB that allows the definition of arbitrary files that are additionally measured by the GRUB. This extension is necessary, since the operating system kernel (e.g., the Linux kernel) is not at all the only security-critical component of the operating system. This way, e.g., Linux kernel modules, configuration files, or important data files can be integrated into the measurement.

4.4 Lessons Learned

The current version of tGRUB is able to measure its own integrity and the integrity of the operating system's basic components. The additional code needed to transform GRUB into tGRUB is quite small, but its integration into the existing one is tricky, because there are some limitations that have to be regarded:

- The first problem was that the size of the bootsector is only 512 bytes. This is sufficient for the code of the original stage1, but our TCG-extended version is already too large. The current specifications of TCG-related BIOS functions are very unhandy and waste a lot of the rare memory. Because of this, it was necessary to split tGRUB into two different versions: One for booting from floppy disk, the other one for booting from hard drive. By improving the BIOS functions such that less memory is required, the TCG would make the development of TCG-enabled bootloaders much easier.

- The second problem is the way the TCG functions (for hashing and writing into a PCR) have to be used: The TCG-related functions offered by the BIOS are only available in real mode assembler, but GRUB's stage2 is written in C and protected mode. This aspect made it necessary to perform CPU mode switches and leads to the problem of making data accessible in both modes.

As already mentioned in the introduction, TCG only provides trusted booting but not secure booting. To prevent that users always have to carry another trusted device to be able to perform remote attestation, we are currently extending the GRUB by a mechanism that warns the user if a platform configuration is loaded that was not already accepted by the user.

Finally, it can be said that tGRUB is another core step towards secure booting. Together with a TCG-enhanced BIOS, two out of three boot components can be called trustworthy now. But in order to finalize the chain of trust, the operating system has to be made secure as well.

5 Secure User Interface

When using security critical applications (e.g., for generating digital signatures) user interfaces of end-user devices, e.g., personal computers, mobile phones, and PDA's, play a security critical role, since they have direct access to critical information, e.g., passphrases, personal data, or confidential documents. While other components, e.g., the harddisk or the network driver, can be used by tunneling (cryptographically protecting) critical data, user interfaces have access to unencrypted data to be able to interact with the user: they render confidential images and movies, have access to sound data (e.g., music tracks) and read every data entered over the keyboard, mouse or similar user input devices. This important security weakness, that particularly leads to loss of privacy, has been identified in the past and investigated in the context of different applications. However, no secure user interface for computing platforms is publicly available yet.

Besides establishing a *trusted path* that protects input and output content, user interfaces have to provide a number of other security services. For instance Trojan horses should be prevented from deceiving users by faked dialogs (see, e.g., Figure 5), and security critical applications such as digital signatures should be provided with a trusted viewing functionality ensuring that the content to be signed or verified cannot be manipulated by malicious applications.

The realization of such a system requires the combination and interplay of various components to achieve the desired security properties of an ideal "trusted viewer" for the real world applications.

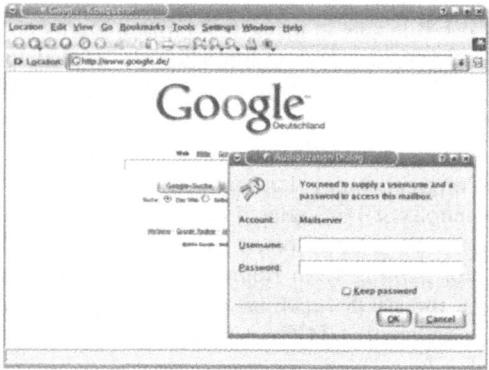

Figure 5: Example of a faked dialog. Using conventional user interfaces,
users are unable to decide whether the password dialog is authentic or faked by the webbrowser.

Due to the lack of secure user interface designs and implementations in widely used computing environments, we have developed a new secure user interface for the PERSEUS security software layer. This interface provides a trusted path. We kept both the design and the implementation as small as possible to keep the trusted computing base small and thus to reduce the probability of security-critical errors. Additionally, a reduced complexity makes porting to other platforms easier. The secure user interface implementation does not enforce security policies. Instead, it is designed in such a way that the provided functions, e.g., the clipboard used for copy & paste, implicitly enforce the same security policy as the underlying security kernel.

The simple design allows to use the secure user interface implementation for mobile devices with small displays, e.g., mobile phones, PDA's, and smartphones. For larger displays, the implementation provides a minimal windowmanager functionality to be able to share the display between multiple applications. Both variants follow conventional GUI design rules as far as possible. The functionality is only restricted if the used behavior can lead to security problems, e.g., to prevent that the user interface creates new information flows. The implementation provides the following security-critical properties:

- Strict isolation between windows of different applications. The secure user interface ensures that applications cannot modify or spoof contents of other windows.

- Applications cannot define the content of their headline. Since only the secure user interface can access these memory regions, application authentication is provided. We are currently implementing a labeling strategy according to Epstein [Epst90] that additionally ensures that window contents are only drawn if the appropriate headline is visible. In this way, we can prevent Trojan horse attacks based on covered labels, i.e., when a malicious window covers a security-critical window.

- Controlled information flows. Whether copy & paste can be performed between two applications depends on the given security policy. If an information flow between application A and B is not permitted, the secure user interface also ensures that users cannot (accidentally or because of an attack) transcript information from one window to another as shown in Figure 6: An information flow from the red window to the green focused window is allowed (left), while an information flow in the other direction is prevented by erasing the window contents if the window focus changes (right).

- A passphrase service that (i) prevents that malicious applications can access critical passphrases, (ii) increases the security of passphrases and (iii) eases the use of them.

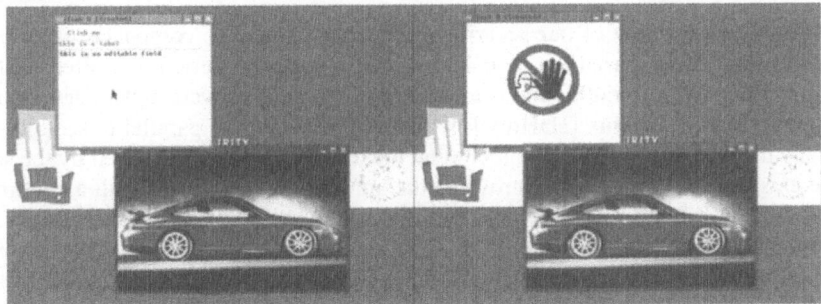

Figure 6: This picture shows the visual information flow protection realized by the PERSEUS secure user interface. In this example, information flows from the top-left window to the bottom-right window are prevented.

The minimal design reduces the complexity of the implementation to the factor hundred compared to conventional user interface implementations, e.g., X-Windows [ScGe92], and to the factor ten compared to other secure implementations like Trusted X [EMO+93]. The current C++ implementation consists of about 6000 lines of code and is available under the GNU General Public License.

6 Realization

We now describe the security architecture required for a computing platform which can offer the properties and services mentioned in previous sections. Such a platform allows the realization of a trusted viewer which is a fundamental component of secure digital signature applications.

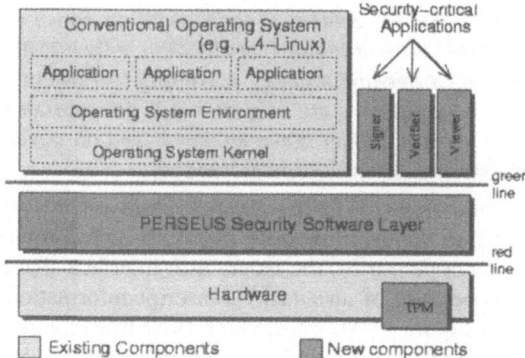

Figure 7: Overview over the PERSEUS security architecture. properties and services mentioned in previous sections. Such a platform allows the realization of a trusted viewer which is a fundamental component of secure digital signature application.

Figure 7 gives an overview of our security architecture. The core component is an efficient security software layer based on a μ-kernel. This security kernel is called PERSEUS [PRS+01a], [PRS+01b], [SaSt03] and is located between the hardware and a conventional operating system (e.g., L4-Linux [HaHo98], [Hohm96]) that runs in parallel to security-critical services and the signature application including the trusted viewer. Controlled by the software layer, the existing operating system provides the application developers with a common ABI (Application Binary Interface) and users with the usual environment (they are used) to execute uncritical applications. By using more than one Linux client operating system, applications can be separated into compartments that are isolated from each other by the PERSEUS layer.

The basic idea of the μ-kernel approach is to minimize the operating system kernel and to implement outside the kernel whatever possible [Lied92], [Lied95], [LDE+01]. In this way, nearly all operating system services can be extracted into separated processes - providing isolation between them and to the μ-kernel through conventional memory protection mechanisms (see Figure 8).

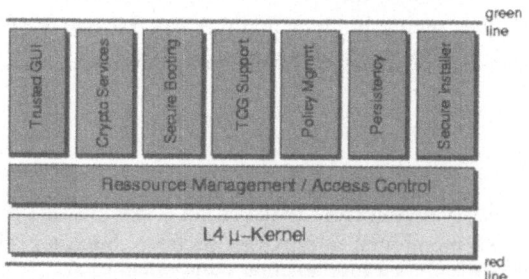

Figure 8: The PERSEUS Security Software Layer is based on a μ-kernel and provides security-critical services as isolated processes

The use of a μ-kernel has the following advantages compared to conventional operating system architectures:

- Operating system services act independent from each other. Therefore it is possible to follow the least privilege paradigm and assign only those rights that are necessary to perform their task. Malfunction or malicious misbehavior is locally isolated. Moreover, it allows us to measure exactly the services (and thus the information) that are used by a rendering engine.

- The complexity of μ-kernels is drastically reduced compared to monolithic kernels. For instance, the L4 μ-kernel [Lied92] contains only about 7000 lines of code, while the current Linux kernel contains more than 2.5 Million source code lines.

- Since a μ-kernel provides only elementary functions based on concepts that change only slowly, the μ-kernel code has the chance to become stable over time.

- The reduced complexity of μ-kernels makes it possible to prove the correctness of the implementation using formal methods. Moreover, the μ-kernel implementation makes an evaluation, e.g., according to the Common Criteria [Comm99] cost-effective, since re-evaluations are expensive in costs and time.

For a more detailed discussion on μ-kernels, see, e.g., [Härt02], [Lied95], [PRS+01a], [ShSF99]. Another core component of our security architecture is the hardware extension as specified by the Trusted Computing Group (TCG), e.g., Trusted Platform Module (TPM) or Microsoft's Next-Generation Secure Computing Base (NGSCB) [LaGr03].

The signature application consists of the following three components: The first one is a *management unit* that generates a cryptographically secure signature key, creates digital signatures, and performs verifications using the functions provided by the TPM. It should be noted that the Linux kernel and Linux applications cannot access the cryptographic keys used by the management unit due to the security properties provided by the underlying platform. The second component is a *rendering engine,* realized as plug-in to be able to support multiple document formats, that converts a document into a bitmap. The underlying μ-kernel allows us to prevent that the rendering engine accesses other processes than the signature application. Therefore, it can access state variables (e.g., the current time) only through the interface provided by the signature application. The rendering engine not necessarily has to be trusted, since the signature application (i) completely controls the input and output and (ii) ensures that the same rendering engine is used by both signer and verifier. The third component is the presentation unit that shows the rendered bitmap and results of signature verifications process using the TrustedGUI provided by the secure user interface. The secure signature application realizes the following functions:

Signing: If the user invokes a signature generating process, the signature application (i) computes the hash value of the rendering engine H_{RE}, (ii) locally stores all state variables $V := V_1 \ldots V_n$ used by the rendering engine to render the bitmap and (iii) concatenates them, together with a certified hash value (H_P) of the platform configuration denoted by $cert_{TPM}$ (created by the TPM on startup) to the hash value H_D of the document D to be signed. Then the signature application sends (D, V, $cert_{TPM}$, H_{RE}) and the signature sig_{sk} (H_D, V, $cert_{TPM}$, H_{RE}) to the verifier where sk denote the secret signing key.

Verification: When verifying a signature on a document D, the verifier can first verify (according to $cert_{TPM}$) whether the computing platform used to create signatures was trustworthy. Then the signature application checks according to the hash value H_{RE} whether the required rendering engine implementation is available. If positive, the signature application invokes it to render D and returns the signed state variables $V_1 \ldots V_n$ (instead of the actual ones) whenever the rendering engine requests them. The result is an identical bitmap than the one produced by the rendering engine of the signer platform.

7 Conclusion

Due to the security vulnerabilities of the existing operating systems we cannot achieve the strong security targets required for critical applications such as digital signatures - a fact hindering the wide deployment and acceptance of digital signatures. Trusted Computing technology offers many useful security features for building more secure IT-systems. These features alone do not solve the security weaknesses of the existing computing platforms. They can only be effectively used in combination with a secure operating system. In this paper we presented our work on a security architecture based on which many security problems of the existing computing platforms can be solved. The core components of this platform are (i) a security software layer PERSEUS, which is located between the hardware and an existing operating system (currently Linux), and (ii) the hardware extension specified by TCG. In particular, we discuss how the security services of this platform, such as a secure graphical user interface, secure booting, isolation of applications, etc., can be used to fulfill the requirements on digital signature applications when deployed in legal transactions. The security services of our platform can also be used in the context of policy enforcement amongst others for Digital Rights Management (DRM) systems.

References

[ADSW99] N. Asokan, H. Debar, M. Steiner, M. Waidner: Authenticating Public Terminals. In: CompNet Journal, Vol. 31, No. 8, 1999.

[CEPW03] Yuqun Chen, Paul England, Marcus Peinado, Bryan Willman: "High Assurance Computing on Open Hardware Architectures". In: Microsoft Research Technical Report MSR-TR-2003-20, March 2003.

[Comm99] Common Criteria Project Sponsoring Organization: „Common Criteria for Information Technology Security Evaluation", Version 2.1, 1999.

[Epst90] Jeremy Epstein: "A Prototype for Trusted X Labeling Policies". In: Annual Computer Security Application Conference (ACSAC), 1990.

[EMO+93] Jeremy Epstein, John McHugh, Hilarie Orman, Rita Pascale, Ann Marmor-Squires, Bonnie Danner, Charles R. Martin, Martha Branstad, Glen Benson and Doug Rothnie: A High Assurance Window System Prototype JCS, Vol. 2, No. 2, 1993.

[Härt02] Hermann Härtig, Security Architectures Revisited: Proceedings of the 10th ACM SIGOPS European Workshop, Saint-Emilion, France, 2002.

[HäHW98] Hermann Härtig, Michael Hohmuth, Jean Wolter: "Taming Linux", In Proceedings of PART, 1998.

[HLM+03] H. Härtig, J. Loeser, F. Mehnert, L. Reuther, M. Pohlack, A. Warg: "An I/O Architecture for Mikrokernel-Based Operating Systems". In: Technical Report TUD-FI03-08-Juli-2003, TU Dresden, July 2003.

[Hohm96] M. Hohmuth, Linux-Emulation auf einem Mikrokern, Master Thesis, Dresden University of Technology, Dept. of Computer Science, 1996

[LaGr03] LaGrande: Technology Archtitectural Overview, Intel White Paper, Intel, September 2003.

[Lied92]   Jochen Liedke: Clans and Chiefs. A new Kernel Level Concept for Operating Systems, Proceedings of the 12th GI-Fachtagung, 1992

[Lied95]   Jochen Liedke: "On μ-Kernel Construction", In Proceedings of Symposium on Operating System Principles (SOSP), 1995.

[LDE+01]   Liedtke, U. Dannowski, K. Elphinstone, G. Liefländer, E. Skoglund, V. Uhlig, C. Ceelen, A. Haeberlen, M. Völp: "The L4KA Vision", University of Karlsruhe, 2001. White Paper, April 2001

[LoSm01]   Peter Loscocco and Stephen Smalley: Integrating Flexible Support for Security Policies into the Linux Operating System, U.S. National Security Agency (NSA), 2001.

[MiRe04]   S. Micali, L. Reyzin: Physical Observable Cryptography: Proceedings of the Theory of Cryptography Conference, TCC 2004, Vol. 2951, LNCS, 2004.

[MVHC03]   Craig Mundie, Pierre de Vries, Peter Haynes, Matt Corwine, Trustworthy Computing, Microsoft Corporation, Oktober, 2003.

[Pear03]   Siani Pearson: Trusted Computing Platforms - TCPA technology in context, Hewlett-Packard Company, Prestice Hall PTR, 2003

[PRS+01a]   Birgit Pfitzmann, James Riordan, Christian Stüble, Michael Waidner, Arnd Weber: „The PERSEUS System Architecture". In: IBM Technical Report #93381, IBM Research Division, Zürich, 2001.

[PRS+01b]   Birgit Pfitzmann, James Riordan, Christian Stüble, Michael Waidner, Arnd Weber: „Die PERSEUS Sicherheitsarchitektur". In: Verlässliche Informationssysteme (VIS) 2001, p. 1-18, 2001.

[SaSt03]   Ahmad-Reza Sadeghi, Christian Stüble: „Taming "Trusted Computing" by Operating System Design", Proceedings of the 4th International Workshop on Information Security Applications (WISA), Korea, 2003.

[ScGe92]   R. W. Scheiffler and J. Gettys: X Window System. In: Digital Press, 1992

[ShSF99]   Jonathan S. Shapiro, Jonathan M. Smith and David J. Farber: EROS: a fast capability system, SOSP99, 1999.

[Gese01]   Gesetz über Rahmenbedingungen für elektronische Signaturen, BGB, Mai, 2001

[Vero01]   Verordnung zur digitalen Signatur, Nov. 2001

[TCG03]   Trusted Computing Group: „Trusted Platform Module (TPM) Main Specification v1.2", December 2003.

[TyWh96]   J. D. Tygar and A. Whitten: "WWW Electronic Commerce and Java Trojan Horses", Proceedings of the 2nd USENIX Workshop on Electronic Commerce, 1996.

Index

3

3D Secure _____ 194

A

access
   control _____ 34, 40, 75, 136, 139, 186, 199, 210, 323, 329
   management _____ 114, 277
accountability _____ 24, 36, 198, 300
advanced electronic signatures _____ 52, 229, 284
ambient intelligence _____ 60
anomaly detection _____ 79
anonymous communication_____ 82
audit_____ 5, 31, 45, 95, 112, 142, 156, 189, 200, 260, 277, 350
authentication _ 4, 52, 67, 77, 96, 101, 113, 117, 118, 146, 151, 160, 179, 186, 216, 233, 237,
   261, 277, 282, 290, 322, 348
   mechanisms _____ 6, 179
authorisation _____ 4, 77, 143, 190
Authorization Token Layer Acquisition Service (ATLAS) _____ 146
Automatic Teller Machine (ATM) _____ 189

B

barcode _____ 60, 160
Basel II _____ 13, 23, 36
biometric _____ 47, 160, 321
blacklisting _____ 135, 180
browser-based federation _____ 92
bulk encryption _____ 102
business
   privacy_____ 277

C

C++ _____ 140, 357
camera phones _____ 58
certificate_____ 41, 110, 117, 143, 191, 211, 221, 229, 239, 252, 260, 281, 290, 310, 322
   Revocation List _____ 197, 323
certificate and key manager (CKM) _____ 244
closed circuit TV (CCTV)_____ 333
common criteria_____ 27
confidentiality _____ 26, 34, 40, 97, 132, 139, 150, 180, 200, 237, 250, 309, 322, 341

consumer _____ 26, 60, 108, 127, 179, 234, 288, 303
content data _____ 63
contractual data _____ 69
copyright protection _____ 66
CORBA Component Model (CCM) _____ 138
corporate network _____ 102, 186, 209
cost saving _____ 9
Council of Information Sharing and Analysis Centers _____ 271
critical infrastructure protection (CIP) _____ 271
cross boarder
    invoicing _____ 228
cyber crime _____ 179
    laws _____ 179

D

data
    minimisation _____ 64
    reduction _____ 67
    retention _____ 64, 198
    scarcity _____ 64
Data Protection _____ 49, 58, 66, 180, 303, 321, 333
    Authority _____ 59, 183, 333
Decalogue 2004 _____ 333
Department of Homeland Security (DHS) _____ 272
deviation _____ 79, 168
Digital Rights Management (DRM) _____ 66, 104, 360
digital signature _____ 40, 117, 171, 186, 219, 228, 237, 250, 281, 291, 309, 322, 346
document-based federation _____ 91

E

e-business _____ 19, 38, 68, 82, 289, 322
e-Commerce _____ 194, 301
eigenfaces _____ 163
electronic
    exchange _____ 219, 250
    identities _____ 179
    invoicing _____ 219, 228
    mass signature _____ 219
    services _____ 179, 262, 291
    signature _____ 43, 48, 52, 219, 233, 264, 281, 303, 330
    trade _____ 67, 228
Electronic Post Mark (EPM) _____ 267
employee monitoring _____ 76
encryption _____ 40, 53, 63, 67, 97, 101, 131, 157, 162, 193, 210, 221, 231, 237, 250,
    261, 281, 313, 349
end-to-end security _____ 242

enforcement _____ 73, 144, 156, 179, 198, 199, 278, 344, 360
enterprise-wide _____ 4, 30
e-Tariff _____ 305
ethics _____ 81
e-Transformation_____ 299
European
  Bridge-CA _____ 255
  Directive _____ 43, 233, 282
  tax laws _____ 219

F

face compression _____ 161
federation_____ 89, 156, 296
filtering _____ 19, 127, 146, 180, 237
financial services_____ 3, 26, 217, 262, 271, 327
fraud _____ 3, 25, 39, 78, 179, 262
freedom
  of movement _____ 333

G

gateway _____ 103, 128, 193, 237, 238, 264, 297
  scanner_____ 128
generic
  blocking_____ 130
grid computing _____ 148

H

heuristics _____ 127, 348
Homeland Security
  Information Network_____ 280
  Presidential Directive-7 (HSPD-7) _____ 271
human rights _____ 49, 82, 182

I

identification and verification _____ 3
identity
  Cards _____ 47
  federation_____ 89, 296
  management _____ 68, 77, 95, 277, 297
in-depth protection _____ 40
industrial espionage_____ 76, 108, 237
Information Security Forum (ISF) _____ 28
information sharing_____ 83, 200, 271

informational self-determination_____51, 66
insider threat _____75
integrity 25, 34, 36, 40, 49, 67, 97, 128, 139, 150, 162, 188, 206, 209, 219, 229, 237, 250, 260, 261, 278, 282, 309, 322, 346
Internal Rate of Return (IRR) _____15
International Security Trust and Privacy Alliance (ISTPA)_____279
International Standardisation Organisation_____64
interoperability _____43, 48, 119, 138, 155, 184, 309
ISAC Council white papers_____279
IT-ISAC_____278

L

laws and regulations _____27, 220, 336
legal aspects _____44, 228
legislation _____36, 50, 180, 198, 281, 299, 309, 333
legislative initiatives _____179
Liberty Alliance _____77, 94, 156, 293

M

macro virus _____128
malware_____128, 237
Marca do Dia Electrónica (MDDE) _____264
mass mailer _____128
Mobile Signature Service Provider (MSSP)_____293
mobility_____39, 121
monitoring_____8, 27, 41, 75, 127, 198, 271, 333
multi-application smart card _____186
multi-channel_____3, 192

N

Net Present Value (NPV) _____15
netiquette_____183
network security _____217, 304, 321
non-repudiation _____121, 192, 259, 309, 322
notebook _____212

O

open source _____151
operational risk framework _____24
opt out _____72

P

P3P _____ 114, 278
passwords _____ 4, 122, 194, 212, 238
patching _____ 35
payback period _____ 17
PKI _____ 191, 236, 237, 295
  Enabling _____ 117
  experiences in Serbia_____ 321
  systems _____ 321
  Wireless (WPKI)_____ 297
Point of Sale (PoS) _____ 193
policies _____ 8, 24, 41, 95, 101, 112, 139, 142, 148, 198, 218, 240, 257, 273, 301, 315, 346
polymorphism _____ 127
Presidential Decision Directive 63 _____ 271
preventative security _____ 75, 339
principal component analysis _____ 163
privacy
  obligations_____ 198
  standard _____ 64
Privacy Act of 1974_____ 278
proof of origin _____ 188
pseudonymous payment procedures _____ 73

R

Radio Frequency Identification (RFID) _____ 58, 108
  tags _____ 58, 109
reactive security _____ 43, 77
regulatory
  compliance _____ 22, 31
  framework_____ 23, 281
remediation planning_____ 32
Return of Investment (ROI) _____ 3, 13, 227
risk
  assessment_____ 32, 83, 152
  management _____ 13, 30
roles_____ 4, 77, 92, 142, 277, 291

S

SafeGuard Easy _____ 217
Sarbanes Oxley (SOX) _____ 23, 36
secrecy
  of letters_____ 78
  of telecommunications _____ 63
secure
  architecture _____ 42
  e-mail_____ 238, 264, 322

user interface _____ 346
Secure Open Data Storage (SODS)_____ 187
security
    architecture _____ 40, 154, 186, 278, 354
    infrastructure _____ 3, 41, 94
    management _____ 277
    Monitoring_____ 77
    policy_____ 8, 41, 49, 109, 138, 156, 216, 356
Security Assertion Markup Language (SAML) _____ 96
self
    data protection_____ 71
Serbian
    Banking Association _____ 327
signature server _____ 118, 230
signed invoice _____ 221, 229
single sign-on (SSO) _____ 90, 120, 329
smartcard _____ 5, 101, 121, 160, 186, 210, 222, 247, 291, 292, 304, 321, 349
SOAP_____ 94, 155, 225, 250
spam _____ 19, 128, 179
spoofing virus _____ 127
standardization _____ 152, 184, 286, 306
surveillance _____ 75, 333
survey about electronic invoicing _____ 234
system integration _____ 8

T

tamper resistant hardware security module_____ 189
tamper-resistant_____ 349
technology assessment _____ 48, 82
threat management _____ 277
threshold cryptography _____ 237
traffic data _____ 63
transaction _____ 5, 24, 38, 61, 69, 95, 121, 132, 186, 201, 260, 286, 291, 309
transparency _____ 50, 61, 66, 182, 202, 303
trust model_____ 41, 156, 272, 310
trusted
    computing _____ 99, 209, 356
    digital repository _____ 230
    system _____ 331
Trusted Computing Group (TCG)_____ 67, 100, 209, 346
trusted viewer _____ 346
TrustPoint _____ 250
Turk Telekom _____ 301

U

ubiquitous computing _____ 43, 60
Universal Description, Discovery and Integration (UDDI) _____ 251
use-profiles _____ 70
utilization data _____ 69

V

validation _____ 41, 117, 139, 221, 233, 246, 252, 261, 279, 282, 295, 310
VAT _____ 219, 228
   executive order _____ 220
   law _____ 219
video surveillance _____ 78, 333
virus _____ 20, 103, 127, 153, 215, 247
VPN _____ 21, 323

W

warrant _____ 63
wearable computing _____ 64
web
   Service Security _____ 154
   Services _____ 83, 154, 250, 293, 326
whitelisting _____ 135
workplace _____ 23, 75, 78, 91, 333
worm _____ 129
WS-Federation _____ 96, 157
WS-Security _____ 96, 157, 251

X

XKMS _____ 250
XML _____ 91, 138, 207, 246
   Encryption _____ 98
   Signature _____ 98

"ARIS made easy"

Heinrich Seidlmeier
Process Modeling with ARIS
A Practical Introduction
2004. xvi, 192 pp. Softc. € 49,90   ISBN 3-528-05877-3

Contents: Summary of process organization - Computers in organizations - Process optimization with the ARIS Toolset - System administration - Case study of a forwarding agency - Applications based on
business models: document and workflow management - Toolset
based on project execution - Exercises and solutions

This textbook helps beginners learn ARIS and advanced users will
find useful and valuable hints. It complements existing training as
well as self studies. First, the reader learns the basics of process organization as well as the roles and effects of computers in enterprises.
Next, the ARIS methodologies are explained. Finally, the essential
concept, the ARIS views (organization, function, data and process) are
explained and the most common models are introduced. The book
offers many practical modeling examples, exercises, and solutions.

vieweg
Abraham-Lincoln-Straße 46
65189 Wiesbaden
Fax 0611.7878-400
www.vieweg.de

Prices and other details are subject to change
without notice. Please order at your bookstore.